ea
out in
pubs

The world of dining pubs and inns continues to evolve, and our guide is developing with it. We've been picking out the best of British and Irish pubs in the Michelin Guide for eight years, and our team of independent, professional inspectors continue to apply the same high standards for the benefit of our readers. But this year's expanded selection contains a large number of brand-new entries, a few of which are already among the best in the book.

To highlight the pick of the pubs, we've introduced the "We most liked" category. The establishments with a "We most liked" symbol 🖢 on their page all have something about them that we think you'll particularly enjoy: it could be the exceptionally good food, the pleasant setting and character of the pub itself, or just its all-round quality.

But we think all of the pubs are well worth a visit. They vary enormously in style, history and personality and include not just Michelin award-winners but also other local favourites which deserve to be better known. Some chefs and landlords see themselves at the forefront of the "gastropub revolution", others are proud that their pub has stayed unchanged for decades, even centuries, yet all of the pubs provide good food in enjoyable surroundings, and all of them make a really enjoyable meal out. If you're having trouble choosing, in-depth descriptive texts bring out the feeling of each and every one, highlighting what we found most charming and memorable.

Michelin's readers contribute thousands of letters and e-mails every year, sending in praise and criticism, suggestions for the guide itself and recommendations for new entries. We hope you'll keep them coming and help us to make the next edition of Michelin Eating out in Pubs even better. You can also fill in and return the readers' questionnaire form at the back of this guide: either way, we look forward to hearing from you!

contents

Contents

3

ENGLAND

- EAST MIDLANDS
- EAST OF ENGLAND
- LONDON
- NORTH EAST
- NORTH WEST
- SOUTH EAST
- SOUTH WEST
- WEST MIDLANDS
- YORKSHIRE & THE HUMBER

SCOTLAND

WALES

IRELAND

- NORTHERN IRELAND
- REPUBLIC OF IRELAND

MIDLANDS

EAST OF ENGLAND

LONDON

EAST

COUNTRY/REGIONS & COUNTY NAMES

ONE OF OUR FAVOURITE SELECTIONS

TOWN/VILLAGE NAME

NAME, ADDRESS, TELEPHONE, E-MAIL AND WEBSITE OF THE ESTABLISHMENT

025

ENTRY NUMBER

Each pub or inn has its own entry number.

This number appears on the regional map at the start of each section to show the location of the establishment. Blue numbered entries indicate that the pub has bedrooms

COLOURED PAGE BORDER

Introduction

East Midlands

East of England

London

North East

North West

South East

South West

West Midlands

Yorkshire & The Humber

Scotland

Wales

Northern Ireland

Republic of Ireland

PAGE NUMBER

TEXT

East Midlands - Rutland

Stretton

025 The Jackson Stops Inn

Rookery Rd, Stretton LE15 7RA

Tel: (01780) 410237 - Fax (01780) 410280
e-mail: james@jacksonstops-inn.fsnet.co.uk

VISA

Adnams Broadside, Oakham Ales JHB, Timothy Taylor Landlord, Hop Back Brewery Summer Lightning

When estate agent Jackson Stops sold off the Stretton Estate in 1955, their sign was outside what was then The White Horse pub for so long that it became known as the Jackson Stops. An interesting little anecdote which goes some way to explaining why a 17C, rurally set thatched inn should end up with such an unusual name. It's a wonderfully characterful place, rustic down to its Rutland wellies; a low wooden bar is frequented by regulars, but this then gives way to a surprising four dining areas, minimalist with plain décor and vintage scrubbed tables, silver chargers glinting in welcome. A very pleasant atmosphere prevails; the constantly evolving menus offer good value, rustic British cooking.

Food serving times:
Tuesday-Saturday:
12pm-2pm, 7pm-10pm
Sunday:
12pm-2pm
Closed 25 December and New Year and Bank Holiday Mondays
Prices:
Meals: a la carte 20.00/25.95

Typical Dishes
Ham hock and mustard terrine
Herb stuffed chicken
Pear Tart Tatin, vanilla ice cream

8ml Northwest of Stamford by B1081 off A1. Parking

PICTURE OF THE PUB/INN

SYMBOLS

- Meals served in the garden or on the terrace
- A good range of wines served by the glass
- A particularly interesting wine list
- **Rest.** Non-smoking dining room
- No dogs allowed
- **VISA** Visa accepted
- **AE** American Express accepted
- **D** Diners Club accepted
- **MC** MasterCard accepted

East Midlands - Rutland

Wing

026 Kings Arms
13 Top St, Wing LE15 8SE
Tel: (01572) 737634 - Fax: (01572) 737255
e-mail: info@thekingsarms-wing.co.uk - Website: www.thekingsarms-wing.co.uk

room **VISA** **AE** **MC**

Timothy Taylor Landlord, Marston Pedigree, Grainstore Cooking, and 1 guest

Built in the early days of Cromwell's Britain, this delightful place gave the Restoration time to settle before becoming "The Kings Arms", but the cosy bar can't have changed much over the last 350 years or so. Flagstone floors, ancient beams and a big open fire lend true period warmth, while more recent prints and paintings of Rutland and around reflect a local pride that comes across just as clearly on the menu. Fresh and substantial dishes on a traditional base make good use of seasonal produce from our smallest county, and the landlord and team chip in well with relaxed, conversational service. All well away from the main bar, the bedrooms are warm and immaculately kept. Rutland Water is a short drive away.

Food serving times:
Monday-Sunday:
12pm-2pm, 6pm-9pm

Prices:
Meals: a la carte 18.00/28.00
7 rooms : 65.00/75.00

Typical Dishes

Marinated herring fillets

Rib-eye steak, garlic herb butter

Baked chocolate fondant

5mi South of Oakham by A6003.
Parking

41

REAL ALES SERVED

A listing to indicate the number and variety of regular and guest cask beers usually served.

OPENING HOURS
FOOD SERVING TIMES
PRICES
ROOMS

Approximate range of prices for a three-course meal, plus information on booking and annual closures.

Some inns offering accommodation may close in mid-afternoon and only allow guests to check in during evening hours. If in doubt, phone ahead.

Room prices range from the lowest-priced single to the most expensive double or twin.

The cup and saucer symbol denotes breakfast; if no price is shown assume it is included in the price of the room.

Prices are given in £ sterling, except for the Republic of Ireland where €uro are quoted.

HOW TO GET THERE

Directions and driving distances from nearby towns, and indication of parking facilities and any other information that might help you get your bearings.

THE BLACKBOARD

An example of a typical starter, main course and dessert, chosen by the chef.

Whilst there's no guarantee that these dishes will be available, they should provide you an idea of the style of the cuisine.

7

Beer
in the U.K. and Ireland

As most pub-goers know, beers in Britain can be divided not only into Ales and Lagers – which differ mainly in their respective warm and cool fermentations – but also according to their means of storage. Keg beer is filtered, pasteurised and chilled, and then packed into pressurised containers from which it gets its name, while cask beer or "Real Ale", as it is often called, continues to ferment and mature in its barrel.

*B*rewers rightly insist that the final flavour of a beer depends on all sorts of elements, from the variety of yeast to the minerals in the local water, not to mention storage in the pub, but there are three stages of brewing which particularly influence the character of the beer in your glass.

The malting, the way the germinating barley is dried, roasted and milled to make it fermentable, affects the flavour, the 'body' and the colour of the drink: a hotter kiln means a darker malt. This malt is then soaked in hot water to form a porridge-like mash; time and temperature are crucial here. Perhaps most importantly, the addition of hops gives a familiar, faintly astringent tang, with different strains of plant lending different overtones to the final pint. For extra aroma, bunches of hop flowers, called cones, can be added to the beer later, at the end of its vat fermentation or even in the barrel, a process known as "dry hopping".

Traditional Styles

Of the several distinct beer styles in the British Isles, **bitter** is the most popular traditional beer in England and Wales, although now outsold by lager. No precise definition exists and the name is loosely used, but bitters are usually paler and dryer than Mild with a high hop content and, of course, a slightly bitter taste and bouquet, from flowery to citrus, depending on the hop variety.

Mild is largely found in Wales, the West Midlands and the North West of England. The name refers to the hop character as it is gentle, sweetish beer, generally lower in alcohol and often darker in colour.

The great dry **stouts** are brewed in Ireland and are instantly recognisable by their black colour and creamy head: they have a pronounced yeast flavour and sometimes a faint smoky taste. Reddish-black **porter** was revived by the renewed interest in real ale and is still something of a rarity. Originally known as 'entire', this slightly lighter though still substantial beer was said to have been a favourite with London's market porters and deliverymen when it was first brewed in the 18th century.

In Scotland the beers produced are typically full-bodied and malty and are often known simply as Light, **Heavy** or **Export**, which refers to the body and alcoholic content of the ale. The old shilling taxes were levied by roughly the same scale, at rates of 60/- to 80/- and beyond, and still survive in some beer names.

The Continental Connection

Many great European styles are now imitated by UK producers, with greater or lesser success, and publicans are also becoming increasingly discerning in their choices of European imports. Drinkers in Britain's dining pubs might come across fizzy, hazy, tan-yellow **Weizenbier** from southern Germany which can accompany anything from full-flavoured white meats to seafood, or one of the crisp, bitter-edged **lagers** produced in the north, where they are sometimes served with fish.

Belgium's spontaneously fermenting **lambic** is aged in wine barrels for up to three years; when flavoured with fruit and bottle-matured it becomes **gueuze**, a sweet-sharp, bubbly beer quite unlike anything in the British Tradition. The great **abbey beers**, traditionally produced by the Belgian Trappist orders, are usually rich, effervescent and complex and need similarly robust flavours to complement them, while cloudy **white beers** make a refreshing accompaniment to light meals and summer salads. Top-fermented then cold-stored like lagers, **bières de garde** from northern France and Wallonia are sometimes sealed with a Champagne-style wired cork. These amber or nut-brown beers are typically strong and characterful and go well with cheeses or slow-cooked meats.

The **Pub** *of the* **year**

There are more than 500 pubs in the Guide, and all of them, naturally enough, have been selected for the quality of their food. The Pub of the Year, though, serves up something a little out of the ordinary. What special ingredients go into the mix? We wanted to bring together all that's best about eating out in pubs: apart from the excellent cuisine, we were looking for location, ambience, service, the choice of beers and wines, and that certain something which locals and visitors alike immediately recognise as unmistakable star quality.

The Michelin Pub of the Year is loved not just for its pretty, unspoilt village, but also for guaranteed hospitality provided by hands-on owners. It's a place renowned for its plentiful charm and character, in which everything revolves round a delightful bar where the log fire roars… even in May. Enjoying food here is a pre-requisite, so three distinct dining areas never feel superfluous to demand. The bedrooms, too, have that just-so blend of top-notch facilities and pretty-in-chintz warmth. Why, the marmalades, bread, jams and chutneys are even home-made. Proudly standing for over 250 years in the delightfully wild and rolling landscape of Teesdale, our Pub of the Year for 2006 is…

003 ## The Rose & Crown

Romaldkirk DL12 9EB

Tel: (01833) 650213 – Fax: (01833) 650828

e-mail:hotel@rose-and-crown.co.uk – Website: www.rose-and-crown.co.uk

see page 161 for more details

A tour of the region begins with a well-kept secret: the rural beauty of the east. Towards the coast lie acres of silent fens, the gentle countryside of the wolds, and the magnificent silhouette of Lincoln Cathedral, rising above the old city. Nottingham, Derby and the nearby towns shot to fame as centres of industry and science and remain the powerhouses of the region. With Leicester they form an old industrial heartland, regenerated by the first plantings of the National Forest and bordered by rural Rutland, "independent" again since 1997. Then to the west, sombre moors, the pretty 'White Peak' downlands, the Derwent and dramatic Dovedale form some of the country's most picture-perfect landscapes, while Peak architecture reflects every mood and era of its history: Matlock's mills and the moving monuments of Eyam village, Georgian Buxton and the stately archetypes of Chatsworth and Haddon Hall. In the region's pubs, there's a strong local flavour on tap – even Rutland brews its own beer – as well as on the plate. Bakewell tarts, or puddings, are a point of local pride, while only the rich, blue-veined cheese from three East Midlands counties can lay claim to the name of Stilton.

Ashbourne

001 Bramhall's 🛏

6 Buxton Rd, Ashbourne DE6 1EX

Tel.: (01335) 346158

e-mail: info@bramhalls.co.uk - Website: www.bramhalls.co.uk

Bass

D on't be put off by the rather dreary façade, just off Ashbourne's cobbled market square; once inside, it's a different picture. Pick a table in one of the four or five little rooms and snugs and let a well-drilled team do the rest. Keen and helpful staff in denim uniforms serve an appetising menu rounded out with daily specials on the board: cream of white onion soup, monkfish with gnocchi and asparagus and rasperry crème brûlée are typical of a sound modern-classic style. At the back, an enclosed terrace for dining looks down over a stepped garden. If you're planning on staying the night, the usefully equipped bedrooms range from plain to contemporary.

Food serving times:
Monday-Sunday:
12pm-2.30pm,
6.30pm-9.30pm
Closed 25-26 December and 1 January
Prices:
Meals: a la carte 20.00/30.00
🛏 **10 rooms :** 27.50/65.00

Typical Dishes

Red Thai tiger prawns

Fillet of Sea bass, saffron mash

Vanilla brûlée

In centre of town.

Birchover

002 **Druid Inn**

Main St, Birchover DE4 2BL

Tel.: 01629 650302
Website: www.thymeforfood.co.uk

🍷 **VISA** ⓜⓒ

 Druids Ale and a locally brewed guest ale

Taking its name from the mysterious and ancient Druid Rocks above it, the Druid Inn, in the heart of the Peak District countryside, has been a hill-walkers' landmark for many years. Much extended since the 19C, it still has plenty of true rural character in the old bar, which has kept its tiled floor, chunky furniture and flickering firelight, and is that bit more authentic-feeling than the smarter modern dining rooms. Considerate and informal staff somehow keep track of a large menu that ranges from daily pastas and risottos, hot and cold lunchtime sandwiches and pints of prawns, by way of enjoyable and substantial modern classics. This is more than food to keep the cold out: it may not be elaborate, but it's marked by true, balanced flavours and sound culinary understanding, with sensible prices to match.

Food serving times:
Monday- Sunday:
 12pm-2.30pm, 6pm-9.30pm
Closed Sunday dinner
Prices:
Meals: a la carte 20.00/29.00

Typical Dishes

Terrine of ham hock, Stilton and black pudding

Breast of chicken, saute of asparagus and pancetta

Milk chocolate bread

7.5 mi Northwest from Matlock by A6 and 5.5 mi from Bakewell. Parking

Hognaston

003 **Red Lion Inn**

Main Street, Hognaston DE6 1PR

Tel.: (01335) 370396
e-mail: info@lionrouge.com - Website: www.lionrouge.com

 VISA **AE** **MC**

Marstons Pedigree, Bass and weekly guest ale

Nestling in a pretty village in the foothills of the Derbyshire Peaks, this cream-washed extended late 17C inn has a cosy, comfortable appeal, typified by a bar full of objets d'art and ornaments. A 'real' pub ambience predominates, with the warmth of the surroundings enhanced with open fires and a rugged old stone floor. You'll want for nothing: the owner is chatty and enthusiastic, and very much on hand to recommend drinks or dishes from the menu. Classic pub meals here have been given a modern twist: typically, pork sausages with mustard mash and red wine jus. Dine at a candle-lit mix of older wooden tables and chairs. Stay overnight in beamed, individually decorated bedrooms.

Food serving times:
Monday to Sunday:
   12pm-2pm, 6.30pm-9pm
Prices:
Meals: a la carte 17.95/25.95
3 rooms : 65.00/90.00

Typical Dishes

Homemade Hummus
Apricot stuffed loin of lamb
Selection of local cheeses

4.5mi Northeast of Ashbourne by B5035. Parking to rear

Hope Valley

004 **Chequers Inn**

Froggatt Edge, Hope Valley S32 3ZJ

Tel.: (01433) 630231 - Fax: (01433) 631072
e-mail: info@chequers-froggatt.com - Website: www.chequers-froggatt.com

     VISA **AE** **MC**

Charles Wells Bombadier, Greene King IPA, Adnams Broadside

Located at the eastern end of the Peak District, and just in front of the woods that lead to Froggatt Edge, this attractively set pub - a Grade II listed building - is quite a find. It dates back to the 16C and was originally four houses; it's been extensively refurbished yet retains many period features, such as the old stables. The spacious interior has a welcoming feel, typified in the bar by a well-chosen selection of wines by the glass, chalked up on blackboard slates hung around the richly varnished panelled ceiling; chunky stone walls with antique prints all add to the rustic atmosphere. Sit at simple, polished wooden tables and tuck into tasty meals with a distinctive modern feel, backed up by efficient, friendly service. Walkers may be delighted to finish the evening tucked up in very pleasant, cosy bedrooms.

Food serving times:
Monday-Friday:
    12pm-2pm, 6pm-9.30pm
Saturday: 12pm-9.30pm
Sunday: 12pm-9pm
Closed 25 December
Prices:
Meals: a la carte 18.50/26.40
5 rooms : 65.00/90.00

Typical Dishes

Smoked bacon risotto

Braised pork belly, pecorino mash

Plum frangipane

Situated on the edge of the village. Parking

Marston Montgomery

005 Bramhall's at The Crown Inn

Rigg Lane, Marston Montgomery DE6 2FF

Tel.: (01889) 590541

e-mail: info@bramhalls.co.uk - Website: www.bramhalls.co.uk

 Draught Bass, Marstons Pedigree

Just up the road from Alton Towers is a far more relaxing and certainly less energetic alternative: a pleasant pub, hidden away in the village centre. Locals are drawn by the warm and welcoming atmosphere, not to mention the splendid selection of real ales and wines by the glass; exposed rafters and an open fire all add to the happy mix. This simple, cosy interior is further enhanced by plenty of comfy seats and distressed wooden tables. The food served here, off a daily blackboard menu, seamlessly matches its surroundings: tasty and unfussy, with modern twists thrown in for good measure. Bedrooms do the trick, too: they're warm, cosy and contemporary.

Food serving times:

Monday-Saturday:
12pm-2.30pm, 6.30pm-9pm

Sunday: 12pm-2.30pm

Closed 25 December and 1 January

Prices:

Meals: 12.95 and a la carte 20.00/30.00

7 rooms : 50.00/70.00

Typical Dishes

Red thai tiger prawns

Rack of lamb, pea and mint mash

Griottine brûlée

7.5mi Southeast of Ashbourne by A515. Parking

Belton

006 **The Queen's Head** 🛏

2 Long St, Belton LE12 9TP

Tel.: 01530 222359 - Fax: 01530 224860

e-mail: enquiries@thequeenshead.org - Website: www.thequeenshead.org

Marstons Pedigree, Wicked Hathern, Brewsters

A renovation of the old village inn has left little if any trace of a 19C pub; even Her Majesty's severe, Penny-Black profile on the monochrome pub sign looks like a tribute to a design classic rather than a touch of Victorian detail. But it's fairer to appreciate the place for what it is. The transformation, into a smart bar, bistro and restaurant has been complete and thorough: calm whites and creams, chocolate suede and polished wood give a feeling of all-over modernity. It's no surprise to find similar attention to detail in a varied and evolving menu on different modern British themes, though you shouldn't overlook the simpler bar choice of sandwiches, salads, pastas and lunchtime specials. Bedrooms are spacious, contemporary and bright; the two in the attic share a bathroom.

Food serving times:
Monday-Saturday:
12.00pm-2.30pm
Sunday: 12pm-4pm
Monday-Thursday:
7pm-9.30pm
Friday-Saturday:
7pm-10.00pm
Closed 25 December
Prices:
Meals: 15.00 and a la carte 15.00/30.00
🛏 **6 rooms :** 60.00/100.00

Typical Dishes

Seared scallops and wild mushrooms

Fillet of beef, truffle and celeriac puree

Cappuccino brûlée

6 mi West of Loughborough by A6 on the B5234. On the Diseworth/Breedon rd. Parking

East Midlands - Leicestershire

21

Breedon-on-the-Hill

007 ## The Three Horseshoes Inn

Breedon-on-the-Hill DE73 8AN
Tel.: 01332 695129 - Fax: 01332 695128

 🍴 ✂ **VISA** **M©**

Marstons Pedigree, Courage Directors, Theakstons mild and Caledonian Deuchars

A 230 year-old establishment of dubious heritage: was it an inn, a public house or maybe just houses? Whatever its provenance, The Three Horseshoes is one third of a stalwart trio in a noteworthy village, famed for its church perched atop a quarry cliff visible for miles around, and opposite an 18th Century lock-up. It's a welcoming pub: there's a locals bar with an open fire, where you can quite happily mingle and enjoy a pint. Food, though, is the main emphasis here. Apart from the bar, there are two dining areas with coir matting, walls filled with a variety of pictures, crafts and artefacts, and plenty of space to take it all in. Large mismatched dining tables and odd chairs complete the quirky picture. Nothing quirky about the menus…large blackboards offer ample choice of carefully sourced and combined ingredients in dishes more akin in style to restaurant than pub.

Food serving times:
Monday-Saturday:
  11.45am-2pm,
  5.30pm-9.15pm
Closed 26 December and 1 January
Prices:
Meals: a la carte 20.00/35.00

Typical Dishes

Chicken and black pudding terrine, apple chutney

Braised lamb shank, mustard mash

Chocolate and Whisky trifle

4mi Southwest of Castle Donington by Breedon rd off A453. Parking ❯❯

Bruntingthorpe

008 Joiners Arms

Church Walk, Bruntingthorpe LE17 5QH

Tel.: (0116) 2478258

e-mail: stephen@joinersarmsbruntingthorpe.co.uk - Website: www.thejoinersarms-bruntingthorpe.co.uk

🍷 *VISA* ⓜⓒ

Greene King IPA

B e warned: you might not even recognise the Joiners Arms as a hostelry at all: its smart little whitewashed 18C exterior only bears the most discreet of pub signs. Once inside, any lingering doubts are soon banished: there's a surprising amount of contemporary design, married successfully to wooden beams, recently returned to their natural oak. Drinkers relax on velvet-upholstered furniture; diners can recline on cushioned pews at closely-spaced wood tables. The menu choice is quite small but appealingly formed, incorporating daily changing blackboard specials that are good value, tasty and accomplished, making the most of seasonal ingredients. Service is friendly and polite.

Food serving times:
Tuesday-Saturday:
  12pm-2pm, 6.30pm-9.30pm
Sunday: 12pm-2pm
Closed 25 December and
Bank Holidays
(booking essential)
Prices:
Meals: a la carte 19.50/30.00

Typical Dishes

Rillette of pork, apple
chutney

Blade of beef, horseradish
mash

Chocolate fondant

Between Leicester and Husbands
Bosworth off A5199. Parking

Hallaton

009 ## Bewicke Arms

1 Eastgate, Hallaton LE16 8UB
Tel.: (01858) 555217 - Fax: (01858) 555598

 VISA

Flowers IPA and beers from the Grainstore Brewery

Visit Hallaton on Easter Monday and you won't forget the experience in a hurry. That's the day of the annual Bottle Kicking and Hare Pie Scramble when locals jostle for pieces of pie and teams of men from Hallaton and neighbouring Medbourne engage in a manic free-for-all trying to capture three wooden casks. The 17C Bewicke Arms provides a pleasant change of pace from the strange goings-on. It is rusticity itself: solid stone floor, hop bines, open fires and exposed rafters. Produce from the region, selected on a seasonal basis, forms the hearty backbone to the weekly changing blackboard menus; chatty, friendly service is guaranteed.

Food serving times:
Monday-Saturday:
    12pm-2pm, 7pm-9.30pm
Sunday: 12pm-2pm
(booking essential)
Prices:
Meals: a la carte 15.95/19.50
3 rooms : 40.00/55.00

Typical Dishes

Mushrooms, goat's cheese and tomato

Chicken in boursin cheese and cream sauce

Cappuccino meringue

8mi Northeast of Market Harborough by B664. Parking

Knossington

010 **The Fox and Hounds**

6 Somerby Road, Knossington LE15 8LY

Tel.: (01664) 454676 - Fax: (01664) 454031
Website: www.foxandhounds.biz

 No real ales offered

This lovely, ivy clad 18C former coaching inn makes an ideal refuelling stop after a visit to Rutland Water. Set in a small, pretty village, it's the very picture of a rural Leicestershire pub, with low ceilings, beams and wood tables at the front for al fresco meals. Drinkers relax on stools at the bar; diners make for one of two coir-carpeted rooms with polished wood tables and a choice of cushioned chairs or pew-style banquettes. Daily changing menus comprise good value, modern rustic dishes with local produce in much evidence. Try, perhaps, breast of chicken with chick peas, broad beans and lentils, or grilled calves liver with green beans and tapenade. Warm attentive service is a pleasant plus.

Food serving times:
Tuesday: 7pm-9.30pm
Wednesday-Saturday:
12pm-2.30pm, 7pm-9.30pm
Sunday: 12.30pm-3.30pm,
7pm-9.30pm
Closed 25 December
(booking essential)
Prices:
Meals: a la carte 30.00/50.00

Typical Dishes

Chicken liver parfait, balsamic onion

Calves liver, leeks, bacon and sage

Coffee panna cotta

4mi West of Oakham by A606 and Braunston rd. Parking

Stathern

011 **Red Lion Inn**

2 Red Lion St, Stathern LE14 4HS
Tel.: (01949) 860868 - Fax: (01949) 861579
e-mail: info@theredlioninn.co.uk - Website: www.theredlioninn.co.uk

Grainstore Olive Oil Bitter and guest ales

Though it's hard to put your finger on what makes the Red Lion such a quietly likeable place, the comfortable sitting room, with today's papers over the arms of the leather sofas, is a nice, understated invitation to make yourself at home. A rural inn to the core, filled with wooden antiques, rustic ornaments and bunches of dried flowers, its able, well-priced cooking easily steps out of old pub convention and manages to keep its well-defined contemporary country style while still rotating its dishes day by day: it's a winning formula, but never comes across as formulaic. Try an appetising lemon and herb risotto or herb-crusted cod, served at neat, gingham-clad tables in what was once the pub's skittle alley, or in the little courtyard at the back.

Food serving times:
Monday-Saturday:
12pm-2pm, 7pm-9.30pm
Sunday: 12pm-3pm
Closed 1 January
(booking essential)
Prices:
Meals: 15.50 and a la carte 19.50/28.00

Typical Dishes

Pork and black pudding terrine

Baked fillet of cod, tomato fondue

Sticky toffee pudding

8mi North of Melton Mowbray by A607. Parking

Thorpe Langton

012 Bakers Arms

Main St, Thorpe Langton LE16 7TS

Tel.: (01858) 545201 - Fax: (01858) 545924

e-mail: thebakersarms@tiscali.co.uk - Website: www.thebakersarms.co.uk

  VISA M©

Langton Bakers Dozen

This pleasantly relaxed pub hidden away in a Leicestershire village has a wonderfully appealing 16C thatched appearance; inside, the appeal also harks back to olden days. Scrubbed pine tables - candlelit in the evenings - exposed timbers, pew seats, oriental rugs, all of them surrounded by rich red walls, ensure that the atmosphere is intimate and most convivial. It's not really a drinker's pub, though if you want a pint, you're certainly welcome. The Bakers is aimed more for the dining fraternity, who, judging by their numbers, are well satisfied by their experience here. Menus are innovative and well executed, with good use made of seasonal Leicestershire ingredients.

Food serving times:
Tuesday-Friday:
6.30pm-9.30pm
Saturday-Sunday:
12pm-2pm, 6.30pm-9.30pm
(booking essential)
Prices:
Meals: a la carte 18.00/30.00

Typical Dishes

Pan fried scallops with black pudding

Baked halibut, crab linguini

Berry gazpacho

3.75mi North of Market Harborough by A4304 via Great Bowden. Parking

Buckminster

013 Tollemache Arms 🛏

48 Main St, Buckminster NG33 5SA

Tel.: 01476 860007
e-mail: enquiries@thetollmachearms.com - Website: www.thetollmachearms.com

 ⌂ ♿room **VISA** **AE** **M©**

| London Pride, Timothy Taylors |

I n the heart of Rutland, something's cooking…and the small village of Buckminster is reaping the dividends. The Tollemache was gutted in 2004 (as were many of the villagers when it happened) but the refurbished Arms has gone a mighty long way to redress the balance. Admittedly, it now bears little resemblance to its late Victorian coaching inn origins. In fact, the wood floor, stainless steel topped bar, huge leather sofas and contemporary colour scheme are about as far removed from 'traditional' as it's possible to get. But regulars and visitors alike have taken to the 21st century version, not least due to the cooking qualities of chef Mark, who for three years was chef de partie at the famous Le Manoir in Oxfordshire. His menus are modern British, but nothing too complicated to upset a consistent level. Simple, good value rooms await those staying overnight.

Food serving times:
Closed Sunday dinner and Monday
Prices:
Meals: 15.00 and a la carte 21.00/36.00
🛏 **5 rooms :** 45.00/60.00

Typical Dishes

Warm salad of smoked mozarella

Grilled wild sea bass, basil mash

Chocolate pudding

Off the A1 at Colsterworth, 3,75 mi West on the B676. Parking ➤

Lincoln

014 Wig & Mitre

First Floor, 30-32 Steep Hill, Lincoln LN2 1TL

Tel.: (01522) 535190 - Fax: (01522) 532402
e-mail: email@wigandmitre.com - Website: www.wigandmitre.com

Batemans XB, Black Sheep

Superior and diverse: two words which readily spring to mind when describing this 14C hostelry, now a most welcoming café, bar and restaurant. It's close to the cathedral, a natural resting place after climbing Steep Hill, where it's perched. Walk in past the handsome broad-windowed exterior to the relaxed café: newspapers to read, sofas and pews to lounge in, exposed stone walls, oak floorboards, simple tables, appealing bistro style menus. Upstairs, the dining room has a medieval air about it, with an open fire, shelves of old books, antique prints and banquette seats. Wide ranging menus with much appeal might include roast sausages with garlic and black pudding mash and apple cream sauce; or steamed brill with red wine butter.

Food serving times:
Monday-Sunday:
8am-12am

Prices:
Meals: 13.95 (fixed price lunch) and a la carte 22.00/34.00

Typical Dishes

Cheese soufflé

Fillet steak, crispy onion rings

Raspberry and mascarpone brûlée

Close to the Cathedral

29

Woolsthorpe-by-Belvoir

015 The Chequers ⊨

Main Street, Woolsthorpe-by-Belvoir NG32 1LU

Tel.: (01476) 870701
Website: www.chequers-inn.net

Olde Trip

In the gentle Lincolnshire countryside near 19C Belvoir Castle, this sizeable old coaching inn is made up of lounges, snugs and a bar with original features but all furnished in a modern style, as well as a slightly more formal restaurant. The same menu is served throughout, the variations on a classic British theme together with more contemporary offerings; it's worth asking about the lunchtime set menu. A gravel petanque strip in the back garden should stimulate some healthy competition, and the cricket pitch in the pub grounds hosts village matches from May to September. Alternatively, friendly local staff can also point you in the right direction for a walk towards Grantham. Out in the converted stable block, four neat, pine-furnished rooms in cottage patterns offer useful facilities.

Food serving times:
Monday-Sunday:
  12pm-2.30pm, 7pm-9.30pm
Closed Sunday dinner in winter
Prices:
Meals: 12.50 and a la carte 18.00/28.00
⊨ **4 rooms :** 49.00/59.00
⌓ 5.00

7.5mi West of Grantham by A607. Parking

Typical Dishes

Smoked chicken and Parma ham salad

Roast saddle of lamb

Chocolate fondant, pistachio ice cream

Lowick

016 Snooty Fox

16 Main St, Lowick NN14 3BH
Tel.: (01832) 733434 - Fax: (01832) 733931
e-mail: thesnootyfox@btinternet.com

Old Speckled Hen, Green King IPA, Ruddles County

This spacious inn dates back to 16C; it started life as the local Manor House, and is reputedly haunted by a horse and its rider killed in the Battle of Naseby, a dozen or so miles to the west. Its carved beams are of particular note, but then again, for those who've tasted them, so are the locally renowned rotisserie grill menus and home-made favourites like pasties and cottage pies. You can eat around the sizable bar or in the elegant main dining room. If you're going for meat, select the size of your cut from a nicely stocked chilled cabinet, but if you're after the vegetarian option, then you won't be disappointed either. Prices are keen and the cooking's very good. It's all run, most unsnootily, by experienced and welcoming owners.

Food serving times:
Monday-Sunday:
  12pm-2pm, 6.30pm-9.30pm
Closed dinner 25-26
December and 1 January
Prices:
Meals: a la carte 16.80/23.95

Typical Dishes

Deep fried Brie de Meaux, roast onion jam

Blade of Scotch beef

Hot banana tart with caramel sauce

Village off A6116. Parking

Oundle

017 **The Falcon Inn**

Fotheringhay, Oundle PE8 5HZ

Tel.: (01832) 226254
Website: www.huntsbridge.com

🍴 🍷 ✂ **VISA** **AE** **①** **⓶**

Adnams Best, Greene King IPA and 1 guest ale

Richard III and Mary Queen of Scots aren't a bad couple of names to help draw in the punters: one was born here, one died here (not in the pub, you understand, but in the village of Fotheringhay). Those not aware of the history will still succumb to the warmth of this characterful place, run with professionalism and great personality. Though modernised, it still feels like a all-round good pub: open fires, spindle back chairs, fresh flowers, framed prints picking up on the history, and tubby wood tables. A spacious conservatory offers a formal air, Lloyd Loom chairs, and some impressive cooking from the modern British repertoire: Greek feta burger with light raita and crisp chips, or smoked haddock with potato and chive tart.

Food serving times:
Monday-Sunday:
 12pm-2pm, 6.30pm-9.30pm
Prices:
Meals: 16.50 and a la carte
19.50/29.00

Typical Dishes

Soup of Spring peas, mint
and pancetta

Grilled John Dory, capers
and olives

Panna cotta with cherries

3.75mi North of Oundle by A427 off A605. Parking

Caunton

018 Caunton Beck

Main Street, Caunton NG23 6AB

Tel.: (01636) 636793 - Fax: (01636) 636828
e-mail: email@wigandmitre.com - Website: www.wigandmitre.com

    VISA AE

Marstons Pedigree, Batemans XB, Black sheep special

With the parish church opposite and the beck itself running alongside, this end of Caunton wouldn't look quite right without a neat village pub to complete the picture. Spacious and airy, with exposed brick walls, open fires and a big counter bar, this sympathetically designed modern place is actually bigger than it looks; a smart dining room offering a more formal alternative and soundly prepared lunches and dinners on a traditional base. A typical selection might take in leek and cheese soufflé or monkfish with crispy pancetta, but don't overlook the bar menu, particularly if you're after something a bit lighter or simpler: a keen young team are on hand if you just can't decide.

Food serving times:
Monday-Sunday:
8am-12am

Prices:
Meals: 13.95 and a la carte 22.00/32.00

Typical Dishes

Garlic and rosemary sardines

Rack of lamb, aubergine confit

Honeycomb and caramel crème brûlée

Located on the A616, 6mi past the sugar beet factory. Parking

Colston Bassett

019 Martins Arms

School Lane, Colston Bassett NG12 3FD
Tel.: (01949) 81361 - Fax: (01949) 81039

 🍷 VISA AE MC

Batemans, Marstons Pedigree, London Pride

Blessed indeed are the cheesemakers, for we're right in the heart of "Stilton country", and the owners of the Martins Arms are as proud as anyone of Nottinghamshire's most famous culinary export. Tucked away at the heart of this sleepy rural village, the big pub with the warm and welcoming atmosphere varies its appealing modern menu with the seasons, but cheese connoisseurs will want to try the generous ploughmans lunches or a tasty starter of Stilton rarebit: other dishes from a wide-ranging repertoire, generally with a more complex and contemporary edge, might include pigeon with mushroom ravioli or strawberry mousse. Lunches and dinners are served in a smart, semi-panelled dining room with lovely Queen Anne style chairs, but the spacious bar is equally appealing, with a carved wooden fireplace and rustic brickwork and furnishings.

Food serving times:
Monday-Saturday:
    12pm-2pm, 6pm-10pm
Sunday: 12pm-2pm
Closed dinner 25 December
Prices:
Meals: a la carte 19.95/33.00

East of Cotgrave off A46. Parking ⟫

Typical Dishes

Crab mayonnaise

Braised tournedos of beef, parsnip puree

Hot chocolate fondant

Halam

020 Waggon and Horses

Mansfield Rd, Halam NG22 8AE

Tel.: (01636) 813109 - Fax: (01636) 816228
e-mail: w-h@btconnect.com

✗=rest **VISA** **MC**

Thwaites Best, Bomber and Bloomin

Between Nottingham and Mansfield, just to the east of Sherwood Forest, the Waggon and Horses draws in an appreciative mix of East Midlanders and passers-by, many of whom have heard about its good local reputation. It's no more than due recognition for the owners, who are members of the Campaign for Real Food and try to offer as much fresh, local produce as possible. The pub itself is quite small with low-beamed ceilings and heavy wooden tables; cricket memorabilia betrays the fact you're not so far from Trent Bridge. The dining area, adjacent to the bar, is the place to try out extensive menus: blackboard specials change daily, and the modern, style of the cuisine, allied to the freshness of the ingredients, guarantees a legion of fans.

Food serving times:
Monday-Saturday:
  12pm-2.30pm, 6pm-9.30pm
Sunday: 12pm-2.30pm
Closed 25-26 December
Prices:
Meals: 14.50 and a la carte
20.00/28.00

Typical Dishes

Red mullet marinated in fennel

Calves liver, crispy pancetta

Rhubarb and vanilla brûlée

1.75mi West of Southwell, opposite the school. Parking

Nottingham

021 **Cock and Hoop**

25 High Pavement, Nottingham NG1 1HE
Tel.: 0115 3523231 - Fax: 0115 852 3223
Website: www.cockandhoop.co.uk

 VISA Ⓜⓒ

 Cock & Hoop, Deuchars IPA, Fullers London Pride, Adnams

Known by many names over the last two centuries, the Cock and Hoop has at last come full circle. The cobbled streets of the redeveloped Lace Market have had a change in fortune too, and the refurbished pub fits in well: an old-fashioned front of mullioned windows and brick-and-timber between two dignified 18C neighbours. Inside is a clutch of tables by a brass-edged bar and, downstairs, a much larger lounge and dining area, panelled in pale modern wood. The familiar modern British cuisine works in a few daily variations, but the core of the menu is tasty and substantial cooking in fair quantity – it's the kind of place where you can have one or two courses and feel well satisfied. Pleasantly chatty staff, all in black, keep the place running smoothly.

Food serving times:
Monday-Thursday: 12pm-7pm
Friday-Saturday: 12pm-6pm
Sunday: 12pm-9pm
Closed 25-26 December and 1 January
Prices:
Meals: a la carte 18.00/26.00

Typical Dishes
Smoked chicken and Parma ham salad
Saute of sea bream, new season white asparagus
Pear and almond tart

Adjacent to Lace Market hotel. NCP Stoney St and free on-street parking after 6pm

Clipsham

022 ## The Olive Branch

Main St, Clipsham LE15 7SH

Tel.: (01780) 410355 - Fax: (01780) 410000
e-mail: info@theolivebranchpub.com - Website: www.theolivebranchpub.com

     VISA

 Grainstore Olive Oil, Timothy Taylor Landlord

Gourmets will have their taste buds suitably satiated at this rurally located inn. But, as Rutland residents have appreciated for some years now, there's so much more to this cosy firelit pub than the admittedly first-rate cooking. For instance, the neat pergola doubles as a terrace in good weather, while back inside there's an irresistible mix of country style attractions – church pew seats, open wood fires, and roughly painted walls with sepia prints, cookery books and assorted curios. And the food? Perfectly judged, seasonally inspired dishes – a flavourful mix of the old and new, with plenty of flexibility and originality in the end result. Three charmingly endowed dining areas enrich the enjoyment factor.

Food serving times:
Monday-Sunday:
   12pm-2pm, 7pm-9.30pm
Closed 26 December and 1 January
(booking essential)
Prices:
Meals: 17.00 and a la carte 20.50/32.50

Typical Dishes

Tiger prawn tempura, sweet chilli mayonnaise

Braised shoulder of lamb, rosemary butter beans

Tiramisu, espresso ice cream

9.5mi Northwest of Stormford by B1081 off A1. Parking

Hambleton

023 **Finch's Arms**

Ketton Rd., Hambleton LE15 8TL

Tel.: (01572) 756575 - Fax: (01572) 771142
e-mail: finchsarms@talk21.com - Website: www.finchsarms.co.uk

   VISA

 Timothy Taylor Landlord, Oakham ales, Grainstore ales

It doesn't matter why you come to the Finch's; you're not likely to find the experience unrewarding. Some tourists want to see its location: alone, surrounded by the vast expanse of Rutland Water. Others want to relax on the splendid hillside terrace and check out the views from another angle. But many arrive wanting to enjoy the pub's atmosphere: an inviting rusticity in keeping with its surroundings; there are open fires, coir carpets, scrubbed, candle-lit wooden tables, and pew-style benches. The more formal rear dining room has solid stone-topped tables. Rather complex menus have an appealing quality full of fresh, seasonal ingredients: typically, ballottine of guinea fowl with prunes. A weekly changing blackboard menu is more down-to-earth. Impressive bedrooms have a French country feel.

Food serving times:
Monday-Sunday:
12pm-2.30pm,
6.30pm-9.30pm
Closed 25 December
Prices:
Meals: 11.50 and a la carte
15.00/25.00
 6 rooms : 65.00/75.00

Typical Dishes

Gambas 'à la plancha'

Rack of lamb, rosemary sauce

3mi East of Oakham by A606. Parking

Lyddington

024 **Old White Hart**

51 Main Street, Lyddington LE15 9LR
Tel.: (01572) 821703 - Fax: (01572) 821965
e-mail: mail@oldwhitehart.co.uk - Website: www.oldwhitehart.com

 VISA

Fullers London Pride, Greene King Abbott, IPA

Among the happy throng of drinkers at this wonderfully unstuffy, unfussy pub you'll find a surprising number of petanque players, drawn by the – probably unique – 10-lane boules court. Of course, you don't need to be a sporty type to appreciate the delights of this pretty Rutland village inn. The gardens offer plenty of outdoor seats, but in winter you'll prefer the roaring fires, welcoming beamed bar and nice feeling of intimacy which ensues. When you're hungry, dine on good value lunch menus or, later, a seasonal à la carte with plenty of choice. The daily changing blackboard fish specials are tasty and renowned: try, perhaps, the Grimsby haddock or mussels in white wine and garlic. Well-kept bedrooms await those staying overnight.

Food serving times:
Monday-Saturday:
 12pm-2pm, 6.30pm-9pm
Sunday: 12pm-2pm
Closed 25 December
Prices:
Meals: 12.95 and a la carte 18.00/38.00
5 rooms : 55.00/85.00

Typical Dishes

Liver parfait, fig compote

English lamb, redcurrant jus

Jam roly poly, custard

1.5mi south of Uppingham off A6003. By the village green. Parking

Stretton

025 ## The Jackson Stops Inn *We most liked*

Rookery Rd, Stretton LE15 7RA

Tel.: (01780) 410237 - Fax: (01780) 410280

e-mail: james@jacksonstops-inn.fsnet.co.uk

🛩️ 🍷 ✂️ *VISA* ⓜ©

Adnams Broadside, Oakham Ales JHB, Timothy Taylor Landlord, Hop Back Brewery Summer Lightning

When estate agent Jackson Stops sold off the Stretton Estate in 1955, their sign was outside what was then The White Horse pub for so long that it became known as the Jackson Stops. An interesting little anecdote which goes some way to explaining why a 17C, rurally set thatched inn should end up with such an unusual name. It's a wonderfully characterful place, rustic down to its Rutland wellies; a low wooden bar is frequented by regulars, but this then gives way to a surprising four dining areas, minimalist with plain décor and vintage scrubbed tables, silver chargers glinting in welcome. A very pleasant atmosphere prevails; the constantly evolving menus offer good value, rustic British cooking.

Food serving times:
Tuesday-Saturday:
12pm-2pm, 7pm-10pm
Sunday: 12pm-2pm
Closed 25 December and New Year and Bank Holiday Mondays
Prices:
Meals: a la carte 20.00/25.95

Typical Dishes

Ham hock and mustard terrine

Herb stuffed chicken

Pear Tart Tatin, vanilla ice cream

8mi Northwest of Stamford by B1081 off A1. Parking ⟩⟩

Wing

026 **Kings Arms**

13 Top St, Wing LE15 8SE

Tel.: (01572) 737634 - Fax: (01572) 737255

e-mail: info@thekingsarms-wing.co.uk - Website: www.thekingsarms-wing.co.uk

room **VISA** **AE** **MC**

 Timothy Taylor Landlord, Marston Pedigree, Grainstore Cooking, and 1 guest

Built in the early days of Cromwell's Britain, this delightful place gave the Restoration time to settle before becoming "The Kings Arms", but the cosy bar can't have changed much over the last 350 years or so. Flagstone floors, ancient beams and a big open fire lend true period warmth, while more recent prints and paintings of Rutland and around reflect a local pride that comes across just as clearly on the menu. Fresh and substantial dishes on a traditional base make good use of seasonal produce from our smallest county, and the landlord and team chip in well with relaxed, conversational service. All well away from the main bar, the bedrooms are warm and immaculately kept. Rutland Water is a short drive away.

Food serving times:
Monday-Sunday:
12pm-2pm, 6pm-9pm
Prices:
Meals: a la carte 18.00/28.00
 7 rooms : 65.00/75.00

Typical Dishes

Marinated herring fillets

Rib-eye steak, garlic herb butter

Baked chocolate fondant

5mi South of Oakham by A6003. Parking

*W*ith culinary tastes ranging from fresh samphire-shoots to cockles, smoked eel and Cromer crab, it's easy to get a flavour of the East of England. It's a region with strong brewing traditions and some of England's most charming pubs, but it's also a place of rich historic roots and a deep attachment to rural life. Here you'll find the medieval wool towns of Lavenham, Coggeshall and Saffron Walden and the old trading centres of Norwich and King's Lynn, Ely's distant tower and the Palladian splendour of Holkham Hall. Be part of the world-famous Aldeburgh music festival or the first Classics of the racing season at Newmarket; cast off into the waterways of the Norfolk Broads or lie back in a punt and drift down the Cam past the beautiful Cambridge colleges. Stroll through the fields of a lavender farm or strike out into the wilds, under the great open sky of the coast and the salt marshes, and spot basking seals, a flight of curlew or the rare wildlife of the broadland meadows. Wherever you go exploring, it's bound to be an inspiration. "They made me a painter and I am grateful", Constable once said of the walks along the Stour near his boyhood home. We can't guarantee the same for everyone, but you'll certainly work up an appetite along the way…

Bolnhurst

001 ## The Plough at Bolnhurst

Kimbolton Rd, Bolnhurst MK44 2EX

Tel.: 01234 376274

e-mail: theplough@bolnhurst.com - Website: www.bolnhurst.com

   VISA

Batemans XB, Fullers London Pride

Razed to the ground nearly two decades ago, the pure white Plough has been lovingly and sympathetically restored to something like its original 14th century glory and was reopened in the summer of 2005. The charming interior offers an inglenook, thick rustic walls, and wood and stone floors in three main seating areas with reassuringly low ceilings and exposed beams. You can't help but feel utterly relaxed. Step outside and there's a duck pond, spacious gardens and two extensive terraces. Local produce is keenly sought and carefully prepared on menus which also pay due homage to the seasons. There's an eclectic feel to what's on offer: amongst the modern dishes, look out too for old favourites that have stood the test of time.

Food serving times:
Closed 25 December, Sunday dinner and Monday except Bank Holidays

Prices:
Meals: 15.00 (fixed price lunch) and a la carte 20.00/28.00

Typical Dishes

Seared scallops, pea and mint purée

Slow braised pork belly, bubble and squeak

Sticky toffee pudding

South of village on B660. Parking

Houghton Conquest

002 **Knife and Cleaver**

The Grove, Houghton Conquest MK45 3LA

Tel.: (01234) 740387 - Fax: (01234) 740900

e-mail: info@knifeandcleaver.com - Website: www.knifeandcleaver.com

  ⊱rest

Fuller's London Pride, Batemans XB and Stowford Press Cider

This 17C redbrick inn is situated right opposite the church. It's lovely on a July day, when those in the know find a white metal table out in the garden, but the bar is also most inviting with a warm log fire, deep purple décor and black timbers - settle down on mahogany chairs, stools or even a small sofa. The area at the side – the old darts room – now looks rather contemporary, and minimalist, too, with just four tables. Menus go across the board from traditional to modern, light to substantial. Alternatively, a conservatory restaurant, which overlooks the garden, offers a fine choice of fish from an altogether more serious selection. Best produce is paramount. Pleasant bedrooms, in former stables, are individually styled and carefully furnished.

Food serving times:

Monday-Saturday:
  12pm-2.30pm, 7pm-9.30pm

Sunday and Bank Holiday
Mondays :   12pm-2.30pm

Closed 27-30 December
(bar lunch Saturday)

Prices:

Meals: 15.95/22.00 and a la carte 22.25/35.40

🛏 **9 rooms :** 53.00/78.00

Typical Dishes

Seared king scallops

Rack of Welsh lamb, mint risotto

Dark chocolate tart, mascarpone ice cream

6.5mi South of Bedford by A6. Near All Saints Church. Parking

47

Milton Bryan

003 ## The Red Lion

Toddington Rd, Milton Bryan MK17 9HS

Tel.: (01525) 210044 - Fax: (01525) 211564
e-mail: paul@redlion-miltonbryan.co.uk - Website: www.redlion-miltonbryan.co.uk

      VISA **MC**

Greene King IPA, Abbot, Old Speckled Hen and 1 guest ale

You can't miss this place in early summer, when the white-gabled, redbrick pub is polka-dotted with a truly extravagant show of overflowing hanging baskets: the old English pub in Glorious Technicolor. Inside, the wood-floored, bare-brick public bar offers a tasty lunch menu of all-time pub favourites, but there's greater seasonal variety in the more formal restaurant, the friendly tenants gladly going the extra mile to find good ingredients for their Thai fishcakes, pheasant confit and a crisp and creamy leek and goat's cheese tart. For friendly neighbourhood atmosphere, it takes some beating, and there's real warmth and thoughtfulness to the service, too.

Food serving times:
Monday-Saturday:
    12pm-2.30pm, 7pm-9.30pm
Sunday: 12pm-2.30pm
Closed 25-26 December and
Monday dinner in winter
Prices:
Meals: a la carte 17.50/27.50

Milton Bryan is South of Woburn by A4012. Parking

Typical Dishes

Caramelised onion and cherry tomato tartlet

Roast cod, saffron mash and salsa verde

Toffee and peach meringue

Old Warden

004 ## Hare & Hounds

Nr Biggleswade, Old Warden SG18 9HQ

Tel.: (01767) 627225 - Fax: (01767) 627588
Website: www.thehare&houndsoldwarden.co.uk

Eagle IPA, Charles Wells Bombardier, Adnams

Such a sincerely friendly welcome at the bar is always a good sign: you'd be welcome to stop here for a pint, but such enjoyable and fairly-priced food is just too good to miss. Three chic but cosy country dining rooms, decorated in tweeds, floral patterns and soft autumnal colours, are an appropriate setting for rustic cooking with a good modern and traditional balance. Plentiful and full-flavoured dishes come and go – it all depends on the season and a handful of trusted local suppliers – but appealing blackboard specials supplement the menu: try a rich, crisp spiced duck confit with lentils and bacon or the Shuttleworth pork plate of fillet, belly and sausage. It's the staff who really make the difference, though: discreetly attentive and genuinely enthusiastic about the dishes they serve.

Food serving times:
Tuesday-Saturday:
   12pm-2pm, 6pm-9.30pm
Sunday: 12pm-3pm
Open Bank Holiday Mondays
Prices:
Meals: a la carte 20.00/30.00

Typical Dishes

Smoked duck pancake, chilli jam

Chicken breast, wild mushroom butter sauce

Caramelised Lemon tart

3.5mi West of Biggleswade by A6001 off B658. Parking

Shefford

005 **The Black Horse** 🛏

Ireland, Shefford SG17 5QL

Tel.: (01462) 811398 - Fax: (01462) 817238
e-mail: blackhorseireland.com

🛖 ♈ ✂ **VISA** **MC**

Fuller's IPA and 1 guest ale

Food serving times:
Monday-Saturday:
  12pm-2.30pm, 6.30pm-10pm
Sunday: 12pm-2.30pm
Closed 25-26 December and
1 January
Prices:
Meals: a la carte 14.00/22.00
🛏 **2 rooms :** 55.00

Y ou'd be hard put to find fault with this 17C white pub not far from the A1. For starters, it boasts a charming garden with bench seats and stylish patio, while inside the feel is no less comfortably rustic. The front bar's old and new beams are warmly off set by polished tables; an adjacent dining room boasts a stylish country feel. Main dining is at the rear in a 21C extension: again, very cool and contemporary, with an African theme predominating. The same menu is served throughout and changes every three months. Well-executed, modern dishes with a classic base ensure the Black Horse retains a serious dining tag. Two bedrooms, neat, up-to-date and compact, guarantee the satisfaction factor remains high.

Typical Dishes

Marinated mushrooms, parmesan risotto

Trio of pork, pink peppercorn sauce

Orange polenta cake

1.75mi Northwest of Shefford by B658 and Ireland Rd. Parking

Steppingley

006 The French Horn

Steppingley MK45 5AU

Tel.: 01525 712051 - Fax: 01525 714067
e-mail: paul@thefrenchhorn.com

Old Speckled Hen

The pretty hamlet of Steppingley boasts this late 18th century pub that features a beautiful period restaurant from the 1950s that's metamorphosed via a super recent makeover. Original character remains in the front bar, where flag flooring and rustic beams are the order of the day. But it's the main dining room that's taken the regulars by pleasant surprise. There are stylish dark leather chairs, dark varnished solid wood tables, bright, modern oil paintings and contemporary lighting. The food is very well regarded. Menus change seasonally and skilfully combine a classic base with the chef's individual flair. Presentation is strong and flavours intense, raising the standard to above the pub norm. To build up a hunger before your visit, take a leisurely stroll through the glories of nearby Woburn Park.

Food serving times:
Monday-Saturday:
12pm-2.30pm,
6.30pm-9.30pm
Sunday: 12pm-3pm
Closed Sunday dinner
Booking essential
Prices:
Meals: a la carte 26.40/31.40

Typical Dishes

Twice baked Roquefort soufflé

Fillet of pork, mustard and cider jus

Warm chocolate cake

4.5 miles from Woburn through The Park. Between junctions 12 and 13 of M1. Parking

Woburn

007 **The Birch**

20 Newport Rd, Woburn MK17 9HX
Tel.: (01525) 290295 - Fax: (01525) 290899
Website: www.birchwoburn.com

  rest **VISA** **AE** **MC**

Adnams, Fuller's London Pride

This established dining pub, like much else in Woburn, sits confidently in the superior category. Locals and visitors mingle contentedly in an establishment that offers a very agreeable ambience, from the pleasant outside decking terrace to the stylish mix of furnishings within; these include mosaic and pine tables and rugs on the floors. At the back, the dining area covers two levels, not counting the conservatory extension: Mediterranean style décor gels comfortably with wooden chairs and tables. All eyes are on an open kitchen in the corner, where the satisfying modern dishes, particularly meat and fish, are conjured up from the grill. An interesting evening à la carte menu is balanced with lighter lunchtime dishes.

Food serving times:
Monday-Saturday:
12pm-2.30pm, 6.15pm-10pm
Sunday: 12pm-2.30pm
Closed 25-26 December and
1 January
(booking essential)
Prices:
Meals: a la carte 18.95/27.95

Typical Dishes

Mussel and smoked salmon risotto

Duck breast wrapped in parma ham

Chilled lime and tequilla

0.5mi North on A5130. Parking

Broughton

008 ## The Crown

Bridge Rd, Broughton PE28 3 AY

Tel.: (01487) 824428 - Fax: (01487) 824912
e-mail: simon@thecrownbrougton.co.uk - Website: www.thecrownbroughton.co.uk

   VISA **MC**

 Adnams Broadside, Greene King IPA, City of Cambridge Hobson's Choice

This soft-hued brick pub nestles in the archetypal English country village scenario: next to the church, surrounded on all sides by rustic repose. Owned by the village, it boasts a large lawned garden and paved terrace with benches. Inside, the 21C has come calling: it's essentially one room divided by a fireplace, with modern tiled floor, pine furniture, bare tables and farmhouse chairs. The clean, uncluttered ambience is enhanced with bright bay windows, mustard walls and golden wood beams which create a sunny, open feel. Menus – which change monthly and feature blackboard specials at lunch and dinner – are keenly priced and modern with a classic French base.

Food serving times:
Wednesday-Sunday:
    12pm-2pm, 6.30pm-9pm
Closed 1-11 January
Prices:
Meals: 13.50 and a la carte
18.00/27.00

Typical Dishes

Warm venison salad

Skate wing, capers and lemon butter

Toffee panna cotta

6mi Northeast of Huntingdon by B1514 off A141. Opposite the village church. Parking

Fowlmere

009 ## The Chequers

High Street, Fowlmere SG8 7SR

Tel.: (01763) 208369 - Fax: (01763) 208944

Adnams, Archers, Nethergate

There's history at every turn in this fascinating 16C inn, built into the timbers and displayed on the walls: Spitfires and Mustangs are frozen in time in old photographs of Fowlsmere airfield and even the colours of the sign comemmorate the pub's finest hour, mirroring the chequerboard insignia of the British and American fighter squadrons who made this their local during the Second World War. Sound, satisfying cooking on a traditional base includes Dover sole, a hearty smoked haddock, cheese and tomato bake and homemade date pudding; you can eat in the conservatory, overlooking the garden, in the beamed and galleried dining room or in the bar itself. After dinner, settle down by the fire and try one – or more – of the thirty malt whiskies: the long-standing owners will be happy to recommend a personal favourite.

Food serving times:
Monday-Sunday:
   12pm-2pm, 7pm-9.30pm
Closed 25 December
Prices:
Meals: a la carte 23.00/32.50

Off B1368. Parking

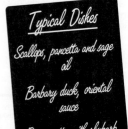

Typical Dishes

Scallops, pancetta and sage oil

Barbary duck, oriental sauce

Panna cotta with rhubarb

Great Staughton

010 The Tavern on the Green

12 The Green, Great Staughton PE19 5DG

Tel.: 01480 860336 - Fax: 01480 869426

e-mail: thetavernonthegreen@btinternet.com

  VISA

Green King IPA, Abbot, Ruddles County, Ale Fresco, Potton Gold and Village Bike, Hopback Summer Lightening

A note on the bottom of the menu says: "Taxis are very scarce around here – book in advance." They could just as easily be offering advice to prospective diners, because the Tavern on the Green's reputation is spreading fast. Close to Grafham Water, it's a pleasant pub, the hub of a proudly rural village. Any claims to traditionality, though, disappear once inside: the open interior has a distinctively modern feel, enhanced by comfy leather tub chairs and effusive arrangements of lilies. There are three main dining areas with wood tables and a warm, relaxing ambience. Chilled meat is on display: you can buy steak dishes by 25 gram weight, and there's a wide selection. If your tastes differ, very good value daily set menus are also on offer, supplemented by blackboard specials. The seasonal, modern dishes are underscored by a host of favourites.

Food serving times:
Monday-Sunday:
12pm-2pm, 6.30pm (7pm Sunday)-9.30pm
Closed dinner 25 December and 1-2 January
Prices:
Meals: 13.95/15.00 (not Sunday lunch or Saturday dinner) and a la carte 18.00/25.00

On A45 northwest of St Neots. Parking.

Typical Dishes

Serrano ham with wood roasted Spanish pepper

Fillet of Cornish lamb, olives and herbs

Chocolate and almond torte

Hemingford Grey

011 **The Cock**

47, High St, Hemingford Grey PE28 9BJ
Tel.: (01480) 463609 - Fax: (01480) 461747
e-mail: info@cambscuisine.com - Website: www.cambscuisine.com

 🍷 ✂ *VISA* Ⓜ🄲

> *Woodfordes Wherry, Elgoods Black Dog Mild, City of Cambridge Hobson's Choice, JHB Oakham Ale*

This lovely 17C village pub has been stripped back to basics by its owners, and given a new lease of life in the process. Locals flock to the pubby part, which revels in its original simplicity. A separate room, it specialises in real ale, and has won several accolades in this department. Don't expect food at the bar: if you're here to satisfy an appetite rather than slake your thirst, step into the main dining area, spacious and soft-toned with wooden floors and a comfy, traditional tables and chairs. A wood burning stove crackles, and saleable oil paintings might tempt you into a purchase. The menu is individual and offers a good choice of British and European dishes, on top of a well-priced light lunch selection. Specialities are fresh fish blackboard specials, and the hallmark sausage board.

Food serving times:
Monday-Friday:
 12pm-2.30pm, 7pm-9.30pm
Saturday-Sunday:
 12pm-2.30pm,
 6.30pm-9.30pm
Closed 25-26 December
Prices:
Meals: 11.95 and a la carte
18.85/29.85

Typical Dishes

Sardines, fennel and radish salad

Chump of lamb, salsa verde

Meringue with lemon curd and passion fruit

5mi South East of Huntingdon by A1198 off A14. Parking

Horningsea

012 Crown and Punchbowl 🛏

High St, Horningsea CB5 9JG

Tel.: (01223) 860643 - Fax: (01223) 441814
e-mail: rd@cambscuisine.com - Website: www.cambscuisine.com

   VISA AE MC

City of Cambridge Hobsons Choice

When is a pub not a pub? Answer: when it comes in the guise of the Crown & Punchbowl. This marriage of two buildings, one 17C, the other 19C, looks and feels like a pub, but doesn't actually have a bar, so anyone revisiting from 200 years ago would wonder what had happened to the village inn. It's certainly been given a modern makeover: wooden floors, farmhouse tables and chairs, rattan seats, neutral décor, contemporary lighting. Lovely old beams will take you back, though. Menus are a mixture of traditional, modern and international; favourite features include the sausage mix and match board and fresh fish blackboard. Clean, modern bedrooms keep the modish feel intact.

Food serving times:
12pm-2.30pm, 6.30pm-9pm
Friday-Saturday:
6.30pm-9.30pm
Closed Sunday dinner
Prices:
Meals: a la carte 16.00/30.00
🛏 **5 rooms :** 59.95/79.95

Typical Dishes

Venison carpaccio

Guinea fowl , creamed cabbage

Rhubarb panna cotta

4mi Northeast of Cambridge by A1303 and B1047 on Horningsea rd. Parking

Keyston

013 **The Pheasant**
Village Loop Road, Keyston PE28 0RE
Tel.: (01832) 710241
Website: www.huntsbridge.com

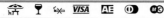

Adnams Best and 2 guest ales

A tip for drivers tearing along the A14 on the Cambridgeshire and Northamptonshire borders: turn off at Keyston and sample a taste of this gloriously thatched inn. A dining pub writ large, The Pheasant consistently serves a range of good value, eclectic dishes in three agreeable dining areas. Regulars mingle in the airy, timbered bar with its open fire, muskets on the wall and well-spaced wooden tables, but if the going gets too busy there, then the rear section – decorated with a mix of pictures and prints - is just as pleasant a place to eat. Interesting, modern à la carte menus with international influences are never less than accomplished and offer plenty of balanced flavour. Helpful, efficient service is a given wherever you decide to eat.

Food serving times:
Monday-Sunday:
 12pm-2pm, 6.30pm-9.30pm
(booking essential)
Prices:
Meals: a la carte 19.00/29.00

Typical Dishes

Salad of Portland crab

Shoulder of lamb, fricassée of beans and vegetables

Banana and toffee crumble

3.5mi Southeast of Thrapstone by A14 on B663. Parking

Madingley

014 Three Horseshoes

High St, Madingley CB3 8AB
Tel.: (01954) 210221 - Fax: (01954) 212043
Website: www.huntsbridge.com

Adnams, Hobsons Choice, London Pride

This picture-perfect thatched pub is an ideal bolt-hole for visitors slightly overwhelmed by tourist numbers in Cambridge. It's located in a village just to the west of the city, and presents an elegant, centuries-old exterior to the world: it used to be the local smithy. The interior, though, comes right up to date. There's a stylish, airy ambience, attributable in part to the pale floorboards, modern log fire and sage green walls, though the alert service has something to do with it too. Eat in the bar - which does a well-priced, short grill menu - or in the smartly set conservatory at the back. It has painted chairs and stylish cloth-clad tables, and menus are innovative, full of interesting combinations.

Food serving times:
Monday-Sunday:
  12pm-2pm, 6.30pm-9.30pm
Prices:
Meals: a la carte 32.00/45.00

Typical Dishes

Portland crab, dill and lemon

Salmon, spiced chick peas and gremolata

Caramelised lemon tart

4.5mi West of Cambridge by A1303. Parking

Spaldwick

015 ## The George

5, High St, Spaldwick PE28 0TD
Tel.: (01480) 890293 - Fax: (01480) 896847

 ❖✗ ✗ **VISA** Ⓜ︎Ⓔ︎

Fuller's London Pride, Adnams Broadside, Theakstons Old Peculier

This early 16C inn is defined on the exterior by its characterful, crooked appearance, but inside refurbishment has been going on apace, and the renovated airy interior now has a bold, clean and uncluttered contemporary look. Lilac and aubergine walls blend with exposed black beams, tiled and wood floors, scrubbed wood tables, and leather armchairs around a lovely fireplace, with the inn's history framed above. The restaurant – also spacious – blends old ceiling timbers with pink hued leather banquettes and rich oil paintings: a stylish statement indeed. Menus here are modern European with solid British classics. You can also take your pick from the blackboard.

Food serving times:
Monday-Sunday:
   12pm-2.30pm, 6pm-9.30pm
Closed dinner 25 December and 1 January
Prices:
Meals: a la carte 17.95/31.95

Typical Dishes

Smoked salmon, red pepper ice cream

Duck breast, black pudding, braised red cabbage

Baked passion fruit

7.5mi West of Huntingdon by A141 off A14. Parking

Stilton

016 Village Bar (at Bell Inn)

Great North Rd, Stilton PE7 3RA

Tel.: (01733) 241066 - Fax: (01733) 245173

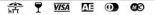

JHB Bitter, Greene King IPA and Abbot Ale, Fuller's London Pride

You know you're in for a cheery experience the moment you come upon this part 16C inn with garden: its swinging red bell pub sign almost beckons you in off the street. The separate Village Bar is the heart and soul of the place, charmingly rustic in its appeal: rough stone walls, flag flooring, large wooden tables with benches and a mix of chairs. Local memorabilia all adds to the characterful mix. It shares its menu with the adjoining Courtyard bar. Expect robust cooking, international influences embellishing a firm traditional base. Hearty portions are guaranteed, and Stilton cheese turns up in soups, dumplings, quiche and dressings. Bedrooms are in the Bell Inn proper: some are deluxe, all are individually styled and well kept.

Food serving times:
Monday-Sunday:
  12pm-2pm, 6.30pm-9.30pm
Closed 25 December
Prices:
Meals: 10.95/25.95 and a la carte 16.00/26.00

Typical Dishes

Chicken roulade, potato and olive salad

Braised English lamb, Stilton dumplings

Prune and Armagnac tart

In centre of village. Parking

Sutton Gault

017 ## Anchor Inn

Sutton Gault CB6 2BD

Tel.: (01353) 778537 - Fax: (01353) 776180
e-mail: anchorinn@popmail.bta.com - Website: www.anchor-inn-restaurant.co.uk

 VISA **AE** **MC**

City of Cambridge Hobson's Choice, Boathouse Bitter

Standing by the bridge over the New Bedford River, this lovely, ever-popular inn can claim to be as old as the Levels landscape itself: the story goes that it was built to house Vermuyden's navvies, who ditched and drained the Cambridgeshire marshes back in the 1650s. Today, gas lamps and open fires light several charming little rooms, and a strong local reputation rests on the tasty cooking. Blackboard specials have a particularly seasonal flavour and the Modern British repertoire finds room for some ambitious Mediterranean touches: typical dishes include Cromer crab, halibut with spinach and artichoke risotto, and sticky toffee pudding with rum and raisin ice cream. Conscientious and personable staff certainly know their regulars, but see to it that everyone is well looked-after

Food serving times:
Monday-Friday:
12pm-2pm, 7pm-9pm
Saturday: 12pm-2pm
6.30pm-9.30pm
Closed 26 December
(fixed price lunch only Sunday)
Prices:
Meals: a la carte 27.00/33.00
2 rooms : 50.00/115.00

Typical Dishes

Dates in bacon, mustard cream sauce

Poussin and Asparagus with lemongrass and watercress sauce

Off B1381; follow signs to Sutton Gault from Sutton village. Pub is near the New Bedford River. Parking

Blackmore

018 Leather Bottle

The Green, Blackmore CM4 0RL

Tel.: (01277) 823538

e-mail: leatherbottle@tiscali.co.uk - Website: www.theleatherbottle.net

 Adnams and various guest ales

A pleasant, well-run place and something of a family enterprise, the Leather Bottle has that confidence-inspiring neighbourhood feel to it: the guest beer mats decorating the walls of the little public bar will be invitation enough to any real ale converts and, in these welcoming surroundings, even sceptics might be tempted to try a half. Diners arriving in good time can choose between a table in the simply styled conservatory overlooking the garden or near the wood burner in the front bar, where a frequently changing menu blends traditional British and eclectic Mediterranean styles, with satisfying results: simple snacks and a handful of daily specials lend a touch of variety. Smooth but unpretentious service.

Food serving times:
Monday-Saturday:
12pm-2pm, 7pm-9pm
Sunday: 12pm-4pm
Closed 26 December and
1 January

Prices:
Meals: 14.00 and a la carte
17.50/30.00

2.75mi Southeast of High Ongar by A414. Parking in front of the pub

Typical Dishes

Smoked red mullet salad

Lamb's liver and bacon

Cointreau and coconut parfait

Clavering

019 **Cricketers** 🛏

Clavering CB11 4QT

Tel.: (01799) 550442 - Fax: (01799) 550882

e-mail: cricketers@lineone.net - Website: www.thecricketers.co.uk

 🍽 🍷 ⚞ **VISA** **AE** **MC**

Adnams, Adnams Explorer, Ridleys IPA

How many landlords could get Jamie Oliver to do the washing-up for pocket money? Mr and Mrs Oliver have been running this well-established local since The Naked Chef was in short trousers and not much has changed over the years: old beams, velour seats, a few newspaper cuttings and a lot of satisfied regulars. Gastro-pilgrims expecting an audioguide and photos of Jamie's dad inventing the Botham Burger will just have to like it for what it is, though that's easily done, and a nicely balanced menu is bound to put a smile on their faces – dishes range from dependable classics to a few recipes from the local hero. If you'd like to stay the night, the bedrooms in the pavilion are traditionally styled and those in the courtyard are more modern.

Food serving times:
Monday-Sunday:
    12pm-2pm, 7pm-10pm
Closed 25-26 December
Prices:
Meals: a la carte 15.00/26.00
🛏 **14 rooms :** 70.00/100.00

Typical Dishes

Avocado pear and crabmeat thermidor

Monkfish fillet, red wine butter sauce

Traditional English trifle

On the B1038. Parking ▸▸

Dedham

020 ## The Sun Inn

High St, Dedham CO7 6DF

Tel.: (01206) 323351

e-mail: info@thesuninndedham.com - Website: www.thesuninndedham.com

 room **VISA** **MC**

Earl Soham Victoria, Crouch Vale Gold, Buffys

O pposite its contemporary, the 15C village church, this handsome inn is an understated blend of tradition and up-to-date style; despite recent renovations, it still feels surprisingly unspoilt. Behind a suitably cheery sunshine-yellow façade, polished period oak and bright modern bouquets fill the spacious front and back rooms. Pick a table, then choose from an affordable, well-sourced menu which changes day by day, adopting an original approach to Italian, Spanish and Maghreb traditions; antipasti platters are good for sharing, but you may find it hard to part with a forkful of chicken tagine, Tuscan sausage on spicy black beans or light and juicy cannellini and sage risotto. Thoughtfully appointed modern rooms include one with a four-poster bed. Walks up to the River Stour and Constable's beloved Flatford start right outside the door

Food serving times:
Monday-Sunday:
12pm-2.30pm,
6.30pm-9.30pm
Closed 25-27 December
Prices:
Meals: a la carte 15.00/25.00
4 rooms : 55.00/120.00

Typical Dishes

Mushroom and baby beetroot bruschetta

Pork chop with aioli

Rhubarb fool

In the centre of the village opposite the church. Parking

Earls Colne

021 Carved Angel

Upper Holt Street, Earls Colne CO6 2PG

Tel.: (01787) 222330 - Fax: (01787) 220013
e-mail: info@carvedangel.com - Website: www.carvedangel.com

      VISA MC

Greene King IPA, Adnams Bitter and guest ales

Relaxed and full of character, this 15C inn has been stylishly updated to the last detail: a bright conservatory extention, subtle lighting, sprays of flowers, foodie pictures on the sage green walls and strings of little blackboard menu plaquettes hanging down from the beamed ceiling. These offer plenty of choice, detailing neatly presented modern gastropub standards and traditional dishes, some with a subtle continental influence – a typical selection might well include lamb chops, smoked haddock rarebit, roast poussin with a watercress sauce, crispy duck spring roll and pistachio crème brûlée. Service is unobtrusive and pleasant, but even at quieter times they stick rigidly to their rule about ordering everything from the bar.

Food serving times:
Monday-Saturday:
11.30am-2pm, 7pm-9pm
Sunday:
12pm-3.00pm, 7pm-9pm
Closed 26 December
Prices:
Meals: 12.95 and a la carte 17.95/25.00

Typical Dishes

Duck bresaola, redcurrant and apple

Herb crusted roast cod with chunky chips

Chocolate cake with pistachio

On sharp bend just outside of the town. Parking

Fuller Street

022 Square & Compasses

Fuller Street CM3 2BB

Tel.: (01245) 361477
Website: www.squareandcompasses.co.uk

  VISA

Ridleys IPA and either Nethergate's Suffolk County or a guest ale

For those who like their pubs with plenty of character, this is an absolute gem. Bringing a little piece of Cold Comfort Farm eccentricity to the wilds of Essex, a bizarre collection of rural odds and ends includes a stuffed owl, old riding tackle, in fact, almost everything but a square and compasses. Ancient farm implements hang from the walls and the photo of a farmer who used them also tells a story. It could so easily feel unnerving or "over-local", but it turns out to be welcoming and extremely cosy, thanks in part to the polite staff behind the bar. A blackboard and a printed menu list lots of dishes available in either starter or large size portions, with local game and traditional British recipes well represented; a simpler menu on Sunday evenings concentrates on pies and quiches.

Food serving times:
Tuesday-Saturday:
　　12pm-2.30pm, 7pm-9pm
Sunday:　　　　　　12pm-3pm
Closed Sunday dinner and Monday
Prices:
Meals: a la carte 17.50/28.00

Typical Dishes

Duck, Port and raspberry pâte

Honey glazed chump of lamb

Mango and apricot cheesecake

Between Chelmsford and Braintree off A131. Parking

High Ongar

 023 **The Wheatsheaf**

King St, High Ongar CM5 9NS
Tel.: (01277) 822220 - Fax: (01277) 822441

Greene King IPA

Pretty and well-restored it may be, but The Wheatsheaf wouldn't be half the place it is without its hard-working staff; cordial, well-informed and eager to please, but in a very genuine, down-to-earth way. They serve four rooms – decorated with ornaments, bric-a-brac and floral fabrics – surrounding a central bar, but if you feel like an open-air summer lunch, ask them if there's a free table in the garden. A classically based British menu, notable for its well-combined but nicely defined flavours, varies from one day to the next, but past dishes have included a rich and fluffy goat's cheese and pecan soufflé, cod with a cheese and bacon crumble crust and rhubarb jelly and ice cream, with caramelised oranges for a zingy foil.

Food serving times:
Tuesday-Friday:
12pm-1.45pm,
6.30pm-8.45pm
Saturday: 6.30pm-9.30pm
Sunday: 12pm-3pm
Closed from 26 December for 2 weeks, 1 week June and 1 week October (booking essential)
Prices:
Meals: a la carte 23.00/35.00

Typical Dishes

Scallops, guacamole and bacon

Roast guinea fowl, honey and garlic

Home made ice creams

2mi East by A414 on Blackmore rd. Parking

Horndon-on-the-Hill

024 **The Bell**

High Rd, Horndon-on-the-Hill SS17 8LD

Tel.: (01375) 642463 - Fax: (01375) 361611
e-mail: info@bell-inn.co.uk - Website: www.bell-inn.co.uk

☐ ⚬ *VISA* AE ⓜⓒ

Greene King IPA, Bass, Crouchvale Brewers Gold, Adnams White Adder, Archers Golden Arrow

Monkfish with veal and snail fritters, ox cheek ravioli with crab sauté and truffle froth: there's no doubting the high culinary ambition behind The Bell's daily-changing modern European menu. At its most complex, the cooking can seem a little overwrought, but there's no denying that the extra effort and attention raise simpler dishes – like Caesar salad or ribeye with parsley sauce – comfortably above pub average. The rather serious approach to good eating sits surprisingly well with the comfy, traditional décor and a long family history, and this characterful and well-established place is efficient, upbeat and busy, particularly at lunchtime.

Food serving times:
Monday-Sunday:
12pm-1.45pm,
6.30pm-9.45pm
Closed 25-26 December and Bank Holidays
Prices:
Meals: a la carte 22.95/26.95
⊨ **5 rooms :** 85.00
☕ 9.50

Typical Dishes

Langoustine ravioli

Duck with red onion tart

Assiette of desserts

3mi Northeast of Grays by A1013 off A13. Parking

Mistley

025 **The Mistley Thorn**

High Street, Mistley CO11 1HE
Tel.: (01206) 392821 - Fax: (01206) 390122
e-mail: info@mistleythorn.co.uk - Website: www.mistleythorn.com

 🍷 ⤬ **VISA** **MC**

Adnams, Greene King IPA, St Peters Organic

Though the exceptionally likeable young staff are only too happy for people to drop in for a drink – and maybe a plate of oysters – you're missing a real treat if you don't stay for dinner in the strikingly contemporary setting of this restyled Georgian pub. Well-composed menus of carefully presented cooking – with conspicuous depth and freshness of flavour – make a strong case for sourcing imaginatively, locally and organically, and include dishes like East Anglian asparagus, shrimp and herb mousse, tender lamb chops on a borlotti and artichoke stew, and a light Chez Panisse chocolate cake: the owner's cookery classes in "the Mistley Kitchen" reveal some, but not all of the secrets. Of the five bedrooms, two front-facing ones look out towards the Stour.

Food serving times:
Monday-Sunday:
　　　　12pm-2.30pm,
　　　　6.30pm-9.30pm
Closed 25 December
Prices:
Meals: 13.50 and a la carte
15.50/22.50
5 rooms : 70.00/90.00

Typical Dishes

Smoked haddock chowder
Chicken, cider mustard sauce
Jack Daniels pecan tart

On B1352 not far from Mistley Towers. Parking

Aldbury

026 Valiant Trooper

Trooper Rd, Aldbury HP23 5RW
Tel.: (01442) 851203 - Fax: (01442) 851071

 VISA MC

 Fullers London Pride, Timothy Taylor Landlord and guest beers

This is another traditional pub that benefits from its close proximity to the Ridgeway Path, so a healthy gathering of walkers can be guaranteed at most times. Even closer than the Ridgeway is the local duck pond; the pub's red, black and white bulk is a short walk away. The rustic bar boasts not only a real fire but also a welcoming wood burner; quarry tiled floors and scrubbed tables and chairs enhance the effect. Dining happens in an area at the back, which has seen a modicum of modernisation: the newer feel is accentuated by minimalist décor. Blackboard plaques announce traditional menus with some international influence, at a reasonable price. There's a good selection of lighter dishes, too: many a rambler has felt the benefit of one of the pub's hearty jacket potatoes.

Food serving times:
Monday-Saturday:
 12pm-2pm, 6.30pm-9.15pm
Sunday: 12pm-2pm
Closed 25 December
Prices:
Meals: a la carte 17.00/28.00

Typical Dishes

Prawn, crab and crayfish salad

Steak, kidney and ale pie

In centre of village. Parking

Cottered

027 The Bull of Cottered

Cottered SG9 9QP
Tel.: (01763) 281243

 VISA MC

Greene King IPA and Abbot Ale

In a pretty village blighted by a busy A road, you need somewhere to keep your spirits up. The Bull is that place: a well looked-after and neighbourhood pub in the old tradition that's genuinely eager to please and worth a visit for its understated friendliness and recently extended and refurbished to provide a more stylish and comfortable dining environment. If you're stopping by at lunchtime, expect anything from homemade burgers, ploughman's or jacket potatoes to full meals – good "beer-friendly" pub meals, in other words. Dinner, though, sees the addition of tasty and sustaining seasonal British dishes like steak, calves' livers with Roquefort cheese or rack of lamb, plus a couple of daily specials.

Food serving times:
Monday-Sunday:
  12pm-2pm, 6.30pm-9.30pm
Prices:
Meals: a la carte 17.50/27.50

Typical Dishes

Wild mushroom risotto

Lamb and Parma ham, rosemary gravy

On A507 in the centre of the village. Parking at the front of the pub

Frithsden

028 The Alford Arms

Frithsden HP1 3DD

Tel.: (01442) 864480 · Fax: (01442) 876893
e-mail: inn@alfordarmsfrithsden.co.uk · Website: www.alfordarmsfrithsden.co.uk

 Marstons Pedigree, Flowers Original, Brakspear, Morrell's Oxford Blue

The quiet hamlet of Frithsden has a frequent tendency to see its population inflate like the hot-air balloons floating over its beautiful surrounding countryside. This is due in part to the popularity of this attractive brick pub, which is based quite close to the Ridgeway Path and regularly offers pints, sustenance and a comfy seat to walkers and saddle-sore cyclists. It's a small and stylish inn, and a good neighbourhood feel pervades the place with a confident, modern gastropub style much in evidence. There's a "free-for-all" drinking area at the front bar, but tables are reserved in the rear dining area. Well-priced menus change seasonally, and the fresh ingredients are evident in a tasty, varied dining pub selection.

Food serving times:
Monday-Saturday:
  12pm-2.30pm, 7pm-10pm
Sunday:
  12pm-3pm, 7pm-10pm
Closed 25-26 December
Prices:
Meals: a la carte 17.50/25.00

Typical Dishes

Smoked bacon, bubble and squeak

Lamb rump with minted hollandaise

Banana tarte Tatin

4.5mi Northwest of Hemel Hempstead by A4146. By the village green. Parking

Hertford

029 **The Hillside**

45, Port Hill, Bengeo, Hertford SG14 3EP

Tel.: (01992) 554556 - Fax: (01992) 583709

e-mail: justin624@hotmail.com - Website: www.thehillside.co.uk

 VISA **AE** **MC**

Put on the brakes as you head out of Hertford and pay a visit to this cosy, intimate, recently refurbished 17C pub, nestling contentedly – as its name suggests – on a hillside. The small beamed bar with comfy leather sofa is a charming haven for drinkers; for diners, there's a sunny, surprisingly airy restaurant with leather banquettes and bare tables decorated with bright flowers. Paintings – for sale – brighten the walls. Contemplate what takes your fancy while waiting for chef's cheery wife to serve a modern menu of brasserie dishes with pronounced global reach alongside more traditional staples. There's also an interesting little organic deli and farm shop next door.

Food serving times:
Monday-Saturday:
12pm-2.30pm, 6.30pm-10pm
Sunday: 12pm-2.30pm
Prices:
Meals: a la carte 25.00/40.00

North 0.25mi on B158. Parking

Typical Dishes

Seared scallops, cauliflower purée

Lamb rump, mint oil

Panna cotta with stewed rhubarb

Reed

030 **The Cabinet at Reed**

High St., Reed SG8 8AH

Tel.: (01763) 848366 - Fax: (01763) 849407
e-mail: p.bloxham@btinternet.com - Website: www.thecabinetinn.co.uk

 Greene King IPA, Adnams, Regatta, London Pride

This pretty 16C clapboard inn suits Reed to perfection, but since its refurbishment it's more than just a village pub in the traditional sense. So while the bar proper still has all the charm of a rustic local, with a little snug to one side, the real focal point is the quietly chic, contemporary dining room beyond, with elegant tables featuring outsize glassware – the red wine glasses actually hold a whole bottle, although that's not really the idea. An enthusiast and populariser to the core, the owner, Paul Bloxham, makes a natural TV chef, sometimes continuing the performance in his demonstration kitchen on the terrace: his interesting, upmarket Modern British menu would not look out of place in a West End restaurant. Change of ownership at time of going to print.

Food serving times:
Tuesday-Saturday:
  12pm-2.30pm, 6.30-10.30pm
Closed 25 December
Prices:
Meals: 14.95 and a la carte
25.00/35.00

Typical Dishes

Ham hock and foie gras
presse

Brill, stewed peppers and
butter beans

Bitter chocolate souffle

3mi South of Royston, just off the A10 London to Cambridge road. Parking

Ware

031 ## Jacoby's

Churchgate House, 15 West St, Ware SG12 9EE

Tel.: (01920) 469181 - Fax: (01920) 469182
e-mail: info@jacobys.co.uk - Website: www.jacobys.co.uk

 VISA **AE** **MC**

No real ales offered

Carefully renovated into a modern bar and restaurant, this Grade II listed timber framed house, dating back to the late 15C, boasts tremendous history and character: in its time, it's been an inn, a bakery and maltings and even a motorcycle repair shop. It stands opposite St Mary's church; in the summer, you'll want to look for a place on the pleasant pavement terrace which faces the square. The stylish front bar has leather armchairs and sets a buzzy tone for the rest of the place. Dining is on two levels: go upstairs for the more intimate tables. Menus change frequently, providing well-executed, mix and match options: good British classics with strong Mediterranean influences alongside dishes with a wider global reach. Service is prompt, young and keen; booking's advisable at weekends.

Food serving times:
Monday-Saturday:
11.30am-2pm,
6.30pm-9.30pm
Closed 24 December-
3 January
Closed Monday lunch
Prices:
Meals: a la carte 24.50/32.00

Typical Dishes

Salmon gravad lax,
Portland crab mousse

Fillet of pork, cheese
crumble

Assiette of cheese

In the town centre, just off the High St. Public car park opposite

Bawburgh

032 Kings Head

Harts Lane, Bawburgh NR9 3LS

Tel.: (01603) 744977 - Fax: (01603) 744990
e-mail: anton@kingshead-bawburgh.co.uk - Website: www.kingshead-bawburgh.co.uk

     VISA **AE** **①** **M©**

Adnams, Woodfordes Wherry and guest beers

Only a short drive out of Norwich but already well into the countryside, this traditional place has plumped for Edward VII as its royal figurehead, the under-represented pub monarch perhaps getting the nod here for his generous appetite and his Sandringham connections. The old bon vivant would be baffled by the fruit machines, but drawn instinctively to the casual but comfortable dining room leading off from one side of the main bar. The daily changing menu blends modern European with traditional dishes: an equal mix of traditional and modern recipes might offer anything from bangers and burgers to potted crab, chicken salsa verde with pasta and peppers or maple and pecan cheesecake. Once the woodburning stove is fired up on winter afternoons, it's also pleasant enough for a quiet pint.

Food serving times:
Monday: 12pm-2pm
Tuesday-Saturday:
    12pm-2pm, 6.30pm-9.30pm
Sunday: 12.30pm-2.30pm
Closed for food 25 December
Prices:
Meals: 16.50/21.00 and a la carte 21.00/30.00

Typical Dishes

Feta and pickled orange salad

Spicy Moroccan chicken breast

Boozy apricot trifle

5mi Northwest of Norwich by B1108. Parking

Blakeney

033 **White Horse** ⊨

4 High St, Blakeney NR25 7AL

Tel.: (01263) 740574 - Fax: (01263) 741303
e-mail: enquiries@blakeneywhitehorse.co.uk - Website: www.blakeneywhitehorse.co.uk

     🍺 🍷 rest 🚭 **VISA** ⓶

Adnams Southwold, Broadside, Woodfordes Wherry, Nelsons Revenge

Estuary, saltings, quayside, and a gaggle of tourists from the Capital make up much of the character of 21C Blakeney. It's further defined by this popular part-17C pub of flint-and-brick which draws in the locals and weekenders a-plenty. They gather round a split-level bar and sup good real ale at wooden tables, chairs and banquettes – an appealing conservatory provides a smart alternative. Go to the rear, to the former stables, to eat: the food is proudly local in nature and naturally enough, seafood is the staple here. For those not climbing back into their 4X4s, there's the option of small, cosy bedrooms.

Food serving times:
Closed 2 weeks mid January
Prices:
Meals: a la carte 17.00/30.00
⊨ **9 rooms :** 70.00/130.00

Typical Dishes

Crab cakes with cucumber salad

Roast black bream, salsa verde

Figs in red wine syrup

Off A149 following signs for the Quay, beside the church. Parking ›

Brancaster Staithe

034 **The White Horse**

Main Rd, Brancaster Staithe PE31 8BY

Tel.: (01485) 210262 - Fax: (01485) 210930

e-mail: reception@whitehorsebrancaster.co.uk - Website: www.whitehorsebrancaster.co.uk

     VISA

Adnams Best, Regatta, Fuller's London Pride, Woodfordes Wherry

This popular North Norfolk inn is the place to go for views: from the sun deck or the big conservatory there are stunning vistas of the distant tidal marshes that stretch flat as dinner plates to the horizon. Weekenders up from London appreciate the palette here: muted colours with pastel tints. Fresh flowers abound and modern paintings light up the walls. There's a bar area at the front, which is solely for drinkers, with cushioned wicker armchairs and sofas, but the rest of the open-plan interior is set up for dining, and menus are full of tasty local seafood, such as oysters, potted shrimps, cod, crabs and mussels. Norfolk meats also make a appearance. Spacious, uncluttered bedrooms are worth it for the views; the North Norfolk Coast Path meanders along the bottom of the garden.

Food serving times:
Monday-Sunday:
   12pm-2.30pm, 6pm-10pm
Prices:
Meals: a la carte 25.00/28.00
15 rooms : 72.00/132.00

Typical Dishes

Foie gras with quince

Sea trout, broad beans and thyme

Hazelnut and ricotta torte

On A149. Parking

Burnham Market

035 The Hoste Arms

The Green, Burnham Market PE31 8HD

Tel.: (01328) 738777 - Fax: (01328) 730103

e-mail: reception@hostearms.co.uk - Website: www.hostearms.co.uk

  VISA **MC**

 Greene King Abbott, Woodfordes Wherry, Woodfordes Nelsons Revenge

The popularity of this bright yellow coaching inn has almost come to define the charming north Norfolk town of Burnham Market: set on the picturesque Green, its 17C quirks have been fully restored; in startling contrast, there's an intriguing wing decorated in Zulu style, and a new Moroccan garden terrace. The bar is an invariably bustling place, and the sound of champagne corks popping is not uncommon; you'll find similar levels of volume and bonhomie in the restaurant. The staff respond well to being busy, and are invariably attentive and friendly, with good attention to detail. Fairly-priced menus offer a mix of global styles, with much local produce in evidence. There's an excellent wine selection featuring 180 bins.

Food serving times:
Monday-Sunday:
  12pm-2pm, 7pm-9pm
(booking essential)
Prices:
Meals: a la carte 19.25/33.95
36 rooms : 82.00/248.00

Typical Dishes

Scallops, oyster butter sauce

Lamb, cannellini beans and merguez sausage

Liquorice rice pudding

Overlooking the green. Parking

Burnham Thorpe

036 The Lord Nelson

Walsingham Rd, Burnham Thorpe PE31 8HL

Tel.: (01328) 738241 - Fax: (01328) 738241
e-mail: enquiries@nelsonslocal.co.uk - Website: www.nelsonslocal.co.uk

    VISA M©

Greene King IPA, Abbot, Woodfordes Wherry, Nelsons Revenge and guest beers in summer

Named in honour of Burnham Thorpe's most illustrious son, and perhaps Britain's first modern celebrity, this 17C inn honours the Victor of the Nile with just enough in the way of pictures and memorabilia: too much swashbuckling nauticalia would clutter up this shipshape little place. Three low-ceilinged parlours, one with a Battle of Trafalgar mural, lead off from a firelit taproom with a tiny cubby-hole of a bar: the landlord opens up the timbered barn, with chunky pine tables and benches, if the pub itself starts to feel overcrowded. Simple, fresh, good-value dishes, both classic and modern, could include grilled red mullet with tapenade or chicken with a red wine and parsley sauce.

Food serving times:
Monday-Saturday:
12pm-2.30pm, 7pm-9pm
Sunday: 12pm-3pm
Closed dinner 25-26 December, 1 January and Monday October-June except Bank Holidays

Prices:
Meals: 23.95 (set price dinner) and a la carte 20.95/30.40

Typical Dishes

Smoked eel and baby squid salad

Pork loin with apple and peanut crust

Trio of chocolate

2mi South of Burnham Market by B1355. Parking

Coltishall

037 King's Head

26 Wroxham Rd, Coltishall NR12 7EA

Tel.: (01603) 737426

 VISA AE M©

Adnams Best, Marstons Pedigree, Courage Best

One of the nicest things about this rather ordinary looking pub in deepest Norfolk is its attractive setting – diners with window tables can look out onto the meandering River Bure. Elsewhere within, a relaxed air pervades. Open fires crackle beneath solid timbers and pieces of fishing and boating memorabilia hang from the ceiling, lending a particularly atmospheric air at night: meals can be ordered in the bar as well as the dining room. Seafood specialities take pride of place with the Norfolk catch freshly served each day or, as an alternative to fish, chef's special meat dishes.

Food serving times:
Monday-Sunday:
12pm-2pm, 7pm-9pm
Closed 26 December
Prices:
Meals: 9.95 and a la carte
21.50/29.50

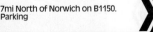

Typical Dishes

Chicken liver and foie gras parfait

Trio of pork, mashed potatoes

Blood orange jelly

7mi North of Norwich on B1150.
Parking

Erpingham

038 Saracen's Head

Wolterton, Erpingham NR11 7LX

Tel.: (01263) 768909 - Fax: (01263) 768993

e-mail: saracenshead@wolterton.freeserve.co.uk - Website: www.saracenshead-norfolk.co.uk

   VISA **AE**

Adnams Best Bitter, Woodfordes Wherry

Charmingly faded and quirky by turns, this individualistic 19C former coaching inn is in the middle of nowhere and loses nothing by its isolation. It contains an impressive walled garden and courtyard set back from two busy, bustling bar rooms and a boldly red-painted parlour filled with odd pictures, bric-a-brac and little wooden tables and chairs with plastic tablecloths. Traditional dishes come dressed in local ingredients such as mussels from Morston and crab from Cromer: unpretentious, country dishes that draw in regular shoals of satisfied customers from miles around. Bright, modest bedrooms nevertheless share the owner's mild and endearing eccentricity.

Food serving times:
Monday-Saturday:
12.30pm-2pm, 7.15pm-9pm
Sunday:
12pm-3pm, 7pm-10.30pm
Closed 25 December and dinner 26 December
Prices:
Meals: a la carte 17.00/25.00
6 rooms : 45.00/85.00

Typical Dishes

Crostini of baby anchovies

Medallions of venison with red fruits

Brown bread and butter pudding

West 1.5mi on Wolterton Hall rd. Parking

Itteringham

039 **Walpole Arms** We most liked

The Common, Itteringham NR11 7AR

Tel.: (01263) 587258 - Fax: (01263) 587074
e-mail: goodfood@thewalpolearms.co.uk - Website: www.thewalpolearms.co.uk

  VISA **MC**

Adnams Bitter, Broadside, Woodfordes Wherry, Wolf

Blickling Hall sets an awesome architectural benchmark in this part of Norfolk; in its more modest way, the nearby part-18C Walpole Arms reaches out in empathy. It's hugely characterful and inviting, with a warm ambiance, roaring fires, exposed brick walls and heavy timbers marking out the bar as a great place for modern dining. New, varied menus are devised daily; the accomplished kitchen interweaves Italian and Spanish ideas. Extensive use is made of local and seasonal ingredients; the owners heartily take on board recommendations from their fishmonger and game supplier. There's a more formal restaurant beyond the bar, but no let-up on the character front, with linen-clad tables and exposed roof trusses lending it an appealing air.

Food serving times:
Monday-Saturday:
    12pm-2pm, 7pm-9.30pm
Sunday: 12.30pm-2.30pm
Closed dinner 25 December
Prices:
Meals: a la carte 19.00/25.00

Typical Dishes

Tart Tatin of beetroot and smoked eel

Pork belly, butter beans, chorizo and gremolata

Rhubarb and apple cobbler

5mi Northwest of Aylsham by B1354. Signposted The Common. Parking

Norwich

040 **1 Up at the Mad Moose Arms**

2 Warwick St, Norwich NR2 3LD

Tel.: (01603) 627687

e-mail: madmoose@animalinns.co.uk

     VISA **AE** **D** **MC**

 Adnams Broadside, Greene King IPA, Abbott Ale, Wolf Brewery Golden Jackal

Just eccentric enough to stand out from the suburban herd, this Victorian tavern wears its bright, cheerful modern refit surprisingly well, particularly in the simply styled first-floor dining room, which feels a little cut off, for better or worse, from the young, full-volume crowd in the bar downstairs. Flavourful modern cooking at a fair price takes in dishes like seared scallops with chilli jam, roast duck in cinnamon jus, served on spring greens, and banana tart – if you've ever eaten at the Wildebeest Arms across the city, you'll have an idea of what to expect. The chatty service from a smart, black-shirted team is well organised and evenly paced.

Food serving times:
Monday-Sunday:
12pm-2pm, 6pm-10pm
Closed 25 December
Bar meals only Saturday lunch and Sunday dinner
Prices:
Meals: a la carte 18.95/27.95

Typical Dishes

Ham hock and morcilla terrine

Venison with truffle cream

Peanut butter parfait

 In residential area West of city centre. Designated parking bays lunchtime, street parking in the evening

Ringstead

041 **The Gin Trap Inn**

6 High St, Ringstead PE36 5JU
Tel.: 01485 525264 - Fax: 01485 525321
e-mail: gintrap@aol.com - Website: www.gintrapinn.co.uk

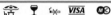

Adnams, Woodfordes Wherry, Timothy Taylor Landlord, Youngs Bitter, Admirals Revenge

Two old iron ploughs crown the modest doorway of this whitewashed inn, which dates back to 1667. In all those years it can rarely have looked and felt so inviting: a proper country pub, warm and comfortable, with a real fire stoked up in the stove on frosty winter evenings. The bar, with its glossy wood-topped tables, and the smartly set dining room feel like two halves of the same whole: the modern British restaurant dishes are well prepared and full of flavour, but no less care goes into a really appealing choice of generous pub classics, good and simple. If you're thinking of staying the night and exploring Hunstanton and the coast in the morning, this could be the place: the bedrooms are a very tasteful blend of subtle country patterns, and two bathrooms have luxurious roll-top baths.

Food serving times:
Moday-Sunday:
12pm-2pm, 6pm-9pm
Prices:
Meals: a la carte 17.75/34.00
3 rooms: 70.00/160.00

3,25 miles East of Hunstanton by A149. Parking.

Typical Dishes

Chicken liver and foie gras parfait

Fillet of Angus beef, Madeira and truffle jus

Iced chocolateo parfait

Snettisham

042 The Rose and Crown 🛏

Old Church Rd, Snettisham PE31 7LX

Tel.: (01485) 541382 - Fax: (01485) 543172
e-mail: info@roseandcrownsnettisham.co.uk - Website: www.roseandcrownsnettisham.co.uk

 ⚡room **VISA** **MC**

 Adnams Broadside, Greene King IPA, Fuller's London Pride, Bass

A buzzing, convivial place at its best, though first-time guests may struggle to get their bearings in a maze of cosy, rustic bars and brightly styled rooms, where quirky decorative details and bric-a-brac give just a hint of well-composed muddle. Whatever you do, don't plan on a quick dinner – for all its good intentions, the service can start to unravel on busy evenings, leaving some diners feeling slightly lost – but go prepared to flag down waitresses and allow time for a drink and a chat between courses. The menu is a conversation piece in itself. Asian influences mingle with Modern European dishes and the out-and-out traditional. There is a well-priced lunch menu and good choice on the à la carte. Tidy, interestingly appointed bedrooms, in a colourful style you'll recognise from downstairs, and good breakfasts.

Food serving times:
Monday-Friday:
    12pm-2pm, 6.30pm-9pm
Saturday-Sunday:
    12pm-2.30pm, 6.30-9.30pm
Prices:
Meals: a la carte 16.00/25.00
🛏 **16 rooms :** 60.00/100.00

Typical Dishes

Red pepper, cous-cous and feta salad

Crispy cod, guacamole and champ potatoes

Chocolate brownies

11mi North of King's Lynn by A149.
Parking

Stoke Holy Cross

043 **Wildebeest Arms**

82-86 Norwich Rd, Stoke Holy Cross NR14 8QJ

Tel.: (01508) 492497 - Fax: (01508) 494353

e-mail: wildebeestl@animalinns.co.uk

    🅷🆃🆃 🍷 🚭 **VISA** **AE** **D** **MC**

Adnams Best Bitter

Dark wooden furniture and sunny yellow ragwashed walls, allied to soft lighting and a slight African theme, lend a homely, comfortable feel to this smoothly run rural pub. The invariably friendly and efficient service is a notable plus; meals are served at substantially proportioned "tree-trunk" tables or, if preferred on brighter days, in the garden. If reputation is everything, then these days The Wildebeest has it in spades: cooking from the open kitchen is of a modern style and has both the quality and price to bring in punters from miles around East Anglia. Menus are exceptional for a pub; they're particularly well-compiled, blending a classic base with French and British elements. Wines, too, are eye-catchingly well-priced. Because of its high regard locally, this is a pub where booking is essential, especially for dinner.

Food serving times:
Monday-Sunday:
    12pm-2pm, 7pm-9pm
Closed 25-26 December
Prices:
Meals: 14.95/18.50 and a la carte 20.00/33.00

Typical Dishes

Pan-fried pigeon breast

Fillet of sea bass, samphire, prawn and tarragon beurre blanc

Chocolate fondant

5.75 mi South of Norwich by A140. Parking

West Runton

044 The Village Inn

Water Lane, West Runton NR27 9QP
Tel.: (01263) 838000 - Fax: (01263) 838999

Adnams, Broadside, Hancocks and Timothy Taylor

West Runton's sand and shingle beach – good for rock pool paddling and fossil hunts along the foreshore – is only a short walk away, making the neatly kept Village Inn an extremely popular choice in high season, so arrive early to secure a place in the comfortable, dark-toned rear dining room or in one of the cosy corners around the bar, or a picnic table on the lawn. A really reasonably priced menu on a traditional base ranges from lunchtime sandwiches and baguettes to tasty crab and leek tartlet on a light roquette salad, crispy, pink liver with sautéed pancetta and green beans, and delicately creamy cheesecake. The formal restaurant – "The Nineteenth" – serves a more elaborate dinner menu from Tuesday to Saturday.

Food serving times:
Monday-Sunday:
    12am-3.00pm, 6pm-9pm
Prices:
Meals: a la carte 16.00/25.00

Typical Dishes

Home-made soup

Chicken breast with white
wine and tarragon

Cheesecake

On A149. Parking

Bramfield

045 ## Queen's Head

The Street, Bramfield IP19 9HT

Tel.: (01986) 784214 · Fax: (01986) 784797

e-mail: qhbfield@aol.com · Website: www.queensheadbramfield.co.uk

    rest *VISA* AE MC

Adnams Bitter, Broadside, Crones Organic Cider

Organic food is the name of the game at this neat and tidy, 'proper' pub not far from Southwold and the Suffolk coast. Nobody seems to know quite how old the Queens Head is, but going by the exposed roof trusses and mighty fireplaces in one of the hugely rustic rooms – a former barn – we're talking about a few hundred years at least. Good value menus take a particular delight in showing off the organic nature of extremely local ingredients: pork, venison and beef are from nearby farms. Settle down to eat at scrubbed pine tables and chairs. In the summer months, the pretty garden is worth discovering with its dome-shaped willow bower, but at colder times of the year settle down in front of a blazing fire with a pint of ale from down the coast road.

Food serving times:
Monday-Saturday:
12pm-2pm, 6.30pm-10pm
Sunday:
12pm-2pm, 7pm-9pm
Closed 26 December
Prices:
Meals: a la carte 16.95/27.00

Typical Dishes

Goats cheese, beetroot and smoked duck breast salad

Lamb à la Grecque

Mango, banana and coconut pavlova

3mi South of Halesworth on A144. Parking

Buxhall

046 The Buxhall Crown

Mill Road, Buxhall IP14 3DW

Tel.: (01449) 736521 - Fax: (01449) 736528
e-mail: trevor@buxhallcrown.fsnet.co.uk - Website: www.thebuxhallcrown.co.uk

   VISA **AE** **MC**

Greene King IPA, Tindalls Best Bitter, Mauldons, Woodfordes Wherry

Without a sixth sense for country pubs, you'd do well to find the Crown by chance, but all the more reason to seek it out, especially on a quieter weekday. One half of the pub is always set for dining, with plenty of intimate corners and a big fire, but you can also eat in the classic old bar, where many of the regulars drop in for a pint of the usual and a quiet smoke. There's an almost homely, family feeling to the place as gently helpful staff shuttle between the bar and kitchen, bringing out well-heaped plates of hearty cooking: notwithstanding a few modern touches, it's the traditional foundations that come across in dishes like Bailey's cheesecake with strawberries and raspberries or thick, pink lamb cutlets with pea purée and plenty of seasonal veg.

Food serving times:
Tuesday-Saturday:
12pm-2pm, 6.30pm-9pm
Sunday: 12pm-2pm
Closed 25-26 December and bank holidays
Prices:
Meals: a la carte 18.00/27.00

From Stowmarket, follow the road to Buxhall across Rattlesden Junction. Parking in Mill Bar Restaurant

Typical Dishes

Aubergine timbale

Roast duck leg, Grand Marnier sauce

Chocolate fondant

Fressingfield

047 ## The Fox & Goose Inn

Church Rd, Fressingfield IP21 5PB
Tel.: (01379) 586247 - Fax: (01379) 586106
e-mail: foxandgoose@uk2.net - Website: www.foxandgoose.net

Adnams Best

I n the heart of this country village and beside the duck pond, this capacious black and white pub with fine leaded windows has become something of a favourite with Suffolk diners. Its well-established credentials guarantee a bustling ambience. Drinkers are catered for with a few tables near the entrance, but the main hub centres around the most welcoming two-roomed dining area of wooden floors, black beamed ceiling and fine floral drapes. There's an extensive menu choice, both fixed price and à la carte, and the pricing is reasonable. Local ingredients are used where possible on traditional menus overlaid with modern twists.

Food serving times:
Tuesday-Sunday:
      12pm-2pm, 7pm-9pm
Closed 27-30 December and 2nd week in January
(booking essential)
Prices:
Meals: 13.95 and a la carte 25.00/32.00

Typical Dishes

Calves liver, onion tempura

Lamb loin, peach and fennel chutney

Raspberry and white chocolate crème brûlée

4mi South of Harleston on B1116.
Parking

Horringer

048 The Beehive

The Street, Horringer IP29 5SN

Tel.: (01284) 735260

 VISA

 Greene King IPA, Old Speckled Hen

S taggeringly rich and deeply eccentric, even by the standards of the Regency gentry, the 4th Earl of Bristol spared no expense on Ickworth House and its Italianate gardens, now owned by the National Trust. His ideal local would probably have been a neoclassical gastro-folly, but The Beehive, just down the road, brings us back down to earth in the very best sense. An attractive, traditional brick and flint house, its old timbers and flagstones set off nicely with a bright, modern décor, it always seems to have one last inviting corner waiting and an old wooden table free. A good-sized blackboard menu, with its share of lighter dishes, combines predominantly British themes with a subtle taste for the modern and the exotic – perhaps His Lordship would have approved after all. Well run by long-standing landlords.

Food serving times:
Monday-Saturday:
    12pm-2pm, 7pm-9.30pm
Sunday: 12pm-2pm
Closed 25-26 December
Prices:
Meals: a la carte 20.00/27.00

Typical Dishes

Ballottine of Salmon

Fillet of sea bream, dill cream sauce

Banana parfait, toffee sauce

3.5mi South West of Bury St. Edmunds by A143

Lavenham

049 Angel 🛏

Market Pl, Lavenham CO10 9QZ

Tel.: (01787) 247388 - Fax: (01787) 248344
e-mail: angellav@aol.com - Website: www.theangelhotel-lavenham.co.uk

🛏 🍷 ✕ **VISA** **AE** **MC**

Nethergate Suffolk County, Adnams, Greene King IPA, Adnams Broadside

History's timbered face appears at every turn in the gorgeous old town of Lavenham, and the Angel wears one of its more delightful countenances. This charming inn has stood in the market square since 1420 and receives a never-ending stream of curious tourists and relaxed locals. There's a pubby bar with several dining areas including lots of timbers, simple wooden tables and a log fire. On the first floor is the Solar, which contains a rare fully pargetted ceiling constructed in the early 1600s, featuring the remains of early wall paintings on some of its beams. This has great views of the Guildhall and Church and is now a residents' sitting room. Hearty, varied menus employ seasonal, local produce, while well-kept bedrooms provide effortlessly comfortable accommodation.

Food serving times:
Monday-Sunday:
12pm-2.15pm,
6.45pm-9.15pm
Closed 25-26 December
Prices:
Meals: a la carte 15.00/20.00
🛏 **8 rooms :** 55.00/85.00

In town centre. Parking ⟫

Typical Dishes

Smoked salmon and trout salad

Steak and ale pie

Steamed syrup sponge pudding

Levington

050 The Ship

Church Lane, Levington IP10 0LQ
Tel.: (01473) 659573

  VISA

Adnams Best, Broadside, Greene King IPA

In an age of rebranding, some pub names still go deeper. The salt of the Suffolk marshes is in the very timbers of this part 14C thatched inn, which stands in sight of the estuary. Though built from the broken-up hulks on the coast and full of seafaring pictures, curiosities and keepsakes, it now feels just too neat and cosy ever to have been a smugglers' haunt, but read the old newspaper cutting on the wall and you'll find the atmosphere of excisemen and contraband hangs about you a little more thickly. Relaxed, smiling and attentive service recalls you to the present for an appetizing menu with a good balance tilted in favour of the traditional: seafood includes Cromer crab and fresh griddled plaice with crispy salad. Save a space for homemade puddings like apple and rosemary crumble with custard.

Food serving times:
Monday-Saturday:
11.30am-3pm,
6.30pm-9.30pm
Sunday: 12pm-3.30pm
Closed 25-26 December and 1 January
Prices:
Meals: a la carte 15.00/24.00

6mi Southeast of Ipswich by A14. Parking

Typical Dishes

Seared scallops, asparagus and hollandaise

Brochette of chicken and king prawns

Roast rhubarb, cinnamon

Lidgate

051 **The Star** *we most liked*
The Street, Lidgate CB8 9PP
Tel.: (01638) 500275 - Fax: (01638) 500275

☂ *VISA* AE M©

🍺 | *Green King Abbot Ale and IPA*

This part 16C village inn may just prove the point: any fusion of traditions will work if you understand both well enough. Its three intimate rooms and snugs are full of restful, old-English charm, braced with ancient beams worn smooth and warmed by drowsy inglenooks. Absolutely the last place, in fact, that you would expect to find sparklingly fresh Iberian cooking. The day's menu comes on blackboards that offer a good variety of simply stated Spanish and Mediterranean dishes. Even locally sourced wild boar and venison are prepared to authentic recipes: at once hearty, piquant and satisfyingly different. Suffolk summers seldom feel properly continental: even so, the terraced garden is very pleasant once the weather finally gets it right.

Food serving times:
Monday-Saturday:
        12pm-2pm, 7pm-10pm
Sunday: 12pm-2pm
Closed Sunday dinner
Spanish
Prices:
Meals: 12.50 (fixed price lunch) and a la carte 25.50/35.00

Parking. 7mi southeast of Newmarket on the B1063 ▶▶

Typical Dishes

Prawns in garlic

Paella

Pavlova

Monks Eleigh

052 The Swan

The Street, Monks Eleigh IP7 7AU
Tel.: (01449) 741391

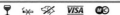

Adnams Best, Broadside and Green King IPA

Heading, perhaps, for the Tudor delights of Lavenham, there's every chance you'll come across this attractive little 16C roadside pub with its thatched roof and honey yellow façade. Stop off and step inside. The interior is as fresh as the country air, with rustic olive tones and shiny wooden floors. It's a charming mix of the old and the new, undertaken with understated style. You won't be let down by the food, either. The chef and landlord specialises in innovative menus that treat local ingredients with the utmost respect: fish, for instance, is the day's catch from the coast. Early dinners come at bargain prices – a great time to sample the homemade seasonal game dishes. When you've left the pub, remember to look round the quaint little streets of Monks Eleigh itself.

Food serving times:
Wednesday-Sunday:
 12pm-2pm, 7pm-9.00pm
Closed 25-26 December and
1 January
Prices:
Meals: a la carte 16.75/37.50

Typical Dishes

Salad of potato, bacon and
black pudding

Spicy Moroccan chicken
breast

Glazed lemon tart

3.5mi Southeast of Lavenham on
A1141. Parking

Nayland

053 White Hart Inn

11 High Street, Nayland CO6 4JF

Tel.: (01206) 263382 - Fax: (01206) 263638
e-mail: nayhart@aol.com - Website: www.whitehart-nayland.co.uk

 VISA AE ① ⓜⓒ

No real ales offered

Floodlit at night, this very pleasant, well-run part-15C former coaching inn has a charming position on the high street of a typically homely Suffolk village, amid colour washed houses, overhanging timbers and patches of cobblestone. Dining is really what the White Hart is all about, and the smooth, considerate service certainly reflects this as much as the layout. Exposed beams divide the welcoming, terracotta-tiled dining room into three distinct areas, with a cosy back bar for pre-prandial relaxation. Menus are modern and accomplished, and may include millefeuille of baby spring vegetables with tomato and basil butter sauce, or rolled loin of suckling pig with seasonal greens and Calvados sauce; the bread and butter pudding is made to the chef's mother's own secret recipe! Beamed bedrooms are pleasantly creaky but very comfortable.

Food serving times:
Monday-Sunday:
12pm-2.30pm,
6.30pm-9.15pm
Closed 26 December-9 January
Prices:
Meals: 14.95 and a la carte 19.50/28.50
6 rooms : 74.00/105.00

Opposite the church. Parking

Typical Dishes

Courgette flower filled with salmon mousse

Salt marsh lamb with basil jus

Strawberry charlotte

Snape

054 Crown Inn

Bridge Rd, Snape IP17 1SL
Tel.: (01728) 688324

     ⌂room ✄ *VISA* Ⓜ©

Adnams Broadside, Trafalgar, Old Ale and Explorer

This gem of a Suffolk pub, with its origins firmly entrenched in the 15C, draws in visitors from upmarket Aldeburgh and The Maltings. They come for the Suffolk ale, the pubby atmosphere enhanced enormously by standing timbers and rafters, old brick flooring and horseshoe-shaped high-backed settles around a grand brick inglenook, and the heart-warming popular dishes served from the blackboard menu. These have a sharp emphasis on fresh fish, game and organic vegetables supplied by local producers. Quaint bedrooms continue the aged theme, complete with sloping floors, beams and some low, low doorways.

Food serving times:
Monday-Sunday:
12pm-2pm, 7pm-9pm
Closed 25 December and dinner 26 December
Prices:
Meals: a la carte 18.00/28.00
⌂ **3 rooms :** 70.00/80.00

6mi West of Aldeburgh by A1094 on B1069. Parking ❯

Typical Dishes

Smoked chicken, vegetable Thai broth

Wild sea bass, basil risotto

Rhubarb and amaretti torte

Southwold

The Crown

90 High St, Southwold IP18 6DP

Tel.: 01502 722275 - Fax: 01502 727263

e-mail: crown.hotel@adnams.co.uk - Website: www.adnamshotels.co.uk

---

🍷 ✕⊷ ✕✕ **VISA** **MC**

Adnams Bitter, Broadside, Explorer, Regatta

The sophisticated elegance of The Crown sits easily within the beguiling surrounds of delightful Southwold. Its mellow yellow tones have graced the high street for many a year, standing proudly adjacent to the Adnams Sole Bay brewery. This smart, intimate old coaching inn is the ideal stopping-off point for a pint with the Suffolk locals in the compact oak-panelled rear bar where, not surprisingly, a nautical edge permeates. Get to the front bar early if you want to bag a seat for dining: it can get packed in there. Or choose a more formal option in the intimate, linen-clad restaurant. The same daily changing menu is served throughout: a well-established and well-prepared mix of modern and more classical dishes, which find favour with East Anglians and the metropolitan influx alike. Individually styled bedrooms.

Food serving times:
Monday-Sunday:
12pm-2.30pm, 6.30pm-9.45pm

Prices:
Meals: 29.50 ((fixed price dinner)) and a la carte 20.00/35.00

🛏 **14 rooms :** 83.00/122.00

Typical Dishes

Asparagus, Parma ham and parmesan

Roasted black bream, ginger and soy dressing

Gratin of gooseberries

In the centre. Parking ⟫⟫

Southwold

056 The Randolph

Wangford Rd, Reydon, Southwold IP18 6PZ

Tel.: (01502) 723603 - Fax: (01502) 722194

e-mail: reception@therandolph.co.uk - Website: www.therandolph.co.uk

 ✗rest ✗ **VISA** MC

Adnams Bitter, Broadside and regularly changing ales

It's a wrench setting foot out of glorious Southwold, but a mile up the road is this sturdy old Victorian stalwart, built by the grandfather of the chairman of the local brewery. It's been given a startling and successful 21C makeover, the big, open-plan bar is suffused with light and furnished with contemporary wicker chairs and leather sofas; deep, bold colours lead you into the dining room where the emphasis is on extremely local produce: those who supply fish, game and the like often stay on for a pint of ale in the bar. Food is traditional and robust: apart from the aforementioned, you might tuck into steaks or toad-in-the-hole. If you're not staying in one of the comfy bedrooms, then what could be better than a post-prandial walk round the greens, beach huts and lighthouse of Suffolk's finest…

Food serving times:

Tuesday-Saturday:
   12pm-2pm, 6.30pm-9pm

Prices:

Meals: a la carte 18.00/26.00

🛏 **10 rooms :** 55.00/100.00

Typical Dishes

Pigeon breast, apple rösti and red wine jus

Smoked haddock, bubble and squeak

Chocolate fondant

Parking

Stoke-by-Nayland

057 **Angel Inn** 🛏

Polstead St, Stoke-by-Nayland CO6 4SA

Tel.: (01206) 263245 - Fax: (01206) 263373
e-mail: the.angel@tiscali.co.uk - Website: www.horizoninns.co.uk

🏧 🍷 ❌ 🚭 **VISA** **AE** **MC**

Greene King IPA, Abbot, Adnams and weekly changing guest beers

Parts of this 16C inn in the heart of Constable country creak with age: not surprisingly, a traditional air is worn with pride. It's heavily beamed and timbered, with exposed brickwork and roaring fires, and a cheerily informal bar that leads through to a sitting room where you can recline in deep sofas. Dine in the main bar or repair to the Well Room, which contains the house's original well and a superb beamed ceiling. Menus here are the same as elsewhere, but the pervading atmosphere is a touch more tranquil and formal. Seasonally influenced dishes abound with locally sourced meat, fish and game prepared in a modern British style. It's the kind of place you might not want to leave, so stay on in one of the traditionally and individually styled bedrooms.

Food serving times:
Monday-Saturday:
 12pm-2pm, 6.30pm-9.30pm
Sunday: 12pm-9.30pm
Closed 25 December and
1 January
Prices:
Meals: a la carte 16.50/25.00
🛏 **6 rooms :** 60.00/85.00

Typical Dishes

Smoked duck and cream cheese roulade

Griddled skate

Rhubarb and apple crumble

On B1068. Parking

Stoke-by-Nayland

058 The Crown

Stoke-by-Nayland CO6 4SE
Tel.: (01206) 262001 - Fax: (01206) 264026
e-mail: crown.eoinns@btopenworld.com

   VISA **MC**

Adnams Best, Greene King IPA, Exmoor Stallion, Ringwood Forrester

"1530" is stamped on the outside of this promising-looking pub, but its comfortable and stylish interior – with a mis-match of sofas, leather armchairs and farmhouse chairs at broad tables – owes much to a recent sympathetic refit. Such is its local reputation that several spacious dining rooms soon fill with a mix of couples, friends and families, particularly for long lunches at weekends and holidays, so booking really is a must. With a new menu every fortnight, the hearty cooking keeps pace with the seasons and brings a regional touch to a couple of daily specials – plus a catch of the day – and a wider range of surefire gastropub classics: a handful of these come in either starter or main portions. The Crown is owned by a firm of wholesale vintners, and its wine shop sells an interesting selection, as well as local homemade chocolates

Food serving times:
Monday-Thursday:
  12pm-2.30pm, 6pm-9.30pm
Friday-Saturday:
  12pm-2.30pm, 6pm-10pm
Sunday:
  12pm-3.30pm, 6pm-9pm
Closed 25-26 December
(booking essential)
Prices:
Meals: a la carte 17.00/27.00

Village centre at the junction of B1068 and B1087. Parking

Typical Dishes

Smoked game terrine, Cumberland sauce

Suffolk hot pot

Strawberry and white chocolate mousse

*I*t's Britain's cultural centre, a business superpower and a fashionista's paradise, but where do you go to find the heart of London itself? Amid the money and the power of Westminster and the City, the mini-Manhattan of Canary Wharf or the bars and studios of Shoreditch and Hoxton in between? Down by Tate Modern and The Globe on rejuvenated Bankside, in the Thames meadows of Richmond and Kew or at the top of the London Eye? The boutiques on New Bond Street or the market stalls of Borough and Billingsgate? Dreaming in the Pavilion End at Lord's or paddling on the Serpentine? In leafy Greenwich, chic Kensington and Chelsea or the glitzy streets of Soho? Wherever you start within this changing patchwork of neighbourhoods, somewhere between The Mall and Metroland, the capital's pubs are moving with the times. Away from the bright lights, brassy Victorian gin-palaces, quiet mews bars and old local boozers are being restored and reborn as London's newest gastronomic gems, bringing good-value informal dining closer to home…

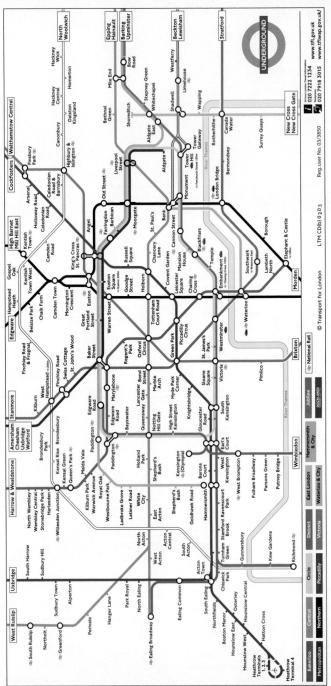

Kensal Rise

001 The Greyhound

64-66 Chamberlayne Road, Kensal Rise NW10 3JJ

Tel.: (020) 8969 8080 - Fax: (020) 8969 8081
e-mail: thegreyhoundnw10@aol.com

VISA *MC*

Charles Wells Bombardier, Adnams Broadside, Courage Directors, London Pride

Once the London campus for the School of Hard Knocks, Kensal Rise is on the up, helped along by enterprising efforts like this. The old neighbourhood pub stood derelict for a year before a group of young friends – with a big picture of a greyhound, but nowhere to hang it – set to work on its restoration. To one side it's a bar, with club chairs and comfy chesterfields for slow drinking and snacking, and on the other side, it's more like a classic gastropub, with reclaimed furniture and black leather banquettes setting a slightly more formal tone. Enjoyable cooking in tried-and-tested, Modern British style takes in crispy belly pork, roast cod on pea purée and caramelised pork chops with lemon and rosemary. Sheltered rear terrace.

Food serving times:
Tuesday-Friday:
　　　　　　12.30pm-3pm,
　　　　　　6.30pm-10.30pm
Saturday:　　12.30pm-4pm,
　　　　　　6.30pm-10.30pm
Sunday:　　　12.30pm-7pm
Closed 25-26 December and 1 January
Prices:
Meals: a la carte 18.00/28.50

Typical Dishes

King scallops, bubble & squeak

Wild sea bass, tomato, red onion and basil salad

Passion fruit panna cotta

Nearest tube: Kensal Green

Willesden Green

002 The Green

110a Walm Lane, Willesden Green NW2 4RS

Tel.: (020) 8452 0171 - Fax: (020) 8452 0774
e-mail: info@thegreennw2.com - Website: www.thegreennw2.com

VISA **M©**

 No real ales offered

Actually a converted Conservative Club snooker room, The Green has kept its airy period proportions, but green baize is out and leather banquettes and stripped wood are in: a bustling but pleasantly low-key bar in the modern gastropub manner, its dining room a touch smarter than out front. The chef and co-owner's Caribbean heritage and an Anglo-French fine dining apprenticeship are both discernable in the generous modern cooking, but the influence is more subtle, and the balance more natural, than you might expect: bream with fried plantain and salsa appears next to duck confit on pak choi or chicken liver parfait, while the lighter selection served in the bar and on the front terrace might feature jerk chicken and coleslaw or gastropub staples like Caesar salads and steak sandwiches. Bright, spontaneous and "au fait" service.

Food serving times:
Monday-Sunday:
11.30am-10.30pm
closed 25 December
Prices:
Meals: a la carte 15.00/25.00

Typical Dishes

Caramelised Onion tart with goats cheese

Pan fried jerk chicken, sauteed plantain and guacamole salad

Nearest tube: Willesden Green

Hampstead

003 The Hill

94 Haverstock Hill, Hampstead NW3 2BD

Tel.: (020) 7267 0033

Website: www.geronimo-inns.co.uk

 VISA **MC**

 No real ales offered

Haverstock Hill, to be precise, where this substantial Victorian pub has been turned around from a workaday drinking haunt to something far trendier: strings of fairy lights twinkle against oxblood-red walls and stylish twentysomethings make themselves at home in old armchairs and sofas. One half of the big, high-ceilinged bar is given over to dining and a smaller room to one side – with one wall covered in black and white photos – is also just for food. Chatty, T-shirted staff serve a good choice of modern Mediterranean cooking with the odd Far Eastern touch: tiger prawns are mixed with coriander and paw-paw salad; prosciutto-wrapped chicken and mozzarella comes with tasty Parmentier potatoes. Laid-back yet lively – a good evening out.

Food serving times:
Monday-Saturday:
   12pm-3pm, 7pm-10.30pm
Sunday: 12.30pm-9pm
Closed 25-26 December and
1 January
Prices:
Meals: a la carte 16.00/24.00

Typical Dishes

Sauteed squid with chilli

Roast duck breast, garlic
French beans

British cheeses

Nearest tube: Belsize Park/Chalk Farm

Hampstead

004 The Magdala
2A South Hill Park, Hampstead NW3 2SB
Tel.: (020) 7435 2503 - Fax: (020) 7435 6167

    VISA ⓂⒸ JCB

Greene King IPA, Abbot Ale, Fuller's London Pride

A stroll on Hampstead Heath reaches a perfect finale with a visit to this deliciously characterful pub, with its two surprisingly rustic bars, appealing neighbourhood ambience - and one rather dark secret, in that it's the place in the 1950s where Britain's last execution victim, Ruth Ellis, shot her lover. Original stained glass windows allow the sunshine to flood through; flickering candles lend a more romantic evening glow. You can eat downstairs or up: the former has an open kitchen, the latter an elegant, formal feel, but it's only open at weekends. Interesting, honest cooking with well-sourced ingredients provides the backbone of a solid dining-pub menu.

Food serving times:
Monday-Friday:
12pm-3.00pm, 6pm-10pm
Saturday and Sunday:
12pm-10pm
Closed 25 December
Prices:
Meals: a la carte 17.75/27.00

Typical Dishes
Pan fried mackerel, paprika and garlic
Chicken, butternut squash risotto
Chocolate parfait

Street parking or nearby Heath car park. Nearest tube: Belsize Pk/ Hampstead Heath National Rail

Hampstead

005 The Wells

30 Well Walk, Hampstead NW3 1BX

Tel.: (020) 7794 3785 - Fax: (020) 7794 6817

e-mail: info@thewellshampstead.co.uk - Website: www.thewellshampstead.co.uk

   VISA Ⓜ©

Fuller's London Pride, Wadsworth 6X, Brains SA, Everards Tiger, Butcombe Gold

This attractive 18C inn sits very easily in a smart part of Hampstead equidistant between the High Street and the Heath. Wander in and relax instantly into one of the dark leather sofas arranged in cosy corners; drinks are ordered from a smart modern bar running centrally across the room. Upstairs it's a bit more formal, with three adjoining rooms linked by burgundy walls and linen covered tables. Menus are from a classical French repertoire, carefully prepared and well balanced. Recent recommendations include roast monkfish minestrone or loin of hare with red cabbage and celeriac purée. What we have here is not quite a pub, not quite a restaurant, but something satisfying in-between.

Food serving times:
Monday-Saturday:
12pm-3.30pm, 7pm-10.30pm
Sunday:
12pm-3pm, 7pm-10pm
Closed 25-26 December
Prices:
Meals: 13.95/29.50

Typical Dishes

Seared tuna with mustard

Lamb with pearl barley risotto

Dark chocolate mousse

Limited metered parking on Christchurch Hill. Nearest tube: Hampstead

Primrose Hill

006 **The Engineer**

65 Gloucester Ave, Primrose Hill NW1 8JH

Tel.: (020) 7722 0950 - Fax: (020) 7483 0592

e-mail: info@the-engineer.com - Website: www.the-engineer.com

   VISA

Timothy Taylor Landlord and a regular changing guest ale

A mid tall terraces in an ever-smarter part of town, this elegantly remodelled Victorian tavern is a neighbourhood pub of a very modern kind. Locals lounge over late lunch and pints in a front bar, filled with light from the broad windows, and even with the intimacy of linen and candlelight, there's an easy, come-as-you-are style about the chic dining room. There's also a little walled terrace at the back. Eclectic cooking, in gratifyingly massive portions, draws freely on global influences: dishes with a robust Pacific Rim or Modern European edge might include quail with polenta or squid on papaya, cucumber and mint salad. Efficient and friendly service.

Food serving times:
Monday-Friday:
　　12pm-3pm, 7pm-11pm
Saturday-Sunday:
　　12.30pm-4.30pm,
　　7pm-11.30pm
Closed 25 December
Prices:
Meals: a la carte 23.50/28.75

Typical Dishes

Feta, watermelon and grape salad

Lamb chump, minted pea purée

Banana pavlova

Parking meters outside. Nearest tube: Camden Town/Chalk Farm

Primrose Hill

 007 **The Queens**

49 Regent's Park Rd, Primrose Hill NW1 8XD

Tel.: (020) 7586 0408 - Fax: (020) 7586 5677
e-mail: mail@thequeens49.fsnet.co.uk - Website: www.geronimo-inns.co.uk

  VISA

Youngs Bitter and Special

C hief among the places that defined the style, and substance, of the capital's gastropubs, this surprisingly down-to-earth local landmark continues as buzzing as ever, and not dining out on past successes, either. With its gauze of hazy blue-grey smoke and the Premiership highlights on in the corner, the basement bar remains an everyday-chic, urbanite drinking den and upstairs the balcony overlooking Primrose Hill is still one of the most popular square metres in North London. In the dining room, simple, close-set linen and paper-clad tables give half a glimpse of jars and rolling pins in the open kitchen, which serves up robust, almost rustic, modern classics like steak and chips and moules portugaise: a regularly changing choice is chalked up on the boards.

Food serving times:
Monday-Sunday:
12pm-3pm, 7pm-10pm
Prices:
Meals: a la carte 25.00/35.00

Typical Dishes

Salt and pepper squid
Char grilled sirloin steak
Almond pavlova

Nearest tube: Chalk Farm

Tufnell Park

008 Junction Tavern
101 Fortess Rd, Tufnell Park NW5 1AG
Tel.: (020) 7485 9400 - Fax: (020) 7485 9401

Fuller's London Pride, Deuchars IPA and weekly changing guest ales

Halfway between Tufnell Park and Kentish Town stands this noble Victorian edifice, now given a modern makeover, guaranteeing swarms of North Londoners making a beeline for its doors: it's become so popular that it could be worth booking at weekends. This is a typical grand 19C metropolitan pub, with a high ceiling and ornate wood panelling and though it still has its split, two-room bar, you're free to eat in either. One is more an informal bar with a conservatory extension; the other a proper dining area with a stainless-steel, open-plan kitchen and array of mismatched tables. Cheerful young staff serve generous portions of robust dishes with tasty, fresh ingredients sourced from local markets.

Food serving times:
Monday-Friday:
 12pm-3pm, 6.30pm-10.30pm
Saturday:
 12pm-4pm, 6.30pm-10.30pm
Sunday:
 12pm-4pm, 6.30pm-9.30pm
Closed 24-26 December and 1 January
Prices:
Meals: a la carte 20.00/27.00

Typical Dishes

Potted shrimps

Organic salmon, Jersey Royals

Valrhona dark chocolate mousse

On-street parking after 6.30pm Monday-Friday and all day weekends. Nearest tube: Tufnell Park

City of London

009 The White Swan

108 Fetter Lane, City of London EC4A 1ES

Tel.: (020) 7242 9696

e-mail: info@thewhiteswanlondon.com - Website: www.thewhiteswanlondon.com

Greene King IPA, Adnams Regatta, Youngs bitter

Just off Fleet Street, the old Mucky Duck has completed an elegant transformation. A lively, free-spending after-work crowd can make the ground floor a busy press of suits and pints, but the vast mirror, reflecting the white sweep of the mezzanine and the big blackboards, makes this handsome, part-panelled bar feel bigger than it really is. In the quieter dining room upstairs, a long mirrored ceiling again gives a sense of space, while elegant, close-set tables and low-backed leather chairs lend a smart brasserie atmosphere. The bar menu with pub classics and a few earthier Old English dishes – pheasant pie, pork cheeks on mash and pints of prawns – makes way for a European and British daily repertoire that might include monkfish fricassee or lamb with gnocchi and root veg. Tidy if rather formal service. Good value for The City.

Food serving times:
Monday-Friday:
　　　12pm-3pm, 6pm-10pm
Closed Bank Holidays
Prices:
Meals: a la carte 22.00/30.00

Typical Dishes

Sautéed duck hearts

Roast guinea fowl Wellington

Chocolate millefeuille

NCP car park nearby or free on street parking after 6pm. Nearest tube: Chancery Lane

Acton Green

010 **The Bollo**

13-15 Bollo Lane, Acton Green W4 5LR

Tel.: (020) 8994 6037
e-mail: thebollopub@btinternet.com

Greene King IPA, Abbot and Old Speckled Hen

A lready a popular neighbourhood meeting-place, this handsome redbrick tavern is at its best on bright summer days, when a buoyant crowd of drinkers and diners fill the spacious bar and make themselves at home on the terrace. There's a slightly smarter rear dining room – its wood panelling, burgundy walls and tan leather banquettes rather suit the pub's Victorian dimensions – but the full menu is served throughout. A core of suitably generous gastropub favourites needs no introduction, but the daily changing menu finds room for more eclectic and original dishes in the same forthright, full-flavoured style: their tasty, medium-rare tuna with braised peas, chorizo and celery is worth looking out for.

Food serving times:
Monday-Sunday:
    12pm-3pm, 7pm-10.15pm
Closed 25-26 December
Prices:
Meals: a la carte 19.00/22.00

Typical Dishes

*Fregola, king prawns,
mussels and clams*

Tuna with wild garlic mash

Amaretto parfait

Parking meters outside. Nearest tube: Chiswick Park

Ealing

011 Ealing Park Tavern

222 South Ealing Rd, Ealing W5 4RL

Tel.: (020) 8758 1879 - Fax: (020) 8560 5269
e-mail: keooi@btconnect.com

 Five guest ales changing weekly

The M4 thunders along close by, but visitors to the Ealing Park Tavern are oblivious to its presence. This typically Victorian pub looks large on the outside, and is cavernous within. It's split into two, with a large, pubby bar, and a high-ceilinged dining area, and light floods through large windows looking out onto the road. Despite its London location, there's a modern-rustic flavour to the cooking, which lures the locals in droves. The buzzy atmosphere is enhanced with an open-plan kitchen, old wooden tables and chairs and colourful modern artwork on the walls. Daily changing menus might offer goats cheese with mixed bean salad for a starter, with rump of lamb, rösti and rosemary jus next up.

Food serving times:
Monday-Sunday:
    12pm-3pm, 6pm-10.30pm
Closed Monday lunch
Prices:
Meals: a la carte 20.00/22.00

Typical Dishes

Pork, black pudding and smoked chicken terrine

Slow roast pork belly

Sticky date pudding

On street parking. Nearest tube: South Ealing

London - Ealing

119

Hackney

012 Cat & Mutton

76 Broadway Market, Hackney E8 4QJ

Tel.: 020 7254 5599

e-mail: info@catandmutton.co.uk · Website: www.catandmutton.co.uk

  VISA AE M⊙

Adnams, IPA, Youngs

In Broadway Market's trendier moments, Hackney's old drinking habits feel a world away and, to most of the Cat and Mutton's regulars, the names of Carrington and Toby, etched on its windows, must seem about as up-to-date as medieval stained glass. It still looks like a Victorian corner pub on first sight, but inside it's one large space: the plain, clean lines of the counter, the brick walls, the open kitchen, and the retro school chairs are lit up by those massive windows. A slate board announces the day's menu: snackier at lunchtime, with rarebit or hot sandwiches next to more substantial dishes. All in all, the cooking is robustly tasty; produce from the Saturday farmers' market is worked in well, and anyone showing up for a late, late Sunday lunch, deep into the afternoon, could find themselves staying for the live DJ in the evening.

Food serving times:
Closed 25-26 December, Sunday dinner and Monday lunch

Prices:
Meals: a la carte 18.00/30.00

Typical Dishes

Roast quail, pomegranate seeds

Grilled pork fillet with Puy lentils

Cheese

Nearest rail: London Fields

Fulham

013 The Farm

18 Farm Lane, Fulham SW6 1PP

Tel.: (020) 7381 3331
e-mail: info@thefarmfulham.co.uk - Website: www.thefarmfulham.co.uk

  VISA **AE** **MC**

 London Pride

Don't misjudge The Farm by its offer of a football lunch menu, served before match-days at nearby Stamford Bridge: The Farm sums up the "nouveau" pub as much as Chelsea stand for "nouveau" football. Lustrous dark wood, dark-chocolate leather and subtle, sidelong lighting give the bar and dining room an ultra-stylish look, particularly at the back where smartly set tables aspire to the height of chic. Confident and flavoursome cooking introduces a French and Italian tone to a steady Modern British style; service is efficient, and its element of restaurant poise hardly feels out of place. It's just what the locals wanted: a good-spirited pub-full of them can always be found doing justice to the well-composed cocktail list, enjoying a few bar snacks or meeting up for dinner.

Food serving times:
Monday-Saturday:
    12pm-3pm, 6pm-10.30pm
Sunday:
    12pm-3.30pm, 6pm-10pm
Prices:
Meals: a la carte 21.00/27.00

Typical Dishes

Deep fried goat's cheese

Roast chicken breast with asparagus and herb butter

Baked lemon ricotta cheesecake with raspberries

Nearest tube : Fulham Broadway.
Difficult street parking

Fulham

014 The Salisbury

21 Sherbrooke Rd, Fulham SW6 7HX

Tel.: (020) 7381 4005 - Fax: (020) 7381 1002
e-mail: thesalisbury@longshotplc.co.uk - Website: www.thesalisbury.com

∇ _VISA_ AE M©

Fuller's London Pride, Charles Wells Bombardier

Assured of a special place in the affections of many Fulhamites, this stylish, smartly modernised corner pub remains the locals' preferred choice for a spur-of-the-moment midweek beer or a little leisurely brasserie eating. Without aspiring to be the neighbourhood's communal living room, The Salisbury mixes in a touch of relaxing, take-us-as-you-find-us spirit with its efficiency and good management, and though it starts busy and gets busier, a natural split between the dining room and the sofas and easy chairs of the bar means there's generally no need for anxious seat–bagging. A tasty, neatly done gastropub repertoire proves just familiar enough: spring rolls with prawns and beetroot might be followed by minute steak-frites with Béarnaise and apple and cinnamon mousse with ice cream.

Food serving times:
Monday-Sunday:
12.30pm-2.30pm, 7pm-11pm
Closed 25, 26 and 31 December
Prices:
Meals: a la carte 19.45/26.15

Street parking nearby. Nearest tube: Fulham Broadway/Parsons Green

Typical Dishes

Gravlax of Salmon

Warm salad of crispy duck

Home-made chocolate doughnuts

Hammersmith

015 **Anglesea Arms**

35 Wingate Rd, Hammersmith W6 0UR
Tel.: (020) 8749 1291 - Fax: (020) 8749 1254

  VISA

 Fuller's London Pride, Greene King IPA, Old Speckled Hen, Adnams Broadside

Though hidden away in deepest Hammersmith, the secret of one of London's original gastropubs is long since out, and a wait at the bar, and at table, is not uncommon on busier days, though decent service smooths things over well. Undoubtedly food-focused, there's still something of the residential street-corner pub about the place, with a sizeable bar at the centre and its dozen close-spaced dining tables kept off to one side, expectantly facing a bustling open kitchen. Capable and full-flavoured cooking in distinctly modern style encompasses dishes like home-cured gravadlax, duck with roast figs and celery and a smooth summer fool with biscotti.

Food serving times:
Monday-Sunday:
12.30pm-2.45pm,
7pm-10.15pm
Closed 23-31 December
(bookings not accepted)
Prices:
Meals: 12.95 (lunch) and a la carte 22.00/31.00

Typical Dishes

Gravadlax, oyster beignet

Duck breast, cauliflower purée

Passion fruit shortbread

Nearest tube: Ravenscourt Park/ Goldhawk Road

Shepherd's Bush

016 Havelock Tavern

57 Masbro Rd, Brook Green, Shepherd's Bush W14 0LS

Tel.: (020) 7603 5374 - Fax: (020) 7602 1163
Website: www.thehavenlocktavern.co.uk

Brakspear, Marstons Pedigree, Fuller's London Pride

It may not look too enticing on the corner of this unassuming West London street, but inside, the Havelock is buzzing. Formerly two shops, there are still big windows looking out onto the street. It gets very, very busy here, so for drinkers or diners, the message is simple: arrive early. Many come for the rather classy food to be had, and most tables are snapped up by seven o'clock. Menus change daily and might include pork with lentils, spinach and mash; Thai fish cakes with chilli dipping sauce; or smoked salmon with soft flour tortillas, avocado salsa, coriander and lime. Despite the bustling atmosphere, staff are friendly and attentive and obviously used to being at full stretch.

Food serving times:
Monday-Saturday:
 12.30pm-2.30pm, 7pm-10pm
Sunday:
 12.30pm-3pm, 7pm-9.30pm
Closed 22-26 December and Easter Sunday
(bookings not accepted)
Prices:
Meals: a la carte 18.00/24.00

Typical Dishes

Welsh rarebit

Char grilled ribeye steak, tarragon butter

Nectarine and almond tart

Pay and display parking during the week, free parking at weekends. Nearest tube: Kensington Olympia

Highgate

017 The Bull

13 North Hill, Highgate N6 4AB

Tel.: 0845 456 5033 - Fax: 0845 456 5034

Website: www.inthebull.biz

VISA MC

Highgate IPA, Timothy Taylor

Since the spring of 2005, denizens of one of London's most sought-after areas have been flocking to this smart Grade II listed pub standing proudly on North Hill. In keeping with Highgate's rather quirky image, it's a pub 'in reverse': the ground floor's the dining room, while upstairs is where the more serious drinking is done, in the company of striking floor to ceiling windows, a real fire and a relaxed style of décor, enhanced by an original American pool table. You eat downstairs at banquette seats in a smart, spacious area with good views of the chefs at work in the open kitchen. Menus are very appealing: simple European dishes, mostly English with a strong Gallic undercurrent, all home-made using top quality seasonal ingredients.

Food serving times:

Tuesday-Saturday:
12pm-2.30pm(-3.30pm Saturday); 6pm-10.30pm

Sunday:
12pm-3.30pm, 6.30pm-9.30pm

Closed 25 and 26 December.

Prices:

Meals: 17.95 and a la carte 40.00/120.00

Typical Dishes

Carpaccio of sea bass

Fillet of veal

Honeycomb parfait with amaretto ice cream

Free parking on road outside pub

Highgate

018 ## Rose & Crown

86 Highgate High St, Highgate N6 5HX

Tel.: (020) 8340 6712 - Fax: (020) 9340 0770
e-mail: johnkrimsonbars@aol.com

London Pride

I n the midst of Highgate's lifestyle shops and restaurant chains, the 300 year old Rose and Crown often passed unnoticed until its recent makeover, now signified by the "RC" monogram sign swinging above the door and the calm palette of reds and creams inside. Smaller, less hectic and more neighbourly than many, the bar now does a stronger line in Pimm's cocktails than in session pints, while a little dining room and secluded garden terrace are similarly relaxed. Here, sound, subtly seasonal cooking on a familiar modern theme adds classic French ideas and a light Asian influence: as well as the balanced à la carte, an accessibly priced lunch and early dinner menu make this a good spur-of-the-moment choice.

Food serving times:
Tuesday-Friday:
12pm-2.30pm, 6pm-10pm
Sunday:
12pm-5pm, 6pm-10pm
Prices:
Meals: a la carte 13.95/23.50

Typical Dishes

Carpaccio of beef

Sea bass fillet with red pepper oil

Apple and orange crumble

On street parking, free except for between 10am-12pm. Nearest tube: Highgate/Archway

Chiswick

019 The Devonshire House

126 Devonshire Rd, Chiswick W4 2JJ

Tel.: (020) 8987 2626 - Fax: (020) 8995 0152
e-mail: info@thedevonshire.co.uk - Website: www.thedevonshirehouse.co.uk

 🍷 *VISA* AE 🅜🅒

 No real ales offered

At the quiet residential end of a West London road close to the A4, this Victorian pub has reaped the benefits of a pleasant conversion: a young crowd creates a bustling atmosphere in what is now a stylish dining pub. Some of the original character is retained by way of the high ceiling and large windows. Elsewhere, the feeling is contemporary and spacious, with wooden floors, navy blue banquettes and chocolate brown leather chairs. Interesting, contemporary menus offer a succinct but balanced choice and might include, for starters, summer salad with smoked haddock brandade, tomato and chive vinaigrette; for mains, escalope of pork Milanese; and, as a refreshing dessert, nougatine glace with fresh raspberries. Obliging and efficient service.

Food serving times:
Tuesday-Friday:
 12pm-2.30pm, 7pm-10.30pm
Saturday:
 12pm-3pm, 7pm-10.30pm
Sunday:
 12pm-3pm, 7pm-10pm
Closed 24-26 December and 1 January
Prices:
Meals: a la carte 20.85/33.90

Typical Dishes

Asparagus with fried egg and crispy bacon

Fillet of sea bass, caponata of peppers

Caramelised apple tart

Parking available on the street.
Nearest tube: Turnham Green

Archway

020 **St John's**

91 Junction Rd, Archway N19 5QU

Tel.: (020) 7272 1587 - Fax: (020) 7687 2247

e-mail: *coppershack@excite.com*

 VISA AE

Up to 3 real ales served

This one-time scruffy, edgy boozer, down from Archway tube, looks sharp and bright again as a smartly run gastro-local. Broad picture windows light up the long counter bar, its real buzz provided by a lively mix of regulars and others at stools and scrubbed tables, but squeeze your way through to the big double doors on the right to see the place at its best. The high-ceilinged former snooker hall, in fine period proportion, is now a bustling dining room and open kitchen, hung with tall mirrors and big blackboard menus; laid-back, convivial and modestly stylish, it's just the place for varied, fresh-tasting dishes in decent quantity, including some tasty chargrills. Spirited staff in t-shirts and aprons shuttle to and fro with baskets of fresh bread, providing swift and friendly service.

Food serving times:
Monday-Friday:
12pm-3pm, 6.30pm-11pm
Saturday:
12pm-4pm, 6.30pm-11pm
Sunday:
12pm-4pm, 6.30pm-9.30pm
Closed Monday lunch
Prices:
Meals: a la carte 18.00/25.00

Typical Dishes

Borscht, sour cream

Caramelised duck, watercress salad

Dark chocolate tart, Columbian rum

Nearest tube: Archway

Finsbury

021 The Peasant

240 St John St, Finsbury EC1V 4PH
Tel.: (020) 7336 7726 - Fax: (020) 7490 1089
Website: www.thepeasant.co.uk

🍷 **VISA** **AE** **MC**

Charles Wells Bombardier, Archers of Swindon and 1 monthly changing guest ale

N o-one charting the rise of the gastro-revolution could miss out The Peasant. This upmarket founding father between Smithfield and The Angel is a landmark pub in more ways than one, and if the cooking has evolved over time, the recipe for success has stayed the same: daily changing menus of robust, well-presented cooking combine fresh ingredients and a marked Mediterranean influence. The pub's original glory days came over a century ago and hints of handsome, high-Victorian style remain, from the broad arched windows and lofty ceilings to the tiled floor, but the defining quality is the bustling atmosphere of happy Londoners at full volume. Even when it's packed out, more often than not, well-organised staff keep their cool and their smiles, but head for the linen-laid tables upstairs if you want quieter, more intimate dining.

Food serving times:
Monday-Sunday:
12pm-10.30pm
Closed 24 December-
2 January
(booking essential)
Prices:
Meals: a la carte 24.00/30.00

Parking meters opposite. Nearest tube: Farringdon/Angel ❯❯

Typical Dishes

Seared organic salmon, green tea noodle salad

Roast cannon of lamb

Chocolate brownie 'French Vanilla' ice cream

Finsbury

022 The Well

180 St John St, Finsbury EC1V 4JY

Tel.: 020 7251 9363 - Fax: 020 7404 2250

e-mail: drinks@downthewell.co.uk - Website: www.downthewell.co.uk

 VISA **AE** **MC**

Finsbury locals may not glance twice as they pass this predictable looking pub-on-a-corner in a trendy part of St John Street not unacquainted with food-and-drink destinations. But regulars in The Well know they're on to a good thing here. Big black canopies hang out over the pavement providing shelter for drinkers at al fresco benches next to slide-open screen windows. Inside, it's small, busy and buzzing: all around is the ambience of the metropolitan gastropub with wooden floorboards, exposed brickwork and mismatched wood furniture. It's the food that lifts it above the average, with everything from the 'pie of the week' to sophisticated, accomplished dishes in the modern British vein: all the fish and shellfish are from Billingsgate down the road. Downstairs a sexy lounge with fish tanks and brown sofas draws a more louche crowd.

Food serving times:
Monday-Friday:
    12pm-3pm, 6pm-10.30pm
Saturday: 10.30am-4.30pm,
                    6pm-10.30pm
Sunday: 10.30am-4.30pm,
                    6pm-9.30pm
Closed 25 and 26 December,
1 January
Prices:
Meals: a la carte 20.00/28.00

Typical Dishes

Pea and mint soup

Pork belly with cassoulet

Potted lemon cream

Nearest tubes: Farringdon, Barbican, Angel

Islington

THE DRAPERS ARMS — Dining Room

023 Drapers Arms

44 Barnsbury St, Islington N1 1ER

Tel.: (020) 7619 0348 - Fax: (020) 7619 0413
e-mail: info@thedrapersarms.co.uk - Website: www.thedrapersarms.co.uk

    VISA

Erdinger Werbrau, Charles Wells Bombardier

An impressive and substantial stone façade announces this proud looking Georgian pub tucked away in one of fashionable Islington's quiet side streets. It was once a ramshackle boozer, but in the last few years has undergone something of a "gastropub" rebirth: rough wooden floors, plenty of space to air-kiss, shiny leather sofas, tables and booths sited along walls made over with a contemporary palette. A delightful rear courtyard terrace is great for summer smooching, and food comes with the guarantee of a light, precise touch: white gazpacho with chilli tiger prawns; gnocchi with Gorgonzola; salmon and cod fishcake with spinach and tartare sauce.

Food serving times:
Monday-Saturday:
12pm-5pm, 6pm-10pm
Saturday-Sunday:
12pm-5pm, 6pm-9pm
Closed 25-26 December, 1-2 January
Prices:
Meals: a la carte 17.50/24.50

Typical Dishes

Artichoke tart
Sausage and mash
White chocolate cheesecake

Nearest tube: Highbury and Islington

Islington

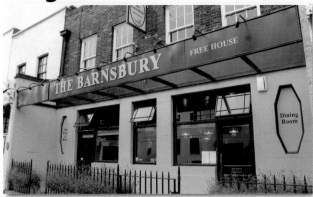

024 The Barnsbury

209-211 Liverpool Rd, Islington N1 1LX

Tel.: (020) 7607 5519 - Fax: (020) 7607 3256

e-mail: info@thebarnsbury.co.uk - Website: www.thebarnsbury.co.uk

Timothy Taylor Landlord, Fuller's London Pride and 1 monthly guest ale

A block or so back from busy Upper Street, The Barnsbury takes things at a more laid-back pace than its larger neighbours. Easy to spot in summer, with a line of flowering lavender fringing the front railings, this agreeable gastrobar keeps up the same downplayed chic on the inside. It's appealingly simple, with a central counter bar surrounded by pews, old stripped tables and chairs, cool cut-glass goblet chandeliers and quarterly changing tableaux on the walls, which are painted in signature shades of dusky duck-egg blue. Genuinely helpful staff, as smiling and at ease as the regulars, happily make the effort to talk you through the menu, a selection of robust modern pub dishes served in unstinting portions.

Food serving times:
Monday-Sunday:
    12pm-3pm, 6.30pm-10pm
Closed 25-26 December and 1 January
Prices:
Meals: a la carte 19.00/26.50

On-street parking after 6.30pm.
Nearest tube: Highbury and Islington

Typical Dishes

Chicken liver parfait

Veal chop with sauteed spinach

Rhubarb and ginger crumble

Islington

025 **The House** *We most liked*

63-69 Canonbury Rd, Islington N1 2DG

Tel.: (020) 7704 7410 - Fax: (020) 7704 9388
e-mail: info@inthehouse.biz - Website: www.inthehouse.biz

Adnams ales

Around the back of the Town Hall in residential Islington, a pleasant and unassuming bar which is popular with the locals. There's a subtle change of tone in the dining room, however: smart linen, flowers, candlelight and even the artwork should prepare you for similar aspiration and attention to detail in a menu that shows the chef's West End restaurant experience. From the open kitchen come carefully composed and full-flavoured dishes: good-sized slices of crispy duck on a soy-dressed watercress salad, herb-crusted cod with noodles and a creamy mustard and chive velouté, and rich, smooth chocolate and orange parfait. A lunchtime list includes shepherd's pie and a modern take on the all-day breakfast.

Food serving times:
Tuesday-Friday:
12pm-2.30pm
Saturday:
12pm-3.30pm, 6pm-10.30pm
Sunday:
12pm-3.30pm,
6.30pm-9.30pm
Closed 24-26 December and 1 January
Closed Monday lunch
Prices:
Meals: 17.95 (fixed price lunch) and a la carte 30.00/50.00

Typical Dishes

Crab and ginger spring rolls

Rib of beef with a shallot crust

Chocolate pudding, vanilla ice cream

Parking meters outside or free after 6.30pm. Nearest tube: Highbury and Islington

Islington

026 **The Northgate**

113 Southgate Rd, Islington N1 3JS

Tel.: (020) 7359 7392 - Fax: (020) 7359 7393

e-mail: thenorthgate@hppubs.co.uk

    VISA Ⓜ©

Deuchars IPA, Fuller's London Pride and regularly changing guest ales

The Northgate looks like the kind of ordinary corner pub you walk past every day, but ask around and you won't want to pass up a visit to this neighbourhood stalwart. A traditionally proportioned front room mixes scrubbed tables and wood floors with eye-catching works of modern art; a big central bar separates it from a slightly smarter dining room to the back. There's no hard and fast split, though, and locals who pull up a stool for a half may well end up staying for one of the daily specials; you can also eat out on the street-side terrace. Blackboard menus offer a cross-section of modern cooking, often working in Mediterranean ideas and flavours to good effect: unusually for a London pub, they also bake their own bread.

Food serving times:

Monday-Friday:
6.30pm-10.30pm

Saturday:
12pm-4pm, 6.30pm-10.30pm

Sunday:
12pm-4pm, 6.30pm-9.30pm

Closed 25-26 December and 1 January

Prices:

Meals: a la carte 18.00/25.00

Unrestricted street parking Sunday, after 6.30pm Monday-Saturday.
Nearest tube: Essex Road/ Canonbury National Rail

Typical Dishes

Pan fried duck livers, balsamic red onion

Confit of duck, chilli glaze

Red wine poached pear tart

Islington

027 The Social

33 Linton St, Islington N1 7DU

Tel.: (020) 7354 5809 - Fax: (020) 7354 8087

e-mail: managers@thesocialn1.com - Website: www.thesocial.com

   VISA

Charles Wells Bombardier, Eagle IPA, Erdinger Weißbräu

D on't be put off by the slightly confusing sign here. It says "Hanbury Arms" on the outside because it's a listed building; look beneath that for "The Social", a name with a seriously fashionable reputation that rests on the DJ's choice of music and a spark of Islington chic as much as on the appetising food. An open-plan kitchen divides the restaurant and a buzzing bar: lots of Japanese lager is drunk, but the über-cool ambience is softened by wood panelled walls. Modern pub menus make the place worth a visit: a good range covers everything from steak sandwiches to confit of duck, and prices have a sensible look about them.

Food serving times:
Monday-Friday:
6pm-10pm
Saturday-Sunday:
12pm-5pm, 6pm-9pm
Closed 25-30 December
(booking essential)
Prices:
Meals: a la carte 17.50/24.50

Typical Dishes

Artichoke tart

Sausages and mash

White chocolate cheesecake

Street parking available after 6.30pm and weekends. Nearest tube: Essex Road/Angel

Chelsea

028 **Admiral Codrington**

17 Mossop St, Chelsea SW3 2LY

Tel.: (020) 7581 0005 - Fax: (020) 7589 2452
e-mail: admiralcodrington@longshotplc.com - Website: www.theadmiralcodrington.co.uk

Charles Wells Bombardier, Black Sheep

This well-established, fashionably located pub is something of a traditional gathering point for the well-heeled neighbours. Its main bar is invariably packed in the evenings, when a pair of shoulder pads can prove a useful fashion accessory. Lightly push your way to the back and you'll find a very pleasant small dining area with wood floor, soft lighting and even a retractable glass roof. Large banquettes, in a modern floral fabric resembling tapestry, can be a haven after the scrum through the bar. The menus are changed quarterly and provide a very good choice: there's strength in depth in the fine range of modern dishes. Pleasant, efficient service is a certainty.

Food serving times:
Monday-Friday:
12pm-2.30pm, 7pm-11pm
Saturday:
12pm-3.30pm, 7pm-10.30pm
Sunday:
12pm-4.30pm, 7pm-10.30pm
Prices:
Meals: a la carte 20.00/35.00

Typical Dishes

Foie gras and chicken liver parfait

Cod in soft herb crust

Passion fruit cheesecake

Nearest tube: South Kensington

Chelsea

029 Builders Arms

13 Britten St, Chelsea SW3 3TY

Tel.: (020) 7349 9040
Website: www.geronimo-inns.co.uk

 Fuller's London Pride, Adnams

Down a quiet Chelsea side street, just off the King's Road, this neat and tidy cream-washed terraced bar can seem impossibly crowded in the early evening, but squeeze through to the less smoky back rooms and a more orderly sense prevails: here you can find bookshelves, wing-back armchairs and slightly surreal oil paintings which create an easy, offbeat lounge ambience for the young King's Road set. There are warming colours everywhere, enhanced by an open fire, and matted flooring adds to the contemporary feel. Relaxed but super-efficient staff haven't let the pub's popularity go to their heads, serving up modern dishes in endless succession, and somehow it all works. Lunch times are much quieter than evenings so arrive early for dinner. And bear in mind that Sundays in this part of the world are particularly busy so do plan ahead.

Food serving times:
Monday-Friday:
12pm-2.30pm, 7pm-9.45pm
Saturday-Sunday:
12pm-3pm, 7pm-9.15pm
Closed 25-26 December and 1 January
(bookings not accepted)
Prices:
Meals: a la carte 17.00/26.00

Typical Dishes

Warm pigeon salad

Cornish crab spaghettini

Treacle sponge and custard

Parking meters available on adjacent roads. Nearest tube: South Kensington

Chelsea

030 **Chelsea Ram**

32 Burnaby St, Chelsea SW10 0PL
Tel.: (020) 7351 4008 - Fax: (020) 7351 5557
e-mail: theram@hotmail.com

 🍷 **VISA** **MC**

Youngs Bitter, Special, Ram Rod, Winter Warmer, St. George

Standing out like a hardy reminder of old London near the rather soulless enclaves of Chelsea Harbour, this solid citizen of a dining pub draws in the punters like a magnet: it's on a corner so it's hard to miss it. Walk in and a feeling of good cheer is instantly awakened. This could be something to do with the bright, airy interior with warm yellow hued walls, or the light that pours in through the etched glass windows. Maybe it's just the knowledge that good beer is on handpump and interesting menus lurk round the back in intimate dining alcoves - an internationally influenced choice of dishes is up for grabs: start off, maybe, with Thai duck salad and follow it up with smoked haddock, black pudding and crushed potato. The shelves of old books might serve to remind you that in a past incarnation this was a junk shop.

Food serving times:
Monday-Saturday:
   12pm-3pm, 6.30pm-10pm
Sunday:
   12pm-4pm, 6.30-9.30pm
Prices:
Meals: a la carte 18.00/21.00

Typical Dishes

Carpaccio of beef

Sea bass ratatouille, saffron sauce

Pear and chocolate Bakewell tart

Pay and display parking available nearby. Nearest tube: West Brompton

Chelsea

031 Cross Keys

1 Lawrence St, Chelsea SW3 5NB

Tel.: (020) 7349 9111 - Fax: (020) 7349 9333

e-mail: cross.keys@fsmail.net - Website: www.thexkeys.co.uk

  Wadworth 6X, Courage Directors

At a fashionable address just up from Cheyne Walk, this is more than just a local pub, whatever the inn sign and 200 year-old façade might suggest on first sight. A spacious bar, brightened by tall windows, mirrors and a curly iron chandelier and open to the gallery above, caters well for drinkers, but the glass–roofed dining room is in a style of its own: tables are spread beneath the branches of a tree, while wicker hurdles, sheaves of grass and a frieze of farming tools are best described as Chelsea Ironic-Rustic. Upstairs, you'll either love or try to ignore a faintly kitsch mix of modern and neo-Classical: the gaping Bacchus-head fireplace on the top floor is particularly impressive. More importantly, though, flavourful, generous standards and specials from the open kitchen strike a real chord with a smart crowd of local diners.

Food serving times:

Monday-Sunday:
    12pm-3pm, 7pm-11pm

Closed 23-28 December and Bank Holidays

Prices:

Meals: a la carte 24.50/28.00

Typical Dishes

Chilled tomato and crab soup

Pork belly with truffle mash

Prunes with Armagnac and praline

Nearest tube: Sloane Square

Chelsea

032 **Lots Road Pub & Dining Room**

114 Lots Rd, Chelsea SW10 0RJ

Tel.: (020) 7352 6645

e-mail: lotsroad@thespiritgroup.com - Website: www.thespiritgroup.com

London Pride, Wadworth 6X, Adnams

Tucked away between Chelsea Harbour's flats and offices and the old gasworks, this refitted gastropub is a friendly, informal and surprisingly busy place – if you happen to be passing, the logic seems to go, you've every right to make yourself at home. Old schoolroom chairs and tables follow the curve of a quadrant-shaped bar-room, and while you can also get a good plate of something and a cold beer sitting at the metal counter, the most intimate place to dine is easily missed, with smart tables off to the other side; a few deep armchairs also beckon for a slow drink. Young, T-shirted staff stay on the move from table to open kitchen, serving a daily changing menu of contemporary dishes like sea bream with fennel.

Food serving times:
Monday-Friday:
12pm-3pm, 5.30pm-10.30pm
Saturday-Sunday:
12pm-10.30pm

Prices:
Meals: a la carte 18.00/26.00

Typical Dishes

Pan fried scallops

Roasted rump of lamb, thyme gravy

Sticky toffee pudding

Nearest tube: West Brompton

Chelsea

033 Swag and Tails

10-11 Fairholt St, Knightsbridge, Chelsea SW7 1EG

Tel.: (020) 7584 6926 - Fax: (020) 7581 9935
e-mail: theswag@swagandtails.com - Website: www.swagandtails.com

Adnams, Charles Wells Bombardier

Just a two-minute walk from Harrods, down a charming mews, hides this cosy little inn with its colourful hanging baskets and smart blue shutters. It makes a neat contrast to the more garish pubs in this part of London. Despite the compact proportions, it falls into two distinct sections: a front half, embellished with wood and pine, brick walls and eponymous swagged curtains; and a rear tiled conservatory with imposing posters and swish down-lighting. Seasonal modern dishes please sophisticated palates while simpler, more popular items are also available.

Food serving times:
Monday-Friday:
 12pm-3pm, 6pm-10pm
Closed Bank Holidays
Prices:
Meals: a la carte 26.00/30.00

Typical Dishes

Assiette of Foie gras, fig chutney

Szechuan peppered duck leg

Caramel panna cotta

Parking meters at the end of the street, or on single yellow line after 6.30pm. Nearest tube: Knightsbridge

Chelsea

034 **The Phoenix**

23 Smith St, Chelsea SW3 4EE

Tel.: 020 7730 9182

e-mail: mail@geronimo-phoenix.fsnet.co.uk - Website: www.geronimo-inns.co.uk

Adnams Best

Even the most "comfortable" of London neighbourhoods has need of a superior kind of local, and the Phoenix gets the full approval of a friendly young crowd, all shopped-out from an afternoon on the King's Road or just kicking back on a balmy weekend evening. A retro tweak or two stops the stylish bar from feeling too uncongenially modern: only in Chelsea could this be thought of as 'shabby chic', but suede, stripped-back floorboards and some suitably clunky old wooden chairs give it a nicely lived-in feel. It's never less than pleasantly busy and, unlikely as it seems, the street-side seats have become one of the area's alternative "destinations". Extensive Modern British menus and a few specials serve their public well. Service is polite, friendly and never off-hand.

Food serving times:
Monday-Sunday:
   12pm-2.45pm, 7pm-9.45pm
Prices:
Meals: a la carte 15.00/28.00

Typical Dishes

Eggs Benedict

Roast chump of Welsh lamb

Warm chocolate and praline brownie

Tube: Sloane Sq

Chelsea

035 The Pig's Ear

35 Old Church St, Chelsea SW3 5BS

Tel.: 020 7352 2908 - Fax: 020 7352 9321

e-mail: hello@thepigsear.co.uk - Website: www.thepigsear.co.uk

     VISA **AE** **MC**

Uley Brewery 'Pigs Ear', St. Austell Tinners

Around the corner from the King's Road, the lightly refurbished Pig's Ear still mixes in plenty of traditional style in a likeable ground-floor bar, with the odd pig-themed picture and ornament here and there. They're also represented on the menu – pigs' ears are not unknown as a starter, and are one of the more extreme examples of a taste for slightly uncommon but properly used ingredients. The bar menu works equally well if you want a set lunch or just a main course, though be warned that it can get very busy in here: you may need a little luck or determination to grab a space. If the panelled first-floor dining room offers more peace and quiet, and a more structured menu, the style of cooking carries over – hearty cuisine with a rustic edge.

Food serving times:
Monday-Saturday:
   12.30pm-3pm, 7pm-10pm
Sunday:
   12.30pm-4pm, 7pm-10pm
Prices:
Meals: a la carte 16.00/22.00

Typical Dishes

Poached duck egg with English asparagus

Bavette steak with French fries

Chocolate tart

Nearest Tube: Sloane Sq (25 mins. walk)

Earl's Court

036 **Hollywood Arms**

45 Hollywood Rd, Earl's Court SW10 9HX

Tel.: (020) 7349 7840 - Fax: (020) 7349 7841

VISA AE MC

Timothy Taylor Landlord, TEA, Fuller's London Pride

An intelligent renovation of this handsome old pub seems to have struck just the right balance: original glasswork has been preserved while fine fabrics, neo-Gothic arches and even the period-patterned wallpaper pay discreet modern homage to the more restrained school of Victorian design. Beyond the stylish bar - polished tables and club chairs - is a softly lit dining room serving a concise, Mediterranean influenced menu with some original touches: flavourful dishes include tender veal with a piquant lemon and caper sauce and a warm salad of artichokes, butter beans, aïoli and soft-boiled egg. Smooth, helpful service really adds to the enjoyment.

Food serving times:
Monday-Sunday:
12pm-11pm
Prices:
Meals: a la carte 17.00/24.00

Typical Dishes

Fishcakes with spinach and buerre blanc

Hollywood supreme burger

Vanilla ice cream with mars bar sauce

Pay and display parking nearby.
Nearest tube: West Brompton

Wimbledon

037 The Fire Stables

27-29 Church Rd, Wimbledon SW19 5DQ

Tel.: (020) 8946 3197 - Fax: (020) 8946 1101
e-mail: thefirestables@thespiritgroup.com

🍷 🚭 **VISA** **AE** **MC**

London Pride

A mongst the trendy natives of Wimbledon, this is seen as a rather smart and stylish addition to the eateries of SW19. They're not wrong: The Fire Stables is handily set in the centre of the village, and is a dining pub writ large, the contemporary décor being modish but not clinical. There's a high vaulted ceiling with a startling abstract painting on the wall. Furniture is a pleasing mix of modern and retro: leather sofas, dark wooden artefacts and floorboards, a coal fire. The rear restaurant serves locally renowned, heart-warming menus. How about the moist, fresh, tasty lamb burger with herbs, light mayonnaise and thick cut, home cooked chunky chips? Followed by feather light panna cotta with caramelised blood orange salad? Enough people are smitten, even though it's not the cheapest place around, so get there early.

Food serving times:
Monday-Sunday:
    12pm-3pm, 6pm-10.30pm
Prices:
Meals: 15.50 (fixed price lunch)
and a la carte 24.00/30.00

Pay and display parking outside.
Nearest tube: Wimbledon

Typical Dishes

Chicken liver parfait

Rack of lamb, pistou vegetables

Chocolate torte, espresso ice cream

Barnes

038 The Bridge
204 Castelnau Road, Barnes SW13 9DW
Tel.: (020) 8563 9811
e-mail: thebridgeinbarnes@btinternet.com - Website: www.thebridgeinbarnes.co.uk

  rest **VISA** **AE** **①** **MC**

 Charles Wells Bombardier, Ruddles, Adnams Broadside

Smartly refurbished a few years back, The Bridge's smart gold lettering and sign proclaim a welcome change of direction for this reformed boozer. With polished tables and chairs dotted around a horseshoe counter bar, the original proportions remain, while the old fireplace and the arch of the ceiling fit the cool but casual look of the retro lounge and its palms, leather sofas and chandelier. Even in the more formal dining area, however, the hint of smartness is less important than the approachable, pleasantly lived-in feel of the place. There's also a neat decked terrace set aside for summer dining and a light seasonal shift in the menu of contemporary gastropub favourites. Though it's set back from the river, don't go expecting a slow, peaceful pint on Boat Race day!

Food serving times:
Monday-Sunday:
12pm-3.30pm,
5.30pm-10.30pm
Closed 25 December
Prices:
Meals: a la carte 20.00/28.00

Near Hammersmith Bridge, opposite Lonsdale Road. Parking in Arundel Terrace. Nearest tube: Hammersmith

Typical Dishes

Seared scallops, pea and bean saute

North African lamb shank

Passion fruit panna cotta

East Sheen

039 ## The Victoria

10 West Temple Sheen, East Sheen SW14 7RT

Tel.: (020) 8876 4238 - Fax: (020) 8878 3464

e-mail: reservations@thevictoria.net - Website: www.thevictoria.net

      VISA **AE** **MC**

Courage, Directors

The age-of-empire pub sign still hangs outside The Victoria, but any resemblance to a suburban boozer stops at the door. Restyled in clean lines and natural colours, a conservatory with linen-clad tables leads out to a terrace and children's play area: it's ideal for diners who like a quick slide or clamber between courses, but a post-lunch family ramble across nearby Richmond Park is better for really letting off steam. Daily changing evening menus combine traditional and Mediterranean-inspired dishes like walnut and rocket penne, brandade-stuffed peppers and sea bass with a bouillabaise sauce; there are one or two weekend lunch specials and understanding staff can suggest a few smaller failsafe options for young gastronomes. It's worth knowing that they're also open for morning coffee and buns: a big hit with mums and toddlers alike.

Food serving times:
Monday-Friday:
12pm-2.30pm, 7pm-10pm
Saturday:
12pm-3pm, 7pm-10pm
Sunday:
12pm-4pm, 7pm-9pm
Closed 4 days at Christmas
Prices:
Meals: a la carte 18.00/28.00
7 rooms : 98.50

Typical Dishes

Smoked eel and bacon salad

Charolais sirloin steak, onion gravy

Chocolate and Seville orange tart

Parking. Nearest station: Mortlake/
North Sheen National Rail

Bermondsey

040 The Hartley

64 Tower Bridge Road, Bermondsey SE1 4TR

Tel.: (020) 7394 7023

e-mail: enquries@thehartley.com - Website: www.thehartley.com

Y VISA AE O MC

 No real ales offered

It's already a bit of a sleeper hit with the upwardly mobile young neighbours and local after-work diners, and Bermondsey may soon wonder how it ever got on without the new version of this Victorian redbrick pub, a little one-room place with close-set, rickety bistro tables, an open kitchen and a lightly quirky taste in decoration. No points for guessing the origin of the name: the converted Hartley's factory across the road is remembered in old nanny-knows-best adverts, black and white photos showing a hard day at the marmalade vats and even jars of jam above the spirits rack. Fight down the urge to order toast and choose instead from a concise menu – terrines, steaks, roast poussin and salsa rosso, salmon cakes and chips – or half a dozen daily specials. Friendly staff, and efficient with it.

Food serving times:
Monday-Friday:
12pm-3pm, 6pm-10pm
Saturday:
11pm-4pm, 6pm-10pm
Sunday: 12pm-9pm
Closed 25-26 December
(Sunday lunch - roast menu only)
Prices:
Meals: a la carte 16.00/27.00

Typical Dishes

Pan fried goat's cheese wrapped in courgette

Roast red bream on Greek salad

Lime mousse brûlée

On street parking. Nearest tube: Borough

Waterloo

041 The Anchor & Hope

36 The Cut, Waterloo SE1 8LP
Tel.: (020) 7928 9898

VISA **MC**

Charles Wells Bombardier

Those in the know queue round the bar and out the door for dinner at one of London's most talked-about dining pubs, where a stylish and convivial no-frills attitude extends to communal tables and boiled eggs and celery salt on the bar, yet avoids the charge of inverse pretension. A tiny open kitchen serves up simply presented but very satisfying cooking which is indebted to the French regional traditions and the earthy, rustic cuisine of St John, Clerkenwell, but remains seriously original for all that: try smoked herring with beetroot and horseradish, lamb in hay with braised peas and a sharp rhubarb jelly with vanilla ice cream. When you add impressively calm, well-timed service, even under pressure, and wines by the tumbler and carafe, this represents conspicuously good value for money.

Food serving times:
Tuesday-Saturday:
12pm-2.30pm
Monday-Saturday:
6pm-10.30pm
Closed Christmas-New Year, last 2 weeks August and Bank Holidays
Prices:
Meals: a la carte 20.00/30.00

Typical Dishes

Snails on duck fat toast

Rabbit, wild garlic and Sherry

Marmalade Bakewell tart

Nearest tube: Southwark

Canary Wharf

042 ## The Gun

27 Coldharbour, Canary Wharf E14 9NS
Tel.: (020) 7515 5222 - Fax: (020) 7515 4407
e-mail: info@thegundocklands.com - Website: www.thegundocklands.com

Adnams Broadside, Youngs Ordinary, Brakspear

Restored after a fire, The Gun might have played more on an authentic naval heritage that begins in the era of the Blackwall cannon-foundry, the India Docks and that most saleable of maritime heroes, Lord Nelson. Thank goodness it didn't. The "Horatio" and "Emma" signs on the toilets are a small price to pay: relaid oak, polished black bar panels and white walls, and a print of a magnificent Dreadnought-era destroyer at full steam give it all the maritime London look it needs. Even the charming terrace keeps it real with a view of the Dome and the cement works. Blackboard specials make the most of nearby Billingsgate market, a great local source of fresh fish, and the modern cooking on a classic French base strikes a good balance between finesse and bold pub style. Keen service is neat and well-timed.

Food serving times:
Monday-Friday:
   12pm-3pm, 6pm-10.30pm
Saturday:
  10.30am-4pm, 6pm-10.30pm
Sunday:
  10.30am-4pm, 6pm-9.30pm
Closed 25-26 December and 1 January
Prices:
Meals: a la carte 20.00/33.00

Typical Dishes

Potted duck, pear chutney and sage brioche

Pork chop, celeriac and apple gratin

Nougat glacé

Street parking

Battersea

043 The Greyhound

136 Battersea High St, Battersea SW11 3JR

Tel.: 020 7978 7021 - Fax: 020 7978 0599

e-mail: eat@thegreyhoundatbattersea.co.uk - Website: www.thegreyhoundatbattersea.co.uk

The owner's knowledge and experience, gained as a sommelier, is given full rein in The Greyhound's superb wine list, but its concise contemporary menu deserves to be at least as well known in this corner of South West London. Behind its neat, tile-and-glass frontage in navy and gun-metal grey, the comfortably remodelled pub divides into a stylish bar and a cosy, nicely lit dining room which opens on to a courtyard: great to have up your sleeve in summer. Even if you're not eating, there's an understated buzz out front, not to mention some interesting beers, but with such a well-priced set lunch on offer, plenty of people take them up on the deal. As in the evening, dishes make use of carefully selected, largely organic produce.

Food serving times:
Closed 24-27 December,
31 December-3 January,
Sunday dinner and Monday

Prices:
Meals: 15.00/31.00 and a la carte 42.00/55.00

Typical Dishes

Wild Scottish salmon carpaccio

Herdwick mutton loin

White peach, crème fraîche mousse, lemon thyme jelly

Nearest station: Clapham Junction

Bayswater and Maida Vale

044 **The Waterway**

54 Formosa St, Bayswater and Maida Vale W9 2JU
Tel.: (020) 7266 3557 - Fax: (020) 7266 3547
e-mail: info@thewaterway.co.uk - Website: www.thewaterway.co.uk

Fuller's London Pride, Courage

With bright-painted barges moored along the canal, the trees in full leaf and the church spire beyond, the deck terrace of this smart gastrobar seems far removed from the pressures and cares of Travelcard zones 1 and 2. Cool young locals chat, clink beers and Pinot Grigio and relax on garden chairs and slatted benches; heaters take the last chill out of the spring air. To the right of the bar, a smart team provides relaxed and efficient restaurant-style service, coasting around a chic dining room where leather banquettes, blond wood and elegant lights set the tone. A concise but nicely weighted modern menu offers dishes like braised lamb with Parmesan polenta, crisp, golden salt cod cakes with aioli, or coffee and praline brulée. Civilised fun.

Food serving times:
Monday-Sunday:
12.30pm-3.30pm,
6.30pm-10.30pm
Prices:
Meals: a la carte 19.00/27.00

Typical Dishes

Foie gras and chicken liver parfait

Milk poached plaice mousseron mushrooms

Warm chocolate cake

Parking. Nearest tube: Warwick Avenue

Regent's Park & Marylebone

045 **The Abbey Road**

63 Abbey Road, St John's Wood, Regent's Park & Myarlebone NW8 0AE

Tel.: (020) 7328 6626 - Fax: (020) 7625 9168

e-mail: theabbeyroad@btconnect.com

 VISA **AE** **MC**

 Greene King IPA and Abbott Ale

The Beatles may have made the name famous, but owners Nick and Rob have built up a loyal following of their own with this rather grand gastropub down the road from the recording studios. Its corner location guarantees conspicuousness; so does its striking columned façade. A patio terrace with wooden benches, canopy and heaters brings out summer drinkers in swarms. Inside, the bustling front bar leads through to a snazzy duck-egg blue main dining room, with French posters, high ceiling and ornate mirrors: large windows let you see and be seen. Modern menus are in the Mediterranean style; on Sundays a roast and brunch is up for grabs. Everyday dishes might include courgette and pine nut ravioli with saffron for starters, followed by roast cod with mixed pepper coulis and spinach; to finish, perhaps, deliciously moist chocolate torte.

Food serving times:
Monday-Saturday:
         12.pm-10.30pm
Sunday: 12,30pm-10pm
Closed 25 and 31 December
Prices:
Meals: a la carte 20.00/25.00

> Some on-street parking, free after 6pm. Nearest Tube: St John's Wood/ Maida Vale

Typical Dishes

Tuna carpaccio

Rack of lamb, pea purée, vine tomatoes

Strawberry gratin

153

Victoria

046 The Ebury (Brasserie)

Ground Floor, 11 Pimlico Rd, Victoria SW1W 8NA

Tel.: (020) 7730 6784 - Fax: (020) 7730 6149

e-mail: info@theebury.co.uk - Website: www.theebury.co.uk

🍷 ✂ *VISA* AE ⓜⓒ

 Fullers London Pride

The ground floor of this refurbished Victorian redbrick pub is now a rather smart meeting place, with floor-to-ceiling windows looking out to the pavement, and a striking and sizable walnut bar being the centre of attention for those who want to look in: it does have just a hint of the "place to be seen" about it. Much of the space is laid out as a comfortably modern room with stylish tables and chairs, but one end is set aside with small leather sofas, another has become a smart seafood bar. Cooking covers the spectrum, and you can get anything from Welsh rarebit and salads to full modern menus blending the continental brasserie and Modern British kitchen. Service is attentive and quite formal, but pleasantly so. More metropolitan good living from the people who brought you The Wells and The Waterway.

Food serving times:

Monday-Sunday:
12pm-3.30pm,
6.30pm-10.30pm

Closed 24-26 December and 1 January

Prices:

Meals: a la carte 21.00/34.00

Typical Dishes

Beetroot cured gravadlax

Grilled black bream, saffron vierge

Apple tart Tatin, buttermilk ice cream

On street parking after 6.30pm.
Nearest tube: Sloane Square

P. Gajic / Michelin

- **a.** ✕✕ *A comfortable restaurant*
- **b.** ❀ *A very good restaurant in its category*
- **c.** 😊 *Good food at moderate prices*

Can't decide?
Find out more with the Michelin Guide Collection!

- A collection of 12 titles
- 20 000 restaurants around Europe
- 1 600 town plans
- The best addresses in every price category

Discover the pleasure of travel with the Michelin Guides.

A better way forward

*S*trengthened by the iconic BALTIC Centre, the Millennium Bridge and the Angel of the North, the sense of identity which binds Newcastle, Gateshead and the region around them has made northeastern unity a modern reality. In the days of the mighty border fiefdom, Northumbria's independent spirit took shape in the castles of Bamburgh and Alnwick and the splendour of Durham Cathedral, though the most celebrated symbols of the region date back still further. The ruins of Lindisfarne Priory and lonely Inner Farne, just off the beautiful Northumberland coast, recall the austerity and learning of the first monastic settlers, and from Housesteads to Wallsend, Hadrian's Wall is the cornerstone of Northern history. But the North East doesn't stop here – to the surprise of many visitors from further south! Some of England's most impressive working countryside can be found in the vast man-made pinewoods of Kielder Forest and the rolling line of the Cheviots: these weathered volcanic slopes are renowned for flavourful Cheviot lamb, while Kielder is known for its venison. Other specialities include fresh and smoked fish and, of course, Newcastle's famous Brown Ale, the national beverage of the "Geordie Nation"!

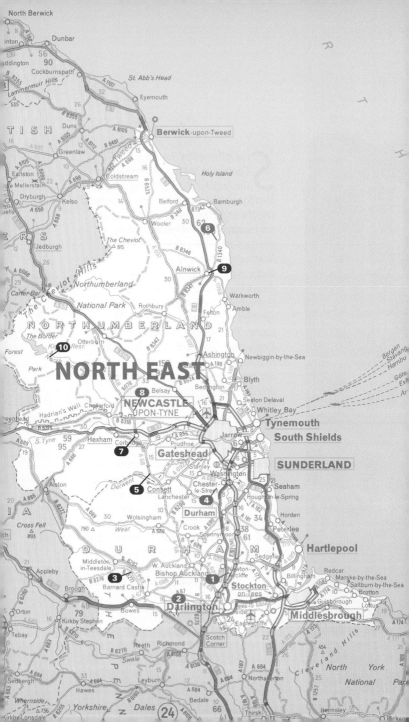

Aycliffe

001 The County

13 The Green, Aycliffe DL5 6LX

Tel.: (01325) 312273 - Fax: (01325) 308780
Website: www.the-county.co.uk

    VISA AE MC

Charles Wells Bombardier, Old Raby, Theakstons Best, Johnsmiths Magnet and weekly changing guest ales

Attention to detail comes first in what must surely be one of Northumbria's most keenly run pubs: that's clear from the warm welcome and the pub itself – three neat, cheerfully coloured rooms with chairs and two-seater pews at polished pine tables. There's further proof in the seasonally changing cooking, as the landlord leads by example in the kitchen, producing piquant, balanced dishes like tomato cake with peppered goat's cheese and balsamic vinegar, fillets of sea bass with a tangy, sticky ratatouille chutney and vegetable spring rolls on sweet chilli noodles. Well-drilled staff with a spring in their step are always discreetly helpful, and make the whole thing seem even more of a bargain.

Food serving times:
Monday-Saturday:
    12pm-2pm, 6pm-9.15pm
Sunday: 12pm-2pm
Closed 25-26 December and 1 January
(booking essential)
Prices:
Meals: a la carte 19.90/32.40

Typical Dishes

Smoked salmon, beetroot and cucumber salad

Red snapper, pink peppercorn and rosemary dressing

Lemon posset

5.5mi North of Darlington on A167. Parking

Hutton Magna

002 ## Oak Tree Inn

Hutton Magna DL11 7HH
Tel.: (01833) 627371

 VISA **MC**

Timothy Taylor Landlord, Black Sheep Best Bitter, Charles Wells Bombardier

Personally run by an amiable couple, this whitewashed part-18C inn fits in perfectly in this unpretentious little village on Hutton Beck. Its simple interior – beamed ceiling, leather-seated pews and food-themed pictures on the walls – gives it an intimate atmosphere, helped along by some keen and friendly service. The blackboard changes daily, with lunch a concise, 'best-of' version of the dinner menu, but there's a consistent theme to the robust cooking: cauliflower soup with Parma ham, garlic and thyme grilled chicken and strawberry and white chocolate trifle are among the British classics to be given an understated modern twist.

Food serving times:
Tuesday-Sunday:
7pm-9.30pm
Closed 25-26 December and 1 January
Dinner only except Sunday-booking essential
Wednesday-Saturday
Prices:
Meals: 22.00 (Sunday lunch) and a la carte 28.00

Typical Dishes
Salmon and smoked trout
Roast pigeon, boudin noir and foie gras
Chocolate fondant, pistachio ice cream

6.5mi Southeast of Barnard Castle by B6277 off A66. Parking

Romaldkirk

003 **Rose and Crown**

Romaldkirk DL12 9EB

Tel.: (01833) 650213 - Fax: (01833) 650828
e-mail: hotel@rose-and-crown.co.uk - Website: www.rose-and-crown.co.uk

    VISA **MC**

Theakson Best, Black Sheep

Our 2006 Pub of the Year was built in 1733 and bears its age with much dignity, and not a little ivy cladding. The inn's stone features sit in the centre of a pretty, unspoilt village, staring out over the green which still boasts original stocks and water pump. Everything revolves around the charming bar with its reassuring grandfather clock, Jacobean oak settle, ancient farm tools and log fire, which roars magnificently, even in May! This is a deliciously relaxing spot to eat, but you can also choose two other rooms to dine: the formal, oak-panelled, linen-clad restaurant, or red-walled, brasserie-styled Crown Room. Cuisine counts for much here: daily changing menus reflect the seasons, with local meat and game forming the core of English dishes cooked with culinary good sense. Relax afterwards in the snug, lounge, or slip upstairs to superior bedrooms that strike the right balance between chintzy allure and restful country style.

Food serving times:
Monday-Sunday:
  12pm-1.30pm, 7.30pm-9pm
Closed 24-26 December
Prices:
Meals: 26.00 and a la carte 14.00/22.00
12 rooms : 75.00/126.00

3.5mi Southeast of Middleton-in-Teesdale on B6277. On the village green, next to the church. Parking

Typical Dishes

Smoked mackeral mousse

Confit of lamb, mint pesto

Espresso panna cotta

Waldridge

004 Inn on the Green

Waldridge DH2 3RY
Tel.: 0191 3890439

  ♒ ♈ ✂ **VISA** **AE** **MC**

Weekly changing real ales

Just outside Chester-le-Street in the village of Waldridge stands this slightly forlorn looking establishment on the village green. But the deceptively ordinary façade hides a surprising gem of an interior. Smart and contemporary, it boasts an appearance straight from the early 21st Century style template: browns, chocolates and creams charm the eye from all angles, while the lounge invites you to nestle on squashy sofas. Church candles add an extra element of intrinsic calm. The rear split-level dining room continues the modish theme. Concise menus are from the modern British repertoire. Northumbrian ingredients are proudly in the mix: you could well find Durham Crown rump steak with forest mushroom duxelle, or Northumberland beef fillet on the main course menu. To nurture an appetite, pay a visit to the nearby Waldridge Fell Country Park beforehand.

Food serving times:
Tuesday-Saturday:
    12pm-2pm, 6.30pm-10pm
Prices:
Meals: a la carte 17.95/24.25

Typical Dishes

Tempura prawns, chilli jam

Fillet of beef, red wine glaze

White chocolate and raspberry crème brûlée

1.75mi West of Chester-le-Street on Waldridge rd. Parking ❯❯

Carterway Heads

005 Manor House Inn 🛏

Carterway Heads DH8 9LX

Tel.: (01207) 255268

🍷 ✂ *VISA* AE M©

Theakstons Best, Courage Directors, Charles Wells Bombardier and locally brewed guest ales

A personally owned and run pub with a growing reputation for good, honest homecooked food: a separate dining room overlooking the countryside allows you to forget the inn's on a busy road, but you'll find more of a local atmosphere in the trim little wood-fitted bar – good for a pint and a game of darts with the locals if you're feeling confident; a characterful lounge with comfy banquettes and views over the fields has the best of both worlds. Amiable staff serve an interesting, extensive menu: look out for medallions of pork with leek and Calvados and their nourishing ham broth, an ideal starter on a cold night. Pleasant, conveniently appointed bedrooms make a handy stopover if you're heading on north of the border, while a short drive west takes you to Derwent Reservoir, with lakeside walks through rolling moorland and pine forest.

Food serving times:
Monday-Sunday:
  12pm-2.30pm, 7pm-9.30pm
Closed dinner 25 December
Prices:
Meals: a la carte 18.00/27.00
🛏 **4 rooms :** 38.00/70.00

Typical Dishes

Chicken liver pâté

Scallops in smoked bacon, chilli jam

Sticky toffee pudding

3mi West of Consett at junction of B6278 and A68. Parking

Christon Bank

 Blink Bonny

Christon Bank NE66 3ES
Tel.: (01665) 576595

VISA MC

Hadrian Brewery and guest ales offered

Named after the famous 19C racehorse which won the Derby and the Oaks, this 200 year-old, stone-built inn sits at the T-junction of a rural Northumbrian village by the main East Coast railway line. A passionately run place, it places a real emphasis on local produce throughout a varied menu: the owner's brother-in-law has a fishing boat and the pub's medley of fish and shellfish, including langoustines, mussels and crab, depends in part on his daily catch. The dining room is bright, colourful and modern, but elsewhere there's a stronger traditional air and a curious quirk of history: the wooden bar is from the second-class lounge of one of the Titanic's sister ships. The large fire roars here in winter – perfect for a cosy after-dinner drink.

Food serving times:
Monday-Saturday:
6.30pm-9pm
Sunday: 12pm-3pm
Lunch served July-mid October
Prices:
Meals: a la carte 20.00/30.00

Typical Dishes

Crab, salmon and prawn tartlet

Hock with ginger glaze

Sticky toffee pudding

8mi North of Alnwick on B1340. Parking

Corbridge

007 **The Angel of Corbridge**

Main St, Corbridge NE45 5LA

Tel.: (01434) 632119 - Fax: (01434) 633496
e-mail: info@theangelofcorbridge.co.uk - Website: www.theangelofcorbridge.co.uk

VISA AE

Black Sheep, Mordue Workie Ticket, Radgie Gadgie

Personally owned and run for the first time in over 100 years, this renovated coaching inn now offers some of the best-value food for miles around, even if its friendly, unassuming bar isn't the first place you'd think of looking. Chalked up above the counter, the well-judged dishes are classically tasty: the tomato and pesto tart, double-baked cheese and spinach soufflé and bitter lemon tart combine lightness and delicacy with pronounced, balanced flavour, and for every more modern main – bream in saffron broth with fennel and pancetta – there's a traditional favourite like Corbridge sausage and mash. Quality food and good value, with polite and well-meaning service.

Food serving times:
Monday-Sunday:
12pm-2.30pm, 6pm-9.30pm
Closed 25-26 December
Prices:
Meals: a la carte 30.00/45.00
5 rooms : 55.00/79.00

Typical Dishes

Scallops
Confit of duck
Bread and butter pudding

In the town centre. Parking

Great Whittington

008 Queens Head Inn

Great Whittington NE19 2HP
Tel.: (01434) 672267

 🖛 🚫 *VISA* MC

Queens Head Bitter, Black Sheep

In the rolling wooded countryside near Hadrian's Wall lies this quiet village and its characterful pub, personally run for over 20 years. Exposed stone walls and old-English fixtures and fittings give the firelit bar a unpretentious, well-ordered atmosphere, and a neat dining room with a mix of banquettes, pews and old spokeback chairs has the same feeling of everything neatly in its place. Suitably traditional cooking has a real Northumbrian flavour to it – home-made pâtés, roast pork with caramelised apples, bread-and-butter pudding – and the service is as polite as you could wish.

Food serving times:
Tuesday-Saturday:
12pm-2.30pm, 7pm-9pm
Sunday: 12pm-2pm
Closed 1 week in Spring
Prices:
Meals: a la carte 19.00/30.00

Typical Dishes

King scallops, balsamic and herb dressing

Halibut, tomato and fennel fumé

Iced nougatine

6mi North of Corbridge by A68 off B6318. Parking

Newton on the Moor

009 Cook and Barker Inn ⊨

Newton on the Moor NE65 9JY
Tel.: (01665) 575234 - Fax: (01665) 575234
Website: www.cookandbarkerinn.co.uk

 🍴 ⚭ ⚭ **VISA** **AE** **MC**

 Timothy Taylor Landlord, Black Sheep, Fuller's London Pride, Theakston's XB, Cook and Barker branded ale

To recommend the Cook and Barker simply as a useful stop for motorists ploughing up and down the A1 doesn't do justice to this big, friendly pub, which has been run by the same team for over 15 years. Traditional country style extends through a series of split-level rooms, main bar and a spacious restaurant, and onto an extensive menu. There's nothing revolutionary here and while a blackboard of daily specials rings the changes, most people seem happy with something classic: deep-fried Brie with apple and raisin chutney, a mixed grill and a slice of cappucino cheesecake, served by a considerate and friendly local team who are clearly used to being kept busy. Bedrooms vary in size and style, but all are comfy and dependable.

Food serving times:
Monday-Sunday:
    12pm-2pm, 6pm-9pm
Closed dinner 25 December
Prices:
Meals: a la carte 25.00/35.00
⊨ **19 rooms :** 47.00/70.00

Typical Dishes

Guinea fowl terrine

Chicken with red pepper and spinach stuffing

Vanilla crème brûlee

5mi South of Alnwick by A1. Parking ▶

Stannersburn

010 Pheasant Inn 🛏

Falstone, Stannersburn NE48 1DD

Tel.: (01434) 240382 - Fax: (01434) 240382
e-mail: enquiries@thepheasantinn.com - Website: www.thepheasantinn.com

🍷 ✕ ✕ **VISA** **MC**

Timothy Taylor Landlord, Speckled Hen, Wylam Gold Tankard and Whistle Stop, Marstons Pedigree

This impressive, ivy-clad inn boasts 17C origins; its neighbour can claim even earlier roots, but then that neighbour is the Northumberland National Park. Tradition is a byword at the Pheasant Inn: the owners have been here for nearly 20 years, and run it as keenly now as the day they arrived. There's a two-roomed bar with low beamed ceiling, polished wood tables, cluttered knick-knacks reflecting local history, and the glint of lovingly cared-for brass. The pine furnished dining room is the place for good, old fashioned, tried-and-tested cooking, where you can expect grand portions of popular favourites such as fish from North Shields quay or home-made game and mushroom pie. An old barn conversion next door has been turned into simply furnished, comfy bedrooms.

Food serving times:
Monday-Sunday:
    12pm-2.30pm, 7pm-9pm
Closed 25-26 December,
Monday and Tuesday
November-March
Prices:
Meals: a la carte 14.45/21.20
🛏 **8 rooms :** 45.00/75.00

Typical Dishes

Pickled herring with salad
Fillet of trout, garlic prawns
Treacle sponge pudding

0.5mi Northeast crossing North Tyne river. Parking ⟫

D. Pazery / Michelin

a. *Muséum National d'Histoire Naturelle (Paris)*

b. *Natural History Museum (London)*

c. *Museum für Naturkunde (Berlin)*

*S*tretching from the Cheshire plains to the Solway Firth, this region defies all easy definitions. Roman Chester, the busy Pennine market towns and the peaceful and scenic West Cumbrian coast are North-West England at its most traditionally picturesque, though there's a very different history to be traced in the decline and renewal of Liverpool's Albert Dock and in the shimmering modern metal of Salford Quays. Lancashire's towns, built for industry and "King Cotton", are now at least as well-known for their cross-Pennine rivalries in football, rugby and the Roses Match as for Lowry's busy cityscapes. Most famous by far, though, is Cumbria's Lake District which, at its best and quietest, remains both a challenging wilderness and a picture of serenity. Bikes, boats, trains, bridle paths and hiking trails will all get you closer to the beauty of Derwentwater and Buttermere and the bleak grandeur of Striding Edge. Local specialities like hot pot, black pudding, Morecambe shrimps, Cumberland sausage, Cumberland sauce and air-dried ham, sticky toffee pudding and Cheshire cheese have all spread well beyond the bounds of the region, but taste as good as ever after all that fresh North Country air...

Alderley Edge

001 **The Wizard**

Macclesfield Rd, Alderley Edge SK10 4UB
Tel.: (01625) 584000 - Fax: (01625) 585105

No real ales offered

The National Trust has a good presence in these parts in the shape of Hare Hill and the local watermill. The Wizard – named after a children's book called "Wizard of Alderley Edge" – has proved an institution worth preserving in its own right. It's a 200 year-old pub which, these days, has restaurant sensibilities. Standing on the edge of a woodland park, it earns a tick in the box on most rustic counts: beamed, flagged and wood floors, with heavy wooden tables and chairs located everywhere. Very good value lunches and evening à la carte, the cooking's interesting and precise. Try grilled black pudding on mash with poached egg and mustard cream, cod with buttered spinach and salsa verde, or sea bass with red chard, avocado salad, lemongrass and coriander.

Food serving times:
Tuesday-Saturday:
    12pm-2pm, 7pm-9.30pm
Sunday: 12pm-2pm
Closed Christmas-New Year
Prices:
Meals: 22.95 (Sunday lunch)
and a la carte 20.00/45.00

1.25mi Southeast on B5087. Parking

Typical Dishes

Scallops, sweet chilli, citrus salad

Fish filo parcel, leek veloute

Iced Malteser parfait, chocolate sauce

Aldford

002 The Grosvenor Arms

Chester Rd, Aldford CH3 6HJ

Tel.: (01244) 620228 - Fax: (01224) 620247
e-mail: grosvenor.arms@brunningandprice.co.uk - Website: www.grosvenorarms-aldford.co.uk

 Flowers IPA, Weetwood, Deuchars IPA, Robinsons

Victorian visitors to the then recently built Grosvenor Arms would find it hard to relate their experience with a modern day excursion. They might recognise the lawned gardens of this spacious, red brick establishment, set in a rural village close to the River Dee, but the bustling, wood-furnished outside dining terrace and conservatory extension would be an eye-opener, to say nothing of the huge, modern interior and busy comings-and-goings of the ever-friendly staff. The Grosvenor owes much of its recent reputation to interesting menus, which combine contemporary and rustic cooking, as typified by butterbean, bacon and watercress soup, duck breast with herb potato cake and sweet and sour beetroot, or parsnip, red onion and goats' cheese tart. What would the Victorians have made of all that?

Food serving times:
Monday-Saturday:
12pm-10pm
Sunday: 12pm-9pm
Closed for dinner 25-26 December and 1 January
Prices:
Meals: a la carte 15.65/29.20

Typical Dishes

Corned beef hash cake

Steakburger with chips

Crème brûlée

3.5mi South of Chester by B5130. On the main village road. Parking

Bunbury

003 Dysart Arms

Bowes Gate Rd, Bunbury CW6 9PH

Tel.: (01829) 260183 - Fax: (01829) 261286

e-mail: dysart.arms@brunningandprice.co.uk - Website: www.dysartarms-bunbury.co.uk

Thwaites, Weetwood Eastgate, Phoenix Arizona, Roosters Yankee and regularly changing selection

Next to the impressive part-14C parish church, this trim, redbrick house, standing four-square by a little lane, is handsome enough in itself, particularly when floodlit at night. Away from the central bar, Victorian portraits, engravings and memorabilia line the white walls and polished wood, Persian rugs and floor-to-ceiling bookshelves give the place a spacious, country feel: broad French windows flood the back room with sunlight on bright days and lead out to benches and tables on the lawn. Fresh, tasty cooking ranges from pie and ploughmans to dishes with a more modern edge, including sweet potato and pepper tarte Tatin and seafood casserole. Though busy with eaters and drinkers in the early evening, it's usually a little quieter after 8.30.

Food serving times:
Monday-Sunday:
12pm-9.30pm
Closed 25 December
Prices:
Meals: a la carte 15.40/27.70

3.25mi South by A49 then take Bunbury Mill rd. Parking

Typical Dishes

Red pepper, feta, olives and tomatoes

Salmon, sweet fennel sauce

British cheeses

Burleydam

004 The Combermere Arms

Burleydam SY13 4AT

Tel.: 01948 871223 - Fax: : 01948 661371

e-mail: combermerearms@brunningandprice.co.uk - Website: www.brunningandprice.co.uk

Deuchars IPA, Hydes Mild, Woodlands Oak Beauty, Phoenix Black Bee, Flowers Original

A clever merging of styles allows the old and the new to link stylistic arms here. There are old beams on view as you step inside, but beyond them the adjoining rooms have been opened up around the central bar, and skylights added, so that everything's open and airy, although you can still find a snug spot if that's what you're after. Walls are covered in pictures of every style and hue. There's an informal menu, and you can eat anywhere you like: lots of choice right across the board means a good selection from sandwiches to more substantial dishes; the wine list is worthy of note, too. This is the ideal dining spot for bigger parties, as some truly cavernous tables are up for grabs. Service is efficient from staff who are used to being busy.

Food serving times:
Monday-Sunday:
12pm-9.30pm

Prices:
Meals: a la carte 16.50/26.40

Typical Dishes

Pear and walnut dolcelatte salad

Grilled dover sole

Home-made apple pie, vanilla ice cream

4.25mi East of Whitchurch on A525. Parking

Chester

005 **Old Harkers Arms**

1 Russell St, Chester CH3 5AL

Tel.: (01244) 344525 - Fax: (01244) 344812

e-mail: harkers.arms@brunningandprice.co.uk - Website: www.harkersarms-chester.co.uk

London Pride, Wapping Bitter and Weetwood ale and up to 7 guest ales

Especially on busy Saturday nights, it's hard to believe that this big, friendly canalside bar was half-derelict not so many years ago. Steel beams, brick pillars and tall sash windows hint at its past as a Victorian warehouse and the heavy restoration, from the ground up, kept the long, open-plan interior, adding hundreds upon hundreds of old framed cuttings, period prints, cover pages and photographs. It's got the right atmosphere for just meeting up for drinks, though a large blackboard menu covers lunchtime sandwiches, snacks and tasty, modern gastropub standards including chicken stuffed with spinach and ricotta and seared salmon on chive and yoghurt mash.

Food serving times:
Monday-Saturday:
12pm-9.30pm
Sunday: 12pm-8pm
25-26 December
Prices:
Meals: a la carte 14.00/25.00

Typical Dishes

Twice-baked goat's cheese soufflé

Pork and herb sausage

Coffee and walnut cheesecake

Between A51 and the canal. Limited parking on City Rd

Cotebrook

006 **Fox and Barrel**

Fox Bank, Cotebrook CW6 9DZ
Tel.: (01829) 760529 - Fax: (01829) 760529

       VISA **AE**

John Smiths Cask, Marstons Pedigree, Bass

It may look pretty ordinary on the outside, but step into the neat front bar and you'll recognise the atmosphere of a personally run pub with a friendly husband and wife team keeping things ticking over, pulling pints and pointing out any daily specials to the diners. They certainly know what their regulars like: as well as light meals and sandwiches, there's a traditional menu built around sound, substantial English dishes, and while this still offers decent variety, you can't go far wrong with braised beef on horseradish mash, followed by a trifle. The panelled, open-plan dining room can feel a bit less intimate than the lounge, but there's plenty of likeable neighbourhood spirit here too, especially when the local jazz quintet play New Orleans classics on Monday nights.

Food serving times:
Monday-Sunday:
  12pm-3pm, 6.30pm-9.30pm
Closed 25 December
Prices:
Meals: a la carte 15.00/30.00

Typical Dishes

Avocado and prawn salad

Rump of lamb, champ

Black cherry mille-feuille

1.5mi Northeast of Tarporley by A49.
Parking

Frodsham

007 **Netherton Hall**

Chester Road, Frodsham WA6 6UL
Tel.: 01928 732342 - Fax: : 01928 739140
Website: www.nethertonhall.com

 ⊱rest ✗ *VISA* **AE** **MC**

🍺 *Timothy Taylors Landlord*

Hiding under its all-enveloping greenery, Netherton Hall is a large Georgian farmhouse, its interior now converted into three relaxing and pleasantly busy dining areas. Books and knick-knacks line the walls throughout and a collection of mix and match wooden tables seem to add a homely atmosphere. It's also worth knowing that there's also plenty of room to eat in the spacious garden. Food is definitely the focus here, with an unusually large choice written up on the blackboards: it's all freshly prepared, and the list can change twice a day. A freely ranging mix of traditional and European ideas guarantees plenty of good, sustaining cooking. The steady, well-run atmosphere of the place is most noticeable in the service, which is invariably alert and smooth.

Food serving times:
Monday-Friday:
    12pm-2.30pm, 6pm-9pm
Friday-Saturday:
    12pm-2.30pm, 6pm-9.30pm
Sunday: 12pm-7.30pm
Closed 25-26 December
Prices:
Meals: a la carte 25.00/35.00

Typical Dishes

Monkfish tail in Parma ham, salsa verde

Rump of venison, juniper and port

Baked raspberry and vanilla

0.75 miles Southwest on A56. Parking

Higher Burwardsley

008 ## The Pheasant

Higher Burwardsley CH3 9PF

Tel.: (01829) 770434 - Fax: (01829) 771097

e-mail: info@thepheasaninn.co.uk - Website: www.thepheasantinn.co.uk

     VISA AE

Weetwood ales

There's been an inn on this elevated site since the 17C; certainly, few pubs can enjoy such enviable views as those afforded from The Pheasant. Its appealing sandstone and timber frame sits atop the Peckforton Hills, giving it astonishing vistas over the Cheshire Plain to Liverpool and the Welsh Hills. Whilst beamed and open-fired, it also boasts a smart, modern feel after refurbishment a few years ago; everyone's made to feel welcome, particularly the many walkers who pass this way. Food is hearty and nourishing, ideal if you've been working up a hiker's hunger. Sandwiches get a modern twist; more accomplished dishes boast interesting and original combinations. An adjacent sandstone barn now houses attractively furnished bedrooms, and, yes, they all have the excellent view.

Food serving times:
Monday-Sunday:
12pm-10pm

Prices:
Meals: a la carte 20.00/28.00
10 rooms : 65.00/80.00

Typical Dishes

Monkfish and tiger prawns in sweet chilli jam

Pork loin, leek mash and redcurrant sauce

Warm waffle, honey-comb

2.5mi Southeast of Tattenhall. Parking

Little Barrow

009 The Foxcote

Station Lane, Little Barrow CH3 7JN
Tel.: (01244) 301343 - Fax: (01244) 303287

No real ales offered

From the outside, this traditional looking inn certainly gives the impression of being somewhere to sink a pint. Wrong! This is now a dining pub, pure and simple, though the courteous, friendly staff and relaxed atmosphere certainly create a very gentle, local feel. The Foxcote is in a tiny Cheshire village off the beaten track, its interior given over to dining tables with gingham cloths; seafood and country prints line the walls. A vast number of blackboards greet you upon arrival: they mostly list seafood dishes featuring a broad variety of ingredients prepared in an accomplished, modern manner. Vegetarians and meat eaters are not forgotten, though, and are well catered for on the blackboards.

Food serving times:
Monday-Saturday:
　　12pm-2pm, 6pm-9.30pm
Sunday:　　　　12pm-2pm
- Seafood -
Prices:
Meals: 9.95 (fixed price lunch) and a la carte 17.00/26.00

Typical Dishes

Tower of avocado crab and brawn shrimp

Baked cod, king prawn tempurar

Sticky toffee pudding

6.5mi Northeast of Chester by A56 on B5132. Parking

Lower Whitley

010 Chetwode Arms

Street Lane, Lower Whitley WA4 4EN
Tel.: (01925) 730203

 Jennings Cumberland, Charles Wells Bombardier, Marstons Pedigree, Cains Bitter

Popularity is clearly nothing new to this neighbourhood favourite, where a brisk, personally led team are well used to a full house of contented diners. The brick-built former coaching inn still welcomes its regulars for a pint, and there are few better places for it than the inviting front bar: old framed prints, real fires, even the Victorian style tiled floor all add a bit of unassuming charm. Find a simply set table in one of the three former bar-parlours and choose from a blackboard menu that might list Bury black pudding with mustard mash or liver and onions: honest, unfussy and full of appetising Northern flavour, if ever there was cooking tailor-made for a decent local ale, this is it.

Food serving times:
Monday-Sunday:
12pm-3pm, 6pm-9pm
Closed 25 December and 1 January
Prices:
Meals: a la carte 20.00/35.00

6.5mi Northwest of Northwich by A533 off A49. Parking

Typical Dishes

Grilled goat's cheese and honey salad

Fillet of beef Stroganoff

Sticky toffee pudding

Ambleside

011 **Drunken Duck Inn** 🛏 *We most liked* 😊

Barngates, Ambleside LA22 0NG

Tel.: (01539) 436347 - Fax: (01539) 436781
e-mail: info@drunkenduckinn.co.uk - Website: www.drunkenduckinn.co.uk

🍷 ✕rest 🚭 **VISA** **AE** **MC**

Barngates Catnap, Cracker, Tag Lag, Chesters Strong and Ugly, Pride of Westmorland

A handsome inn that takes its name from a story involving a 19C landlady, a leaky barrel and a gaggle of unsteady ducks: true local history or an old taproom canard? Either way, this trusty Lakeland landmark still marks the old crossroads, in the midst of stunning fell and high peak scenery. Its lovely rustic bar with open fire is a haven for walkers, particularly those who like real ale, as The Duck has an on-site micro-brewery producing four beers on handpump, and local waterfowl are kept well away these days. The beers can be enjoyed in one of the cosy, beamed rooms which radiate from the bar, while meals are served in two pleasant dining rooms with polished wooden tables: a modern style menu has a seasonal base and an elaborate, eclectic range. Bedrooms are snug and of fine quality.

Food serving times:
Monday-Sunday:
    12pm-2.30pm, 6pm-9pm
Closed 25 December
Prices:
Meals: a la carte 25.95/39.95
🛏 **16 rooms :** 71.25/210.00

Typical Dishes
Potted Flookburgh shrimps
Noisettes of Herdwick lamb, redcurrant glaze
Warm waffles, 'Tag Lag' ice cream

3mi Southwest of Ambleside by A593 and B5286 on Tarn Hows road. By the crossroads at the top of Duck Hill. ➤➤

Beetham

012 Wheatsheaf Inn

Beetham LA7 7AL

Tel: (015395) 62123 - Fax: (015395) 64840

e-mail: wheat,beeth@aol.com - Website: www.wheatsheafbeetham.com

   VISA

Jennings Cumberland, Tirrel Bragham, Cragrat

Stained glass windows, old prints of country life and prize sportfish from the Cumbrian rivers and lakes, mounted in glass cases, all add to the genuine charm of this part-16C inn, its beamed bar set with polished tables and spokeback chairs and filled with a warm and bustling atmosphere. An extensive menu – served downstairs and in the quieter first floor dining room – begins with reliable pub standards and interesting sandwiches, but also finds room for a few more dishes with a modern edge. Pastel-toned bedrooms with neat fittings and tapestry-style fabrics are all named after nearby areas: you should find them homely and practical, even if local geography isn't your strong point.

Food serving times:

Monday-Saturday:
12pm-2pm, 6pm-9pm

Sunday:
12pm-3pm, 6.30pm-8.30pm

Closed 25 December and Sunday dinner January-April (fixed price meal 6pm-7pm)

Prices:

Meals: 12.95 ((Sunday lunch) and a la carte 16.90/28.00

6 rooms : 55.00/69.50

Typical Dishes

Potted Wheatsheaf shrimps

Pork fillet, chestnuts and cider

Sticky toffee pudding

Off the A6, 1mi south of Milnthorpe. Parking

Cartmel Fell

013 ## Masons Arms

Strawberry Bank, Cartmel Fell LA11 6NW

Tel.: (015395) 68486 - Fax: (015395) 68780
e-mail: info@masonsarms.com - Website: www.strawberrybank.com

 Hawkshead bitter and Gold, Black Sheep, Timothy Taylor Landlord

The characterful downstairs bar and its layout of little snugs, parlours and open fires in the old ranges are all clues to the history of the Masons Arms, originally built as a cottage and converted in the 1800s. This smaller, family scale can make it feel a little crowded at the busiest times, so head upstairs to the restaurant if you want a touch more comfort and formality, or take a seat outside. From the heights of Strawberry Hill there are charming views to be had from the rear garden or the front terrace, handsomely equipped with broad canopy parasols, lights and heaters to bring a hint of café culture to the Lakes. A popular menu – the same at lunch and dinner – combines British standards like Stilton mousse and chutney or chicken, leek and ham pie with international favourites like Caesar salad, lasagne and barbecue ribs.

Food serving times:
Monday-Sunday:
12pm-2pm, 6pm-9pm
Prices:
Meals: a la carte 18.00/28.00

3.75mi North East of Newby Bridge by A590 off A592. Parking

Typical Dishes

Black pudding, egg, bacon and mustard sauce

Salmon and scallops, garlic butter

Warm lemon cream

Casterton

014 **Pheasant Inn**

Casterton LA6 2RX

Tel.: (015242) 71230 - Fax: : (015242) 74267
e-mail: pheasantinn@fsbdial.co.uk - Website: www.pheasantinn.co.uk

  VISA ⓂⒸ

Theakston Best Bitter, Black Sheep, Dent Aviator

Halfway between the Lake District and the Dales lies the agreeable little village of Casterton and, at its centre, this traditional 18C inn at the foot of the fell. With its easy pace and a very open and natural warm welcome, it seems to draw on the best of the village's character, and its collection of local artefacts and farming prints are reminders that this part of Cumbria still earns part of its living from the land. There's a room set aside for dining, but you can also choose from a full menu - with surprisingly varied daily specials – in the three traditionally appointed bars and lounges: very comfortable, especially when they stoke up the fires. Tasty, homely dishes, from sandwiches, grills and filling stews to baked crab and honey-roast ham, seem entirely in keeping here. Inviting, good-sized bedrooms.

Food serving times:
Monday-Sunday:
      12pm-2pm, 6pm-9pm
Closed dinner 25 December
Prices:
Meals: a la carte 14.00/26.00
10 rooms : 38.00/90.00

Typical Dishes

Egg mayonnaise, fresh asparagus

Crispy ducking, sage and onion stuffing

Chocolate and Grand

In the centre of the village. Parking ➤➤

Castle Carrock

015 **The Weary**

Castle Carrock CA8 9LU

Tel.: (01228) 670230 - Fax: (01228) 670089
e-mail: relax@theweary.com - Website: www.theweary.com

 VISA AE M3

Occasionally one local guest ale

Two minutes' drive from the beauty spot of Talkin Tarn, this white-painted pub looks the picture of pretty Lake District gentility – until you open the front door. Striking modern lighting, chic wood and slate and dashes of zingy modern colour make the restyled front bar look anything but weary: you can take a seat on the sofa and dine here, or head through to the conservatory and a smart walled terrace. With a nod to local tradition, a sizeable modern menu finds room for toffee pudding or a starter of black pudding and apple mash with whisky sauce, but also takes in vegetable tempura, chilli and garlic sea bass and a Pernod parfait with cassis pear. Fine bedrooms certainly don't let the side down, with more bold colourways plus stylish bathrooms and flat-screen televisions.

Food serving times:
Tuesday-Sunday:
       12pm-2pm, 6pm-9pm
Closed 25-26 December and 1 January
Monday residents only
Prices:
Meals: a la carte 22.75/35.00
5 rooms : 55.00/85.00

Typical Dishes

Chorizo tapas

Tuna steak, red onion marmalade

Raspberry souffle

4mi south of Brampton on B6413. Parking

Coniston

016 **The Black Bull Inn**

1 Yewdale Rd, Coniston LA21 8DU

Tel.: (015394) 41335 - Fax: (015394) 41168

 VISA

Coniston Bluebird and XB, Old Man Ale, Blacksmiths Ale from own microbrewery

There's no mistaking this sizeable 16C coaching inn at the foot of the Old Man, not with the sign of a hefty-looking bull hanging below the eaves. From blackened timbers to stone floor, it's a decent, personally run inn of the old school, though with far more depth of character than most. The pleasant dining room is neatly kept, but the bar itself just edges it for warmth and personality, and beer experts will waste no time in pulling up a stool and ordering its great speciality. Of the pints produced on-site, none is more renowned than Bluebird: it shares its name with Donald Campbell's record breaking hydroplane and a memento recalls the triumph and loss of the speed-king on nearby Coniston Water. With its true local flavours, honest and homely Lakeland cooking makes a fine accompaniment to an ale; try local beef followed by apple pie.

Food serving times:
Monday-Sunday:
12pm-9pm
Closed 25 December
Prices:
Meals: a la carte 15.25/22.50
15 rooms : 45.00/90.00

Typical Dishes

Goat's cheese and tomato stack

Roast duckling

Sticky toffee pudding

On A593. Parking

Great Salkeld

017 **Highland Drove Inn**

Great Salkeld CA11 9NA

Tel.: (01768) 898349 - Fax: (01768) 898708
e-mail: highlanddrove@btinternet.com - Website: www.highland-drove.co.uk

   VISA M©

Theakstons Black Bull, John Smiths Cask and various guest ales

Approaching the Lake District from the north, this is an ideal stop-off point before the inevitable encounter with the tourist masses. It's a pleasant whitewashed pub in a tiny village in the heart of the Eden valley, and dates back hundreds of years. There are beams and a good selection of cask ales, but what really catches the eye is the content of the menus. Dishes are changed on a daily basis and revolve around local meat, game and fish. Sea bass, salmon fillet and brill regularly share the honours with mallard duck, rack of lamb and spiced Elizabethan pork; look out too for the steaks from herds reared in Cumbria. Suitably replenished, you'll need no reminding that you're in first-class walking country. Comfy bedrooms await those staying on.

Food serving times:
Tuesday-Sunday:
12pm-2pm,
Monday-Sunday:
6.30pm-9pm
Closed 25 December
Prices:
Meals: 15.95 (lunch) and a la carte 16.95/27.50
5 rooms : 32.50/65.00

Typical Dishes

Seafood plate

Honey glazed duck, blackcurrant sauce

Sticky toffee pudding

6.75mi North of Penrith by A686. Parking

Loweswater

018 **Kirkstile Inn**

Loweswater CA13 0RU

Tel.: (01900) 85219 - Fax: (01900) 85239
e-mail: info@kirkstile.com - Website: www.kirkstile.com

Coniston Bluebird, Yates and Melbreak and Grasmoor brewed on site

A part-16C inn in a picture-perfect setting: an isolated and beautiful valley between Loweswater and Crummock Water. If you can tear yourself away from the view, head inside to the welcoming beamed bar or a more formal dining room and choose a lighter lunch – from sandwiches upwards – or more substantial cooking at dinner. Fresh Cumbrian produce, organic where possible, is the cornerstone of their traditional cooking: decent, substantial dishes like Lakeland rump steak or beef and ale pie – plus a couple of specials – find favour with locals and visitors and certainly suit the home-brewed beers. Simple tidy accommodation with lovely hill views; two rooms suitable for families. Needless to say, there's good climbing and walking nearby.

Food serving times:
Monday-Sunday:
          12pm-2pm, 6pm-9pm
Closed 25 December
Prices:
Meals: a la carte 13.00/18.00
11 rooms : 45.00/86.00

Typical Dishes

Goat's cheese in filo pastry

Steak and Kidney pudding

Cumberland rum Nicky

Located between Loweswater and Crummock Water. Parking

Portinscale

019 The Farmers

Portinscale CA12 5RN
Tel.: (017687) 73442

  VISA MC

 Jennings Bitter, Cumberland Ale, Sneck Lifter, Crag Rat, Red Breast

On the face of it, this slate-built village pub looks much the same as it ever was: a few tables out front, a tiny beer garden behind and a neat, stone-flagged bar with stools and tables occupied by the regulars, who make up the backbone of the pub's darts and quiz teams and sup their pints to the quiet click of dominoes. But the remainder of the pub, decorated in bright Mediterranean tones, is given over to dining; besides the lunchtime ciabattas, galettes, ploughmans and homemade breads, a more adventurous main menu offers pancetta wrapped salmon on olive ratatouille, and rhubarb and white chocolate fool. Very helpful service binds together this deserving combination of the modern and the traditional.

Food serving times:
Monday-Sunday:
12pm-2pm, 6pm-9pm
Prices:
Meals: a la carte 17.50/23.50

Typical Dishes

'Tattie' scones, haggis and garlic butter

Fillet steak, horseradish mash

Parkin, caramel sauce and ice cream

1.5 miles West of Keswick by A66. Limited parking in the village

Tirril

020 ## Queens Head Inn

Tirril CA10 2JF

Tel.: (01768) 863219

e-mail: tirrelpub@yahoo.co.uk - Website: www.queensheadinn.co.uk

✂ **VISA** **M**

Up to 4 ales from Tirril brewery, plus 1 guest ale

When not wandering lonely as a cloud, the great William Wordsworth also dabbled in the more profitable world of property management. God's gift to the Lakes Tourist Board signed away the family's stake in this charming 18C inn in 1836 and the contract still hangs in the atmospheric bar, along with such un-Wordsworthian curios as a hunting horn, a First World War shell and a diving helmet. Ullswater trout and local lamb feature on a hearty but carefully prepared menu which works much better on the plate than on the page: lamb and rosemary pie and steak and ale pudding show the same full-flavoured style. The pub also hosts a Cumbrian Beer and Sausage weekend every August. Four rooms for dining include a pleasant conservatory, ideal in summer.

Food serving times:
Monday-Sunday:
 12pm-2pm, 6pm-9.30pm
Closed dinner 25-26 December
Prices:
Meals: a la carte 17.50/25.00
🛏 **7 rooms :** 40.00/70.00

Typical Dishes

Brie tartlet

Salmon and prawns, tarragon sauce

Apricot and passion fruit parfait

3mi South West of Penrith by A6 on B5320. Parking

Troutbeck

021 ## Queens Head

Troutbeck LA23 1PW

Tel.: (015394) 32174 - Fax: (015394) 31938
e-mail: enquiries@queensheadhotel.com - Website: www.queensheadhotel.com

🍷 ✗=room **VISA** **M©**

🍺 *Coniston Bluebird, Hawkshead Best, Barngates Cracker, Tirrel Academy*

Not many pub bars are built around superbly carved Elizabethan four-poster beds. In fact, this 400 year old posting inn boasts probably the only one in the country. The place has charm and character to spare. You might get lost in the warren of beamed and panelled rooms, in which cobwebbed musical instruments hang, and beribboned stuffed beasts gaze. You'll come across old cushioned settles, stone walls and a roaring open fireplace. The upstairs dining room has capacious windows for even bigger views over valley and moor. Settle down at scrubbed oak tables and extinguish countryside appetites with imaginative, well-cooked, tasty Northern food with traditional and modern options, served by staff eager to please. You might want to stay the night: bedrooms boast antique furnishings and terrific views.

Food serving times:
Monday-Sunday :
   12pm-2pm, 6.30pm-9pm
Closed 25 December
Prices:
Meals: 15.50 (fixed price) and a la carte 15.50/28.95
🛏 **14 rooms :** 120.00

Typical Dishes

Beetroot cured salmon, blinis

Lamb shank, wine jus

Ginger pudding, marmalade ice cream

4mi North of Ambleside by A592. Parking

Ulverston

022 **Bay Horse** 🛏

Canal Foot, Ulverston LA12 9EL

Tel.: (01229) 583972 - Fax: (01229) 580502
e-mail: reservations@thebayhorsehotel.co.uk - Website: www.furness.co.uk/bayhorse

✗=rest **VISA** **AE** **M◯**

Pride of Pendle, Jennings bitter, Moorhouses Premiere, Cumberland

Commanding views of the Lancashire and Cumbria Fells are just one reason to recommend this well-established little inn by Ulverston Sands. The bar area, well known for its capacious horse's head of stone, has a smart ambience, afforded by plush built-in wall banquettes, stylish wooden armchairs, beams and open fire. An adjacent conservatory houses a more formal linen-clad restaurant, which boasts fine views over Morecambe Bay. Tasty, effectively prepared cooking finds favour with appreciative diners, who have long admired the flavourful, seasonal menus, typified by roast fillet of halibut, or Cumberland sausage with date chutney, cranberry and apple sauce. Bedrooms - snug and with a host of extras - have the enviable coastal view.

Food serving times:
Tuesday-Sunday:
12pm-2pm
Monday -Sunday: 7.30pm
One sitting for dinner
7.30pm for 8pm
Prices:
Meals: 29.50 and a la carte 20.00/40.00
🛏 **9 rooms :** 80.00/115.00

Typical Dishes

Smoked duck and mango salad, Cumberland sauce

Fillet steak strips, ginger and soy sauce

Cape brandy pudding

2.25mi East of Ulverston by A5087, turning left at Morecambe Tavern B&B and beyond industrial area, on the coast. Parking

Watermillock

023 Brackenrigg Inn

Watermillock CA11 0LP

Tel.: (017684) 86206 - Fax: (017684) 86945
e-mail: enquiries@brackenrigginn.co.uk - Website: www.brackenrigginn.co.uk

 ✗rest **VISA**

 Coniston Bluebird, Jennings Cumberland Ale, Theakstons, Black Sheep, Tirril Old Faithful

Commanding fine views of the lakes and mountains, the Brackenrigg Inn is sure to appeal to Lakeland pub lovers, for many reasons. Its open main bar has changed a little since it welcomed the post coach in the 18C, but its comfy seats, dartboard and promising line of bar taps still sends the right message to the tired traveller. Meals are also served in two more formal adjoining rooms and the appealing, full-flavoured cooking casts its net surprisingly wide. They aim to offer something for everyone, serving potato, chorizo and trout salad or salmon with basil and asparagus alongside well-known favourites, snacks and daily specials. Well marshalled service directed by the experienced patrons – still as keen and amiable as ever – binds the whole place together.

Food serving times:
Monday-Sunday:
12pm-2.30pm, 6.30pm-9pm
Prices:
Meals: a la carte 16.85/24.95
17 rooms : 33.00/98.00

Typical Dishes

Spring rolls

Chump of lamb, goats cheese mash

Sticky toffee pudding

On A592 besides Ullswater. Parking

Yanwath

024 The Gate Inn

Yanwath CA10 2LF
Tel.: 01768 862386 · Fax: 01768 899892
e-mail: enquiries@yanwathgate.com · Website: www.yanwathgate.com

 rest *VISA* AE

> Jennings Cumberland Ale, Tirril Bewshers

This charming drovers' inn, built back in 1683, takes its name from the tollgate which once stood outside. If you're unfortunate enough to be caught by a Lakeland downpour, or find yourself cold and lunchless on the hills, this is the kind of place you dream of finding. The old taproom, in the light of candles and an open fire, looks wonderfully inviting, with scrubbed wooden tables and thoughtful, welcoming service from behind the bar, but the panelled dining room beyond is no less pleasant – the friendly owner willingly takes a hand in both to keep things going according to plan. Seasonal cooking is never less than generous, concentrating on nourishing, substantial recipes and organic or free-range ingredients. Good value pub food with a sound slice of local character.

Food serving times:
Monday-Sunday:
 12pm-2.30pm, 6pm-9.30pm
Prices:
Meals: a la carte 21.00/32.00

Typical Dishes

Black pudding and haggis, grain mustard sauce

Fillet of beef fricasse of wild mushrooms

Marbled chocolate cheesecake

2,5mi Southwest from Penrith by A6 and B5320. Parking

Manchester

025 ## The Ox

71 Liverpool Rd, Castlefield, Manchester M3 4NQ

Tel.: 0161 839 7740

e-mail: gmtheox@barbar.co.uk - Website: www.theox.co.uk

  VISA AE MC

 Tim Taylors Landlord, Deuchars IPA, Boddingtons, Pheonix, Joseph Holts

Food serving times:

Monday-Saturday:
    12pm-3pm, 6pm-9.30pm

Sunday: 12pm-6.30pm

Prices:

Meals: 13.95 (Sunday lunch) and a la carte 21.85/26.00

Manchester's museums and the local Granada studios provide a steady flow of drinkers and diners to The Ox, as well as incognito appearances by a few television celebrities. Apart from the massive, block-bold "OX" monogram, stamped like a cattle-brand between the eaves and glowering in at the windows, it's an understated corner pub, more pleasant and homely than the logo suggests. An open though still intimate-feeling bar room leads on to a traditionally styled dining area, and this is where The Ox sets itself apart from its neighbours: the menu has an unmistakeably eclectic touch, with a number of lightly fusion-influenced dishes in among the more familiar gastropub favourites. Fresh and popular food served unpretentiously.

Typical Dishes

Rabbit and pheasant terrine

Grilled poussin, honey and mustard glaze

Blueberry souffle, shortbread

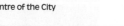

Centre of the City

Oldham

026 The White Hart Inn(Brasserie)

51 Stockport Rd., Lydgate, Oldham OL4 4JJ

Tel.: (01457) 872566 - Fax: (01457) 875190
e-mail: bookings@thewhitehart.co.uk - Website: www.whitehart.co.uk

 VISA AE MC

Timothy Taylor Landlord, JW Lees, Tetleys, Copper Dragon, IPA

Between the town centre and Saddleworth Moor, this great local favourite - built in 1788 to provide hospitality for cross-Pennine travellers - remains ever-popular; in part a tribute to the attentive staff who provide a pleasant but quite formal style of service. Two rooms off the main bar – one larger and slightly more comfortable – are set aside for lunch and dinner, but share the same likeably no-frills décor of bricks, beams and open fires. New to the White Hart in 2005 is the lavish Oak Room, proof positive of the inn's burgeoning appeal. Overall there's a friendly mix of drinkers and diners, although the focus is very definitely on the owner's locally renowned cooking. On an expanding menu you'll find full-flavoured cooking in the Modern British vein. It's good value, and they occasionally offer a special set-price lunch and early evening menu.

Food serving times:
Monday-Saturday:
  12pm-2.30pm, 6pm-9.30pm
(booking essential)
Prices:
Meals: 14.50 (before 7pm) and a la carte 24.00/31.00
12 rooms : 95.00/120.00

Typical Dishes

Crispy prawns and smoked salmon

Fillet of beef, wild mushrooms

Baked chocolate mousse

3mi East of Oldham by A669 on A6050.
Parking

Wrightington Bar

027 ## The Mulberry Tree

Wrightington Bar WN6 9SE
Tel.: (01257) 451400 - Fax: (01257) 451400

VISA MC

No real ales offered

Not a pub for the traditionally-minded lover of beams and foaming ale. Nevertheless, what it lacks in traditional character, it makes up for in ample size and ultimately in the quality of the food. The rather cavernous open plan interior has a spacious bar with simple tables and chairs occupying one end, and a large, more formal linen-clad restaurant at the other. Both share a warm, buzzy atmosphere as well as the same range of specials, and this is where the pub comes into its own: the satisfying modern cooking demonstrates sound experience and culinary know-how and portions are, by any standards, generous. Local, seasonal ingredients are to the fore in the quality cuisine which pays due homage to global influences. Keenly-priced menu.

Food serving times:
Monday-Sunday:
12pm-2pm, 6pm-9pm
Closed 26 December
Prices:
Meals: a la carte 25.00/28.00

Typical Dishes

Black pudding on an English muffin

Roast belly pork, apple and cider jus

Strawberry shortbread

3.5mi Northwest of Standish by A5209 on B5250. Parking

Fence

028 The Forest Inn

Cuckstool Lane, Fence BB12 9PA

Tel.: (01282) 613641 - Fax: (01282) 698140
Website: www.forestinn.co.uk

VISA MC

Black Sheep, Thwaites, Moorhouses IPA

Fresh-tasting and seasonal in character, the food at the Forest Inn has plenty of generous country flavour to it. Lighter, simpler lunches and more substantial dinners, most with a hearty, traditional base, are prepared with equal care, and it's no surprise that word has reached well beyond the little Lancashire village. If the setting of fields and trees comes as a relief after the madness of the M86, the plain-fronted inn looks respectable but nondescript. A contemporary interior, however, complete with comfortable leather chairs, blond wood dining tables, modern art and hushed, neutral colours feels much less stark than it sounds and the service lends real warmth to the place: a dedicated local team is never short on friendliness or effort when helping out the family owners.

Food serving times:
Tuesday-Saturday:
                12pm-2.30pm
Sunday: 12pm-8pm
Closed Monday
Prices:
Meals: a la carte 28.00

Typical Dishes

Thai fishcake, sweet chilli dip

Goosnargh duck breast, blackcurrant sauce

Fruit pavlova

3 miles Northeast of Padiham by A6068, then 0.5miles Southwest by A6248. Parking

Forton

029 Bay Horse Inn

Forton LA2 0HR
Tel.: (01524) 791204
e-mail: wilkicraig@aol.com - Website: www.bayhorseinn.com

Pendle Witches Brew, Lancaster Bomber, Black Sheep

With service from a cheery local team, enthusiastic, all-action management from the chef, well-chosen regional produce and big helpings of homemade everything, this hidden 18C inn has personality in abundance. A lovely rustic bar, filled with framed menus and sporting memorabilia and warmed by an open fire, leads into a smart, airy dining room. Pick whichever suits you best and choose from a quarterly menu, a list of chalkboard specials or the daily-changing sandwich board: Lancashire hotpot terrine, Morecambe Bay shrimps and Cumbrian roast beef sum up an appealing modern-rustic range with a forthright Lancastrian flavour.

Food serving times:
Tuesday-Saturday:
12pm-2pm, 7pm-9.30pm
Sunday: 12pm-2pm
Closed 25 December, 1 January
Prices:
Meals: 17.50 ((fixed price lunch)) and a la carte 20.00/ 35.00

Typical Dishes

Morecambe bay shrimps
Lancashire hot pot
Bread and butter pudding

1.25mi North by A6 on Quernmore Rd. Parking

Mitton

030 The Three Fishes

Mitton BB7 9PQ

Tel.: 01254 826888 - Fax: 01254 826026
Website: www.thethreefishes.com

 VISA AE MC

Thwaites Original, Thwaites Bomber, Bowland Brewery Sawley Tempted, Moorhouses Black Cat

Pies and hotpots, platters of tongue and brisket, black pudding and potted Morecambe shrimps – a look at the Three Fishes menu is the stuff of northern dreams. It's rare to find cuisine so thoroughly rooted in a region, but the richly savoury and heartening Lancastrian recipes are given pride of place here, prepared in a kitchen which is stocked by a host of hand-picked local suppliers, and served in a very spacious, modern and totally non-smoking pub. Find a table then order at the bar – this is such beer-friendly food that it's worth trying a north-western cask ale to go with it. This updated pub has come a long way since it served passengers from the river Ribble ferry, but its change of tack has been a definite success, so be warned: it gets very busy.

Food serving times:
Monday-Thursday:
    12pm-2pm, 6pm-9pm
Friday-Saturday:
    12pm-2pm, 6pm-9.30
Sunday: 12pm-8.30pm
Closed 25 December
Prices:
Meals: a la carte 15.00/19.50

Typical Dishes

Crumpet, Lancashire curd, beetroot salad

Hot pot, pickled cabbage

Manchester custard, raspberry jelly, bananas

Parking; northwest: 2.5mi on B6246

Tunstall

031 Lunesdale Arms

Tunstall LA6 2QN
Tel.: (015242) 74203 - Fax: (015242) 74229

Black Sheep, Hartleys Cumbria Way

This rural dining pub with Cumbria to the north and Yorkshire to the west is making friends across the board, and across the borders. What was probably once a licensed room of the old village hall now feels pleasantly, deliberately modern; uncluttered and bright with chunky tables and chairs dotted around, squashy sofas facing a vast fireplace and a combined family and games room for post-lunch pool or table football. Eat – or drink – where you like: a blackboard menu changes as seasons and local suppliers dictate, but sharp, simple, flavourful dishes like spinach, pea and mint soup with homemade bread, goujons of cod, or broccoli, mustard and cheese tart make good, nourishing lunches, while a larger dinner selection could take in chicken with pesto or herb-crusted fennel with garlic butter.

Food serving times:
Tuesday-Friday:
    12pm-2pm, 6pm-9pm
Saturday-Sunday:
    12pm-2.30pm, 6pm-9pm
Closed 25-26 December
Prices:
Meals: a la carte 15.50/21.45

Typical Dishes

Pate, homemade chutney

Steak and kidney pie

Cappuccino crème brûlee

4mi South of Kirkby Lonsdale on A683. Parking

Whitewell

032 **Inn at Whitewell**

Forest of Bowland, Whitewell BB7 3AT

Tel.: (01200) 448222 - Fax: (01200) 448298

VISA MC

Timothy Taylor, Bowland Brewery, Copper Draggon

A delightful location in a river valley in the Forest of Bowland means that a visit is always going to be special. The pub itself is an extended 14C cottage which once served as a coaching inn; nowadays it's very personally run with a endearing eccentricity which surfaces at the unlikeliest moments! It has considerable charm downstairs with a lovely faded bar full of eyecatching curios, a reception-cum-shop and an intimate restaurant overlooking the River Hodder and Trough of Bowland. Dishes have a traditional base and make good use of sound Lancastrian produce: ask for a table in the restaurant or just pull up a chair in the bar. The large, comfortable bedrooms really are the pick of the place - they boast plenty of style, and some have real peat fires. All have CD players and fittings that touch on the highest inn standards.

Food serving times:
Monday-Sunday:
12pm-2pm, 7.30pm-9.30pm
Prices:
Meals: a la carte 18.25/36.00
24 rooms : 70.00/150.00

Typical Dishes

Scallops, red wine juice

Fillet of beef, parsley crushed potatoes

Sticky toffee pudding

6mi Northwest of Clitheroe by B6243. Parking

Liverpool

033 Floor One at the Baltic Fleet

33a Wapping, Liverpool L1 8DQ
Tel.: 0151 708 4345 - Fax: 0151 643 8304

  VISA **M**

 From own microbrewery: Wapping, Bowsprit, Summer Ale, Smoked Porter and guest ales

Close to the Albert Dock and dwarfed by the massive silhouette of the Anglican Cathedral, the odd, wedge-shaped Baltic Fleet cuts a lost and unpromising figure from the outside, but locals need no introduction to one of the city's most famous pubs, which now has a growing gastronomic reputation too. The microbrewery in the basement produces a rotating list of real ales to supply a no-frills traditional bar on the ground floor, while the simply styled dining room upstairs displays a sizeable blackboard menu beside the Liverpudlian-themed art and photographs it offers for sale. Straightforwardly appealing cooking sells best, and steaks, wild boar sausages and even haggis are all among the favourites, though the choice changes regularly.

Food serving times:
Monday-Sunday:
12pm-2pm
Tuesday-Saturday:
6pm-9.30pm
Prices:
Meals: a la carte 12.00/23.00

Typical Dishes

Black pudding with caramelised apple

Roulade of pork, sage and Parma ham

Sticky toffee pudding

Close to Albert Dock. Street Parking

B. Kaufmann / Michelin

- **a.** *Hollywood Studios (California)?*
- **b.** *Tabernas Mini Hollywood (Spain)?*
- **c.** *Atlas Film Studio (Morocco)?*

THE GREEN GUIDE

THE GREEN GUIDE

New edition

Spain
Balearic and Canary Islands

With hotels and restaurants

MICHELIN
Travel Publications

Can't decide?

Then immerse yourself in the Michelin Green Guide

- Everything to do and see
- The best driving tours
- Practical information
- Where to stay and eat

The Michelin Green Guide: the spirit of discovery.

*N*ot content with seven historic counties, the South East has always looked further for inspiration. This, after all, is the region that gave the world a prince's Indian pavilion facing the Brighton seafront, the pretty redbrick streets of Sandwich, bridging the Channel to Holland and Germany, and Waddesdon Manor, a perfect Loire Chateau just off the A41. Yet these are as much an image of "Englishness" as the domes and spires of Oxford or Kent's white-capped oasthouses amid the hop-poles and apple orchards of the Weald. Here in the South East you'll find the start of the Cotswolds and the freedom of the South Downs Path, the ancient vantage of White Horse Hill and the rural calm of Royal Berkshire's riverside villages, while Canterbury and Winchester, Blenheim, Chartwell and Windsor all have their special place in British history. For a change of pace, fast or slow, the quiet countryside or the colourful cultural life of Brighton are both within an hour from the capital. The South East is also a place to dine well: Whitstable oysters, delicately flavoured Romney Marsh lamb and Aylesbury duck, not to mention a long brewing tradition, are just some of its specialities.

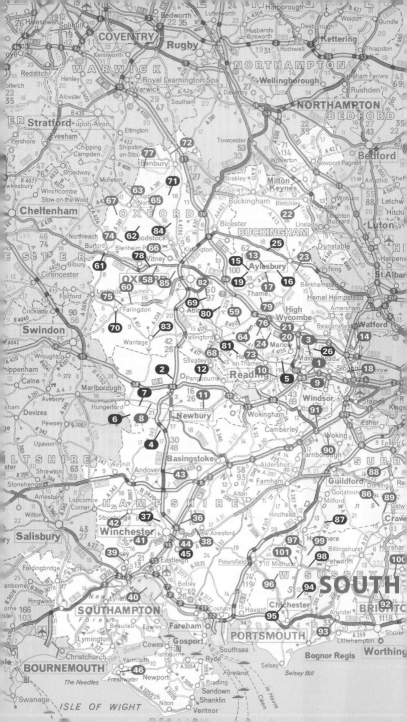

Bray-on-Thames

001 ## Hinds Head

High St, Bray-on-Thames SL6 2EB
Tel.: 01628 626151 - Fax: 01628 623394

Ÿ ✄ **VISA** ⓜⓒ

Green King IPA, Abbot Ale and weekly changing guest ale

Cross Heston Blumenthal's dedication with the warm, true-grained charm of the English pub and you have a recipe for success. The ground-breaking modern cuisine of the Fat Duck, four doors away, is little reflected in the pub's menu, but the team at the Hind's Head do share the owner's fascination with the lost glories of English cookery: try a glass of pear cider or a sip of mead with satisfying and full-flavoured dishes that include pies and puddings, syllabubs and trifles. The most imaginative choices are based on favourites from the old royal kitchens downriver at Hampton Court. The pub itself has its origins in the 1600s – with its beams, panelled walls and real fire, it feels wonderfully inviting – but it's more used to keeping up with 21C demand, so arrive early.

Food serving times:
Monday to Saturday:
 12pm-2.30pm,
 6.30pm-9.30pm
Sunday and Bank Holidays:
 12pm-4pm
Closed 25 December,
1 January
and dinner Bank Holidays
Prices:
Meals: a la carte 20.50/26.50

Typical Dishes

Pea and ham soup

Oxtail and kidney pudding

Treacle tart with milk ice cream

Parking 》

Chieveley

002 The Crab at Chieveley

Wantage Rd, Chieveley RE20 8UE

Tel.: (01635) 247550 - Fax: (01635) 248440
e-mail: info@crabatchieveley - Website: www.crabatchieveley.com

London Pride, Arkell Moonlight

Down a country road, surrounded by waving fields of wheat and well-ordered countryside, The Crab doesn't look like the kind of place to rock the boat, but country pub preconceptions are best forgotten here. The old fishing nets give you a clue to the menu – an extensive choice of seafood served in the more casual Fish Bar and a surprisingly formal dining room. The real surprise, though, is reserved for diners who decide to stay the night. Ten bedrooms in the modern annex eclipse the average inn for originality and luxury. Decorated in the style of famous hotels from Raffles to Sandy Lane in Barbados and La Mamounia in Marrakesh, each one is equipped with DVD players and other delightful extras: ground floor rooms have their own private terrace with a hot tub!

Food serving times:
Monday-Sunday:
   12pm-2.30pm, 6pm-10pm
- seafood -

Prices:
Meals: 16.50/19.50 (fixed price lunch) and a la carte 19.50/ 45.00

10 rooms : 120.00/ 170.00

Typical Dishes

Scallops with caramelised apples

Crab crusted cod chunk

Hot chocolate fondant

2.5mi West of Chieveley by School Road on B4494. Parking

Cookham

003 The Ferry

Sutton Rd, Cookham SL6 9SN
Tel.: 01628 525123
Website: www.ferry.co.uk

 rest VISA AE ① MC

 Timothy Taylor, Fullers London Pride

In terms of location, it's hard to imagine a pub more enviably situated than The Ferry, which stands alongside the meandering Thames overlooking Cookham Bridge. It even has its own landing stage for those who like to arrive in a bit of style. Some don't even make it inside, but are tempted to linger on the lovely wood furnished dining terrace, but those who do venture through the front doors are hardly short-changed. The pub boasts a part-14th century interior, and its recent restoration offers modernised, rustic charm. There's a smart snug with leather seats, a bar with sofas to snuggle into, and two restaurants with good views over the river. Appealing menus wander through the gastro universe, from snacks to pasta and pizza, and on to rotisserie and grill, all of which can be walked off afterwards with a nice stroll along the Thames Path.

Food serving times:
Monday-Sunday:
    12pm-2.30pm, 6pm-9.30
Prices:
Meals: a la carte 21.00/34.00

Typical Dishes

Goats cheese tart tatin

Rib eye steak, bearnaise and fries

Sticky toffee pudding, fig and date ice cream

2 mins walk from the centre of the village by the river. Parking

Highclere

004 ## The Yew Tree

Hollington Cross, Andover road, Highclere RG20 9SE

Tel.: (01635) 253360 - Fax: (01635) 255035

e-mail: gareth.mcanish@theyewtree.net - Website: www.theyewtree.net

Fuller's London Pride, Timothy Taylor Landlords Best

The rustic black and white pub outside Highclere looks the very picture of an English country inn, but it's carved out more than just a traditional role in village life. As well as its blackboard menus and dishes of the day, the well-restored part-17C bar still offers full measure to its drinkers, but the four classically elegant dining rooms at the back add candlelight and white linen to the same handsome period décor. Though a clear split between the two helps each keep their true atmosphere, the lunch and dinner menus are the same in both halves: a typical selection might take in lamb with champ and red onion marmalade, chicken en papillote and gravadlax - a taste of home for the amiable owner.

Food serving times:
Monday-Sunday:
                    12pm-3pm

Prices:
Meals: 15.50 (lunch and 6pm-7pm) and a la carte 20.00/57.00

6 rooms : 60.00

Typical Dishes

Risotto of crayfish

Grilled rib-eye steak, l'escargot d'ail

Raspberry soufflé

Parking

Hurley

005 **Black Boys Inn**

Henley Rd, Hurley SL6 5NQ
Tel.: 01628 824212
e-mail: info@blackboysinn.co.uk - Website: www.blackboysinn.co.uk

🍷 ✂ *VISA* ⓜⓒ

Brakspears Bitter

This part-16C inn is already showing the benefits of a thorough-going renovation: it's intimate, relaxing, and obviously run with real pub know-how. A delightful, soft-toned main bar centres on an open stove. True to form, the gently helpful, conversational service strikes just the right note: the friendly team are justifiably proud of their good food and will talk you through the daily specials, which might include fresh Newlyn fish, salt-marsh lamb and good seasonal game. The concern for fine ingredients is typical of a pub which even draws its own water from its own well, but the result is the sort of flavourful, well-prepared cooking which is very easy to enjoy. Extremely comfortable and pleasantly furnished modern bedrooms – some in converted outbuildings – really stand out for value.

Food serving times:
Monday-Saturday:
    12pm-2pm, 7pm-9pm
Sunday: 12pm-2pm
Closed 2 weeks Christmas
Prices:
Meals: a la carte 21.00/27.00
🛏 **8 rooms :** 65.00/75.00

Typical Dishes

Salcombe crab gateau

Rump of English lamb, marjoram scented cannellini beans

Raspberries with lemon

1,5 miles Southwest on
A4130. Parking

Inkpen

006 Swan Inn ⊨

Craven Rd, Lower Green, Inkpen RG17 9DX

Tel.: (01488) 668326 - Fax: (01488) 668306
e-mail: enquiries@theswaninn-organics.co.uk - Website: www.theswaninn-organics.co.uk

   VISA

Butts Jester, Traditional, Maggs Magnificent Mild and a guest beer

This enthusiastic husband and wife team don't do things by halves, managing a likeably down-to-earth community pub – with darts or quiz night on Thursdays – as well as running the 100% organic farm just down the road in this pretty corner of Berkshire. It supplies home-made sausages and tender sirloins, as well as the nicely matured steak for their locally renowned beef and ale pies. Next door is their farm shop, stocking more home-reared meats and much else besides. A small, neatly set restaurant to the rear is traditional in style with a menu of familiar favourites to match; simple bedrooms in pine and patchwork overlook the fields.

Food serving times:
Monday-Sunday:
12pm-2pm (-2.30pm weekends), 7pm-9.30pm
Closed 25-26 December
Prices:
Meals: a la carte 16.00/29.00
⊨ **10 rooms :** 50.00/90.00

Typical Dishes

Prawns in Pernod

Sirloin steak, mustard and red wine jus

Tuscan pudding

3.5mi Southeast of Hungerford by Inkpen rd. Parking

Kintbury

007 ## The Dundas Arms

Station Rd, Kintbury RG17 9UT

Tel.: (01488) 658263 - Fax: (01488) 658568
e-mail: info@dundasarms.co.uk - Website: www.dundasarms.co.uk

 VISA

Ramsbury Gold, Adnams, West Berks Good Old Boy, Mr Chubb's Lunchtime Bitter

After supplying Kintbury with sustaining dinners and its daily pint for over three decades, the long-standing landlord knows he's among friends in the bar. Never ones to pass up a good thing, the locals arrive on the dot for filling dishes like fried skate with capers and jacket wedges or roast duck with apple and cider sauce, and a friendly, familiar atmosphere prevails. It can get just a little too busy and smoky for some tastes, in which case the trick is to ask if they're opening the rear restaurant, usually reserved for more formal dinners. But on a summer afternoon, there's only one place to be. A lovely double terrace borders the edge of the Kennet and the canal: watch the narrowboats passing the lock as the stopping trains roll away to Bedwyn and the Wessex Downs. Five neat, light bedrooms face the river.

Food serving times:
Monday: 12pm-2pm
Tuesday-Saturday:
12pm-2pm, 7pm-9pm
Closed 25 December

Prices:
Meals: a la carte 17.00/27.00
 5 rooms : 75.00/85.00

Typical Dishes

Home potted shrimps
Steak and kidney pie
Bread and butter pudding

3.5mi East of Hungerford by A4. Parking

Marsh Benham

008 The Red House

Marsh Benham RG20 8LY

Tel.: (01635) 582017 - Fax: (01635) 581621
Website: www.theredhousepub.com

No real ales offered

O nce inside this well cared-for thatched inn, there's a choice to be made. To the front, the more casual bar: grab one of several tables by the old mullioned windows, if you can. To the back, pleasant countryside views, courteous, attentive service, smartly set dining tables polished to a high sheen and the option of an à la carte or prix-fixe bistro menu. A classical French influence comes through in rather delicate, carefully presented dishes like chicken and wild mushroom terrine with brioche or a buttery asparagus risotto; they're also very proud of their banoffee pie with cinnamon and nut crumble.

Food serving times:
Monday-Saturday:
  12pm-2.30pm, 7pm-9.30pm
Sunday: 12pm-2.30pm
Closed 25 and 31 December
and 1 January
Prices:
Meals: 16.95 and a la carte
25.50/32.95

Typical Dishes

Scallops with fennel compote

Pork with oyster mushrooms
and wide noodles

Banana, banoffee and
chocolate papillotte

Off the A4 between Newbury and
Hungerford. Parking

Paley Street

009 Royal Oak

Paley Street SL6 3JN
Tel.: (01628) 620541

VISA **M©**

Fuller's London Pride

A pleasant, proudly preserved village pub, but with a difference: framed photos of the owner's father, chatshow legend Michael Parkinson, and his showbiz friends beam affably from the wattle and timber walls. Attentive staff share Parky's talent for putting guests at their ease and serve up classically tasty, no-nonsense cooking with proper seasonal character: dishes could include chicken parfait and grilled sole with asparagus, followed by a lemon tart. A smart yet cosy bar, complete with dedicated regulars, offers a fine selection of wines and real ales and a quietly convivial atmosphere.

Food serving times:
Monday-Saturday:
       12pm-3pm, 6pm-10pm
Sunday: 12pm-3pm
27 December-2 January
Prices:
Meals: 19.50 and a la carte
23.00/30.00

Typical Dishes

Poached asparagus wrapped parma ham

Duck, fried noodles

Apple, raisin and cinnamon crumble

3.5 mi Southwest of Bray-on-Thames by A308, A330 on B3024. Parking

Wargrave

010 St George & Dragon

High Street, Wargrave RG10 8HY

Tel.: (01189) 405021 - Fax: (01189) 405024
e-mail: stgeorgeanddragon@hotmail.com - Website: www.stgeorgeanddragon.co.uk

 VISA **AE** **MC**

 Timothy Taylor Landlord

S ummer visitors to this delightfully modern and relaxed pub should make sure they arrive early: the enviably located raised deck terrace is a perfect spot to watch life go by on the neighbouring River Thames, but a place here is at a premium. Don't worry if your best bet is to stay inside – this is a textbook contemporary pub with a central bar, copper topped tables, tub chairs and several inviting log fires on colder days. To make the most of the river views, the main restaurant with open kitchen is around the side: heavy wood tables, fine glassware and interesting, modern specialities from the wood-fired oven and spit roast, alongside other up-to-date, globally inspired dishes at a keen price.

Food serving times:
Monday-Saturday:
   12pm-2.30pm, 6pm-10pm
Sunday: 12pm-7pm
Closed 25-26 December
Prices:
Meals: a la carte 18.50/34.35

Moorings on the River Thames, at the end of the garden. Parking

Typical Dishes

Asparagus wrapped in prosciutto, poached egg

Spit roast chicken, Belgian fries and aoli

Chocolate fondant pudding

Woolhampton

011 The Angel

Bath Rd, Woolhampton RG7 5RT

Tel.: (0118) 971 3307
e-mail: mail@a4angel.com - Website: www.a4angel.com

 🍷 ✕ **VISA** **MC**

 No real ales offered

A first impression of the Angel – green window frames in a curtain of ivy – offers no hint of the highly personalised design inside. Tropical plants, flowers, hops and yet more ivy set off some eye-catching modern art and photographs in a series of intimate, candlelit rooms: burgundy, green and ochre, with rows of wine bottles glinting between the beams. Fish and chips aside, much of an ambitious modern repertoire takes French culinary style as its starting point, and delicately presented starters and mains might include tuna on salad niçoise or prawns in lobster broth. Compiling the wine list is clearly a labour of love: some rare vintages – like the empties on the ceiling – may be out of reach to most of us, but the selection includes a more accessible range by the glass and even a homemade sloe gin.

Food serving times:
Tuesday-Saturday:
    12pm-2pm, 6pm-9.30pm
Sunday: 12-2pm
Christmas week
Prices:
Meals: a la carte 18.00/32.00

Typical Dishes

Warm salad of chorizo sausage

Chicken with bacon, herbs and caesar salad

Chocolate and raspberry

Located on the A4 between Reading and Newbury. Parking

Yattendon

012 **Royal Oak**  We most liked

The Square, Yattendon RG18 0UG

Tel.: (01635) 201325 - Fax: (01635) 201926
e-mail: oakyattendon@aol.com

  VISA **AE**

Wadworth 6X, West Berkshire Good Old Boy

Though not a million miles from the roaring intensity of the M4, this very pleasant redbrick former coaching inn could inhabit another age. Sympathetically set in a picture postcard village, its well-appointed lounge with real fire sets the scene, evoking English country house style at its more comfortable and unassuming. Choose from two dining rooms, one in smart, classic style with cloth-clad tables and fine quality cover, the other more pubby and relaxed. Menus, invariably with plenty of choice, change every two and a half months but never stray far from a confidently executed classic base with distinctly modern overtones, their influences stretching globally. Comfortable, pretty bedrooms, with a rather chintzy quality, beckon upstairs.

Food serving times:
Monday-Sunday:
    12pm-2.30pm, 7pm-10pm
Closed 1 January
Prices:
Meals: 15.00 (lunch) and a la carte 28.00/33.00
🛏 **5 rooms :** 110.00/130.00

Typical Dishes

Salad of bouin noir with poached egg

Fillet of sea bass with tortellini of crab

Raspberry crème brulee

In the village centre. Parking

223

Cuddington

013 Crown

Aylesbury Rd, Cuddington HP18 0BB

Tel.: (01844) 292222

e-mail: david@anniebaileys.com

 VISA **AE** **MC**

Fuller's London Pride, Adnams, Red Fox

Locals swarm to this highly renowned village pub, and not just because it's 16C, Grade II listed, and thatched to boot. The interior is a most welcoming place to be, with subdued lighting, small windows and several period fireplaces, though the collection of Victorian prints reveal a lightly quirky side, too. There are four areas in which to relax and mingle; the two most sought-after being around the bar, near the fires, though you can eat wherever you like. Menus mix pub staples, like steaks and lamb casserole, with more contemporary dishes, such as scallops and chilli jus, or chicken saltimbocca with sweet potato mash, while puddings come under the heading 'heart-warming'. Enthusiastic, down-to-earth service is entirely in keeping for a pub with the true "local" ambience.

Food serving times:

Monday-Sunday:
12pm-2.30pm, 6.30pm-9.30pm

Monday-Sunday:
12pm-2.30pm, 6.30pm-9.30pm

25 December

Prices:
Meals: 12.50 (2 courses) and a la carte 19.50/27.00

Typical Dishes

Red onion and goat's cheese tartlet

Smoked haddock with Welsh rarebit

Tarte au citron

West of Aylesbury by A418. Some parking spaces available

Denham

014 The Swan Inn

Village Rd, Denham UB9 5BH

Tel.: (01895) 832085 - Fax: (01895) 835516
e-mail: info@swaninndenham.co.uk - Website: www.swaninndenham.co.uk

Courage Best, Wadworth 6X, Morrell's Oxford Blue

Very much at the heart of one of the loveliest villages in Buckinghamshire, the pretty, ivy-clad Swan Inn is half bar, half restaurant, but it's run in such a pleasant, accommodating spirit that everyone feels welcome; drinkers and diners mingle under the broad umbrellas on the terrace, which leads into a spacious garden. Choose from a menu with a modern edge or daily changing blackboard specials which reflect the season; typical of these are tasty black and white puddings with crispy pancetta, halloumi with saffron vegetables and couscous and a subtly flavoured elderflower and lavender crème brulée.

Food serving times:
Monday-Saturday:
12pm-2.30pm, 7pm-10pm
Sunday: 12pm-3pm, 7pm-10pm

Closed 25-26 December (booking essential)
Prices:
Meals: a la carte 17.75/25.00

Pass through the centre of the village and over the bridge, follow the road and the pub is on the left. Small car park

Typical Dishes

Caramelised goat's cheese and tomato tart tatin

Smoked haddock on asparagus

Rich chocolate fondant

Easington

015 Mole & Chicken

The Terrace, Easington HP18 9EY

Tel.: (01844) 208387 - Fax: (01844) 208250
e-mail: shanepellis@hotmail.com - Website: www.moleandchicken.co.uk

Y ⊱room 🚭 **VISA** **AE** **MC**

Greene King IPA, Hook Norton

The bend in the road of a tiny Buckinghamshire hamlet provides the cosy backdrop to this attractive, wisteria clad country pub. There's a really comfortable ambience here, highlighted by the carefully chosen fabrics in pretty country pub style, roaring fires, beams, decorative candles and scrubbed pine tables and chairs: it's a cosy and intimate place. Menus are changed regularly (apart from the well-established favourites the regulars won't allow to go!). Good modern dishes are served in hearty sized portions: originality is the keyword. Service is locally renowned: staff are known for their enthusiasm. Adjacent cottages provide bright, modern bedrooms, some with countryside views.

Food serving times:
Monday-Sunday:
    12pm-2pm, 6pm-9.30pm
Closed 25 December
(booking essential)
Prices:
Meals: 20.00 (fixed price dinner) and a la carte 20.00/25.00
⊨ **5 rooms :** 50.00/65.00

Typical Dishes

Roasted marrow and stilton soup

Roasted duck with orange sauce

Cheeseboard

2.5mi Northwest of Thame by B4011. Parking

Ford

016 **Dinton Hermit**

Water Lane, Ford HP17 8XH

Tel.: (01296) 747473 - Fax: (01296) 748819

e-mail: dintonhermit@btconnect.com - Website: www.dinton-hermit.com

 Adnams, Brakspears, Wychert

Although it's much less secluded than the name suggests – surely the only hermit with an extensive car park – the gently firelit bar of this listed pub does provide a lovely, if temporary, retreat from the world. Burnished benches, cane-backed chairs, whitewashed walls with bricks and beams make it recognisably traditional in spirit, but there's also a modern sense of clutter-free space about the place. Neatly set dining rooms are in similar style, and the upfront country flavours in a modern pub menu seem to go down well: try braised ham with tarragon and Cheddar sauce or pot-roast guinea fowl with a nutty, zesty sauce. The restored outbuilding now houses the inn's bedrooms: two have Jacobean style four-posters, the others have a pleasing modern look: bright, tidy and individual.

Food serving times:

Monday-Saturday:
12pm-2pm, 7pm-9pm
Sunday: 12pm-2pm
Closed 25 and 26 December

Prices:

Meals: 12.50 and a la carte 20.00/35.00

 13 rooms : 80.00/125.00

Typical Dishes

Asparagus wrapped in parma ham

Grilled lemon sole with prawns, parsley and garlic

Mixed berry crumble

5.5mi Southwest of Aylesbury by A418. Parking

Haddenham

017 **Green Dragon**

8 Churchway, Haddenham HP17 8AA

Tel.: (01844) 291403 - Fax: (01844) 299532
e-mail: paul@eatatthedragon.co.uk - Website: www.eatatthedragon.co.uk

Wadsworth 6X, Dewchars IPA, Notley Wytchert

Personally run with an affable ease which seems to spread through the place, the well looked-after Green Dragon has a reputation for good food, one which now reaches far beyond the picturesque village it still serves so well. An extensive menu – with a few unexpected combinations – ranges from partridge with parsnips and pear sauce or scallops with white wine and vanilla dressing to a few simple but carefully sourced pub classics like chicken and wild mushroom pie and steak and kidney pudding with local ale. Haddenham was once as famous for its ducks as nearby Aylesbury and they still have quite a taste for them here, so look out for confits or roasts among the specials. Light lunches and dinners are served at the same neatly set tables, laid out all around the central bar.

Food serving times:
Monday-Saturday:
    12pm-2pm, 7pm-9.30pm
Sunday: 12pm-2pm
Closed 25 December and 1 January
(booking essential)
Prices:
Meals: 11.95 (2 course dinner menu on Tuesdays and Thursdays) and a la carte 18.00/28.00

Typical Dishes

Confit of duck glazed with pineapple chutney

Halibut with spinach, wild mushrooms and pine nuts

Banana and toffee crumble

By the Green and St Mary's Church. Parking

Iver

018 ## The Swan at Iver

2 High St, Iver SL0 9NG
Tel.: 01753 655776 - Fax: 01753 655090
Website: www.theswanativer.co.uk

  VISA AE ⓘ ⓜⓒ

Green King IPA, Fullers London Pride and 2 guest ales

Over 400 years after it first opened its doors, The Swan is still giving the locals what they want. A warm, informal feeling remains – in fact, it's the first thing you notice – but this big market-town pub has moved smartly and completely with the times: framed photos of Iver's streets in days gone by are among the few concessions to tradition. Expect to find a good crowd of locals in the front bar and a fair number in the dining room at the back, too. You'll have the choice of lunchtime sandwiches or a fixed price menu, slightly more extensive in the evenings. The style is resolutely Modern British: satisfying, well-made dishes of good contemporary cooking, with no unnecessary pretension in its preparation or service.

Food serving times:
Tuesday-Sunday:
    12pm-2.30pm, 6pm-11pm
Closed Sunday dinner and Monday
Prices:
Meals: 25.00

Typical Dishes

Warm salad of smoked haddock

Grilled chicken, mushroom and pinenut ravioli

Champagne fruit salad

3 mi Southwest of Uxbridge by the A408 on the B470. Parking

Long Crendon

019 Angel 🛏️

47 Bicester Rd, Long Crendon HP18 9EE

Tel.: (01844) 208268 - Fax: (01844) 202497
Website: www.angelrestaurant.co.uk

🍽️ 🍷 🛏️=room 🚭 **VISA** ⓘ ⓜⓒ

 Hook Norton, Brakspear, Spitfire, Bass

This attractive part-16C inn is now most assuredly in the quality restaurant-with-rooms category, but qualifies in the pub league due to its bright and cheery bar area with leather sofas. This is where the regulars gather to pay homage to the local beer on draught. Characterful dining areas lead off from here, defined by tiled flooring, bare wood tables and crisp linen napkins. To the rear an air-conditioned conservatory adds another enticing option. Seasonally changing, modern, creative menus have assured the Angel of a grand reputation, enhanced by daily changing fish specials. The word has spread, too, about the bedrooms here. They're decorated on a lavish scale with rich fabrics and wrought iron beds. One even allows you the luxury of a roll-top bath.

Food serving times:
Monday-Saturday:
  12pm-2.30pm, 7pm-9.30pm
Sunday: 12pm-2.30pm
Closed 1 January
Prices:
Meals: 17.95 (fixed price lunch) and a la carte 25.00/35.00
🛏️ **3 rooms :** 65.00/85.00

Typical Dishes

Salad of duck and bacon

Roast fillet of halibut with plum tomato and asparagus

Espresso crème brûlée

1.5mi Northwest of Thame by B4011. Parking

Marlow

020 **Royal Oak**

Frieth Rd, Bovingdon Green, Marlow SL7 2JF

Tel.: (01628) 488611 - Fax: (01628) 478680
e-mail: info@royaloakpub.co.uk - Website: www.royaloakpub.co.uk

Marlow Rebellion IPA, Brakspear, Fuller's London Pride

Though it remains every inch the rural pub, from the old beams to the logs stacked by the wood burners, plenty of well thought-out details lend the Royal Oak an eclectic, but well-adapted, modern atmosphere. A bright conservatory bar feels clean and airy: barmen, spotting the regulars arriving, can get pouring before they've even walked through the door! Beyond, salvaged antique chairs and tables and fine tableware invite an easygoing attitude to good eating, and the charming staff do the same, carrying off what's actually very efficient, personalised service with breezy friendliness. Offering great value for this part of the world, ably judged dishes share a fresh, seasonal, classically balanced taste.

Food serving times:
Monday-Saturday:
12pm-2.30pm, 7pm-10pm
Sunday:
12pm-3pm, 7pm-10pm
Closed 25-26 December
Prices:
Meals: a la carte 17.75/27.25

Typical Dishes
Cornish yarg and sage brûlée

Smoked haddock on spinach
and potato pancake

Honey and cinnamon rice
pudding with roasted fig

From the town centre, head towards Bovingdon Green, pub is on the left as you leave the woods. Parking

Marlow

021 ## The Hand and Flowers

West St, Marlow SL7 3BP
Tel.: 01628 482277

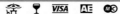

Green King IPA, Old Speckled Hen, Abbot and seasonal ales

The Hand and Flowers was originally a pretty row of period cottages, dating back at least to the 1800s by the look of their black and white timbered facades. A necessary modicum of modernisation inside has left it feeling nice and unspoilt: beams, rough plasterwork and chunky wooden tables in the original bar blend perfectly with modern art and vases of elegant lillies. The classically based cuisine is an equally good balance, excellent in sourcing and preparation and full of richly appealing, sophisticated flavours: professional but unstuffy service helps the enjoyment no end. Any off-hand Gallic shrugs or feigned unconcern are far more likely to be found on the petanque pitch in the back garden, where the pub team enjoys a bit of good-natured competition.

Food serving times:
Tuesday-Saturday
    12pm-2.30pm, 7pm-10pm
Sunday: 12pm-3pm
Closed 26-30 December, 2-8 January
Prices:
Meals: a la carte 23.50/37.00

Typical Dishes

Crab fondant with cucumber and dill chutney

Roast chicken with parmesan risotto

Vanilla crème brulee

On the A4155, follow Henley signs West from the centre of town. Pub on right after 350metres. Parking

Newton Longville

022 Crooked Billet

Newton Longville MK17 0DF

Tel.: (01908) 373936 - Fax: (01908) 631979
e-mail: john@thebillet.co.uk - Website: www.thebillet.co.uk

   VISA AE MC

 Old Speckled Hen, Wadworth 6X, Abott, Hobgoblin, Batemans XXXB, IPA

The Crooked Billet's phenomenal wine list, chosen with passionate connoisseurship to include over 300 wines by the glass, makes remarkable reading and very enjoyable drinking. With their typically helpful friendliness, the owner and his staff are happy to recommend a good match for lunch or dinner, and the well-judged modern cooking does it justice. In fact, it's hard to fault this smoothly run, ever welcoming pub with its thatched roof and pretty gardens: a spacious firelit bar still attracts its locals – you're welcome for a pint or a lunchtime sandwich if that's all you feel like – while the comfortable dining room with a hint of 16C character is a lovely setting for a dinner at leisurely pace.

Food serving times:
Monday: 7pm-10pm
Tuesday-Saturday:
12pm-2pm, 7pm-10pm
Sunday: 12pm-3pm
Closed 25-26 December and 1 January
Closed Monday lunch
Prices:
Meals: a la carte 25.00/50.00

Typical Dishes

Asparagus with seared scallops, parma ham and hollandaise

Lamb fillet, leek and potato cake

6mi Southwest of Milton Keynes by A421. Parking

Stoke Mandeville

023 ## The Wool Pack
21 Risborough Road, Stoke Mandeville HP22 5UP
Tel.: (01296) 615970 - Fax: (01296) 615971

 VISA AE D MC

Tim Taylor Landlord, Fuller's London Pride

An object lesson in how to bring an old pub up to date, the low-ceilinged but now very contemporary bar of this part-thatched pub seems to get more cosy as the night draws in, especially if you've bagged one of the leather tub chairs and copper topped tables, or a spot near the fire. At the back is a sizeable dining room with French doors leading out onto the terrace, and this is where the contemporary influence is really brought to bear. Dishes like duck confit with pak choi and chilli are the exceptions in a repertoire which is more likely to turn to Italian cuisine for its subtle fusion twists: fresh, tasty stone-baked pizzas, grills and dessert treats like lemon polenta cake are all prepared with understanding and care and served by knowledgeable, spontaneous staff who seem genuinely happy to be there.

Food serving times:
Monday-Saturday:
  12pm-2.30pm, 6pm-9.30pm
Sunday: 12pm-8pm
Closed 26 December and 1 January
Prices:
Meals: a la carte 15.00/40.00

South of town on A413 close to the hospital. Parking

Typical Dishes

Asparagus, poached egg, proscuitto with hollandaise

Lamb and dauphinoise potatoes and minted pears

Sticky toffee pudding

Turville

024 Bull & Butcher

Turville RG9 6QU

Tel.: (01491) 638283 - Fax: (01491) 638836
e-mail: info@thebullandbutcher.com - Website: www.thebullandbutcher.com

   VISA Ⓜ️©

 Brakspears Bitter, Hook Norton

Built in the mid-16C, this handsome, half-timbered pub served its first ales to the workmen restoring nearby St Mary's church. Tasty, tried-and-tested bar dishes can be as simple as ploughman's, fish and chips or a "Farmer's Supper and pint", while the table d'hôte might offer confit of duck or shellfish cakes with spicy lentils, unless it's time for a themed dinner: the "Bangers", "South Africa" and "Beaujolais" nights all went down well. Menus and specials are served in the restaurant and in the bar, where a semi-circular table centres on the rediscovered pub well. The charming village of Turville is worth an after-dinner stroll: fans of "The Vicar of Dibley" may find that it all looks strangely familiar…

Food serving times:
Monday-Saturday:
12pm-2.30pm,
6.30pm-9.30pm
Sundays and Bank holidays:
12pm-4pm, 7pm-9.30pm
Prices:
Meals: a la carte 23.00/29.00

Typical Dishes

Seared sirloin salad with mango dressing

Grilled cod fillet

Baked banoffi cheesecake with toffee sauce

5mi North of Henley on Thames by A4130 off B480. Parking

Waddesdon

025 **Five Arrows**

High St, Waddesdon HP18 0JE

Tel.: (01296) 651727 - Fax: (01296) 658596
e-mail: bookings@thefivearrowshotel.fsnet.co.uk - Website: www.waddesdon.org.uk

Fuller's London Pride

Certainly not your everyday local, this delightful late 19C inn is part of a magnificent estate built by Baron Rothschild, complete with attractive gardens and courtyard terrace, and close to Waddesdon Manor, now a National Trust property. Numerous comfy dining rooms centre on a charming bar; they're undeniably characterful and period features like wood panelling and parquet floors fit the studied country-house style to the last detail. Extensive menus offer a mix of British classic and contemporary, and though the service has an element of restaurant smartness, this aristocrat among pubs wears its hint of formality with good grace. As might be expected, very spacious bedrooms offer some stylish touches, along with an almost de rigeur four-poster. It's all very impressive, though maybe not for those who want to "pop out for a swift half."

Food serving times:
Monday-Saturday:
    12pm-2.30pm, 7pm-9pm
Sunday: 12.30pm-2.30pm
Closed 26 December, dinner
31 December and 1 January
Prices:
Meals: a la carte 23.85/32.40
 11 rooms : 70.00/150.00

Typical Dishes

Aubergine, feta and sundried tomatoes

Monkfish with red chard

Chocolate fondant sponge

On A41. Parking

Wooburn Common

026 **Chequers Inn** 🛏

Kiln Lane, Wooburn Common HP10 0JQ
Tel.: (01628) 529575 - Fax: (01628) 850124
e-mail: info@chequers-inn.com - Website: www.thechequersatwooburncommon.co.uk

    VISA **AE** **①** **MC**

Ruddles, Abbot, IPA, Rebellion Smuggler

You're looking for a handsome redbrick inn, but alternatively you could just follow your nose: the famous garden barbecues at The Chequers do all their own advertising, and if you arrive on a sunny evening, your mouth may be watering by the time you reach the front door. Bring your elbows to make your way through a well-dressed knot of post-commute drinkers until around eight, but you should be able to grab a table for sandwiches or a full meal in the bar, or something a touch more adventurous in the restaurant at the back: favourites include ribeye and chips and almond and pear tart with crème anglaise. Bedrooms are perfect for anyone who wants pretty, cottage-style furnishings, but can't be without modems and satellite television. A well run place with real personality.

Food serving times:
Monday-Friday:
12pm-2.30pm, 7pm-9.30pm
(-10pm Friday)
Saturday-Sunday:
12-9.30pm(-10pm Saturday)
Prices:
Meals: 13.95 (2 course lunch menu) and a la carte 25.00/30.00
🛏 **17 rooms :** 72.50/107.50

Typical Dishes

Terrine of duck breast

Loin of Venison

Cheese selection

3.5mi Southwest of Beaconsfield by A40. Parking

South East – Buckinghamshire

237

Alfriston

027 George Inn

High St, Alfriston BN26 5SY

Tel.: 01323 870319

Website: www.thegeorge-alfriston.com

VISA **MC**

Tribute Cornish ale, Old Speckled Hen

The most charming sight on Alfriston's pretty High Street, the overhanging front of the listed, brick-and-timber-built George Inn looks the picture of a good, old-fashioned English pub, and first impressions are confirmed in the front bar, with its strings of hops and its flickering fire. There's even some original 15C art on the walls. A relaxed landlord succeeds in making everyone feel properly at home, from the South Downs walkers who come for pints and ploughmans to a good crowd of locals – many pub cricket club and panto society members among them. Tasty dishes with an international or Asian touch offer plenty of choice and put their faith in the local greengrocer and butcher. Restored rooms are well kept and nicely equipped; at the front, the sound of traffic to and fro on a weekday is noticeable, but no more than that.

Food serving times:
Monday-Sunday:
  12pm-2.30pm, 7pm-10pm
Prices:
Meals: a la carte 12.00/25.00

Typical Dishes

Chicken liver parfait

Confit of pork belly

Sticky fudge and walnut pudding

Two public car parks 150 metres

Bodiam

028 The Curlew

Junction Rd, Bodiam TN32 5UY

Tel.: (01580) 861394
e-mail: enquiries@thecurlewatbodiam.co.uk - Website: www.thecurlewatbodiam.co.uk

Hall and Woodhouse Badger Best, Fursty Ferret

A pub of two halves, but the warm ambience ensures this is a local favourite either way: choose from a good list of snacks and simpler meals in the main bar, its timbers edged with beardy fringes of Sussex hops, or a thoughtfully composed menu on a classic base. Smooth-clothed tables, elegant china and glassware in the dining room suggest a rather formal approach, but it feels entirely appropriate for the tasty cuisine, not to mention the truly comprehensive selection of fine wines – there can't be many roadside stops with a cellar list like this. A short drive takes you to Bodiam Castle.

Food serving times:
Tuesday-Saturday:
12pm-2pm, 7pm-9pm
Sunday-Monday:
12pm-5pm
**Closed 26 December,
1 January and Bank Holidays**
Prices:
Meals: 19.95 and a la carte 32.00

On the B2244 Hawkhurst to Sedlescombe road, by the Bodiam Castle crossroads.

Typical Dishes

Raviolis of smoked haddock with saffron

Fillet steak with black pepper rösti

Chocolate fondant, vanilla ice

239

Danehill

029 ## Coach & Horses

School Lane, Danehill RH17 7JF

Tel.: (01825) 740369 - Fax: (01825) 740369
e-mail: coachandhorses@danehill.biz

Harveys Best, Robinson's Stockport

Rough-hewn stone gives this Sussex hostelry a solid presence, softened somewhat by the magical nearby presence of the Bluebell Railway. The locals love it here; they're still an important part of its character, despite its recent "conversion" into a destination dining pub, and can usually be found having an afternoon ale in the small bar as you enter, dogs at their side. There are two separate dining areas, a top one which enjoys the atmosphere created in the bar, and another in the converted stables, with well-spaced tables, beams adorned with dried hops, and walls decorated with modern art. Particularly welcoming service adds the final touch to seasonally changing modern menus that dance to a distinctly Gallic tune: dishes are robust, frill-free, and full of flavour.

Food serving times:
Monday-Saturday:
12pm-2pm, 7pm-9pm
Sunday: 12pm-2pm
Closed 25 December (pm),
26 December and 1 January
(pm)
Prices:
Meals: a la carte 20.50/24.50

Typical Dishes

Beetroot marinated salmon
with asparagus salad

Pan fried halibut with white
radish

Lime crème brulée

0.75mi North East on Chelwood
Common Rd. Parking

East Chiltington

030 Jolly Sportsman

Chapel Lane, East Chiltington BN7 3BA

Tel.: (01273) 890400 - Fax: (01273) 890400
e-mail: info@thejollysportsman.com - Website: www.thejollysportsman.com

Regularly changing ales, mainly from micro breweries

Once you know the right sequence of narrow country lanes, the trip to the Jolly Sportsman is half the fun; set in the lee of the South Downs, it's just secluded enough for driver and map reader to feel they've earned that first drink. Not that everyone comes from far afield; the enthusiastic team here certainly know the locals, and regulars are as likely to head for the cheerfully painted dining room as prop up the bar. As well they might: dishes from an appetising menu, with a sensible balance and extra variety from the specials list, prove to be well-presented and, as a rule, their clean-cut, direct flavours come over well. Should any of the local artwork on the walls catch your eye over coffee, ask at the bar: if the price is right, it's yours! Pretty rear garden and terrace.

Food serving times:
Tuesday-Saturday:
    12.30pm-2pm, 7pm-10pm
Sunday: 12.30pm-3pm
Closed 24-27 December
Prices:
Meals: 15.75 and a la carte
19.50/29.00

Typical Dishes

Risotto Primavera

Slow-cooked lamb with aubergine stew

Grappa panna cotta

5.5mi Northwest of Lewes by A275 and B2116 off Novington Lane. Parking

241

Fletching

031 The Griffin Inn 🛏

Fletching TN22 3SS

Tel.: (01825) 722890 - Fax: (01825) 722810
e-mail: thegriffininn@hotmail.com - Website: www.thegriffininn.co.uk

 🍷 room 🚭 **VISA** **AE** **①** **MC**

🍺 *Harveys, King of Horsham, Tanglefoot, Woodhouse*

Pubs are meant to lie at the heart of a community, and this one certainly fits the bill. Reassuringly situated in the middle of a smart village, and boasting huge views to Ashdown Forest, the Griffin dates back to the 16C, as witnessed by the open fires, beams and oak panelling. The feel of a local is enhanced by the pool table at the back and the informality when ordering food: no bookings taken, order directly from the bar. Go through to the restaurant and it's something else again: rafters, candlelight and linen-clad tables. Modern menus have pride of place here: European and local dishes are prominent, such as fish risottos and roasted wood pigeon. Up-to-the-minute bedrooms – shared between the main house and garden annexe – are comfortable.

Food serving times:
Monday-Saturday:
12pm-2.30pm, 7pm-9.30pm
Sunday:
12pm-2.30pm, 7pm-9pm
Closed 25 December,
1 January (dinner)
Closed Sunday dinner -
(fixed price Sunday lunch)
Prices:
Meals: 25.00 (Sunday lunch only) and a la carte 20.00/32.00 (approx)
🛏 **8 rooms :** 60.00/130.00

Typical Dishes

Chicken, pigeon and venison terrine

Linguini vongola

Vanilla and Grappa panna cotta

Between Uckfield and Haywards Heath off A272. Parking

Heathfield

032 Star Inn

Church St, Old Heathfield, Heathfield TN21 9AH

Tel.: (01435) 863570 - Fax: (01435) 862020
e-mail: heathfieldstar@aol.com - Website: www.thebestpubsinsussex.co.uk

 Harveys Best, Shepherd Neame Master Brew, Welton's Old Harry

Standing in the grounds of the village church, this ivy-clad 14C pub is particularly charming on fine afternoons, when drinkers and diners have the run of a lovely lawned garden with tree-trunk benches, but don't wait for the first summer sun. Two intimate and ultra-traditional bars, with silver tankards hanging from the beams, are made all the more cosy by a wood-burning stove and an open fire: a couple of tables are tucked into a big inglenook fireplace. One blackboard lists familiar pub meals alongside ploughmans and potatoes, others offer the season's specials; expect decent-sized helpings of robust cooking in either case. The Star is so well regarded in the neighbourhood that it's as well to book, even for a midweek lunch, but at busy times they open the upstairs restaurant; some tables to one side have views of the church.

Food serving times:
Monday-Saturday:
  12pm-2.15pm, 7pm-9.30pm
Sunday:
  12pm-2.15pm, 7pm-9pm
Closed dinner 25-26 December
Prices:
Meals: a la carte 15.00/25.00

South East 2 miles by A265, off B2096. Parking

Typical Dishes

Liver pate with Cumberland Sauce

Duck breast with port and cinnamon sauce

Black pepper meringue

Piltdown

033 Peacock Inn

Shortbridge, Piltdown TN22 3XA
Tel.: (01825) 762463 - Fax: (01825) 762463

 VISA

Harveys Best, Fuller's London Pride, Old Speckled Hen

A quintessentially English pub in the heart of the Sussex countryside, its 16C black and white timbered exterior enhanced by two very neatly trimmed yew trees at the entrance. There are benches at the front, too, and a sign with a brightly painted peacock in full plumage. The rear has a children's play area and large paved terrace, where they sometimes host barbecues in summer. Inside are spacious bar rooms, full of character: log fire, dark beams, brass ornaments and an old framed peacock tapestry in pride of place. A variety of photos cover the walls: those of the owner with celebrity guests testify to the Peacock's enduring popularity and warm atmosphere. Menus are traditional and unpretentious, complemented by chef's blackboard specials, with fresh ingredients from mainly local suppliers. The home-made desserts are warmly recommended.

Food serving times:
Monday-Sunday:
12pm-2.30pm, 6pm-9.30pm
Closed 25-26 and
31 December
Booking advisable at
weekends
Prices:
Meals: a la carte 12.00/30.00

Typical Dishes

Crayfish and smoked salmon

Chicken with cashew nuts,
garlic butter

Fruit crème brûlée

By Shortbridge Lane, off A272.
Parking

Rushlake Green

034 The Horse and Groom

The Green, Rushlake Green TN21 9QE

Tel.: (01435) 830320 - Fax: (01435) 830310
e-mail: chappellhatpeg@aol.com - Website: www.thebestpubsinsussex.co.uk

      VISA AE MC

Harveys Best, Shepherd Neame, Master Brew and 1 monthly changing guest ale

One for the traditionalist in all of us: horsebrasses twinkle, copper kettles gleam and ostlers and riders pose proudly with their glossy steeplechasers in the old prints above the fire. The two cosy, beamed rooms, their candles lit even at lunchtime, are at either end; although the Gun Room, its three fearsome-looking shotguns kept safely in the rack, is set slightly apart from the bar, the same menu is available throughout the pub. Using seasonal produce and market-fresh meat and fish, it's generous country cooking through and through. Full-flavoured roast lamb and other classics are served in good-sized portions and with prompt and friendly staff into the bargain, it's no wonder they're busy.

Food serving times:
Monday-Sunday:
12pm-2.15pm, 7pm-9.15pm
(-9pm on Sundays)

Prices:
Meals: a la carte 20.00/35.00

Typical Dishes

Asparagus with crispy pancetta

Monkfish wrapped in Parma ham

Chocolate pudding

3mi Southeast of Heathfield by B2096. Parking

Wartling

035 **Lamb Inn**

Wartling BN27 1RY

Tel.: (01323) 832116
Website: www.lambinnwartling.co.uk

   VISA **AE** **①** **M©**

 Harveys, Leval Best, London Pride

On the edge of the Pevensey Levels, this part 16C pub is personally run and proudly traditional. Little black-framed windows give it the look of a country cottage from the outside, as do the dark beams and pretty chintz patterns in the little front bar, while the more spacious restaurant is decorated in shades of terracotta and dusky pink. The menu – served throughout – changes weekly, with plenty of thought going into the choice of ingredients and new season's produce, be it Southdown lamb or additive-free beef from the farm right next door. The choice of sausages and pies varies every day, and there's a separate seafood menu. Chirpy and prompt staff serve their guests well.

Food serving times:
Monday-Sunday:
11.45am-2.15pm,
6.45pm-9pm

Prices:
Meals: a la carte 17.40/27.15

Typical Dishes

Prawn and crayfish ravioli

Turbot on grain mash with 3 cheese sauce

Blackberry cheesecake with cherry ice cream

3.75miles Southeast of Herstmonceaux by A271 and Wartling Rd. Parking

Easton

036 Chestnut Horse

Easton SO21 1EG

Tel.: (01962) 779257 - Fax: (01962) 779037

 VISA ⓂⒸ

 Ringwood Best, Courage Best, Chestnut Horse Bitter

Just a short drive from the centre of Winchester, The Chestnut Horse is a real find, with individuality and charm written right through it. For a start, there's the bar, showing its age in the best sense. A log fire, beams and rows of pint pots and jugs bring out the building's 16C character, while two more formal rooms introduce subtle changes of style: "Green" makes a natural setting for lunch, "Red", with dark tones offset by candlelight, is better for intimate dinners, but the pretty rear terrace, with an abundance of plants and flowers, trumps them both on a hot summer's day – friendly staff are happy to guide you round them all before you decide! An extensive menu runs from pub favourites to more modern dishes and a big line-up of specials.

Food serving times:

Monday-Saturday:
12pm-2pm, 6.30pm-9.30pm

Sunday: 12pm-5pm

Closed 25 December

Prices:

Meals: 10.00 (Monday to Saturday lunch) and a la carte 24.00/30.00

Typical Dishes

Avocado and warm bacon salad

Home-made steak and kidney pudding

Vanilla crème brulee

4mi North East of Winchester by A3090 off B3047. Parking

Littleton

037 The Running Horse

88 Main Road, Littleton SO22 6QS

Tel.: (01962) 880218 - Fax: (01962) 886596

e-mail: runninghorse@btconnect.com - Website: www.therunninghorsepubrestaurant.co.uk

  VISA AE

Ringwood Best, Itchen Valley and 1 guest beer

Delightful service from a considerate and well-drilled young team is just one element in a winning formula for the Running Horse, which has changed almost out of recognition from the run-down village pub that finally closed its doors. They re-opened on a radical rehaul – an attractive modern bar and a cleanly styled restaurant, smart wicker-backed chairs, delightful terrace with wrought iron furniture, even trendy new cutlery – and the gamble is paying off, with a good many takers for lighter bar lunches and the sophisticated but well-priced evening menu offering an enjoyable balance of full, fresh flavours.

Food serving times:
Tuesday-Saturday:
  12pm-2pm, 6.30pm-9.30pm
Sunday: 12pm-3pm
Closed 25-26 December and first 2 weeks January
Prices:
Meals: a la carte 27.00/33.00
🛏 **9 rooms :** 85.00

Typical Dishes

Lamb chop, with grilled aubergine and rosemary oil

Grilled tuna with gingered greens

Lemon and raisin cheesecake

2.5mi North West from Winchester by B3049. Parking

Ovington

038 Bush Inn

Ovington

Tel.: 01962 732764 - Fax: 01962 735130
e-mail: thebushinn@wadworth.co.uk

  VISA **AE** **MC**

Wadworths 6X, IPA, JCB, Summersault, Tomstipple, Old Timer and changing guest ales

Well-hidden down a winding country road, near the banks of the river Itchen, the 17C Bush Inn has all the understated friendliness you would hope to find in a family-run pub. Over the years it's accumulated an interesting collection of framed photographs and country memorabilia, and the feeling in the four little rooms, mostly for dining, is an easy and very natural one. Choose a table and pick from the blackboard: with a genuinely appetising range of wholesome, well-made dishes, including daily specials, this could be harder than you'd expect. Friendly service deserves a mention too, but the real bonus here is a lovely garden with plenty of seating: add some sun, and it's just perfect.

Food serving times:
Monday-Sunday:
12pm-2.30pm
Monday-Thursday:
7pm-9pm
Friday-Saturday:
7pm-9.30pm
Closed 25 December
Prices:
Meals: a la carte 22.00/35.00

Typical Dishes
Thai spiced Crabcake
Seabass fillet, saffron and mustard sauce
Roast rack of lamb, herb and mustard crust

5.75 mi East by B3404 and A31. Parking

Romsey

039 Three Tuns

58 Middlebridge St, Romsey SO51 8HL
Tel.: (01794) 512639

 VISA M@

Ringwood Best Bitter, Gales HSB

Romsey town centre has seen various changes over the years, but The Three Tuns remains an engaging constant. It's been in Middlebridge Street for 300 years and the perennial log fire and timbers help it retain its period feel, much to the contentment of a large group of regulars. A facelift, though, is evident in the slate flooring and understated décor. The fairly large bar with vast wooden tables inhabits one side of the pub; a restaurant the other – this has a haphazard, rustic appeal with bare tables of various shapes and sizes alongside mismatched chairs. Relaxed but helpful service will ease you into a modern menu which you'll find characterised by capable, well-judged cooking using first-rate ingredients, not least game from the nearby Broadlands Estate, with lighter dishes available at lunchtime.

Food serving times:
Monday-Saturday:
    12pm-2pm, 7pm-9.30pm
Sunday: 12pm-2pm
Prices:
Meals: a la carte 25.00/33.00

Towards the western end of the town, off the by-pass. Parking

Typical Dishes

Gazpacho of Dorset crab

Gressingham duck breast, fricasse of summer vegetables

Lemon Parfait

Southampton

040 White Star Dining Rooms

28 Oxford Street, Southampton SO14 3DJ

Tel.: (023) 8082 1990

e-mail: manager@whitestartavern.co.uk - Website: www.whitestartavern.co.uk

Fuller's London Pride

N aming their new venture after the Titanic's ill-fated shipping line was a brave move but, a few years on, it's full steam ahead for the team behind the White Star, who are making their London experience count in Southampton's wining and dining district. Neatly redesigned, the former chain pub is now split into an intimate lounge bar - complete with chill-out leather armchairs - and a comfortable dining room, spacious, understated and stylishly functional: all the old tables can be extended if a few more friends show up for dessert. A British/eclectic menu with a pleasantly familiar ring to it goes more free-form at lunch, with no distinction between "starters" and "mains".

Food serving times:
Monday-Thursday:
   12pm-2.30pm, 6.30pm-9pm
Friday-Saturday:
   12pm-3pm, 6.30pm-10pm
Sunday: 12pm-9pm
Closed 25-26 December and
1 January
Prices:
Meals: 14.95/24.95 and a la
carte 19.50/35.00

Typical Dishes

Tempura prawns

Sirloin with sauteed new potatoes

Crème vanille with basil infused strawberries

Parking meters directly outside

Sparsholt

041 **Plough Inn**

Main Road, Sparsholt SO21 2NW

Tel.: (01962) 776353 - Fax: (01962) 776400

 ☂ 🍷 *VISA* ⓂⒸ

Wadworth 6X and JCB, Henry's IPA, Summersault

P roving that people really will go the extra mile for a good pub lunch, the friendly Plough Inn is often packed, even in midweek, so booking is a must. Even at its busiest, though, the atmosphere in the softly lit bars and lounges remains relaxed and warm, and in fine weather, a good-hearted crowd from the village and beyond are only too happy to spread out onto the front terrace and cottage garden, or take a seat on the benches in the field at the back, where the pub's donkeys crop the pasture with Eeyore-ish reserve. Back inside, big blackboard menus of wholesome country cooking offer some subtle variation: after a range of tasty starters, the mains diverge, with lighter pub fare on the one hand and more elaborate entrées on the other.

Food serving times:
Monday-Sunday:
 12pm-2pm, 6pm-9pm
Closed 25 December
(booking essential)
Prices:
Meals: a la carte 18.00/25.00

Typical Dishes

Plaice, salmon and spinach

Chicken with asparagus, wild mushrooms

Roasted plum and almond tart

3.5mi Northwest of Winchester by B3049. Parking

Stockbridge

042 The Greyhound

31 High St, Stockbridge SO20 6EY
Tel.: (01264) 810833 - Fax: (01264) 811184

  VISA

Butcombe

Standing snugly at one end of Stockbridge High Street since time immemorial, this honey-hued old stone pub now tends to attract a rather smartly casual set after a 21C clean-up in which its 18C features were carefully restored and brought to prominence. Country pursuits are a way of life around here, and locals tell tales at the bar of their fishing exploits along the nearby River Test. Bow your head if needs be to make progress through a characterful, low-beamed lounge, to arrive at the bare tables and wood flooring of two dining areas where 'shabby chic' is very chic indeed. It feels like a pub, but quite clearly has restaurant sensibilities reflected in the chef's metropolitan background and modern Anglo-French menus, which are prepared with skill and imagination and served by an enthusiastic brigade of young waiters.

Food serving times:
Monday-Thursday:
12pm-2pm, 7pm-9.30pm
Friday-Sunday:
12pm-2.30pm
Closed 25 and 26 December and 1 January
Prices:
Meals: a la carte 25.00/39.00

Typical Dishes

Gravadlax with new potato and fennel salad

Fillet of Scotch beef with smoked bacon dumplings

Vanilla rice pudding

Parking

Whitchurch

043 Red House Inn

21 London St, Whitchurch RG28 7LH
Tel.: (01256) 895558 - Fax: (01256) 895966

VISA MC

Cheriton Pots

To save any fruitless searches for red houses, what you're actually looking for is a row of 400 year-old whitewashed cottages: as you'll see inside, from the black and white photographs of the market town in bygone days, the conversion took place nearly a century ago. One door leads to the public bar, the other takes you into the restaurant: uncovered pine tables, a big mirror giving a pleasing sense of space and a large brick fireplace by the bar providing a homely atmosphere. Blackboard menus and the more formal printed menu have the same modern style. Weather permitting, tables are also available on the raised terrace outside.

Food serving times:
Monday-Sunday:
    12pm-2pm, 6pm-9.30pm
Prices:
Meals: a la carte 23.00/30.00

Typical Dishes

Seared scallops with chorizo

Lamb rump with couscous, baby carrots and madeira jus

Chocolate pie with berry coulis and crème fraiche

In the village. Parking

Winchester

044 **The Black Boy**

1 Wharf Hill, Winchester SO23 9NQ

Tel.: 01962 861754

  VISA **MC**

Cheriton Pots Ale, Ringwood Best and 2 other guest ales

Fire buckets, reading glasses, door keys, books, corks and radiograms fill the gloriously quirky interior of this personally run pub. After a cordial greeting from the pub dog, settle down in one of the many relaxing corners with real fires and squashy sofas: one snug room is bathed in the gentle warmth of its own Aga. The lunchtime choice is not much more than sandwiches and a couple of hot dishes – tasty enough, and worth trying, but not in the same league as the evening menu, which offers fine seasonal and modern dishes with a touch of imagination. The Black Boy is not the kind of place you'd find by chance, but if you're after a casual, intimate dinner, that's yet another reason to go.

Food serving times:
Wednesday- Sunday lunch:
12pm-2pm
Tuesday-Saturday dinner:
7pm-9pm
Closed 2 weeks Christmas- New Year, 2 weeks September and Sunday dinner to Tuesday lunch
Prices:
Meals: a la carte 24.25/29.40

Typical Dishes

Chicken and duck liver pâté

Fillets of sea bass, herb butter sauce

Warm chocolate fondant, ginger ice cream

To the South of the city centre, near the junction of Chesil St and Quarry Rd.

Winchester

045 **Wykeham Arms**

75 Kingsgate St, Winchester SO23 9PE

Tel.: (01962) 853834 - Fax: (01962) 854411

e-mail: wykehamarms@accommodating-inns.co.uk

  room VISA AE ⊙ ⓶③

HSB, Gales Best Bitter, Butser and 1 guest ale

On a quiet street between the Cathedral and the College stands Winchester's third great institution, the Wykeham Arms. Founded back in the 1700s, it continues to draw a loyal local following but should be first on any visitor's itinerary too: intimate and charming, its comfortable snugs contain an intriguing collection of prints, flags, rackets, straw boaters and other sporting and school memorabilia, as well as old oak desks from the nearby classrooms. Well-informed young staff serve with enthusiasm and a good sense of timing; fresh, appetising cuisine – a modern-classic blend with nicely weighted flavours – puts the region's seasonal produce at the top of the list. Bedrooms are split between the main house – rich colour scheme and historical prints – and the annex across the road; the oak-panelled breakfast room is on the first floor.

Food serving times:

Monday-Saturday:
12pm-2.30pm,
6.30pm-8.45pm

Sunday: 12pm-2.30pm

Closed 25 December

Prices:

Meals: 14.50/18.50 (Sunday lunch only) and a la carte 19.75/30.50

14 rooms : 57.00/135.00

Typical Dishes

Seared scallops with tempura prawns

Roast rack of lamb with rosemary and redcurrant jus

Passion fruit delice with tuile

Near (St Mary's) Winchester College. Access to the car park via Canon Street only

Freshwater

046 Red Lion

Church Pl, Freshwater PO40 9BP

Tel.: (01983) 754925 - Fax: (01983) 754925
e-mail: info@redlion-wight.co.uk - Website: www.redlion-wight.co.uk

Wadworth 6X, Fuller's London Pride, Flowers Original, Goddards

A handsome, part 14C building with little bay windows, this is as traditionally English a pub as any you might find on the slightly larger island across the water, and the characterful country style continues in its rustic interior. Run with a mix of enthusiastic quirkiness and good old fashioned hard work, it continues to do a thriving trade, with the focus squarely on a blackboard menu with daily variations – mostly traditional in its essentials, the pub's cuisine makes good use of its fresh ingredients, including newly-landed Channel fish. On busy days, your best chance of a seat may be in the garden or under the mini-marquee: a fixture since 2000, "the Dome" gets rather more use than the Greenwich version, but is generally reserved for private parties.

Food serving times:
Monday-Sunday:
    12pm-2pm, 6.30pm-9pm
Closed 25 December
Prices:
Meals: a la carte 16.00/25.00

Typical Dishes

Duck and port terrine

Braised lamb shank with minted gravy

Bread and butter pudding

By the saltings of the River Yar. Parking

Biddenden

047 **Three Chimneys**

Hareplain Road, Biddenden TN27 8LW

Tel.: (01580) 291472

  VISA

Adnams Best, Harveys Best

Here's a pub full of Kentish character: it's only down the road from Sissinghurst, so make a day of it and combine a visit to both. The Three Chimneys has been around since about 1420, and its lovely old exterior has a rough thick cream coat. The attractive terrace is packed in summer; at other times, don't miss the definitively rustic bar: yellowing walls, dried hops, absurdly characterful (and original) beams, little burner fire, lots of rough furniture. The restaurant, at the back, is smarter, in a palette of chocolate brown, with leather chairs, sealed wooden floors, painted wood-panelled walls and spacious tables; what's more, it faces the garden (where only Ploughman's are served). Dishes change regularly, from substantial salads to fish and steaks. Puddings are all homemade, in keeping with the warm, genuine feel that pervades here.

Food serving times:
Monday-Saturday:
12pm-1.50pm (Sunday 2.30pm),
6.30pm-9.30pm (Sunday 9pm)
Closed 25 December and 31 December
Prices:
Meals: a la carte 26.00/32.00

West 1.5mi off A262. Parking

Typical Dishes

Home made fishcakes

Salmon, gremolata crust

Dark chocolate and Baileys torte

Bodsham

048 Froggies at the Timber Batts

School Lane, Bodsham TN25 5JQ

Tel.: 01223 750237 - Fax: 01223 750176
e-mail: joel@thetimberbatts.co.uk - Website: www.thetimberbatts.co.uk

VISA *MC*

London Pride, Adnams Southwold, Woodfordes Wherry

A little piece of "la France profonde" in a lovely, creeper-clad, early Tudor pub. This unlikely success story is all down to the charming, French-born landlord who provides gentle bar-room bonhomie, superintends the spit-roast at the summer barbecues and teams up with his son in the kitchen to produce light bar lunches and unfussy and authentic Gallic classics from the regional cookbook. Fine fish and game are sourced locally, but the cheeseboard and the wine list – including a few vintages from a cousin's vineyard by the Loire – are proudly continental. Care and appreciation are obvious, and echoed in the service: staff are genuinely happy to recommend, explain, or provide enthusiastic translations. Frog ornaments decorate the brick pillars and window sills, and a welcoming, cosy feeling prevails.

Food serving times:
Tuesday-Sunday:
    12pm-2.30pm
Tuesday-Saturday:
    7pm-9.30pm

Closed 1 week January, 1 week September, Sunday dinner and Monday except Bank holidays when closed Tuesday
-French-

Prices:
Meals: 20.00 (Sunday lunch) and a la carte 23.00/30.00

Typical Dishes

Stuffed mussels

Confit of duck

Crème brûlée

Off B2068 between Canterbury and Hythe. Close to Wye. Parking

Bridge

049 ## White Horse Inn

53, High St., Bridge CT4 5LA

Tel.: (01227) 830249 - Fax: (01227) 832814

e-mail: thewaltons_thewhitehorse@hotmail.com - Website: www.whitehorsebridge.co.uk

🍷 **VISA** **AE** **MC**

Up to 4 regularly changing ales

Particularly proud of their commitment to small local suppliers, not to mention their Kentish wines from Tenterden vineyards, the team at the White Horse have put together two menus with a common local and traditional theme. One, served in the classically styled dining room with more formal presentation and the little restaurant extras, has a touch more seasonality to it, while the bar menu combines long-standing pub favourites with more modern or original dishes. The British and Irish cheeseboard, with specialities from as close to home as Thanet and as far afield as Cork, deserves a menu in itself, and gets one, complete with tasting notes.

Food serving times:
Monday-Saturday:
    12pm-2pm, 6.30pm-9.30pm
Sunday: 12pm-2pm
Closed 25 December and
1 January
Prices:
Meals: 12.95/23.50 and a la carte 12.95/35.00

5 miles from Canterbury, off A2. Parking.

Typical Dishes

Pork terrine

Chicken with olive crust

Melting chocolate pudding with white chocolate panna cotta

Brookland

050 **Yew & Ewe**

High St, Brookland TN29 9QR

Tel.: 01797 344215 - Fax: 01797 344373

e-mail: info@yewandewe.co.uk - Website: www.yewandewe.co.uk

VISA MC

Adnams Broadside, Heart of Rother, Gadds No. 7

Beside Brookland's interesting parish church – and its churchyard planted with yews – stands the 15C village pub. As a listed building it, too, has tradition on its side, and the renovation inside suggests a careful blend of new and classic pub style. Thick oak tables, smart, worn-effect leather chairs, modern art and ancient sandblasted beams are all part of the comfortable compromise. So too is a combination of menus – a choice of lunchtime bar food appears alongside the main lunch and dinner menu, while on Sundays they stick with a classic roast. The friendly owners also take their beer very seriously and aren't afraid to canvass their regulars: a wish list displays the latest suggestions for guest ales and ciders, while badges and pump clips behind the bar announce coming attractions from the cellar.

Food serving times:

Monday to Sunday:
12pm-2.30pm,
6.30pm-9.30pm

Closed Monday October to June

Prices:

Meals: a la carte 16.00/25.00

Typical Dishes

Crab cakes, chilli and lime dressing

Roasted fillet of monkfish in Serrano ham

Chocolate Pecan brownie

Off A259 between Rye and New Romney. Parking.

Dargate

051 **The Dove** *We most liked*

Plum Pudding Lane, Dargate ME13 9HB
Tel.: (01227) 751360

🏠 ♀ *VISA* Ⓜ︎Ⓒ︎

Shepherd Neame Master Brew

Unremarkable on the outside, this Victorian redbrick pub feels much friendlier once you walk up to the bar: the smiling landlady is only too pleased to sort out drinks, talk you through the menu and find you a table. Three little pine-fitted bar-rooms are warmed by open fires and decorated with black and white photos – a real visual history of village, pub and landlords down the years. A surprisingly extensive menu balances classic and modern influences to good effect: well-judged and richly flavourful dishes with solid French base. Even with one or two slightly pricier dishes, this is excellent value for money.

Food serving times:
Tuesday: 12pm-2pm
Wednesday-Saturday:
                 12pm-2pm, 7pm-9pm
Sunday: 12pm-2pm
(booking essential)
Prices:
Meals: a la carte 23.50/32.00

Typical Dishes

Crevettes with pickled ginger and herbs

Roast duck with crushed new potatoes with tapenade

Apple and almond tart

Just off the A299 between Faversham and Whitstable; turn right at junction, 3/4mi on unmarked road to The Dove. Parking

Igtham Common

052 Harrow Inn

Common Rd, Igtham Common TN15 9EB
Tel.: (01732) 885912 - Fax: (01732) 885912

VISA *MC*

Greene King IPA, Abbot and 1 guest ale

Don't be misled by the Harrow Inn's location, down a sleepy little lane in a Kentish hamlet – you'll have to get here pretty early to be sure of securing a seat in this pretty, part 17C stone and brick pub. An open fire divides the lovely, pleasingly traditional bar, although you might also find a free table in the back dining room and conservatory extension, where a printed menu replicates the list on the blackboard. With its share of more inventive recipes, there's a little more to this good, honest country cooking than you might expect: enjoy a tasty light lunch before a trip to nearby Knowle or the Tudor castle at Ightham Mote. Cheerful service.

Food serving times:
Tuesday-Saturday:
  12pm-2pm, 6pm-9pm
Sunday: 12pm-2pm
Closed 1 January,
26 December, Bank Holiday
Mondays
(fixed price menu Sunday)
Prices:
Meals: 23.95 and a la carte
18.00/30.00

Typical Dishes

Crab spring roll

Lobster ravioli

Lemon meringue roulade

5mi South East of Sevenoaks by A25 on Common Road. Parking

Lower Hardres

053 The Granville

Street End, Lower Hardres CT4 7AL
Tel.: 01227 700402 - Fax: 01227 700925

 Masterbrew and Shepherd Neames seasonal Ale

Though big and open-plan in design, The Granville couldn't be more different from the chain-run drinking hangars of Britain's town centres. Light, well-kept and comfortable, its split into nicely airy sections which still share the good overall buzz of the place, and the service, though wonderfully laid-back, remains personal and helpful. The varied, interesting selection of dishes, frequently changing, is chalked up on the blackboard and delivers all the liveliness, piquancy and balance it promises. A serious regard for ingredients makes for distinct, resonant flavours: greens taste a fresh, chlorophyll green, and the excellent fish, much of it from the Kent coast, is always worth a try. Devotees of The Sportsman, Seasalter, will notice a strong family resemblance.

Food serving times:
Tuesday-Saturday:
12pm-2pm, 7pm-9pm
Closed 25 December
Prices:
Meals: a la carte 17.00/35.00

Typical Dishes

Grilled local baby sole, tartare sauce

Roast chicken and summer chanterelles

Treacle tart, Jersey cream

3mi South of Canterbury on B2068. Parking

Pluckley

054 Dering Arms 🛏

Station Rd, Pluckley TN27 0RR

Tel.: (01233) 840371 - Fax: (01233) 840498
e-mail: info@deringarms.com - Website: www.deringarms.com

 🍷 **VISA** **AE** **DC** **MC**

🍺 *Geachers, Dering and Gold Star*

Step through the heavy, original doors of this mid-19C Dutch-gabled former hunting lodge and experience the genuine feel of a 'local'. A pleasant rural atmosphere is evoked from blazing log fires, reclaimed tables and chairs, farming implements and bars festooned with hops. Emphasis is on the hefty seafood menus. You might find salmon fishcakes with sorrel sauce; monkfish with bacon, orange and cream; or skate wing with capers and black butter. If you're not in the mood for fish, then opt for the likes of duck or the pie of the day. Afterwards, order a pint of real farm cider – the Dering specialises in them - and flop into a leather armchair in the cosy lounge.

Food serving times:
Tuesday-Saturday:
    12pm-2pm, 7pm-9.30pm
Sunday: 12pm-2pm
Closed 26-27 December,
1 January
Prices:
Meals: a la carte 18.00/34.00
🛏 **3 rooms :** 35.00/45.00

Typical Dishes

Chicken livers sauteed with onion, mushroom and bacon

Fillet of red mullet with couscous and saffron sauce

Chocolate fudge cake

1.5mi Southeast of Bethersden rd. Beside the Railway Station. Parking

Seasalter

055 ## The Sportsman *we most liked*

Faversham Rd, Seasalter CT5 4BP

Tel.: (01227) 273370 - Fax: (01227) 262314

 ⚎ 🍷 *VISA* ⓜⓒ

Shepherd Neame Master Brew, Porter, Late Red, Goldings, Bishops Finger

Sheltering in the lee of the sea wall, this rather ramshackle pub doesn't promise much; inside, though, it's a different story. The simple, modern styling in pale pine looks a little stark at first, but as the log fires get going, the front and back bars fill up with a good mix of weekenders and regulars, sheep huddle on the marshes and circling gulls are blown past the window, it starts to feel quite cosy. A chatty, knowledgeable team, led by brothers Phil and Steve, runs the place with real enthusiasm, preparing a good-value blackboard menu centred on well-chosen seafood. Skillful combinations of flavours mean it's hard to put a foot wrong. Excellent quality and value.

Food serving times:
Tuesday-Saturday:
    12pm-2pm, 7pm-9pm
Sunday: 12pm-2pm
Closed 25 December
Prices:
Meals: a la carte 23.00/30.00

Typical Dishes

Crab, asparagus and hollandaise salad

Seabass with cockle and summer vegetable pistou

Brioche with strawberries

2mi Southwest of Whitstable and then 2mi Southwest following coast road. Parking

Speldhurst

056 **George & Dragon**

Spelhurst Hill, Speldhurst TN3 0NN

Tel.: 01892 863125

e-mail: julian@george-and-dragon-speldhurst.co.uk - Website: www.george-and-dragon-speldhurst.co.uk

     VISA M©

An ideal blend of North London pub style and deep-rooted Kentish loyalty, a sentiment fully returned by the regulars, who stop to read the parish news pinned up inside the door. Its interior is increasingly trendy but still fits perfectly and hasn't upset the welcomingly mellow but busy mood. Arty black-and-white shots of the owners' favourite pheasant shooters, chicken rearers and all-England cheesemakers – imagine Mario Testino and Lord Snowdon at the farmers' market – are a tribute to the primacy of fine ingredients. Here, "imported" food comes from the other side of the Medway and the chef regularly sends suppliers gleaning, foraging and rummaging round the county to unearth produce in the wild. Vigorously tasty dishes – combining culinary finesse with flavour in the raw – offers diners a real scope of seasonal originality.

Food serving times:
Monday-Saturday:
12pm-2.30pm, 7pm-10.30pm
Sunday: 12pm-5pm
Prices:
Meals: a la carte 20.00/30.00

3 ,5 mi North of Royal Tunbridge Wells by A26. Parking

Typical Dishes

Smoked eel with beetroot relish

Belly of pork with roasted apple

Elderflower and pear trifle

West Peckham

057 Swan on the Green

West Peckham ME18 5JW

Tel.: (01622) 812271 - Fax: (0870) 0560556

e-mail: bookings@swan-on-the-green.co.uk - Website: www.swan-on-the-green.co.uk

 VISA **AE** **①** **MC**

> *On-site microbrews include Trumpeter Best, Bewick Special, Mild, Ginger and Fuggles*

Pub settings rarely come more attractively old English than this – the Swan's redbrick and ornate gabled exterior sits idyllically by the green, right next to the village's Saxon church. There's no pub garden, but benches perch along the terrace at the front. Inside, a framed history puts the inn's origins at 1526, but it's been given a pleasing modern makeover with pale wood throughout: the dried hops and real fire add a rustic twist. At the back is a micro-brewery, so a selection of unique ales are chalked up on the board behind the bar. There's a loyal local following and menus, featuring an interesting eclectic à la carte, change weekly. Try to visit in summer, when the owners provide blankets for you to eat on the green.

Food serving times:

Tuesday-Saturday:
12pm-2pm, 7pm-9pm

Monday: 12pm-2pm

Closed 25 December, 1 January

Prices:

Meals: a la carte 20.00/27.00

Typical Dishes

Crevettes with chilled poached salmon

Chargrilled fillet steak

Whisky and honey brulee

7.75mi South West of Maidstone by A26 and B2016. Follow sign to church and green. Parking

Barnard Gate

058 The Boot Inn

Barnard Gate OX29 6XE

Tel.: (01865) 881231 - Fax: (01865) 882119
e-mail: info@theboot-inn.com - Website: www.theboot-inn.com

   VISA MC

 Hook Norton Best

The Cotswold stone walls of this eclectic pub are covered with the footwear of the famous from Stanley Matthews to the Bee Gees, though it's not clear what drinks, if any, they ordered at the bar and whether a pint was paid for with a pair of old trainers. However, elsewhere at the Boot, tradition plays a stronger role: snug corners, welcoming fire, beams and flagstones. Tables are rustic to the core, and chairs clatter on bare boards. Eating at lunchtime can be a simple affair - thick cut sandwiches or a plate of gammon and chips - but things get a little more elaborate in the evenings, with a mixture of traditional and more inventive dishes to be enjoyed in the candlelight. Friendly, approachable service comes naturally here.

Food serving times:
Monday-Sunday:
   12pm-2.30pm, 7pm-10pm
(booking essential)
Prices:
Meals: a la carte 18.75/25.95

Typical Dishes

Chicken, coriander, vegetable roulade

Chicken supreme

Rhubarb and vanilla fool

3.25mi East of Witney by B4022 off A40. Parking

Britwell Salome

059 **The Goose**

Britwell Salome OX49 5LG
Tel.: (01491) 612304 - Fax: (01491) 613945

Hook Norton Best Bitter and occasional guest ales

The Goose's kitchen was once famously run by Prince Charles' personal chef, and the former gastronomer-royal has left this lovely period pub in good keeping, passing the spatula to his right-hand man. It remains a charming and astutely judged blend of pub and restaurant, its stylish bar - comfy sofas and a faint aroma of wood smoke - leading on to a dining room with blue glassware, white china and a easy air of good taste. If sparkling, attentive service from a team in Oxford-cloth shirts and aprons deserves a special mention, the food itself steals the show. Waitresses will talk you through an outstanding-value set lunch or introduce a more elaborate but still concise and balanced menu – confidently prepared, deliciously moreish dishes burst with seasonal flavour and show a trust in quality produce that would please HRH. An enclosed rear terrace is perfect for summer dining. A real delight.

Food serving times:
Monday-Saturday:
   12pm-2.30pm, 7pm-9pm
Sunday: 12pm-3pm
Prices:
Meals: 15.00/18.00 and a la carte 22.50/34.50

Typical Dishes

Scallops, with homedried tomatoes and parmesan crisp

Braised lamb, creamed spinach

Hot passion fruit soufflé

Between Watlington and Benson off B4009. Parking

Buckland

060 ## Lamb Inn

Lamb Lane, Buckland SN7 8QN

Tel.: (01367) 870484 - Fax: (01367) 870675
e-mail: enquiries@thelambatbuckland.co.uk - Website: www.thelambatbuckland.co.uk

      rest **VISA** **MC**

Adnams Broadside, Hook Norton

This charming 18C pub luxuriates in a quiet village of Cotswold stone. Family owned for a number of years, it boasts a well-established local reputation and an extremely comfy atmosphere prevails, suitably enhanced by soft lighting, real log fire, and sheep motifs which show up in paintings, curios and even the capet. Choose to eat in a characterful beamed room or more formal linen clad dining area. Either way, the same blackboard menus are served; these consist of accomplished, traditional dishes, typified by locally smoked prawns and salad, loin of pork with wild mushrooms, and raspberry brulée with raspberry sorbet.

Food serving times:
Tuesday-Saturday:
12pm-2.30pm, 7pm-9.30pm
(-10pm Saturday)
Sunday: 12pm-2.30pm
Closed 2 weeks Christmas-New Year
Prices:
Meals: 12.00/18.50 and a la carte 20.00/35.00

Typical Dishes

Sea trout with asparagus

Duck breast with apple and calvados sauce

Petit pot a la crème

Between Faringdon and Kingston Bagpuize off A420. Parking

Burford

061 **Lamb Inn**

Sheep St, Burford OX18 4LR

Tel.: (01993) 823155 - Fax: (01993) 822228

e-mail: info@lambinnburford.co.uk - Website: www.cotswold-inns-hotel.co.uk

Y ⅙⨯rest **VISA** Ⓜ️Ⓒ

 Hook Norton, Wadworth 6X, Butcombe

Weathered local stone announces this strikingly relaxed part 14C inn, set prominently in a picture-postcard market town. The interior is as quietly charming as you would expect: flagstone floors and open log fires in three antique furnished lounges. Go through a separate entrance to a cosy bar where a good selection of real ales is enjoyed by the regulars. A classically formal restaurant reflects the age of the inn: appealing menus mix traditional and modern dishes which range from roast best end of lamb with sweetbreads and bubble and squeak, to smoked cod with cauliflower cheese and mustard potatoes. Bedrooms underwent a refurbishment early in 2004: now you can tumble blissfully into beds clothed in fine Egyptian linen and quality fabrics.

Food serving times:
Monday-Sunday:
  12pm-3pm, 6.30pm-9.30pm
Prices:
Meals: 32.50 and a la carte 21.90/32.95
15 rooms : 115.00/ 235.00

Typical Dishes

Pressed ham hock terrine

Red pepper and goat's cheese risotto

Apple and blackberry pancakes

In town centre. Parking on the street ›

Charlbury

062 **Bull Inn**

Sheep St, Charlbury OX7 3RR

Tel.: (01608) 810689

e-mail: info@bullinn-charlbury.com - Website: www.bullinn-charlbury.com

  VISA **MC** **JCB**

Abbot, IPA, Hook Norton

This charming hostelry has been delighting the locals of Charlbury since the 16C, and in 500 years it hasn't compromised one jot on its traditional appeal. Creeper-clad in summer, it's the quintessential country pub right down to its flagstone floors and inglenook fires. You can whet your appetite before visiting with a stroll along the banks of the River Evenlode, just five minutes' walk away. The rustic bar is divided into three booths with wicker and pine chairs; the restaurant continues the rural theme with more hardy stone floors and rugged pine tables. Concise, fresh menus have earned the Bull a fine local reputation for its cooking: you might find braised lamb shank with a mint and redcurrant gravy; smoked haddock Florentine; or chicken, smoked ham and leek casserole.

Food serving times:
Monday-Sunday:
   12pm-2pm, 7pm-9.30pm
Closed Christmas Day and New Year's Day. Closed Mondays in winter.
Closed Sunday from 4pm
Prices:
Meals: a la carte 16.95/25.00
 4 rooms : 60.00/85.00

Typical Dishes

Roasted pepper filled with ratatouille

Shank of lamb with minted gravy

Chocolate waffles

Parking

Chipping Norton

063 The Masons Arms

Banbury Rd, Swerford, Chipping Norton OX7 4AP
Tel.: (01608) 683212 - Fax: (01608) 683105

Hook Norton Best, Wadworth 6X

A roadside Cotswold inn, raised above the norm by the keenness of a husband and wife team, whose hospitable approach seems to have spread to the rest of the helpful young staff. Dating back to the 1800s, its origins are rather mysterious – quite appropriate for a former Freemason's lodge – but apart from a nod to its Masonic past near the entrance, the interior resonates with bright, 21C country style: more rattan chairs and polished floors than horse brasses and swirly carpets. In contrast, the owner is a great advocate of culinary tradition. For the most part, only local produce makes it into the kitchen, and many methods and recipes described on the blackboard owe as much to the Victorian cookbook as to contemporary cuisine. Robust, flavourful food might include braised oxtail or sea bass in gazpacho sauce. Lovely views from the garden.

Food serving times:
Monday-Sunday:
   12pm-2.15pm, 7pm-9.15pm
Closed 25-26 December
Prices:
Meals: 9.95 (Monday-Thursday) and a la carte 18.00/25.00

Typical Dishes

Goat's cheese, caramalised apples and sweet pepper coulis

Skin of beef with horseradish mash

On A361, North East of the town. Parking

Christmas Common

064 ## The Fox & Hounds

Christmas Common OX49 5HL

Tel.: (01491) 612599

Brakspear, Special, Seasonal, Hook Norton Mild

Ideally set for walkers, with the Chilterns and the Ridgeway Path to hand, the pub's been here in the hills, in what's now rare red kite territory, since the 15C; recent years have seen a bit of updating, including the new restaurant, which has metamorphosed from the old barn. The pub proper retains its tiled and beamed interior, the gentle crackle in the inglenook on all but the hottest days, a delightful, laid-back atmosphere and plenty of quirky appeal. Savoury bar dishes of a traditional stamp cry out for a good ale, organic juice or wine, so try one with your Welsh rarebit or roast ham hock; if you fancy a full meal, blackboards list a mix of modern, traditional and Mediterranean dishes. Local suppliers stock the kitchen and produce for sale here includes everything from pickled onions to beeswax and eggs from 'the man up the road'.

Food serving times:
Monday-Saturday:
    12pm-2.30pm, 6pm-9.30pm
Sunday: 12pm-4pm
Prices:
Meals: a la carte 18.00/29.00

Typical Dishes

Mackerel, warm potato salad

New season lamb, artichoke and mint cous cous

Bitter chocolate tart

South East of Watlington, near Shotridge Wood. Parking

Church Enstone

065 The Crown Inn

Mill Lane, Church Enstone OX7 4NN

Tel.: (01608) 677262 - Fax: (01608) 677394
Website: www.crowninnenstone.co.uk

 🍴 🍷 **VISA**

Hook Norton Best Bitter, Timothy Taylor Landlord, Shepherd Neame Spitfire and a guest ale

Close to the gurgling River Glyme, this 17C pub of Cotswold stone is one of the highlights of a charming little village. It's a well-kept establishment, personally run by a husband and wife team: she keeps things ticking over in the main bar while he does the cooking. Refurbishment has added a modish seagrass carpet across the floor, but other features have stayed reassuringly traditional: a cottagey bar, log fire in stone fireplace, beams and exposed stone. You can eat in two areas: a bright dining room with red hued walls and uncovered pine tables, or a conservatory extension. The lunchtime blackboard menu gives way to a more expansive repertoire in the evening, while charming, attentive service adds an extra dimension to the invariably pleasant atmosphere.

Food serving times:
Monday: 7pm-9pm
Tuesday-Saturday:
                    12pm-2pm, 7pm-9pm
Sunday: 12pm-2pm
Closed 25-26 December and 1 January. Open Bank Holiday Mondays
Prices:
Meals: a la carte 20.00/25.00

Typical Dishes

Scallops and bacon salad
Medallions of beef fillet
Warm chocolate pudding with fudge sauce

3.5mi Southeast of Chipping Norton by A44. Parking

Church Hanborough

066 **Hand & Shears**

Church Hanborough OX29 8AB

Tel.: (01993) 883337 - Fax: (01993) 881392

e-mail: handandshears@tiscali.co.uk

🍷 ✂ **_VISA_** **M©**

Hook Norton Best, Wychwood Hobgoblin

A handsome 17C inn in mellow Oxfordshire sandstone, the Hand and Shears is just the sort of place you hope you'll find in such a pretty village. It looks quite small opposite the parish church, but once inside feels positively spacious. Two richly decorated parlours off the main bar have big scrubbed pine tables for eating and drinking, while to the back an inviting lounge with leather sofas connects to an airy restaurant, its high, beamed ceiling making it look more like a converted barn than a pub. The balanced menu presents re-invented classics and Modern British dishes in equal measure, plus a very affordable set-menu lunch deal and four children's choices.

Food serving times:

Tuesday-Saturday:
12pm-2.30pm,
6.30pm-9.30pm

Sunday: 12.30pm-4pm

Prices:

Meals: a la carte 15.20/30.00

4.25mi South West of Woodstock by A44 off A4095. Opposite the church. Parking

Typical Dishes

Smoked salmon risotto

Fish pie with mussels, hake and prawns

Peaches on brioche, vanilla custard

Churchill

067 The Chequers

Church Rd, Churchill OX7 6NJ

Tel.: (01608) 659393

  VISA

 Hook Norton Best, Old Speckled Hen, Timothy Taylor Landlord, Adnams, Old Hooky

S et on the main road of a delightful Cotswold village, this charming hostelry is idyllically placed opposite All Saints Church. It's been creating quite a buzz since it opened its doors in the spring of 2004, after nine months of refurbishment, having lain idle for five years. An 18C inn lurks in there somewhere; the owners have added in a sympathetic and careful way using honey coloured Cotswold stone. The bustling atmosphere is testament to good local opinion. You can dine in two areas: downstairs – a combination of beams, high arched ceiling and exposed stone; or upstairs, where a cosy lounge is ideal for pre- or post-prandial drinks. Well-balanced menus might include pan fried swordfish with olive beurre blanc, or tenderloin of pork with grilled black pudding.

Food serving times:
Monday-Sunday:
    12pm-2pm, 7pm-9.30pm
Closed 25 December
Prices:
Meals: a la carte 20.00/25.50

Typical Dishes
Smoked haddock kedgeree
Baked port fillet on bubble and squeak
Rice pudding with stewed plums

South West of Chipping Norton by B4450. Parking.

Crays Pond

068 The White Lion

Goring Rd, Goring Heath, Crays Pond RG8 7SH

Tel.: (01491) 680471 - Fax: (01491) 681654
e-mail: reservations@innastew.com - Website: www.innastew.com

 VISA

 Greene King IPA, Abbot, Hook Norton

A stylish mix of old and new has earned this village pub outside Goring a strong local reputation. Part built in 1756, its wooden window shutters and paved terrace give it a modern veneer, but old beams and low ceilings have been retained from a refurbishment in 2003, which now sees smart oak floors combined with burgundy and sage green walls. These are adorned by framed menus from Gordon Ramsay, Le Manoir and the like, some of which were obtained from patrons' visits, others from auction. Soft wall lighting enhances a couple of roaring log fires. Eclectic dishes and good British staples dominate menus which offer a robust, hearty choice and plentiful portions. Everything is cooked freshly to order, from the homemade chips to puddings. This is a busy, popular destination: it could be worth booking at weekends.

Food serving times:
Tuesday-Saturday:
   12pm-2pm, 6pm-9.30pm
Sunday: 12pm-2pm
Closed 25-26 December,
1 January
Prices:
Meals: 16.95 and a la carte
25.00/30.00

2mi East of Goring on B4526. Parking

Typical Dishes

Ham hock rillette

Fillet of turbo with morel
and broad bean risotto

Chocolate and mascarpone
cake

279

Cuddesdon

069 The Bat & Ball Inn

High St, Cuddesdon OX44 9HJ

Tel.: (01865) 874379 - Fax: (01865) 873363
e-mail: bb@traditionalvillageinns.co.uk - Website: www.traditionalvillageinns.co.uk

  ⚲room **VISA**

Marston Pedigree, House LBW and 1 guest ale

ricket lovers will be in their element here, with enough conversation pieces to see them through lunch – and the tea interval. Scorebooks, trophies and old cigarette cards are proudly displayed and batting gloves hang above the window in the flag-floored bar, while the very rafters of the new dining room are braced with ancient stumps and well knocked-in bats: some, with a blackboard slab set into the willow, list the chef's daily specials. British cooking, hearty and plentiful, runs from venison in red wine to cod and chips, by way of salads and lunchtime baguettes or panini, all served at big pine tables by a young team who are casual, friendly and far too modest to mention Australia's defence of The Ashes. For the full Test Match Special experience, they also serve decent slabs of chocolate cake.

Food serving times:
Monday-Friday:
  12pm-2.45pm,
  6.30pm-9.45pm
Saturday-Sunday:
  12pm-9.45pm
Closed 26 December
Prices:
Meals: a la carte 17.00/30.00
7 rooms : 53.00/65.00

Typical Dishes

Garlic mushroom soup

Herb crusted cod, red pepper cream

Chocolate and strawberry shortcake

6mi East of Oxford city centre.
Parking

Faringdon

070 The Trout at Tadpole Bridge

Buckland Marsh, Faringdon SN7 8RF

Tel.: (01367) 870382
e-mail: info@troutinn.co.uk - Website: www.troutinn.co.uk

   ⇔room **VISA** MC

Youngs PA, White Horse, Ramsbury and several guest ales

This attractive old inn stands next to a pretty bridge by the Thames and is locally renowned by the anglers who gather along the riverbanks. You can watch them in action - or inaction - from the Trout's relaxing terrace: on the menus, the eponymous fish itself is caught by a local fisherman. The rustic interior has a number of charmingly refurbished rooms, boasting a mix of old pine and polished tables, assorted chairs, and newspapers and magazines lying invitingly to one side. It's most certainly a pub to stretch out in. Cooking is satisfying and reliable: game and meat come from local estates and farms, with some vegetables picked fresh from the back garden. Tasty, accomplished dishes, including seafood specials on the blackboard, are the result. Smart bedrooms may entice weary rod danglers.

Food serving times:
Monday-Saturday:
12pm-2pm, 7pm-9pm
Sunday: 12pm-2pm
Closed 25-26 December,
31 December, 1 January and
last week in January
Prices:
Meals: a la carte 18.40/31.40
6 rooms : 55.00/80.00

Typical Dishes

Scallops wrapped in pancetta

Lemon sole with fresh herb and lemon butter

Lemon posset

4.5mi Northeast of Faringdon by A417, A420 on Brampton rd. Parking ⟫

Great Tew

071 Falkland Arms

Great Tew OX7 4DB

Tel.: (01608) 683653 - Fax: (01608) 683656
e-mail: sjcourage@btconnect.com - Website: www.falklandarms.org.uk

Wadworth IPA, 6X and seasonal guest ales

A picture-perfect village inn without a scrap of preciousness or pretension. Its 17C Cotswold stone is wreathed in ivy and climbing roses; in the cosy, flag-floored bar, orderly rows of crocks and mugs hang from the beams and polished pint-pot tankards glint in the lamplight. Chalked up on the board are six classic dishes, tasty and fortifying, plus potatoes and baguettes, but plenty of the locals are happy enough with the friendly welcome, a seat on the old settles and benches, a well-kept beer and a bit of old-English aromatherapy: tins of snuff and clay pipes are sold behid the bar. The spiral staircase leads up to six charming, period styled rooms in country patterns.

Food serving times:
Monday-Saturday:
12pm-2pm, 7pm-8pm
Sunday: 12pm-2pm
Restricted opening at Christmas
(booking essential)
Prices:
Meals: a la carte 15.00/25.00
6 rooms : 50.00/110.00

Typical Dishes

Warm tomato, red onion and feta cheese tart

Slow cooked lamb shank

Lemon and thyme crème brulee

6.5mi East of Chipping Norton by A361 and B4022. Parking in village car park or opposite pub

Hanwell

072 The Moon and Sixpence

Hanwell OX17 1HW

Tel.: 01295 730544 - Fax: 01295 730147

e-mail: info@moonandsixpencehanwell.com - Website: www.moonandsixpencehanwell.com

Norton

Interesting times at Hanwell's old village inn, owned and run by two brothers who were determined to give the Moon and Sixpence more than just a quick spit and polish. Even after the most well-meaning makeovers, a new lease of community spirit is never guaranteed, but Hanwell has really taken to its new-look pub. An appealing and wide-ranging menu certainly helps, offering everything from dependable pub classics to more contemporary recipes, all soundly prepared and fairly priced; a barbecue at the back, with a little terrace next to it, gets plenty of use in the summer if the weather plays its part. The real-ale enthusiasts have no complaints either, and its modern bar is as popular as ever.

Food serving times:
Tuesday-Sunday:
    12pm-2pm (-3pm Sunday)
Monday-Sunday: 6pm-9pm
Prices:
Meals: 8.85/20.00 and a la carte 20.00/28.00

Typical Dishes

Black pudding wrapped in bacon

Lamb on sundried tomato and rosemary mash

Bitter chocolate mousse

3,5mi northwest of Banbury by A422 and B4100. Parking

Henley-on-Thames

073 The Three Tuns Foodhouse

5 The Market Pl, Henley-on-Thames RG9 2AA

Tel.: (01491) 573260
e-mail: thefoodhouse@btconnect.com

VISA MC

Brakspear

Henley isn't all about the river and the regatta. There's a smart, buzzing town beyond the bridge, and right in the heart of the market place is this little pub sandwiched between the shops. It's an early 16C hostelry with a traditional appearance: 'foodhouse' has been added to the frontage to denote its recent change of tack. There's a distinct gastro-pub style here. The front bar is quirkily fashionable, while the back has been transformed into a cosy, dining area with rough ceiling beams, a mix of oak tables and old school style chairs and an offbeat clutch of collectables and curios: many of the furnishings are supplied by a local antiques shop. Menu ingredients are also locally sourced. Much market-fresh produce goes into the interesting British and Mediterranean dishes.

Food serving times:
Monday-Saturday:
　　　　12-2.30pm, 7-9.30pm
Sunday:　　　　　12-2.30pm
Closed 25-26 December
Prices:
Meals: a la carte 20.00/35.00

In the town centre. Public parking off Greys Rd and at National Rail station

Typical Dishes
Beef, duck and celeriac terrine

Sea bass, pea and broad bean salad

Chocolate tart

Leafield

074 The Navy Oak

Lower End, Leafield OX29 9QQ

Tel.: (01993) 878496
Website: www.thenavyoak.co.uk

   VISA MC

 Hook Norton, Arkells, Adnams and Wychwood Ales

For five years this solid stone pub lay barren in its leafy environs on the eastern edge of the Cotswolds, awaiting the kiss of life. Along came Alastair and Sarah with big ideas, a warm and personal style, and refurbishment ideas that would kick-start the Navy Oak into a stylish new existence. A glowing fire, cosy seating and warm, modern colours tick all the right boxes on a chilly day when the wind blows in from the hills. There are two main dining areas exuding a fine rustic air. Though not close to the sea, this is a pub with the bracing smell of seafood in its nostrils: Alastair worked for Rick Stein, and the menu reflects his time there. Good value, appealing, daily changing menus are supplemented by a more formal, linen clad dining experience on Fridays and Saturdays.

Food serving times:
Tuesday-Saturday:
12.30-2.30, 7pm-9pm
Sunday: 12.30pm-2.30pm
closed 1-14 January and Monday
Prices:
Meals: a la carte 18.00/30.00

Typical Dishes

Escabeche of red mullet

Best end of lamb, dauphinoise potatoes

Nougatine parfait, fig compote

5.75 miles Northwest of Witney by B 4022 (Charlbury Rd). Parking

Littleworth

075 The Snooty Fox Inn

Littleworth SN7 8PW
Tel.: (01367) 240549

VISA **MC**

 Bass

To the south: the Vale of White Horse. To the north: the Thames Path. Slap bang in the middle: this yellow-painted roadside pub with gardens and a welcoming, if somewhat minimalist, ambience for visitors to this pleasant part of Oxfordshire. The spacious interior fans out into a coterie of private dining areas supported by oak beams, with wooden flooring and polished tables. Further in you can choose a nice, comfy sofa to loll around in as you peruse the huge wine rack beside a modern bar. A blazing, brick-built fireplace adorns the main dining room, where an extensive menu takes a bit of investigating. In the end, you might decide on slow-roasted half-shoulder of lamb glazed with honey, or lamb kidneys turbigo; an interesting range of fish and pasta dishes waits temptingly in the wings.

Food serving times:
Monday-Sunday:
12pm-10pm
Prices:
Meals: 14.50 and a la carte
15.00/25.00

Typical Dishes

Devilled lamb's kidneys
Fillet steak Rossini
Strawberry shortcake

3mi Northeast of Faringdon by A417 off A420. Parking

Maidensgrove

076 **The Five Horseshoes**

Maidensgrove RG9 6EX

Tel.: (01491) 641282 - Fax: (01491) 641086

   VISA

Brakspears Ordinary and Special,

Halfway between the Ridgeway and the upper Thames, this pleasantly down-to-earth pub in 17C redbrick looks out over wooded hills. In summer, you'll want to make straight for the tables in the conservatory, but the same menu is served in the cosy main bar; its low, black-beamed ceiling is papered with old banknotes, some in currencies which haven't aged nearly as well. Tasty dishes might include smoked trout and salmon salad, or pork with Stilton, mango and ginger or scampi and chips: it's substantial cooking on a traditional base and there's always a good turnout for summer barbecues in the garden. The Oxfordshire Way skirts the village, and there are plenty of shorter rambles around the woods, but walkers should make sure they have somewhere to stow their muddy boots. Stonor Park, a part-Tudor manor house, is a few minutes' drive away.

Food serving times:
Monday-Saturday:
            12pm-2pm, 6pm-9pm
Sunday: 12.30pm-3.30pm
Closed Sunday dinner
Prices:
Meals: a la carte 16.00/27.50

Typical Dishes

Goat's cheese filo parcels, onion jam

Calves liver with bacon and onions

Chocolate tart

Near Stonor Park. North of Henley by A4130 on B480, then 0.75mi West. Parking

Sibford Gower

 077 **The Wykham Arms**

Temple Mill Road, Sibford Gower OX15 5RX
Tel.: (01295) 788808 - Fax: (01295) 788806
Website: www.wykhamarms.co.uk

 VISA

Hook Norton

T he pub in this pretty village opened its characterful doors in May 2004 and became an instant hit with Oxfordshire locals and Cotswold tourists. This was a farmhouse 400 years ago. Since then, it's been added to but the thatched roof and hanging baskets mean it's still very pretty and charming. There's a bright interior, accentuated by wood flooring, original inglenook fireplace in the bar, low beamed ceiling and dining areas spread between the bar and other rooms adjacent to it. A separate spacious garden or the terrace is an ideal spot to pop a champagne cork on a summer's day. Dine on inventive modern fare; reworked contemporary British classics with local ingredients a top priority.

Food serving times:
Monday-Sunday:
    12pm-2.30pm, 6pm-10pm
Closed 25 December
Prices:
Meals: a la carte 16.00/28.00

Typical Dishes

Terrine of gammon and blue cheese

Beef with stout juices

Chocolate fondant with peanut butter ice cream

8mi West of Banbury by B4035. Parking

South Leigh

078 **Mason Arms**

South Leigh OX29 6XN
Tel.: (01993) 702485

Telfords Burton Ale

Sensitive vegetarians and critics beware: this may not be the place for you! It's run in highly 'individualistic' style by the owner who keeps a tight reign on what he serves, and whom he serves it to! The pub itself is a charming 15C thatched inn with pleasant gardens in a tranquil village. Inside, much of the interior is given over to the restaurant: antiques are set on both solid wood and linen-clad tables. Three fascinating rooms have dark walls enhanced by paintings, and cigar boxes mingling with old wine bottles: fine vintages and cigars are evidently a personal passion, and appreciation of both is encouraged. Food is quite classically based, on both menu and blackboard specials, and ranges from cottage pie to caviar. If you're staying overnight, two clean, functional bedrooms await.

Food serving times:
Tuesday-Saturday:
    12.30pm-3pm, 7pm-10pm
Sunday: 12.30pm-3pm
Closed 21-31 December,
1 week in Spring and
2 weeks in August.
Prices:
Meals: a la carte 45.00/65.00
2 rooms : 35.00/65.00

Typical Dishes

Fresh scallops

Dover sole

Treacle tart

3mi Southeast of Whitney by B4022.
Parking

Sprig's Alley

079 **Sir Charles Napier**

Sprig's Alley OX39 4BX
Tel.: (01494) 483011 - Fax: (01494) 485311
Website: www.sircharlesnapier.co.uk

Wadworth 6X

The big draw of this attractive flint-built pub-restaurant regularly turns the sleepy Oxfordshire hamlet of Sprigg's Alley into a vibrant, buzzy location. Very much a dining destination, it nevertheless retains a pubby feel with beer from the wood and roaring fires in the low-beamed bar. Individuality is writ large, particularly the elegant restaurant – where most people head – which has commissioned marble sculptures, antique silver and smart linen napkins. It opens onto pleasant gardens, a further attraction for diners once summer's here. Interesting menus showcase game and local produce in a seasonal menu that's prepared with care to a most agreeable standard. Service is never less than engaging, which is one reason why those visitors keep coming back.

Food serving times:
Tuesday-Saturday:
  12pm-2.30pm, 7pm-9.30pm
Sunday: 12pm-3.30pm
Closed 3 days over Christmas
Prices:
Meals: 15.50/16.50 (available weekdays) and a la carte 27.50/ 35.00

Typical Dishes

Kidneys wrapped in parma ham

Sea bass with creamed white beans

Honeycomb parfait

2.5mi Southeast of Chinnor by Bledlow Ridge rd. Parking

Stadhampton

080 Crazy Bear

Bear Lane, Stadhampton OX44 7UR
Tel.: (01865) 890714 - Fax: (01865) 400481
e-mail: sales@crazybearhotel.co.uk - Website: www.crazybearhotel.co.uk

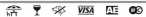

Tanners Jack

A traditional and rather understated pub appearance belies what's going on here. The Crazy Bear has a modern English restaurant upstairs, a Thai restaurant in the basement, a bar with a stuffed "crazy bear" where you can order cocktails, oysters and frozen vodkas (preferably not at the same time) on the ground floor, and bedrooms with zebra striped carpets and walls of peacock blue and purple, not to mention Philippe Starck inspired bathrooms. Of main interest for foodies is the Thai half of the eating equation: prawn in filo pastry with dipping sauce; duck with tamarind crust and Asian greens; and coconut parfait to round things off – good quality, accomplished and tasty dishes.

Food serving times:
Monday-Sunday:
      12pm-3pm, 6pm-10pm
Prices:
Meals: 15.00 and a la carte
21.50/50.00
18 rooms : 65.00/375.00

Typical Dishes

Seared scallops with guacamole

Beef fillet, chips and glazed cherry tomatoes

Chocolate torte

Off Wallingford rd. Parking

Stoke Row

081 Cherry Tree Inn

Stoke Row RG9 5QA

Tel.: 01491 680430 - Fax: 01491 682168
e-mail: info@thecherrytreeinn.com - Website: www.thecherrytreeinn.com

    VISA

Breakspears Bitter and Special

A good dose of personality and enthusiasm from the owners has certainly helped in the renovation of this 17C inn, which has lost none of its relaxing, rural pub character in the process. Lovely polished wooden tables, low-beamed ceilings, scrubbed floors and fires lend an even charm to three main dining areas and two smaller non-smoking ones: there's also a pleasant garden terrace, its wooden benches shaded by broad standing parasols. An appealing blackboard selection of modern dishes changes by the day, typified by variety, good cooking and generous portions. Over in a nearby outbuilding, spacious but very cosy bedrooms, complete with smart fittings and excellent ensuite bathrooms, make this a good choice for an overnight stop.

Food serving times:
Monday-Friday:
12pm-3pm, 7pm-10pm
Saturday and Sunday:
12pm-4pm, 7pm-10pm
Closed 25-26 December and 1 January
Prices:
Meals: a la carte 19.00/26.00
4 rooms : 85.00

Between Henley on Thames and Goring off B481. Parking

Typical Dishes

Grilled asparagus with buffalo mozzarella

Roast fillet of cod, minted mushy peas

Apple tart Tatin Calvados

Toot Baldon

 082 **The Mole Inn**

Toot Baldon OX44 9NG

Tel.: (01865) 340001 - Fax: (01865) 343011
e-mail: info@themoleinn.com - Website: www.themoleinn.com

 VISA **AE** **MC**

Hook Norton, Courage Directors

The sleepy hamlet of Toot Baldon, just outside Oxford, has had a serious wake-up call with the renaissance of this attractive old stalwart as a real top-notch dining pub heavyweight. Huge amounts have been invested in The Mole's stylish refurbishment and it shows. Impressive features include stone tiled flooring, beams galore, cosy lounge area with leather sofas leading into a series of four dining areas, roaring log fires, pine and oak tables, crisp napkins and fine glassware: it's no less than immaculate. Though virtually everything is angled towards eating, drinkers are nevertheless welcomed. Interesting, well-priced cuisine – running from rustic, earthy pub classics to more modern, globally influenced dishes – is prepared with assurance and care. Add light and personable service and the whole experience is positively charming.

Food serving times:
Monday-Saturday:
12pm-2.30pm, 7pm-9.30pm
Sunday: 12pm-4pm,
6pm-9.30pm
Closed 25 December and 1 January
Prices:
Meals: a la carte 20.00/25.00

Located a short distance from both the B480 and A4074. Parking

Typical Dishes

Salad of king prawn with fresh coconut

Oxford bangers and mash, onion jus

Fudge pudding with sesame

Wantage

083 **Boar's Head** 🛏️

Church St, Ardington, Wantage OX12 8QA

Tel.: (01235) 833254 - Fax: (01235) 833254

e-mail: info@boarsheadardington.co.uk - Website: www.boarsheadardington.co.uk

🚻 🍷 ⇆room 🚫 **VISA** **AE** **MC**

Hook Norton, Butts Golden Brown, West Berkshire

Stunning scenery, in the stirring shape of the Vale of White Horse and Lambourn Downs, is tantalisingly close to this pretty little pub in Ardington, an attractive downland village that's just outside Wantage. From the look of the interior, there's nowhere it would rather be: hunting curios and country magazines appear at every turn, pints of Berkshire ale sit on rough pine tables and a good mix of locals at the bar and chattering diners creates a warm, relaxed atmosphere. The menus come from a modern British direction, featuring some well-balanced combinations like entrecôte of Angus beef with corned beef hash, or stuffed fillet of sea bass with scallop mousse. One further recommendation remains: the bedrooms, which are particularly strong for a pub, in bright, breezy colours and no little style.

Food serving times:
Monday-Sunday :
    12pm-2pm, 7pm-9.30pm
Prices:
Meals: a la carte 24.00/40.00
🛏️ **3 rooms :** 75.00/130.00

Typical Dishes

Foie gras terrine

Roast monkfish with chorizo and Shiraz saucer

Assiette of three chocolate puddings

2.25mi East of Wantage by A417. Next to the church. Parking

Wootton

084 **Kings Head**

Chapel Hill, Wootton OX20 1DX

Tel.: (01993) 811340

e-mail: t.fay@kings-head.co.uk - Website: www.kings-head.co.uk

🍷 🍴 **VISA** **M©**

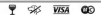

Ruddles County, Old Hooky

Located in a pretty village just outside handsome Woodstock, this attractive 17C Cotswold stone house has a fair degree of charm. Whilst originally an inn, it cottoned on to the possibilities of pub dining in the 1980s and 90s, earning itself a headstart in the gastropub stakes. There's a delightful bar area at the front with roaring fire, where you can eat from a blackboard menu, which might include oriental dishes and fish specials. Cooking is tasty, wholesome and well executed with a smattering of the ambitious. To the rear is a rather stark but still comfortable restaurant with quality napkins. As in the bar, the cooking is impressive, and includes homemade breads and ice creams. The overall feeling of quality and freshness continues to the bedrooms, which are simple but spotless.

Food serving times:

Tuesday-Saturday:
12pm-2pm, 7pm-8.30pm

Sunday: 12pm-2pm

Closed 25 December. Open Bank Holiday Monday

Prices:

Meals: a la carte 18.00/28.00

🛏 **3 rooms :** 65.00/110.00

Typical Dishes

Toasted goat's cheese on roasted tomatoes

Breast of duck

Trio of home-made ice creams

2.5mi North of Woodstock by A44. Parking

Wytham

085 **White Hart** We most liked

Wytham OX2 8QA

Tel.: (01865) 244372 - Fax: (01865) 812950

e-mail: whitehartwytham@yahoo.co.uk

 🍷 **VISA** **AE** **MC**

🍺 *Hook Norton, Fuller's London Pride*

Offering a perfect change of pace from Oxford, the White Hart is the pretty 18C village pub we would all love to have nearby: a relaxing atmosphere and an archetypal interior, right down to the fire in the hearth and the flagstone floor. Ask for a table in the front dining room, or a place on the attractive courtyard terrace warmed by heaters and tall clay ovens when the evening chill sets in. A laid-back but efficient young team provides attentive service of a carefully prepared menu, offsetting restyled classics with more inventive Modern British cooking: you might find a mustard-dressed salad of Stilton, bacon and black pudding, bream with tabbouleh and rocket pesto or fishcakes and mango salsa among the choices. Filled foccacias are a lighter lunchtime option.

Food serving times:
Monday-Friday:
　　12pm-3pm, 6pm-10pm
Saturday-Sunday:
　　12pm-4pm, 6.30pm-10pm
Prices:
Meals: a la carte 18.80/30.00

Typical Dishes

Beef carpaccio with truffle oil

Shoulder of lamb with ratatouille

Dark and white chocolate

3.25 mil North West of Oxford by A420 off A 34 (northbound). Parking

Abinger Common

086 The Stephan Langton Inn

We most liked

Friday Street, Abinger Common RH5 6JR
Tel.: (01306) 730775

 VISA

 Adnams, Fuller's London Pride, Hogs Back

This bustling local favourite, set in a delightful woodland setting, owes its name to a 13C Archbishop of Canterbury and its popularity to a heartily satisfying style of country cooking; it's rightly regarded as one of the best eating destinations in the region. Regulars and walkers to picturesque local landmarks Leith Hill and Box Hill gather at the Langton, despite – or because of – its isolation and position at the end of a particularly elongated Surrey lane. Choose between two areas: a wood fitted pub that's capacious, rustic, and of admirable vintage; or a dining room where modern art peers down on equally creative gastronomic delights. Book in advance for the restaurant or get there early to sample and enjoy the fine cooking on daily changing menus at moderate prices. Good, efficient service from enthusiastic young staff is guaranteed.

Food serving times:
Tuesday-Saturday:
    12.30pm-3pm, 7pm-10pm
Sunday: 12.30pm-3pm
Closed 25 December and 1 week January
Prices:
Meals: a la carte 19.00/24.00

4.5mi Southwest of Dorking by A25. Parking

Typical Dishes

Chicken liver, pigeon and bacon terrine

Roast magret, confit hash, pineapple relish

Buttermilk pudding

Chiddingfold

The Swan Inn

Petworth Rd, Chiddingfold GU8 4TY

Tel.: (01428) 682073 - Fax: (01428) 683259

e-mail: the-swan-inn@btconnect.com - Website: www.swaninnandrestaurant.co.uk

 rest **VISA** **AE** **MC**

Fuller's London Pride, Alton Pride, Hogback TEA

The handsomely mature exterior of this 14C Surrey redbrick village pub belies the extensive and stylish refurbishment which took place here in 2004. Despite the modern makeover, there remains a determinedly rustic atmosphere in most of the dining areas, with their bare wood tables. However, a formal dining room is available with white linen and elegant porcelain, while expansive terraced gardens beckon the summer visitor - dishes remain constant to all eating areas. Chic, understatedly-stylish bedrooms with air-conditioning and marble bathrooms await those staying overnight; their high-tech features, including plasma televisions, DVD players and broadband internet access will appeal to gadget-lovers.

Food serving times:
Monday-Sunday:
12pm-2.30pm, 6.30pm-10pm
Prices:
Meals: a la carte 18.00/27.00
 11 rooms : 65.00/120.00
5.00

Typical Dishes

Seared scallops with lime scented crab

Beef with parsnip puree and braised oxtail

Sticky toffee pudding

On the right hand side of the A283, approaching from the South. Parking opposite

Mickleham

088 **The King William IV**

Byttom Hill, Mickleham RH5 6EL

Tel.: (01372) 372590
Website: www.king-williamiv.com

   VISA

Adnams, Badger Best, Hogsback TEA and 1 monthly changing guest ale

Overhung with trailing creepers, this very traditional, part-tiled pub stands a little way above the hamlet itself, its pretty terrace commanding views of the gentle hills. Where the workers from Lord Beaverbrook's estate once propped up the little taproom bar, you're now more likely to find weekend walkers and locals from round about, drawn by the promise of wholesome, dependable English cooking. Look for the list of modern seafood dishes up on a large blackboard. Personally run by a good-natured team, this is just the kind of unfussy place that would have got the approval of the bluff Sailor King, or his contemporary, the cleric and wit Sidney Smith, nicknamed "The Bishop of Mickleham" for his many visits of the village.

Food serving times:
Monday-Saturday:
    12pm-2pm, 7pm-9.30pm
Sunday: 12pm-5pm
Closed 25 December and Sunday dinner
Prices:
Meals: a la carte 16.40/22.75

Typical Dishes

Chicken liver pâté

Steak, kidney and mushroom pie

Bread and butter pudding

0.5mi North of Mickleham by A24. Difficult off-road parking nearby - allow time and patience!

Ockley

089 **Bryce's**

The Old School House, Stane Str, Ockley RH5 5TH

Tel.: (01306) 627430 - Fax: (01306) 628274
e-mail: bryces.fish@virgin.net - Website: www.bryces.co.uk

� Ψ *VISA* Ⓜ

Fuller's London Pride, Gales Best, Sussex

Just a short walk from the lovely green stands the former village school, now a traditional, personally run pub with a sound reputation in this quietly well-to-do part of Surrey. The spacious if low-beamed bar is the place to go for fresh fish and chips, langoustines and lighter meals, though for something closer to restaurant dining, the more formal room to one side is the better bet. Besides a few meat dishes, it concentrates on fresh seafood, introducing some more adventurous choices on the specials board, like red mullet with spinach and pesto or a puff pastry galette of devilled crab, without dispensing with the classics: there would be an outcry if they tried, albeit a very polite one. As it is, a rather reserved regular clientele soon warm to the friendly and attentive service from a smartly dressed team.

Food serving times:
Monday-Sunday:
12pm-2.30pm, 7pm-9.30pm
Closed 25-26 December, 1-2 January, Sunday dinner in November, January and February
- Seafood -
Prices:
Meals: a la carte 18.40/24.40

On A29. Parking

Typical Dishes

Warm avocado, smoked salmon and scrambled eggs

Fillets of grey mullet, ratatouille and tapenade

Orange and ginger pudding

West End

090 The Inn @ West End

42 Guildford Road, West End GU24 9PW

Tel.: (01276) 858652 - Fax: (01276) 485842
e-mail: greatfood@the-inn.co.uk - Website: www.the-inn.co.uk

🍷 VISA AE MC

Fuller's London Pride, Courage Best

A busy roadside pub where the personable owners really lead from the front, energetically organising everything from themed suppers and wine tastings to just-for-fun boules tournaments in the pleasant garden out back. Even on an ordinary day you're likely to find the place busy, with a few knots of chatting regulars in the neatly overhauled modern bar and most of the diners in the conservatory or the dining room to the left; it's smarter than you might expect from the easy, informal tone of the place. A carefully prepared Modern British à la carte menu and their two or three-course lunch menus stand out as particularly good value: it's worth double-checking first, all the same.

Food serving times:
Monday-Sunday:
  12pm-2.30pm, 6pm-9.30pm
Prices:
Meals: 14.25/27.50 and a la carte 19.50/27.50

2.5mi from M3 on A322. Parking

Typical Dishes

Black pudding with caramelised apples

Fresh fish with smoked salmon buerre blanc

Summer berry pudding

301

Windlesham

091 The Brickmakers

Chertsey Rd, Windlesham GU20 6HT

Tel.: (01276) 472267 - Fax: (01276) 451014

e-mail: thebrickmakers@4cinns.co.uk - Website: www.4cinns.co.uk

 🍷 VISA AE M○

Courage Best Bitter, Hogs Back TEA, London Pride

The very picture of a trim, Home Counties pub, built in Southern brick – naturally – and hung with baskets of flowers in summer. A simply styled room at the front, dominated by its big bar island, leads into a formal but still relaxed restaurant and adjoining conservatory. Sound, well-prepared cuisine weighs modern and traditional approaches to British cuisine and seems to have struck the right balance for its affluent clientele. A polite young team approach the job in hand with cheery enthusiasm. A short drive away is Chobham Common, a rolling heathland nature reserve; sometimes bleak, but a rare piece of quiet wilderness so close to the capital.

Food serving times:
Monday-Sunday:
12pm-3pm, 6.30pm-10pm
Prices:
Meals: 25.95 and a la carte
19.50/31.50

East 1mi on B386. Parking

Typical Dishes

Goat's cheese tart

Duck breast with braised cabbage

Strawberry shortcake with vanilla ice cream

Ashurst

092 Fountain Inn

Ashurst BN44 3AP
Tel.: (01403) 710219

 VISA ⓜⒸ

 Harvey's Sussex and Best, Gales HSB, Fullers London Pride

This whitewashed, tiled former farmhouse, dating from 1572, draws in locals like flies to a trap: Paul McCartney's even been in. It's not hard to see what attracts so many here, apart from the obvious charms of the South Downs. An alluring garden and decked area by a pond is instantly relaxing, a skittle alley at the front fosters a bit of healthy local competition and the scents of the pleasant kitchen garden carry gently on the breeze. It's no less charming inside: the low-ceilinged bar has beams galore and leads into a series of characterful rooms where fires and flagged floors set the tone. Flavourful traditional cooking.

Food serving times:
Monday-Saturday:
    11.30-2pm, 6pm-9.30pm
Sunday: 12pm-3pm
Prices:
Meals: a la carte 12.75/17.20

Typical Dishes

Smoked haddock and prawns, cheese sauce

Sticky toffee pudding

3.5mi North of Steyning on B2135. Parking

Burpham

093 # George and Dragon

Burpham BN18 9RR
Tel.: (01903) 883131

VISA MC

Red River, Arundel King and 1 guest beer

This splendid old pub of mellow stone is set in a South Downs valley with sweeping views across to Arundel Castle on the skyline. Not surprisingly, it's prime walking country, so be prepared to share a pint with someone wearing big muddy boots. There's a large area at the front for outside dining in the sunny months, but at other times you'll want to get inside to sample the beamed bar, scrubbed pine tables and frothing real ale. It's where the regulars like to eat: steaks, pies and the like are on offer. To the left more diners settle into the small but irresistibly formed restaurant, which features an inglenook, full linen on antique tables and appealing mix of polished wood chairs. Menus are balanced, interesting and contemporary, using local produce and prepared with care and no little skill.

Food serving times:
Monday-Saturday:
  12pm-2pm, 7pm-9pm
Sunday: 12pm-2pm
Closed 25 December
Prices:
Meals: a la carte 22.00/35.00

Typical Dishes

Spicy smoked salmon

Scallops, creamy spinach risotto

Mango and paw paw crème brûlée

3mi Northeast of Arundal by A27. Parking

Charlton

094 **The Fox Goes Free**

Charlton PO18 0HU

Tel.: 01243 811461 - Fax: 01243 811946

e-mail: thefoxgoesfree.always@virgin.net - Website: www.thefoxgoesfree.com

  VISA

The Fox Bitter, Ballards Best

Arriving through the pretty village or off the hills, you can't miss this charming brick and flint pub, which is well-loved by its locals and gives them plenty back in return. Music nights, pub quizzes and themed dinners make it more than just a village meeting-place; fresh and hearty pub cooking, from sandwiches and bar favourites up to full meals, mixes contemporary and traditional ideas, and service is very warm and helpful. The dining room, cosy snug, big main bar and garden room have been carefully modernised but are still rich in originality and down-to-earth character, while the picnic tables, out in the sun or under the boughs of the trees, look far out over the start of the South Downs. Well-kept ensuite bedrooms, two reached from behind the bar, are well above pub average.

Food serving times:
Monday-Friday:
 12pm-2.30pm, 6.30pm-10pm
Saturday and Sunday:
            12pm-10pm
Closed 25 December
Prices:
Meals: a la carte 18.50/27.50
5 rooms : 50.00/70.00

Typical Dishes

Baked goats cheese, red pepper coulis

Best end of lamb, garlic mash

Hot chocolate mousse

6,75 mi North of Chichester by A286. Parking

East Lavant

095 ## The Royal Oak Inn we most liked

Pook Lane, East Lavant PO18 0AX

Tel.: (01243) 527434 - Fax: (01243) 775062
e-mail: ro@thesussexpub.co.uk - Website: www.thesussexpub.co.uk

Up to 3 local ales

This elegant but relaxed Georgian pub, within a turbo blast of Goodwood Motor Circuit and close to the Channel and the South Downs, adds up to more than the sum of its parts. It contains not just an exceptionally busy inn with rustic walls of red brick and rafters, but also a barn and cottage – all with tastefully decorated and well-equipped bedrooms – set cosily round a charming courtyard. The pub cuisine is well-renowned in the Chichester area. There's an interesting à la carte choice with south European influence, and the specials board features perennial country pub favourites alongside modern dishes.

Food serving times:
Monday-Sunday:
    12pm-2.15pm, 7pm-9.30pm
Closed 25 December
Prices:
Meals: a la carte 20.00/30.00
6 rooms : 60.00/110.00

Typical Dishes

Crab and tiger prawn cocktail

Smoked haddock and caerphilly cheese

Dark chocolate tart

Off A286 after the hump-back bridge.
Parking opposite the inn

Elsted

096 ## Three Horseshoes

Elsted GU29 0JY

Tel.: (01730) 825746

 VISA **MC**

 Cheriton Pots, Ballards Best, Timothy Taylor Landlord, Hopback Summer Lightning

From Uppark House to the Iron Age trails around Beacon Hill, the high, open downlands of East Sussex can make for exhilarating walking, and there are few more satisfying feelings than the stroll down from the scarp path to this welcoming 16C former drovers' inn, where you can enjoy more far-reaching countryside views from the garden or clink well-earned pints by the warmth of the wood burners. A delightful beamed bar where the beers are racked up in casks fills up quickly at the weekend, when it's as well to get your reservation in early; locals and even one or two escaping Londoners enjoy modern dishes from the blackboard or tuck into homemade pies, puddings and other hearty British favourites. Cordial and kindly service.

Food serving times:
Monday-Saturday:
12pm-2pm, 7pm-9pm
Sunday: 12pm-2pm,
7pm-8.30pm

Prices:
Meals: a la carte 20.00/27.00

Typical Dishes

Mozzarella and bacon salad

Steak and kidney pie

Raspberry and hazelnut meringue

5mi Southwest of Midhurst by A272 on Elsted rd. Parking

Fernhurst

097 King's Arms
Midhurst Rd, Fernhurst GU27 3HA

Tel.: (01428) 652005
Website: www.kingsarmsfernhurst.com

 VISA

 Ringwood 49er, Horsham Best, Hopback Crop Circle, Triple F Moondance, Hog's Back

Renowned locally for its friendly, welcoming atmosphere, the 17th century King's Arms – privately owned and run - stands at the northern edge of the proposed South Downs National Park, and benefits from being surrounded by fields, its own pretty gardens enhanced by the shade of a weeping willow. Inside. all is warmth and rustic character, embellished by the warm glow of a woodburner and a cosy series of comfy eating areas around the bar. You can eat at cushioned wall benches under a long, low mantelbeam. The appealing menu employs Sussex game, fruit and vegetables from the local shop, and fish from market in Portsmouth. Those more suited to liquid refreshment have the benefit of an annual beer festival in the barn.

Food serving times:

Closed 25 December
Prices:
Meals: a la carte 19.50/24.95

Typical Dishes

Grilled asparagus with hollandaise sauce

Cumberland sausage ring, mash and onion gravy

Rhubarb and custard fool

Parking »

Halfway Bridge

098 **The Halfway Bridge Inn** ⨸

Halfway Bridge GU28 9BP

Tel.: (01798) 861281 - Fax: (01798) 861878
e-mail: mail@thesussexpub.co.uk - Website: www.thesussexpub.co.uk

⨸=room **VISA** **AE** **MC**

Cheriton Pots Ale, Gales HSB, Harveys Sussex Best and Arundel Gold

An easy-going, eat-where-you-like policy makes it all the more tempting to drop in and grab a table, but you may not always find your favourite corner free. A bustling crowd know a good thing when they see one, and come in numbers for seasonal cooking at a competitive price: winter dishes, for instance, could include black pudding salad with bacon and mushrooms or duck confit with honey and thyme, but tasty fish and game also make the specials board. To the back of the 17C pub itself – cosy and rustic with its stripped pine floors and log fires – you'll find the old barn, a reminder of the days when this was a coaching halt. Now smartly converted and facing a courtyard garden, it's split into thoughtfully appointed rooms, with vaulted ceilings, a few pieces of antique pine furniture and particularly impressive bathrooms.

Food serving times:
Monday-Sunday:
    12pm-2pm, 6pm-9pm
Closed 25 December
Prices:
Meals: a la carte 18.00/23.00
⨸ **8 rooms :** 55.00/120.00

Typical Dishes

Crispy oriental duck salad

Calves' liver with smoked bacon

Baked blueberry cheesecake

Halfway between Midhurst and Petworth on the A272. Parking available on street outside inn ➤

Lickfold

099 ## Lickfold Inn

Lickfold GU28 9EY

Tel.: (01798) 861285 - Fax: (01798) 861342
e-mail: thelickfoldinn@aol.com

 🍷 *VISA* ⓜⓒ

 TEA, Horsham Best Bitter, Bomadier Premium Bitter

Follow the narrow country road as it winds through the gentle Sussex countryside and eventually you'll catch a glimpse of the Lickfold Inn, a pretty, tile-hung pub dating back to the 1400s. The smart rear terrace, backing on to a mature garden, and the trimly kept bar, with its stone floor, open fires and scrubbed pine tables, are rather less formal than the dining room upstairs, but the same enjoyable modern cooking is available everywhere. Even on a weekday lunchtime you may find the place busy, but it doesn't dilute the informal charm and service is only a little stretched. Concise menu and specials board; ask about their popular summer barbecues.

Food serving times:
Tuesday-Saturday:
  12pm-2.30pm, 7pm-9.15pm
Sunday: 12pm-2.30pm
Closed 25 December
Prices:
Meals: a la carte 19.95/29.95

Typical Dishes

Sweet onion and goat's cheese tarte tatin

Oven-baked fillet of sea bass

Mango crème brulee

6mi Northwest of Petworth by A272.
Parking

Partridge Green

100 The Green Man Inn

Church Rd, Jolesfield, Partridge Green RH13 8JT

Tel.: (01403) 710250 - Fax: (01403) 713212
e-mail: will@thegreenman.org - Website: www.thegreenman.org

Harvey's Sussex Best

It's hard to imagine a more handsomely English-looking redbrick pub, but the winking earth-spirit on the pub sign should tip you off that there's a bit of a twist to this one. A stylish and polished interior is decorated with local prints and largely set for dining, though the busy atmosphere means there's still plenty of informal pub character to it. Locally sourced produce is at the hub of a mainly Modern British menu, but the surprise comes in the appealingly tasty selection of authentic Spanish tapas on offer alongside the lighter lunchtime bar classics. The whole place feels welcoming and well looked-after: charming service is the icing on the cake.

Food serving times:
Closed 26-31 December
Prices:
Meals: 14.95 (lunch) and a la carte 20.00/32.00

Typical Dishes

Seared king scallops with pea veloute

Pork belly with apple mash

Sticky toffee pudding with caramel sauce

Just out of the village on the B2135. Parking

Stedham

101 Nava Thai at Hamilton Arms

School Lane, Stedham GU29 0NZ

Tel.: (01730) 812555 - Fax: (01730) 817459

e-mail: hamiltonarms@hotmail.com - Website: www.thehamiltonarms.co.uk

 🍷 ✂ **VISA** **MC**

 Fuller's London Pride, Young's Best, Ballard's Best

Happily situated in the rolling South Downs, this whitewashed inn boasts an authentic Asian ambience barely a couple of miles from the attractive and quintessentially homespun appeals of Midhurst. The bar area at the front is brimming with Thai artefacts set around polished tables – during the week, this is where lunch is usually served. Adjacent: a homely, comfortable restaurant with a similar interior gets you in the mood for excellently prepared, tasty Thai dishes, monosodium glutamate and additive free. Enjoyment is enhanced by polite service from traditionally attired Thai waiters.

Food serving times:
Tuesday-Saturday:
12pm-2.30pm, 6pm-10.30pm
Sunday:
12pm-2.30pm, 7pm-9.45pm
Closed 1 week January.
Open Bank Holiday Monday lunchtimes
- Thai -
Prices:
Meals: 19.50 and a la carte
15.00/25.00

Typical Dishes

Prawns in filo pastry, chilli sauce

Green chicken curry

Thai egg custard, coconut ice cream

2mi West of Midhurst by A272.
Parking

E. Baret / Michelin - (06 - Roubion)

- **a.** D17 road ?
- **b.** N202 road ?
- **c.** D30 road ?

Which road will get you there?
To find out, simply open a Michelin map!

The Michelin Atlases and m
NATIONAL, REGIONAL, LOC
and ZOOM map series of
clear, accurate mapping
help you plan your route a
find your way.

*A*s anyone west of the Avon will tell you, the historic West Country has been many countries in its time: the ancient land of Celtic saints and Arthurian legend, Drake's home port and the Old England of Hardy's Wessex are rediscovered every year by countless visitors, drawn by sun and surf and the West's astonishing variety. Where else can you find untamed moorland next to semi-tropical fantasy gardens? Which other region combines the magnificent Elizabethan Longleat House with the mysterious standing sarsens at Stonehenge, the genius of Brunel's grand designs and the exquisite style of Georgian Bath, not to mention the ultra-modern Eden Project? Add to this the seaside villages, sandy beaches and hundreds of miles of breathtaking clifftop trails and you have a glimpse of this amazing region, but for a real flavour of the place, get down to the dairy, the quay and the orchard. Come harvest time, Pippins, Dabinetts and Somerset Redstreaks are ripened for slow-matured dry ciders, "real" Cheddar and Blue Vinney cheeses are in every farmers' market and Brixham and Newlyn's fresh and cured seafood appear on the specials boards. But there's much more to West Country cooking than these three famous exports, as you'll soon discover...

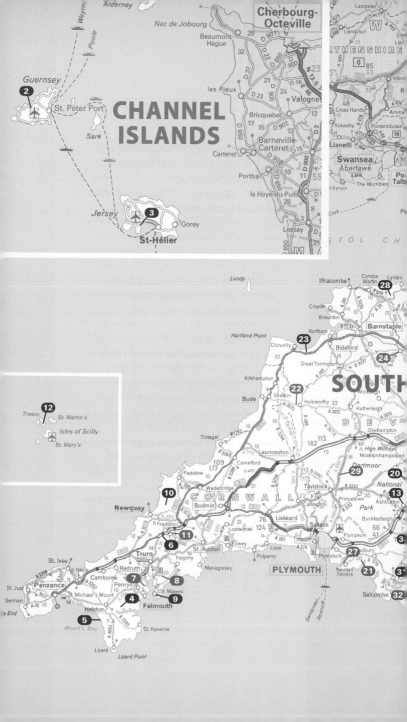

Chew Magna

001 ## Bear & Swan

South Parade, Chew Magna BS40 8SL

Tel.: 01275 331100 - Fax: 01275 332187

e-mail: enquiries@bearandswan.co.uk - Website: www.bearandswan.co.uk

 VISA

 Odyssey, Butcombe Bitter

A sturdy homage to Victoriana in the heart of a small, pretty but truly bustling village. The exterior is of sturdy stone and the 'proper' bar at one end has the same sterling qualities. Here you can enjoy a pint or a tasty snack at chunky rustic tables- mind you- only at lunchtime. In the evenings, the main blackboard menu takes centre stage. This can also be enjoyed in the main dining area at the other end of the bar where a hotchpotch of antique tables and chairs, reclaimed floor boards, and exposed stone work give a pleasant feel. You can watch the chefs at work in their open-plan kitchen as they prepare an ample, modern, eclectic range of dishes that draw diners from far and wide, attracted by locally renowned menus full of tasty West Country produce on daily changing menus.

Food serving times:
Monday-Sunday:
12pm-2pm, 7pm-10pm
Closed Sunday dinner
Prices:
Meals: a la carte 19.50/29.00

Typical Dishes

Warm goat's cheese tart

Guinea fowl breast with black pudding

Pear and almond tart

8.25mi South of Bristol via A37 on B3130. Parking

Kings Mills (Guernsey)

002 **Fleur du Jardin** 🛏

Castel, Kings Mills (Guernsey) GY5 7JT

Tel.: (01481) 257996 - Fax: (01481) 256834
e-mail: info@fleurdujardin.guernsey.net - Website: www.fleurdujardin.guernsey.net

      VISA AE M©

Guernsey Sunbeam and 1 guest ale

Couldn't be more aptly named: this welcoming old inn has good-sized gardens, colourful borders, shrubs, bright hanging baskets and flower barrels. Inside, the laid-back bar and adjacent alcoves sport low beams and thick granite walls confirming their 15C origins: there's well tended Guernsey real ale on draught. But it's the daily menus of local seafood which give the Fleur its standing of quiet renown among tourists as well as locals. The beamed restaurant, with its reassuringly ancient granite fireplace, mixes these with a more eclectic, traditional range of dishes, or you can dine more informally at the bar. After eating, swim off delightful, nearby beaches, and sleep deeply in one of the pub's smart but cottagey bedrooms.

Food serving times:
Monday-Sunday:
  12pm-2pm, 6.30pm-9.30pm
Prices:
Meals: a la carte 15.00/25.00
🛏 **17 rooms :** 47.00/116.00

Typical Dishes

Sauteed scallops, coconut and sweet chilli

Sea bass with fennel beurre blanc

Crème brûlée

3mi West of St Peter Port. Parking

Saint Aubin (Jersey)

003 Old Court House Inn 🛏

St Aubin's Harbour, Saint Aubin (Jersey) JE3 8AB

Tel.: (01534) 746433 - Fax: (01534) 745103
e-mail: ochstaubins@jerseymail.co.uk

🛶 ♈ 🍴 ⌂ **VISA** **AE** ⦾ ⓜⓒ

 Mary Ann

T his atmospheric 15C quayside inn has had a colourful history as a courthouse, merchant's house, and, more recently, bit-part player in the TV series Bergerac. Its traditional whitewashed façade looks beyond the harbour to St Helier. The main hub of activity is the Westward bar, built from the gig of a schooner scuttled off the Hurd Deep. Two areas are kept for dining: a characterful, Georgian glass-paned front room, or a courtyard restaurant at the back. Menus are the same throughout, and are rooted in the popular, tried-and-tested category: the highlight is the local seafood, in simple platters or elaborate specials, but the Old Court House is also good for the likes of vegetable lasagne or wild mushroom and asparagus risotto. Individually decorated bedrooms are colourful, countrified and most have harbour views.

Food serving times:
Monday-Sunday:
12.30pm-2.30pm, 7pm-10pm
Prices:
Meals: 10.00/21.00 and a la carte 20.00/60.00
🛏 **9 rooms :** 40.00/120.00

Typical Dishes

Sauteed local scallops
Fisherman's platter
Jersey ice cream

4mi West of St Helier. Parking opposite ➤➤

Constantine

004 **Trengilly Wartha Inn** 🛏

Nancenoy, Constantine TR11 5RP

Tel.: (01326) 340332 - Fax: (01326) 341121
e-mail: reception@trengilly.co.uk - Website: www.trengilly.co.uk

Sharps Cornish Coaster and 1 local beer

A good place to learn Cornish – that's the Trengilly Wartha (translation: settlement above the trees), because the locals throng here. It's not the easiest place to get to, being at the tail end of some notorious near vertical lanes, but the end product's worth it. This former crofter's abode has been enlarged over the years, but everyone spills out into the garden in summer. The interior is dominated by the airy main bar, which, apart from serving fine ales, also boasts a terrific selection of wines. The scrubbed wood tables and old Cornish settles almost invite you to sit, sup and relax. Dine in a formal restaurant or conservatory where the hearty pub grub is enlivened by daily changing specials boards. Menus are richly influenced by the seasons, and cooking is well honed and solidly skilful.

Food serving times:
Monday-Saturday:
12pm-2.15pm,
6.30pm-9.30pm
Sunday: 12pm-2pm,
7pm-9.30pm

Prices:
Meals: 29.00 (fixed price dinner) and a la carte 14.00/26.00
🛏 **8 rooms :** 50.00/96.00

Typical Dishes

Seared Cornish scallops, pickled ginger

Confit shoulder of lamb, black pudding mash

Marinated Fingals cheese

1.5mi South by Fore St off Port Navas rd. Parking

# Gunwalloe

005 **The Halzephron Inn** 🛏

Gunwalloe TR12 7QB

Tel.: (01326) 240406 - Fax: (01326) 241442
e-mail: halzephroninn@gunwalloe1.fsnet.co.uk

   ⇝rest **VISA**

Sharps Doom Bar, Halzephron Gold, St Austell Tribute

A visit to this extreme south-westerly corner of Cornwall wouldn't be complete without a visit to the Halzephron, staring out imperturbably across Mount's Bay. It knows its place: it's been here 500 years, and is wonderfully snug and rustic. The low ceiling boasts fine old timbers; gleaming copper and original paintings adorn the walls. Knick-knacks, curios and higgledy-piggledy décor enrich four adjoining dining rooms: food's a serious business here, and wide-ranging menus are fiercely Cornish in produce and style. Portions are of the hearty variety; an impressive selection of local real ales is an ideal way to wash down lunch or dinner, followed by a walk on the nearby South West Coast Path. Two neat, cosy bedrooms await.

Food serving times:
Monday-Sunday:
12pm-2pm, 7pm-9pm
Closed 25 December and Sunday and Monday dinner November-March
Prices:
Meals: a la carte 16.90/30.00
🛏 **2 rooms :** 45.00/80.00

Typical Dishes

Smoked duck risotto

Escalope of pork, garlic pommes purées

Baileys panna cotta

3.5mi South of Helston by A3083. Easter to end of September parking in the field adjacent to the inn

Mitchell

006 ## The Plume of Feathers

Mitchell TR8 5AX

Tel.: (01872) 510387 - Fax: (01872) 511124
e-mail: enquiries@theplume.info - Website: www.theplume.info

   VISA

Sharps Doom Bar, Shepherd Neame Spitfire, Oakham JHB

As good a break as you'll find from the drone of the A30, this smartly refurbished part 16C dining pub, away from the visitors' hotspots, comes into its own as an escape from the tourist influx of a Cornish summer, but you'll find a reassuringly good turnout - families and couples, groups of friends - on most days of the year. Set aside from an airy, sympathetically restored bar, several connecting lounges serve as the restaurant, although service is just as alert and organised at the bar. The cooking itself is steady as she goes - there is a sound, classic menu with blackboard specials - but the real draw is the relaxed, everyday atmosphere of the place: they have plenty of regulars, but are always happy to take on a few more. Large, bright bedrooms in the restored barns and stable. A well provides ample pure drinking water and water for the baths and showers.

Food serving times:
Monday-Sunday:
12pm-10pm
Closed 25 December
Prices:
Meals: a la carte 16.00/27.00
🛏 **5 rooms :** 63.75/105.00

Near the junction of A30 and A3076.
Parking

Typical Dishes

Pan fried scallops, orange fumet

Roasted Cornish turbot

Vanilla panna cotta, carpaccio of pineapple

Mylor Bridge

007 Pandora Inn

Restronguet Creek, Mylor Bridge TR11 5ST
Tel.: (01326) 372678 - Fax: (01326) 378958
Website: www.pandorainn.co.uk

  VISA

St Austell HSD, Tribute and Tinners

Sail up Mylor Creek, moor at the pontoon, and you'll have taken the scenic route to this stunningly located pub, which dates back to the 13C. Its charming interior comes courtesy of timbered ceilings for the vertically challenged, shiny stone floors, cosy corners, open fire and seaside pot pourri. Food can be eaten at the bar or at the slightly more formal Andrew Miller restaurant upstairs: hearty pub menus take in a wide range of favourites, but are quite rightly dominated by fresh seafood off the blackboard, so be patient with service. Crab bucket and bait are available at the bar or work off your meal with a relaxed walk along the creekside paths.

Food serving times:
Monday-Sunday:
    12pm-3pm, 6.30pm-9pm
    (9.30pm Friday and Saturday)
Prices:
Meals: a la carte 19.00/25.00

Typical Dishes

Local mussels

Grilled sea bass, niçoise garnish

Chocolate fondant, milk chocolate malt ice cream

3.5mi North of Falmouth on A39 and B3292. Fork left via Restronguet and Weir rd for 1mi. Parking

Philleigh

 008 Roseland Inn

Philleigh TR2 5NB
Tel.: (01872) 580254 - Fax: (01872) 580966

Sharps Doom Bar, Bass, Ringwood

You know you're edging into rural heaven when you come by ferry to this out-of-the-way family-run Cornish pub – the chuch's next-door neighbour for the last 500 years – and step inside from the rose-covered courtyard. Just look around and admire the charming rustic surrounds: exposed black beams, open fires, rugged stone floors and scattered knick-knacks. A fine selection of real ales is on hand – a pint or two will go down exceptionally well with a dish or two from the traditional and unpretentious menus, which owe much of their hearty character to Cornish produce.

Food serving times:
Monday-Sunday:
12pm-2.30pm,
6.30pm-9.30pm

Prices:
Meals: a la carte 15.00/25.00

Typical Dishes

Coconut mussels

Slow roasted shoulder of lamb

Eton Mess

Situated between King Harry ferry and Ruan High Lanes. Parking

St Mawes

009 The Victory Inn

Victory Hill, St Mawes TR2 5DQ
Tel.: (01326) 270324 - Fax: (01326) 272557
Website: www.victory-stmawes.co.uk

 🍷 *VISA* 🆖

Sharps Doom Bar, Bass and London Pride

There are various splendid ways of getting to the Victory Inn. You can reach it by ferry, road or on foot along the harbour; whichever alternative presents itself, the delights of the Roseland and Falmouth Bay are ever-present. This professionally run pub delights in a cosy interior with some charm, not a little enhanced by its enviable position on the Victory Steps next to the harbour. The real ale selection is broad; wander across to the open fire and mingle with the locals over a pint. The dining room is upstairs, a spacious area, with a more formal, contemporary feel and mainly used in the evening. As you might expect, seafood figures strongly on the menu, aided and abetted by Cornish ingredients, all very simple, fresh and unfussy. Tuck into moules marinière, perhaps on one of the few benches outside.

Food serving times:
Monday-Sunday:
12pm-2.30pm, 6pm-9.30pm
- Seafood specialities -
Prices:
Meals: a la carte 15.00/25.00

Typical Dishes

Scallop terrine, elderflower salad

Cumin roasted Cornish mackerel

Hazelnut and chocolate tart

Next to St Mawes harbour. Parking at the harbour car park >>

St Mawgan

010 The Falcon Inn 🛏

St Mawgan TR8 4EP
Tel.: (01637) 860225 - Fax: (01637) 860884
Website: www.thefalconinn-newquay.co.uk

  VISA

 Tribute, HSD, Tinners

Set just inland from the delights of Newquay, in the splendid Vale of Mawgan, this 16C wisteria-clad hostelry rejoices in a totally unspoilt character and a quaint surrounding of antique shops. The bar is cosiness itself: roaring log fire, comfy settles, large antique prints and, naturally enough, pictures of falcons on the walls; you can sit at homely farmhouse tables and chairs. Eat either here, in the French-windowed restaurant, or at a delicious cobbled courtyard in the front. Dishes are based around freshly-caught seafood which arrives on the plate from the nearby beaches at Newlyn; classic dishes also make a solid appearance.

Food serving times:
Monday-Sunday:
    12pm-2pm, 6pm-9pm
Prices:
Meals: a la carte 14.00/20.00
🛏 **3 rooms :** 26.00/74.00

Typical Dishes

Cornish smoked salmon, lemon and chive mayonnaise

St Mawgan sausages, onion gravy

Treacle tart

Follow signs for the airport on A3059 between Newquay and St Colomb Major; the pub is down the hill. Parking

Summercourt

011 **Viners** We most liked

Carvynick, Summercourt TR8 5AF
Tel.: (01872) 510544 - Fax: (01872) 510468

  VISA MC

Sharps Doom Bar

This charming stone-built cottage, with origins stretching back to the 17C, can claim to have been here long before the landscaped encampments of mobile homes or the golf course next door, but it's a much more recent change which has really captured the local imagination. The bar near the entrance remains a good place for beer, nuts and pub chat, and drinkers are positively encouraged, though most will stay for one and head straight for the elegant new restaurant. Pale-toned walls, slate floors and high-backed velvet chairs strike a sophisticated note, taken up in a creative but affordable menu that shows sound culinary understanding: for an example of this generosity and balance, try grilled oysters in lime and chilli or sole in parsley butter with bean salad.

Food serving times:
Tuesday-Saturday
6.30pm-9.30pm
Sunday   12.30pm-3pm
Closed 4 weeks in winter
Prices:
Meals: a la carte 21.70/30.00

Typical Dishes

Scallops with pancetta, parmesan and pesto

Roast loin of venison

Chocolate and hazelnut pudding

At Carvynick Golf and Country Club, 1.5mi North West of the junction of A30 and A3058. Parking

Tresco (Scilly Isles)

012 New Inn 🛏

Tresco (Scilly Isles) TR24 0QQ

Tel.: (01720) 422844 - Fax: (01720) 423200
e-mail: newinn@tresco.co.uk

🍷 ⤨-rest 🚫 **VISA** **M©**

Skinners Tresco Tipple, Betty Stogs and Cornish Knocker Ale

An hospitable stopping off point on your way, perhaps, to the Old Blockhouse or Tresco Abbey Gardens, this stone built former inn may prove difficult to leave. It has a charming terrace garden - with plenty of seating - and views that extend across the beautiful island. In keeping with its surroundings, the traditional bar is packed with nautical memorabilia; other lounges have a friendly, bustling ambience – it's where the locals congregate. Back outside, a large semi-decked sun lounge is a good place to tuck into an extensive "snacky" menu or indulge in blackboard seafood specials. The dining room (remember to book first) is a striking bistro-style restaurant serving traditional favourites. If, indeed, you haven't moved on, bedrooms are simple, well-kept and comfortable.

Food serving times:
Monday-Sunday:
12pm-2pm, 7pm-9pm
(booking essential to non-residents) Accommodation rates include dinner

Prices:
Meals: 29.00 (fixed price dinner) and a la carte 13.00/29.00

🛏 **16 rooms :** 218.00

Near Tresco Stores

Typical Dishes

Seafood brochettes
Char grilled rump steak
Raspberry crème brûlée

Ashburton

013 **Rising Sun**

Woodland, Ashburton TQ13 7JT

Tel.: (01364) 652544 - Fax: (01364) 653628

e-mail: mail@risingsunwoodland.co.uk - Website: www.risingsunwoodland.co.uk

  ✂room **VISA**

Princetown Jail Ale, Teignworthy Reel Ale and regularly changing guest ales,

In the depths of the rolling countryside, this old drovers' inn is one to remember for hot summer afternoons, when families can enjoy some fresh Devon air at one of the terrace picnic tables in the garden, but the cosy and very traditional bar comes into its own at the turn of the year. The blackboard menu gives credit where it's due to a huge supporting cast of Wessex farmers, brewers and other suppliers, and approachable bar staff will happily talk you through the choices. Fresh and appetising dishes could include pigeon or smoked trout salads and sea bass with balsamic sauce – it depends on the season, of course – but their hearty pies are perennially popular; beef and Devon blue cheese and venison with stout and juniper head a short list of favourites.

Food serving times:
Tuesday-Sunday:
12pm-2.15pm, 6pm-9.15pm
Closed 25 December. Open Bank Holiday Monday

Prices:
Meals: a la carte 15.00/22.00
🛏 **6 rooms :** 40.00/68.00

Typical Dishes

Devon blue cheese tart

Torbay dabs, lemon butter

Treacle tart

1.5mi East off the A38 between Exeter and Plymouth. Parking

Beesands

014 The Cricket Inn 🛏

Beesands TQ7 2EN
Tel.: (01548) 580215

   VISA AE M©

Fuller's London Pride, Bass

The owners lovingly call this bright, modernised establishment "the inn by the shore", which rather neatly sums up the fact that you can practically kick one of Start Bay's pebbles from the Cricket Inn's front door. This, of course, guarantees it's a busy watering hole when the sun's shining. It's formed from a couple of fishermen's cottages, and the airy, open-plan interior means there's plenty of room to grab a table and admire the view from one of the many windows. There's a hearty choice of modern British dishes, but in this location you can hardly pass up the seafood, which practically jumps from the Channel to the kitchen. Of the three light, spacious bedrooms, two boast sea views.

Food serving times:
Monday-Sunday:
  12pm-2.30pm, 6pm-9.30pm
(check opening times in winter)
Prices:
Meals: a la carte 14.00/40.00
🛏 **4 rooms :** 40.00/60.00

Typical Dishes

Locally smoked mackerel

Monkfish with coconut and chilli

Chocolate and orange torte

2.25mi South East of Kingsbridge by A379. Parking

Branscombe

015 ## Masons Arms

Branscombe EX12 3DJ
Tel.: (01297) 680300 - Fax: (01297) 680500
e-mail: reception@masonsarms.co.uk - Website: www.masonsarms.co.uk

  rest **VISA** **MC**

Otter Bitter, Old Speckled Hen, London Pride

The picturesque village of Branscombe is one of the joys of the East Devon coast, nestling piecemeal in a deep valley right next to the sea. At its heart lies this 14C creeper-clad inn, visible to anyone up in the hills. It has a wonderfully bustling atmosphere, built around the unspoilt bar where hotel guests and locals mingle with a pint. The hearty ambience is enhanced with the surrounding ancient ships' beams, slate floors, and stone walls; a huge central fireplace is regularly used to spit-roast joints of meat at lunchtime and in the evening: modern British menus are highlighted by crab and lobster landed on Branscombe's beach. Also finding favour are comforting favourites such as casserole of local beef and dumplings with horseradish sauce. Bedrooms are divided between inn and cottages opposite.

Food serving times:
Monday-Sunday:
11pm-2pm, 7pm-9pm
(bar lunch)
Prices:
Meals: 25.00 (fixed price dinner) and a la carte 15.20/27.00
21 rooms: 30.00/150.00

Typical Dishes

Warm chicken and foie gras sausage

Roast fillet of hake, balsamic reduction

Chocolate crème brûlée

In the village centre. Parking

Broadhembury

016 **Drewe Arms**

Broadhembury EX14 3NF

Tel.: (01404) 841267 - Fax: (01404) 841118

🍷 🐾 **VISA** **AE** **M©**

Otter Bitter, Ale, Bright, Head

A delightful village deserves a delightful pub, and in this village tucked away in East Devon they've struck gold. A quintessentially English setting places the 13C Drewe Arms next to a church and opposite a row of cottages the colour of clotted cream. Gloriously unimproved, the interior seems not to have changed for centuries. Unusually, the walls are covered with carved walking sticks, while farming implements and even an eel-catcher's basket hang from the ceiling. The quiet is broken only by the satisfied murmurs of those drinking at the neat little bar or eating in the two dining areas. Fish is the focus of the menus. Typically, you might find marinated herrings, roasted cod with anchovies or salmon fishcakes with tomato and dill sauce; dishes are reassuringly well executed and very tasty.

Food serving times:

Monday-Saturday:
12pm-2pm, 7pm-9.30pm

Sunday: 12pm-2pm

Closed 25 December and 31 December

(booking essential) - Seafood -

Prices:

Meals: a la carte 10.00/30.00

Typical Dishes

Crab thermidor

John Dory, anchovies and caper butter

Lemon posset, cream

5mi Northwest of Honiton by A373. Parking

Dalwood

017 The Tuckers Arms 🛏

Dalwood EX13 7EG

Tel.: (01404) 881342 - Fax: (01404) 881138
Website: www.tuckersarms.co.uk

     VISA Ⓜ©

Otter, O'Hanlon's Firefly, Palmers IPA, Old Speckled Hen

With its neatly trimmed thatch and little low windows, this medieval longhouse looks promising from outside, but it's a particular pleasure to find its style and history still so well reflected in the interior, both in the cosy lounge bar and the dining rooms. Plates and brasses decorate the beams and the venerable old stonework of the fireplace has been preserved. The cooking remains the big draw, though: a very affordable menu with a set-price option doesn't overlook local meat or seasonal game and has a good local reputation for its catch of the day: try smoked salmon cakes or John Dory in a delicate Devon cream sauce with asparagus, and follow it up with a tasty, traditional pudding like date and banana sponge, served with rum and toffee sauce.

Food serving times:
Monday-Sunday:
     12pm-2pm, 7pm-8.45pm
Closed dinner 25 and 26 December
Prices:
Meals: 19.95 (fixed price dinner) and a la carte 10.95/ 23.00
🛏 **4 rooms :** 65.00

Typical Dishes

Smoked haddock rarebit
Chicken with tomato salsa
Lemon meringue pie

3.5mi West of Axminster by B3261, off A35. Parking

Doddiscombsleigh

018 **Nobody Inn**

Doddiscombsleigh EX6 7PS

Tel.: (01647) 252394 - Fax: (01647) 252978
e-mail: info@nobodyinn.co.uk - Website: www.nobodyinn.co.uk

   VISA **AE** **M©**

Nobody Inn Bitter, Otter Bitter, R.C.H. East Street Cream

All roads may not lead to Doddiscombsleigh, but find the lanes that do, and you'll alight on a little piece of history in the rather eccentric shape of the Nobody Inn. An unfalteringly characterful part 16C interior leads you off down a warren of nooks and crannies; a veritable sense of history is all pervading. Food is ordered at the bar and you dine on uncovered tables, sitting perhaps on an ancient settle. Local ingredients are all over the menu, such as fish from Dartmouth, quail from local farms and fruit from nearby orchards. Wine buffs will appreciate sizeable wine list.

Food serving times:
Monday-Sunday:
12pm-2pm, 7pm-10pm
Closed 25-26 December and
1 January
Prices:
Meals: a la carte 19.40/29.90

Typical Dishes

Salad of smoked eel

Grilled fillet of ling with butter beans

Chocolate soufflé cake

10mi Southwest of Exeter by B3212 off B3193. Parking

Exton

019 **The Puffing Billy**

Station Rd, Exton EX3 0PR

Tel.: 01392 877888 - Fax: 01392 876232

e-mail: food@thepuffingbilly.com - Website: www.thepuffingbilly.com

O'Hanlans Firefly

If only all railway pubs were this nice. Round the corner from Exton station and the path along the water, look for its string of pretty flower baskets: the Puffing Billy continues in similarly cheerful mood inside. Highly original artwork, celebrating the owner's love of the seaside and of all things culinary, makes interesting viewing; a coral-coloured banquette and smart modern lighting, hanging from the rafters, further brightens up the dining room. You can also eat in the comfortable bar: in either case, the menu is a broad one, covering lunchtime sandwiches, fine-dining classics and more 'informal' dishes, many of which are available in either starter or main size. If you're interested in seeing how it all happens, a few tables face the open kitchen.

Food serving times:
Monday-Saturday:
12pm-9.30pm
Sunday: 12pm-3.30pm
Closed Sunday dinner
Prices:
Meals: a la carte 16.00/36.00

Brown tourist sign off A376 to Exmouth, 3mi from junction 30 M5. Parking

Typical Dishes

Confit salmon fillet, baby leeks, tomato

Crispy duckling, apples and fig jus

Chocolate fondant

Haytor Vale

020 **Rock Inn**

Haytor Vale TQ13 9XP

Tel.: (01364) 661305 - Fax: (01364) 661242
e-mail: inn@rock-inn.co.uk - Website: www.rock-inn.co.uk

🍷 ⚂room 🚫 **VISA** **AE** **①** **M©**

Dartmoor Best, Old Speckled Hen

In a pleasant little village near the eastern tip of Dartmoor stands this characterful looking pub with a long-standing owner. It was originally a coaching inn dating back to the mid-18C, and this is evidenced by the covered entrance and stone trough beside old stables. There are nooks and crannies a-plenty; the warren of rooms adds to the gloriously rural appeal of the place. Horse-brasses, unsurprisingly, are ubiquitous. Food orders are taken at the bar by a very pleasant team. Cooking is sound and satisfactory with an interesting meat menu, which might include pan-fried local pheasant breast on cider and fennel seed cabbage with a Merlot jus, shallots and roast walnuts, or suprême of Devon chicken on coconut risotto. Accommodation is provided in the shape of surprisingly spacious and well-kept bedrooms.

Food serving times:
Monday-Sunday:
          12pm-2pm, 7pm-9pm
Closed 25 December
Prices:
Meals: a la carte 20.00/35.00
🛏 **9 rooms :** 66.95/106.95

Typical Dishes

Warm goats cheese, tomato confit

Pan fried sea bass

Coffee and Tia Maria brûlée

3.5mi West of Bovey Tracey by B3387. Parking

Holbeton

021 The Dartmoor Union

Fore St, Holbeton PL8 1NE

Tel.: 01752 830288 - Fax: 01752 830296
Website: www.dartmoorunion.co.uk

    rest **VISA**

Otter and Tawny

Once a Victorian workhouse and later a cider press-house, the Dartmoor Union seems to have found its true vocation at last and, although it's still early days, the tradition of pouring home-produced pints looks set to continue with the establishment of a microbrewery. For all the activity inside, the pub can be hard to spot, as there's only a discreet brass plaque on its stone façade. Its bar is spacious and smartly furnished, hung with pictures of old Holbeton: gold inscriptions on the walls – including "manners maketh man" – may or may not inspire a more philosophical tone of pub debate. The dining room to one side offers a large, seasonal selection of modern and traditional dishes including a good value set lunch. The flower-filled terrace is lovely in summer, and so are Coastguards beach and its cliff walks, a short drive away.

Food serving times:
Monday-Saturday:
12pm-2pm
Sunday:
12pm-3.30pm, 6pm-9pm
Prices:
Meals: 13.95 (fixed price lunch) and a la carte 19.15/25.45

Typical Dishes

Honey glazed goats cheese
Pan seared fillet of bream
Chocolate and banana tart

Between Yealmpton and Modbury. Parking

Holsworthy

022 The Rydon Inn

Holsworthy EX22 7HU

Tel.: (01409) 259444 - Fax: (01409) 259186
e-mail: info@rydon-inn.com - Website: www.rydon-inn.com

    VISA

Sharps Doom Bar, Ring o' Bells Triple H

Tired of life out of a suitcase, two world travellers have decided to put down roots in rural Devon. Their joint venture, the Rydon Inn, actually centres on the stylish modern extension to the 300 year old pub, a bright rotunda with big cross-beams and broad picture windows giving lovely views over the fields. The adjoining bar still welcomes a young local crowd for a pint or three on a Friday night, though the restaurant is a touch smarter in tone, its tables set with candles and fresh flowers. Plenty of thought goes into composing an interesting modern menu that might take in lobster ravioli, braised shank of Devon lamb or a creamy blueberry cheesecake. A concise "little ones" menu sees younger diners well catered for.

Food serving times:
Monday-Sunday:
    12pm-2pm, 6.30pm-9pm
Closed 25-26 December
Closed Monday in winter
Prices:
Meals: a la carte 17.00/27.50

Typical Dishes

Whisky-dressed Gravadlax
Pork tenderloin, Calvados jus
Cheesecake

On A3072 1mi West of Holsworthy.
Parking

Horn's Cross

023 The Hoops Inn

Horn's Cross EX39 5DL

Tel.: (01237) 451222 - Fax: (01237) 451247
e-mail: sales@hoopsinn.co.uk - Website: www.hoopsinn.co.uk

Hoops Old and Special Ales, Bass and 2 guest ales

An old wayside inn since the Middle Ages, this sizeable thatched pub still has plenty to offer the passer-by, including those who need a bed for the night – four rooms in the main house are particularly comfortable, but there are a further eight "standard" ones at the back. Its handsome bar preserves its wooden settles, bowed ceiling beams, cups, tankards and porcelains, not to mention traces of the well which once supplied water for home-brewed ales. A wide-ranging menu covers everything from lunchtime ploughmans and bar favourites, through afternoon teas to tasty dishes like seafood pie, lamb with rhubarb jus and sticky toffee pudding. A pretty terrace looks out over the water garden.

Food serving times:
Monday-Sunday:
    12pm-3pm, 6pm-9.30pm
Closed 25 December
Prices:
Meals: a la carte 11.00/35.00
13 rooms : 65.00/140.00

Typical Dishes

Confit duck salad

Shoulder of lamb, rosemary and garlic

Treacle tart

0.5mi West on A39 going to Clovelly. Parking

Knowstone

024 The Masons Arms Inn

Knowstone EX36 4RY

Tel.: (01398) 341231

e-mail: dodsonmasonsarms@aol.com - Website: www.masonsarmsdevon.co.uk

 VISA **AE**

Tawny Real Ale

Nestled most serenely in a tiny hamlet just off the southern tip of Exmoor is this very attractive, yellow painted, part 13C little thatched inn. It's tremendously characterful inside, heavily beamed with flagged floors and a cosy front snug bar where locals gather to sup Exmoor ale drawn from the barrel. Go down some ruggedly ancient stone steps to find yourself in a candlelit dining room: you could be feasting 700 years ago! Rickety wood tables, benches and chairs are haphazardly set about the place; however, there's nothing haphazard about the food, as the new owner comes from a haute cuisine background including 12 years as head chef of the celebrated Waterside Inn at Bray-on-Thames.

Food serving times:
Monday-Sunday:
12pm-2pm, 7pm-9.30pm
Closed Monday lunch
Prices:
Meals: a la carte 23.00/30.00

Typical Dishes

Ham hock terrine

Seared sea bass and sweet peppers

Rhubarb and sweet wine trifle

7mi Southeast of South Molton by A361. Opposite the village church. Parking

Lydford

025 Dartmoor Inn

Moorside, Lydford EX20 4AY
Tel.: (01822) 820221 - Fax: (01822) 820494
e-mail: info@dartmoorinn.co.uk

VISA

Otter, Dartmoor Best

A bracing walk round Lydford Gorge can build a serious appetite, and there's no better way of satisfying it than a visit to this locally renowned inn on the edges of Dartmoor. As befits its location, it boasts a pleasing rustic character, and enough dining areas to satisfy a coachload of gourmands. Open fires and arty prints on the walls create just the right feeling of relaxation. Good value set menus where local produce is much in evidence in modern cuisine influenced by Mediterranean and local styles. On any given day, you might be able to savour chicken liver parfait, followed by lamb shank shepherds pie, finishing with a home-made, naughty but nice chocolate ice cream with chocolate sauce.

Food serving times:
Tuesday-Saturday:
12pm-2.15pm,
6.45pm-10.15pm
Sunday: 12pm-2.15pm

Prices:
Meals: 17.50 (fixed price lunch and midweek dinner) and a la carte 17.50/30.00
3 rooms : 85.00/125.00

Typical Dishes

Crab salad with herb toasts

Ruby Red Devon beef fillet, red wine sauce

Strawberry jam ice cream, lavender biscuits

1mi East on A386. Parking

Marldon

026 ## Church House Inn

Village Rd, Marldon TQ3 1SL
Tel.: (01803) 558279 - Fax: (01803) 664865

Dartmoor Best, Fuller's London Pride, Greene King IPA and Bass

V isitors to Torbay might like to make an excursion from the delights of Torquay and Paignton to this nearby, attractive inn by the church in Marldon: the pub itself is well sign-posted. It's a listed, whitewashed Georgian structure of 14C origins, and its characterful aspect continues inside with beams, rough stone walls and flagstone floors. There's a large central bar with adjoining rooms which tend to be used for dining but you can eat anywhere: you'll find plenty of drinkers mingling with diners. The bustling atmosphere doesn't faze the waiting staff: there's an invariably friendly service. Blackboard menus offer plenty of choice from the traditional to the more modern, with a guarantee that the vegetables have come from the village's allotment!

Food serving times:
Monday-Sunday:
  12pm-2pm, 6.30pm-9.30pm
Prices:
Meals: a la carte 21.00/28.00

Typical Dishes

Warm leek and Stilton tart

Seared monkfish, basil and olive oil

Brandy snap basket with poached strawberries

Off A380 between Torquay and Paignton - well signposted. Parking

Noss Mayo

027 Ship Inn

Noss Mayo PL8 1EW
Tel.: (01752) 872387 - Fax: (01752) 873294
e-mail: ship@nossmayo.com - Website: www.nossmayo.com

Tamar Jail ale, Butcombe Tribute

Go down a winding South Hams road to get to this idyllically located pub, a stirring dash of white in a delightful inlet surrounded by hills. At high tide, entry is via a back door at first-floor level, but when the tide's out, you can scamper over the beach to the front entrance. The oldest part of the Ship dates from the 1700s; now it's a gleaming, modern place with lovely local prints, glossy wood furniture and piles of books and newspapers – there are games to play as well, like Scrabble and chess. Upstairs a maritime air pervades the restaurant. Friendly staff serve up an extensive menu, ranging from the simple to the adventurous with a good helping of local seafood. Afterwards, go for a stroll in the delightful village, cross the inlet to visit the equally charming Newton Ferrers, or set off on a salty walk up the South West Coast Path.

Food serving times:
Monday-Sunday:
12pm-9.30pm
Prices:
Meals: a la carte 15.00/25.00

10.5mi Southeast of Plymouth by A379 off B3186. Restricted parking, particularly at high tide.

Typical Dishes

Warm shrimps on a buttered crumpet

Grilled sea bass, chorizo mash

Chocolate fondant

Parracombe

028 **Fox & Goose**

Parracombe EX31 4PE

Tel.: (01598) 763239 - Fax: (01598) 763621
e-mail: foxandgoose@mrexcessive.net - Website: www.foxgoose.com

      room **VISA** **MC**

Exmoor Ale, Silver Stallion, Fox, Barn Owl Amber Wheat Ale

The pleasant pub by the stream has, like the rest of Parracombe, taken progress at its own pace: you can still make out today's village of quiet, narrow streets in the sepia photos from the pub's early days, hung here and there among the books, plants, prints and hunting trophies of the main bar. The landlord takes charge in the kitchen and makes good use of the ingredients close to hand: blackboard menus list meats supplied by nearby farms, fish from the local boats – turbot, for example, served with a sundried tomato risotto – and homemade ice creams and desserts, including a good, hearty apple pie. Two simple, pine fitted rooms are fine for an overnight stop.

Food serving times:
Monday-Sunday:
12pm-2pm, 6pm (7pm Sunday)-9pm
Closed 25 December
Prices:
Meals: a la carte 20.00/25.00
1 room : 30.00/50.00

Typical Dishes

Smoked fish platter

Venison casserole

Toffee sponge pudding

5mi Southwest of Lynton by B3234 off A39. Parking

Peter Tavy

029 Peter Tavy Inn

Peter Tavy PL19 9NN
Tel.: (01822) 810348 - Fax: (01822) 810835
e-mail: peter.tavy@virgin.net

    VISA

Princetown Jail Ale, Summerskills Tamar, Sharps Doom Bar, Blackawton Tavy Tipple, Sutton Dartmoor Pride

A matter of yards from St Peter's Church, and the River Tavy, this tiny country pub soon fills up; with good-spirited locals clustered round the bar for a chat in the evening, it certainly has the right kind of sound as you open the door. Two dining rooms with very low beams and close-set chairs and benches can be a bit of a squeeze, too, but once you're settled, an attentive landlord and his team will see you well looked-after. Chabichou goat's cheese and pancetta salad, mildly spicy chicken and prawns and sticky toffee pudding with thick Devon cream are typical of a sound menu with a touch more variety than you might first expect. If the weather's set fair, ask about walks around the surrounding moorland to build up a serious appetite!

Food serving times:
Monday-Sunday:
   12pm-2pm, 6.30pm-9pm
Closed for dinner 24, 26 and 31 December and all day 25 December
Prices:
Meals: a la carte 12.65/25.20

Typical Dishes

Goats cheese charlotte

Shank of lamb, gooseberry and mint sauce

Chocolate truffle torte

3mi Northeast of Tavistock by A386. Parking

Rockbeare

030 **Jack in the Green Inn** *We most liked*

London Rd, Rockbeare EX5 2EE

Tel.: (01404) 822240 - Fax: (01404) 823445

e-mail: info@jackinthegreen.uk.com - Website: www.jackinthegreen.uk.com

   **VISA**

Otter Ale, Gotleigh Tawny, Ruddles

This whitewashed pub has been heavily extended, but still retains an air of the traditional with its carpets and beams. The lounge bar has banquette seating and dark wood tables, but the more characterful – and touch more sophisticated – place to eat is the restaurant, which spans three rooms in the oldest part of the premises. You can eat from the range of dishes listed on the blackboard or from a regularly changing fixed price menu, both of which provide good value. Cooking in the modern British style is accomplished and well presented. Typically, expect fillet of smoked haddock topped with welsh rarebit, or rack and braised shoulder of Whimple lamb with Meaux mustard.

Food serving times:

Monday-Saturday:
12pm-2pm, 6pm-9.30pm

Sunday: 12pm-9.30pm

Closed 25 December-5 January

Prices:

Meals: 22.75 (Sunday lunch) and a la carte 20.00/30.00

Typical Dishes

Pithivier and loin of rabbit

Braised belly pork

Fried figs, raspberries and honeycomb

6.25mi East of Exeter by A30. Parking at the back

Slapton

031 ## Tower Inn

Church Rd, Slapton TQ7 2PN

Tel.: (01548) 580216

e-mail: towerinn@slapton.org · Website: www.thetowerinn.com

 ⚲room *VISA* AE MC

Adnams Bitter, Tribute, Badger Tanglefoot and guest beers during the summer

B uilt in 1347, this remarkably preserved inn once belonged to the Collegiate Chantry of St Mary, and the old church tower still keeps watch over a charming pub garden. Inside, inviting flagged and beamed bar-parlours – one with a fireplace stripped back to the old stone – connect with a slightly smarter dining room strung with hop bines. In such characterful old surroundings, it comes as quite a surprise to see a number of more contemporary dishes among the classics: generous, well-prepared platters of piquant antipasti are something of a speciality. Two simple little bedrooms in the annex are designed with stopovers in mind.

Food serving times:
Monday-Sunday:
12pm-2pm, 7pm-9pm
Closed 25 December,
Sunday dinner and Monday
November-March
Prices:
Meals: a la carte 20.00/25.00
 3 rooms : 40.00/60.00

Typical Dishes

Locally smoked fish platter

Lemon and thyme roasted sea bass

West Country cheeses

6mi Southwest of Dartmouth by A379. Parking

Stokenham

032 Tradesman's Arms

Stokenham TQ7 2SZ

Tel.: (01548) 580313 - Fax: (01548) 580657
Website: www.thetradesmansarms.com

Bass, Eddystone, Devon Pride, Brakspear

 glistening seven-mile finger of golden coastline runs along this part of South Hams, and the nearby Tradesman's Arms is the kind of pub whose charm fits in seamlessly with such enviable surroundings. It's a part-thatched, 14C building that used to serve as workmen's cottages. You have the choice of two separate rooms in which to idle away time looking across a green and pleasant South Devon valley, a pint of real ale at your side. There's the main bar with its stone fireplace and beamed ceiling, or a non-smoking alternative. Both rooms serve the same menu, based around fish and game which, naturally enough, are fresh from the most local of sources: typically, Brixham fish or scallops from Start Bay.

Food serving times:
Monday-Sunday:
 12pm-2.30pm, 7pm-9.30pm
(booking essential)
Prices:
Meals: a la carte 14.15/26.15

Typical Dishes

Chicken liver pâte, pear and ginger chutney

Home-made sausages with onion gravy

Warm Devon apple cake

5.5mi East of Kingsbridge on A379. Parking

Strete

033 The Kings Arms

Dartmouth Rd, Strete TQ6 0RW
Tel.: 01803 770377

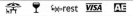

Otter Ale, Adnams

From being slightly rundown – to put it kindly – The Kings Arms has picked itself up in fine style. A white-painted roadside pub with a distinctive balcony, it's easy to spot as you drive up, but this is not its best side, and anyone who has spent a slow, sunny lunchtime in the garden or the pleasant rear terrace is sure to agree. The bar itself, decorated with old local pictures, is fine but small; it's worth going for the extra comforts of the dining room. Two window tables are the prime spots, but bare beams and seats in nautical blue give the whole place a nice, fresh feel. Lunches are slightly lighter but, even here, fish and chips with mushy peas is the odd one out in a menu of modern classics. Dinners make even more use of local, seasonal ingredients, including Devon seafood, meats and cheeses. Fresh, unfussy flavours.

Food serving times:
Monday-Sunday:
    12pm-2pm, 7pm-9pm
Prices:
Meals: a la carte 23.50/30.00

Typical Dishes

Carpaccio of tuna

Fillets of sea bream with crispy pancetta

White chocolate panna cotta

Southwest 4mi from Dartmouth on A379. Parking

Tuckenhay

034 ## The Maltsters Arms

Bow Creek, Tuckenhay TQ9 7EQ

Tel.: (01803) 732350

e-mail: pub@tuckenhay.demon.co.uk - Website: www.tuckenhay.com

  VISA

Princetown IPA, Teignworthy and a selection of guest ales

As implied by its name, this is a former Devonshire malt house dating from the 1800s sited idyllically on the Tuckenhay Creek, when the tide's in, that is. The Maltsters, once owned by TV chef Keith Floyd, is personally run and enjoys a cosy, quaint feel, with a little "pubby" bar and adjacent dining area with further "overflow" room. On busy summer days, a terrace at the side of the creek has its own bar and barbeque. Modern British cooking is the order of the day here, and there's ample choice of meat and local fish dishes, as well as a very good selection of wines by the glass. Families are provided with a "Real Food For Children" menu, so you'd be ill-advised to expect chicken nuggets or even chips.

Food serving times:
Monday-Sunday:
  12pm-3pm, 6.30pm-9.30pm
    (all day in summer)
Prices:
Meals: a la carte 18.00/25.00
5 rooms : 105.00

3.75mi South East of Totnes, near the mouth of the river. Parking

Typical Dishes

Sardines grilled in sea salt

Roast Devon chicken, herby stuffing

Treacle tart

Bridport

035 **West Bay**

Station Road, West Bay, Bridport DT6 4EW
Tel.: (01308) 422157 - Fax: (01308) 459717
e-mail: karen.trimby@btopenworld.com

 room **VISA** **MC**

Copper Ale, Palmers IPA, 200

Sitting just yards from the harbour, there's been a pub on this spot since 1739 and you can still imagine the smugglers and crusty seafarers planning their moonlit jaunts. The front of the bar is still popular with the locals, and the low-beamed ceiling adds to the intimate atmosphere. Behind the bar is the slightly more formal restaurant with its neat arrangement of pine tables and chairs. A blackboard menu offers an extensive range of refreshingly local seafood, which is delivered twice a day. Lunchtime offers a lighter option. In this part of the world, eating al fresco comes naturally, and a summer terrace gives an opportunity to catch up with news from Lyme Bay's fossil gatherers. It's a busy place, so make sure you book first. Four simple bedrooms await upstairs.

Food serving times:
Monday-Saturday:
    12pm-2pm, 6.30pm-9.30pm
Sunday: 12pm-2.30pm
Open dinner Bank Holiday Sundays
booking essential
Prices:
Meals: a la carte 18.85/28.85
4 rooms : 50.00/70.00

Typical Dishes

Scallops, black pudding and fennel

Sea bass with noodles

Vanilla crème terrine, fruit coulis

1.75mi South of Bridport by B3157. Near the harbour. Parking

Corscombe

036 **The Fox Inn**

Corscombe DT2 0NS
Tel.: (01935) 891330 - Fax: (01935) 891330

room   **_VISA_**

Exmoor Ale, Butcombe Bitter and occasional guest ales

Sticky soot, built up over time, lies ingrained on the walls above the fireplaces here. It's one of many endearing features of this mightily charming thatched 17C pub, which boasts several fascinating areas. Two stone floored main bar rooms are intimate and dripping with rural ambience, typified by pews, slate-clad bar and scrubbed pine furniture. Country style imbues the extremely characterful breakfast room, where the first meal of the day is cooked on the Aga; look out for the dog that rests there. A mellow old conservatory has a large table constructed from one strip of oak felled in the 1987 storms. And the food? Dine on well-judged traditional dishes using the best seasonal produce, including well-renowned blackboard fish specials, washed down with something from the reasonably-priced wine list. There are cosy bedrooms, too, endowed with homely charm.

3.5mi Northeast of Beaminster. Parking

Food serving times:
Monday-Sunday:
12pm-2pm, 7pm-9pm
Closed 25 December
Prices:
Meals: a la carte 19.00/28.00
4 rooms : 55.00/100.00

Typical Dishes
Gratin of crab, sea bass and bream

Brill, sweet potato and coriander mash

Sticky toffee pudding

Evershot

Acorn Inn

28 Fore St, Evershot DT2 0JW
Tel.: (01935) 83228 - Fax: (01935) 83707
e-mail: stay@acorn-inn.co.uk - Website: www.acorn-inn.co.uk

  room

Draymens, Ringwood and 1 guest ale

This neat 16C inn in sleepy Evershot still feels like a proper village local, with friendly neighbourhood rivalries kindled at the skittle alley and cooled off with pints of Devon guest ales and ciders, but the oak-panelled main bar, warmed by an open fire in winter, also attracts diners from further afield. Two further rooms in pale wood are just for dining. British pub favourites appear alongside classic dishes with a light modern touch and plenty of local produce; a blackboard menu lists daily changing seafood specials. Recently refurbished bedrooms with designer touches including plasma televisions and separate breakfast room with country style feel.

Food serving times:
Monday-Sunday:
　　　　12pm-2pm, 7pm-9pm
Prices:
Meals: a la carte 20.00/30.00
10 rooms : 75.00/140.00

Typical Dishes
Chicken liver and Port parfait
Moroccan style lamb
Summer pudding, berry ice cream

7mi Northeast of Beaminster by B3163. Parking

Farnham

038 The Museum Inn

Farnham DT11 8DE

Tel.: (01725) 516261 - Fax: (01725) 516988
e-mail: enquiries@museuminn.co.uk - Website: www.museuminn.co.uk

   VISA **MC**

Ringwood Best, Timothy Taylor, Summer Lightening

Standing at the main crossroads of the village, the original, part-thatched Museum Inn has long since received an addition here and an extension there, but the pub as it stands today seems not only smart, bright and well-tended, but seamlessly characterful too. Diners have the choice of four dining rooms, furnished with antique dressers and scrubbed tables and decorated with curiosities from old paintings to stags heads, but as they don't take bookings here, you may be asked to take a seat in the bar first before heading through for classic-contemporary dishes like chicken parfait, duck confit and haddock and mustard risotto. Spacious, quite luxuriously styled bedrooms really are a cut above the average inn; if you don't feel quite ready for bed, the residents lounge might tempt you with a cosy fire and plenty of reading matter.

Food serving times:
Monday-Saturday:
     12pm-2pm, 7pm-9.30pm
Sunday:
     12pm-3pm, 7pm-9pm
Closed 25 December, dinner 26 December and dinner 31 December
Prices:
Meals: a la carte 25.00/32.00
8 rooms : 85.00/140.00

Typical Dishes

Orkney herring fillets

Slow roast belly pork

Crème caramel, pistachio and white chocolate biscuit

7.5mi Northeast of Blandford Forum by A354. Parking

Plush

039 Brace of Pheasants

Plush DT2 7RQ

Tel.: (01300) 348357

e-mail: albu@tinyworld.co.uk - Website: www.thebraceofpheasants.co.uk

 Butcombe, Otter, Palmers, Ringwood, Adnams, Wadworths, Fuller's London Pride

The Giant of Cerne Abbas is not much more than a (giant's) stone-throw from this gloriously secluded 16C thatched inn, which revels in a pleasant rural setting midway between Dorchester and Blandford Forum. In keeping with the surroundings and exterior, the pub – formerly two thatched cottages and a smithy - has a cosy, characterful interior, dominated by the large bar where locals gather to sup pints or partake of the robust, tasty cooking, which has earned a solid local reputation. The same is served in a slightly more formal parlour, or non-smoking dining area for families. There's a pretty rear garden for summer use, with the woods and bridleways of the Piddle valley beyond.

Food serving times:
Tuesday-Sunday:
12pm-3pm, 7pm-9.30pm
Closed 25 December. Open Bank Holiday Mondays
Prices:
Meals: a la carte 22.45/29.25

Typical Dishes

Pan fried foie gras, blueberry sauce

Rack of spring lamb, redcurrant jus

Elderflower meringue

Parking

Arlingham

040 **Old Passage Inn** 🛏

Passage Rd, Arlingham GL2 7JR

Tel.: (01452) 740547 - Fax: (01452) 741871
e-mail: oldpassageinn@ukonline.co.uk - Website: www.fishattheoldpassageinn.co.uk

        VISA *AE* *MC*

Changing Cotswold real ales

Originality is the keyword to this bright green painted inn, perched in an isolated spot where the Severn starts to twist and turn. Any resemblance to a cosy, small-town country inn ends at the dining room, where gastronomic ambitions spiral off on a modern tangent. All efforts go into an accomplished seafood menu; cooking is bold, generous and suitably rustic. A small private dining area at the front can be booked for special occasions. The inn's three bedrooms are funky. They're called Red Mullet, Yellow Finned Tuna and Green Lipped Mussel, and they're all strikingly modern, bright, hi-tec and highly individual. Each has a kingsize bed, and each has a tall DIY cupboard from which, in the morning, Continental breakfast is rather surprisingly, and uniquely, served.

Food serving times:
Tuesday-Saturday:
12pm-2pm, 7pm-9pm
Sunday: 12pm-2pm
Closed 24 December-3 January
Prices:
Meals: a la carte 23.50/33.50
🛏 **3 rooms :** 55.00/95.00

Typical Dishes

Potted shrimps

Pan fried halibut with black truffle

Strawberry and saffron crème brûlée

On the banks of the River Severn, 2.5mi Northwest of Frampton on Severn. Parking

Barnsley

041 Village Pub 🛏

Barnsley GL7 5EF

Tel.: (01285) 740421 - Fax: (01285) 740900
e-mail: reservations@thevillagepub.co.uk - Website: www.thevillagepub.co.uk

   ⇥room **VISA** **MC**

Wadworth 6X and Hook Norton Best

A really special place – too good and too affordable to save for special occasions. Renovated with impeccable taste, five connecting rooms of this part-17C inn lead from gleaming oak floors to spotless flagstones, bright botanical prints and Regency colours to Persian carpets and wingback chairs; the elegant, beamed bedrooms in French country style are every bit as inviting. The real highlight, though, is the daily-changing menu. Dilligently sourced produce, local and organic where possible, and a dash of originality raise appetising modern dishes well above the norm: try tagliatelle with a rich, dark venison and chicken liver sauce, haddock with potato and bacon salad and a deliciously buttery banana cheesecake. Keen and accommodating staff who make sure you're well looked-after.

Food serving times:
Monday-Sunday:
12pm-3pm, 7pm-10pm
Prices:
Meals: a la carte 20.00/30.00
🛏 **6 rooms :** 75.00/125.00

Typical Dishes

Farmhouse terrine and home-made pickles

Rib eye steak garni

Ginger cake, vanilla ice cream

4mi North East of Cirencester, on the B4425

Bledington

042 **Kings Head Inn**

The Green, Bledington OX7 6XQ

Tel.: (01608) 658365 - Fax: (01608) 658902
e-mail: kingshead@orr-ewing.com - Website: www.kingsheadinn.net

☐ ⌖room *VISA* ⓂⒸ

Hook Norton and guest ales

A charming Cotswold setting and a warmly welcoming pub: what could be more idyllic on a perfect summer's day? The Kings Head traces its origins back to the 15C, and in all that time it can rarely have looked more inviting: it certainly entices the Morris dancers who happily congregate each summer on the green outside to perform the Bledington Dances. The place oozes style, with stone and wood floors, real fires and an archetypal modern country pub feel. Printed evening menus identify a solid traditional base, with good use of local produce: meat is bought from a renowned Cotswold butcher, fresh Cornish fish arrives daily, and vegetables are from nearby Evesham Vale. Bedrooms hold the promise of comfy country repose: a low-beamed stairway leads the way.

Food serving times:
Monday-Sunday:
   12pm-2pm, 7pm-9.30pm
Closed 25-26 December
Prices:
Meals: a la carte 20.00/30.00
🛏 **12 rooms :** 55.00/125.00

Typical Dishes

Devilled Lamb's kidneys

Roast saddle of English lamb, minted honey jus

Pear Tart Tatin

4mi Southeast by A436 on B4450.
Parking

>>

Calcot

043 ## The Gumstool Inn

Calcot GL88YJ

Tel.: (01666) 890391 - Fax: (01666) 890394
e-mail: reception@calcotmanor.com - Website: www.calcotmanor.co.uk

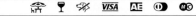

Butcombe Bitter, Cotswold Way, Sharps Doom Bar

The cheerful, civilised Gumstool proudly nurtures its own identity beside an impressive neighbour – Calcot Manor - in one of Gloucestershire's most pleasing locations. It boasts a bustling intimacy, as locals and hotel guests mingle. Gingham curtains, hop bines and a leather armchair by the open fire lend traditional flavours to a generally modern ambience. Rustic but comfy about sums it up. You'll eat well here: bold, imaginative cooking is invariably flavoursome, with influences drawn from the Mediterranean. Dishes can be taken in ample (starter), or generous, portions. Staff create a very relaxed style, but you'll always feel you're being well looked after.

Food serving times:
Monday-Sunday:
12pm-2pm, 7pm-9pm
(booking essential)
Prices:
Meals: a la carte 18.50/25.00
🛏 **30 rooms :** 170.00/235.00

Typical Dishes

Dressed Cornish crab

Confit pork belly, bacon and onions

Orange and lemon pancake

3.5mi West of Tetbury on A4135. Parking

Chipping Campden

044 Eight Bells Inn

Church St, Chipping Campden GL55 6JG

Tel.: (01386) 840371 - Fax: (01386) 841669

e-mail: neilhargreaves@bellinn.fsnet.co.uk - Website: www.eightbellsinn.co.uk

    VISA JCB

Hook Norton Best, Old Hooky, Marston Pedigree, Goffs Jouster, Fullers London Pride

With its typical gables, little leaded windows and steep-pitched roof, the charming 14C Eight Bell Inn stands out even in well-preserved Chipping Campden. It once housed the stonemasons working on the nearby bell-tower, and history is still writ large on the rustic interior. The ancient beams over the bar are now studded with brasses and hung with mugs, and a glass plate set into the floor reveals an old passage running from St. James' Church, thought to have been used for escaping the persecutions of the Reformation or the dangers of the Civil War rather than for discreet exits after last orders. A succinct modern menu and specials board balances the eclectic and the traditional: chunky baguettes are a popular choice at lunch. Pine-fitted bedrooms in bright blues and yellows provide the essentials

Food serving times:

Monday-Thursday:
12pm-2pm, 6.30pm-9pm

Friday-Saturday:
12pm-2.30pm, 6.30pm-9.30pm

Sunday:
12pm-3pm, 7pm-9pm

Closed 25 December

Prices:

Meals: a la carte 19.50/28.50

7 rooms: 50.00/95.00

Typical Dishes

Seared duck livers, crispy Parma ham

Tempura battered king prawns, sweet and sour sauce

White chocolate and rasberry

In centre of town. Unlimited parking on road

361

Chipping Campden

045 **The Kings**

The Square, Chipping Campden GL55 6AW

Tel.: (01386) 840256 - Fax: (01386) 841598
e-mail: info@kingscampden.co.uk - Website: www.kingscampden.co.uk

Hook Norton Best and Hook Norton seasonal bitter

This archetypal Cotswold inn is a real treat. Behind the handsome 17C façade, two surprisingly spacious, antique-furnished rooms, decorated with pictures on a culinary theme, are the perfect place to enjoy a well-balanced menu with a hint of brasserie style – dishes like pork with apple and Calvados, or asparagus salad, make the most of local produce in all its seasonal variety. Countless delightful details raise the bedrooms well above the usual pub standard: impeccably tasteful and never fussy, some even have oak four-poster beds. The pretty rear courtyard, bordered with lavender, is blissfully quiet after the bustle of the town in summer.

Food serving times:
Monday-Sunday:
    12pm-2.30pm,
    6.30pm-9.30pm
Closed 24-25 December
Prices:
Meals: a la carte 15.25/30.35
11 rooms : 85.00/165.00

Typical Dishes

Spiced tiger prawns, sauce vierge

Spring lamb, red wine jus

Chocolate fondant, banana and muscovado ice cream

In centre of town. Residents only parking or parking in the square

Clearwell

046 **The Wyndham Arms**

Clearwell GL16 8JT

Tel.: (01594) 833666 - Fax: (01594) 836450
e-mail: res@thewyndhamhotel.co.uk - Website: www.thewyndhamhotel.co.uk

VISA **M©**

 Freeminer Brewery Speculation Ale, Freeminer Bitter

Visitors are spoiled for choice in this part of the Forest of Dean: the Clearwell Caves and medieval Castle are close at hand, while the Perrygrove Railway is just up the road. Paying a visit to this Cotswold style pub, dating back 600 years, fits in seamlessly on the tourist trail. A pleasant outside terrace is a good spot for summer relaxing; inside, there's much character to admire, particularly in the two-roomed restaurant, which proudly boasts flagstones, bare white walls, rafters, chimney, old bread baking oven in a corner, and paintings for sale on the walls. Hearty, well-cooked, keenly priced dishes keep locals and tourists alike happy: typical dishes might include lightly spiced crab cake with chilli jam; roast rump of lamb on ratatouille with a redcurrant jus; or roasted bell peppers stuffed with couscous.

Food serving times:
Monday-Saturday:
12pm-2pm, 7pm-9.30pm
Sunday:
12.30pm-2pm, 7pm-9pm
Prices:
Meals: a la carte 17.50/27.50
 18 rooms : 55.00/95.00

Typical Dishes

Confit duck leg

Gloucester 'Old Spot' sausages, creamy mash

Apple and rhubarb crumble

By the Cross in the village. Parking

Clifford's Mesne

047 **Yew Tree**

Clifford's Mesne GL18 1JS
Tel.: (01531) 820719

Wye Valley Butty Bach, Fuller's London Pride, Whittington Ale

Allow yourself plenty of time to find this little village, hidden in a wooded corner of the Herefordshire borders. What was once a sadly run-down old pub has been restored through the efforts of a dedicated couple, who have definitely put their mark on the place: dog lovers will be pleased to see man's best friend getting the recognition he deserves in the lounge décor and the five acres of thriving garden are now patrolled by talkative ducks and geese. There's a ringingly enthusiastic welcome for everyone and no effort spared in the service, while regional produce is the key to an appealing modern menu, which is a touch lighter at lunch: try straw-smoked haddock with poached duck's egg or lemon tart with homemade prune and Armagnac ice cream.

Food serving times:
Tuesday-Saturday:
12pm-3pm, 7pm-11pm
Sunday: 12pm-3pm
Closed 2-22 January
Prices:
Meals: 28.50
2 rooms : 55.00/70.00

Typical Dishes

Goujons of Cornish fish

Medallion of Gloucestershire 'Old Spot' pork

Rich lemon tart

2mi Southwest of Newent. Parking

Cockleford

048 **The Green Dragon Inn** 🛏

Cockleford GL53 9NW
Tel.: (01242) 870271

Hook Norton, Butcombe, Courage Directors and 1 monthly changing guest ale

The classic direction "in the middle of nowhere" is a pinpoint indication for this authentic old Cotswold pub in a delightfully remote setting along a country road. A typical honey-gold stone façade serves notice of the warm ambience within: beams, log fire and an authentic rustic style dating back to the 17C. Take your pick of three rooms around the double bar – one is particularly devoted to dining. There's an elaborate choice of menu with a touch of Italian inspiration, so you might find roast fig, taleggio and Parma ham bruchetta for starters, followed by fried gnocchi with white truffle oil, Parmesan and oyster mushrooms for main course. Visitors to the area may wish to stay overnight in plain, simple yet well-equipped bedrooms.

Food serving times:
Monday-Friday:
   12pm-2.30pm, 6pm-10pm.
Saturday-Sunday:
            12pm-10pm

Prices:
Meals: a la carte 20.00/28.00
🛏 **9 rooms :** 57.00/70.00

Typical Dishes

Warm brie and bacon salad

Lamb chops, rosemary and honey glaze

Sticky toffee pudding

5mi South of Cheltenham by A435.
Parking

Coln Saint Aldwyns

049 ## The Courtyard Bar

Coln Saint Aldwyns (at New Inn at Coln) GL7 5AN

Tel.: (01285) 750651 - Fax: (01285) 750657
e-mail: stay@new-inn.co.uk - Website: www.new-inn.co.uk

VISA **AE** **MC**

Wadworth 6X, Hook Norton Best

This delightful, ivy-wreathed 16C inn, with pretty bedrooms in floral patterns, makes a perfect destination for an indulgent long weekend in the country, but you don't have to be a guest to make the most of the Courtyard Bar. Discreetly spaced tables and charming, serenely efficient service would not seem out of place in the more formal restaurant, but there's more than a measure of proper pub intimacy to the place, especially when they fire up the old stove on frosty evenings. Affordable cuisine in contemporary style: ask for a place on the terrace in summer. Welcoming bedrooms.

Food serving times:
Monday-Sunday:
    12pm-2pm, 7pm-9.30pm
(bookings not accepted)
Prices:
Meals: a la carte 20.00/38.00
14 rooms : 95.00/163.00

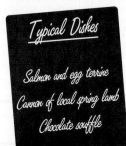

Typical Dishes

Salmon and egg terrine
Cannon of local spring lamb
Chocolate souffle

3mi North of Fairford. Parking

Didmarton

050 **Kings Arms**

The Street, Didmarton GL9 1DT

Tel.: (01454) 238245 - Fax: (01454) 238249
e-mail: bookings@kingsarmsdidmarton.co.uk - Website: www.kingsarmsdidmarton.co.uk

   VISA **M**

Uley Bitter, Bath Ales, Sharpes Doom Bar and Butcombe

This 17C former coaching inn looks most resplendent in its honey coloured overcoat - fitting apparel for a trusted Cotswold family member. Inside is just as good. Hops clamber over beams and local stone merges seamlessly with terracotta walls. A bright and cheerful fire-lit bar with oak settles is perfect for a winter's evening. During the summer months, there's an ideal garden setting for drinks and gentle slumbers. The bright dining room offers a reassuringly hearty menu of tried-and-tested dishes which might include local sausages with buttered mash and onion gravy, or fresh Cornish crab. Smart, pine-fitted bedrooms are good for a pub. Wake refreshed for trips into nearby Malmesbury or Tetbury.

Food serving times:
Monday-Friday:
   12pm-2pm, 7pm-9.30pm
Saturday:
  12pm-2.30pm, 7pm-9.30pm
Sunday:
   12pm-2.30pm, 7pm-9pm
Prices:
Meals: a la carte 15.00/25.00
4 rooms : 45.00/70.00

Typical Dishes
Smoked haddock fishcake, Thai green chilli mayonnaise
Roast rack of Cornish lamb
Lemon cheesecake

5.5mi Southwest of Tetbury on A433. Parking

Ewen

051 **Wild Duck Inn** 🛏

Drake's Island, Ewen GL7 6BY

Tel.: (01285) 770310 - Fax: (01285) 770924
e-mail: wduckinn@aol.com - Website: www.thewildduckinn.co.uk

 🍴 🍷 **VISA** **AE** Ⓜ️Ⓒ

> *Theakston Best, Old Peculier, Sharps Doom Bar, Wells Bombardier, Duck Pond, Courage Directors*

Equally remarkable on the inside and the outside, this privately owned Elizabethan house seems almost too imposing to have started life as a mill, but though the ancient oil paintings do have a hint of stateliness about them, there's an unmistakeable pub atmosphere to the place: intriguing artefacts and bushy swags of hops decorate a series of intimate bar-rooms. Upstairs and in the modern wing, imaginatively styled bedrooms, two with four-poster beds, all share the same richly comfortable ambience. An extensive daily menu, supplemented by blackboard specials, combines modern and traditional dishes and includes a good choice of fresh fish landed at Brixham. Weather permitting, the giant chess set on the terrace offers a more intellectual way to decide who picks up the bill for lunch..

Food serving times:
Monday-Sunday:
　12pm-2pm, 6.30pm-10pm
closed dinner 25 December
Prices:
Meals: a la carte 25.00/40.00
🛏 **12 rooms :** 70.00/150.00

Typical Dishes

Deep fried goats cheese parcel

Monkfish with coconut and chilli sauce

Sticky toffee pudding

3.25mi Southwest of Cirencester by A429. Parking

Frampton Mansell

052 White Horse

Cirencester Rd, Frampton Mansell GL6 8HZ

Tel.: (01285) 760960

Website: www.cotswoldwhitehorse.com

   VISA

Uley Bitter, Hook Norton Best Bitter, Arkell's Summer Ale

From dismal nonentity to bright, modern gastropub, it's been a busy few years for The White Horse, and the friendly, responsive service suggests a team enjoying their success. More cheerful-looking than you would ever guess from the outside, the interior divides into a cosy and very relaxed bar, where they serve snacks and baguettes at lunchtime, and a colourful dining room offering a more ambitious menu. Fairly priced dishes, typically including grilled sardine fillets and roasted tomato, rich chicken liver parfait and sea bass on warm baby vegetables, blend bold, contemporary flavours with a streak of originality. An ever-growing local reputation means it's worth getting there early at weekends

Food serving times:
Monday-Saturday:
12pm-2.30pm, 7pm-9.45pm
Sunday: 12pm-3pm
Closed 24-26 December and 1 January
Prices:
Meals: a la carte 21.00/40.00

7mi West of Cirencester by A419. Parking

Typical Dishes

Seared scallops

Belly of pork, celeriac purée

Crème brulee

Lower Oddington

053 **Fox Inn**

Lower Oddington GL56 0UR
Tel.: (01451) 870555 - Fax: (01451) 870666
e-mail: info@foxinn.net - Website: www.foxinn.net

 ⌂ room *VISA* Ⓜ©

Hook Norton, Abbott, Adnams, Wadworth 6X

A charming village deserves a charming pub, and Lower Oddington has one, an ivy-covered inn not far from the 11C church. 2005's Pub of the Year goes from strength to strength: there's a well cared-for atmosphere in the smartly cosy dining rooms – beams and fireplaces, nooks and crannies, books and candlelight – although the first impression, on most nights of the week, is of friendly chat and activity. Imperturbable young staff have it all under control, even during the busiest lunchtimes, serving enjoyable, flavoursome cooking with its share of British classics like steak and kidney pudding and Bakewell tart. Seafood fans will want to try the potted shrimps, or even ask in advance about their special fish days. Three delightful bedrooms, sumptuously furnished with antiques, are always in immaculate order.

Food serving times:
Monday-Sunday:
    12pm-2pm, 6.30pm-10pm
Closed 25 December and Sunday dinner December-February
Prices:
Meals: a la carte 17.95/27.65
⌂ **3 rooms :** 68.00/95.00

3mi East of Stow-on-the-Wold by A436. Parking

Typical Dishes

Red pepper, goats cheese and tapenade tart

Braised lamb shank with rosemary

Raspberry ripple parfait

Paxford

054 **Churchill Arms**

Paxford GL556XH

Tel.: (01386) 594000 - Fax: (01386) 594005
e-mail: info@thechurchillarms.com - Website: www.thechurchillarms.com

  ⤫room   **VISA**

Hook Norton Best and 1 guest ale

This well-kept, instantly likeable pub is a confirmed local favourite and even at its busiest – when service can start to fray a little at the edges – a laid-back atmosphere still prevails: it's usual to see locals, walkers and visitors to nearby Hidcote Manor propping up the bar and chatting as they patiently bide their time for a table. It's worth the wait; fresh, contemporary, seasonal cooking, using fine ingredients from trusted regional suppliers, is served up at prices which are generous going on philanthropic. Recent successes, typically robust and enjoyable, include asparagus with shallot dressing and smoked goose, crisp, full-flavoured duck confit with cauliflower purée, and a rich chocolate torte. Simple, stylish rooms, half in the modern extension, make a good base for a weekend in the Cotswolds.

Food serving times:
Monday-Sunday:
        12pm-2pm, 7pm-9pm
Prices:
Meals: a la carte 18.00/28.00
🛏 **4 rooms :** 40.00/70.00

Typical Dishes

Pigeon breast with mushroom caponata

Monkfish with chorizo and butternut squash broth

Goats cheese and orange

3mi East of Chipping Campden by B4035. On street parking

Poulton

055 Falcon Inn

London Rd, Poulton GL7 5HN

Tel.: (01285) 850844

e-mail: info@thefalconpoulton.co.uk - Website: www.thefalconpoulton.co.uk

Hook Norton Best, Ramsbury Flint Knapper, Bath Ales Spa

More contemporary inside than the exterior suggests, the thoroughly refitted Falcon has, if anything, gained in neighbourly good nature since its conversion to a dining pub. Relaxed and friendly in atmosphere, there's a main room with a log fire, seagrass carpets, scrubbed pine tables and mix-and-match chairs and pews, and more dining space in the converted skittle alley, from where you can peek into the kitchen and see how lunch is coming on. Two old friends with enthusiasm to burn share the cooking and put their faith in local suppliers; hearty Modern British dishes, never over-elaborate, range from crab cakes or blue cheese and spinach omelette to unstinting helpings of belly pork with lentils, followed by tasty chocolate brownies with ice cream. Well-balanced wine list

Food serving times:
Monday-Saturday:
      12pm-2.30pm,
      6.45pm-9.15pm
Sunday: 12pm-2.30pm
Prices:
Meals: a la carte 18.00/29.00

Village on A417 between Cirencester and Fairford. Parking

Typical Dishes

Seared scallops and pea purée

Navarin of lamb

Pear and almond tart, honey anglaise

Sapperton

056 The Bell

Sapperton GL7 6LE

Tel.: (01285) 760298 - Fax: (01285) 760761
e-mail: thebell@sapperton66.freeserve.co.uk - Website: www.foodatthebell.co.uk

 **VISA**

Hook Norton Best, Uley Old Spot, Butcombe Bitter and Gold

Over the past few years, a dedicated young team have really seen their efforts pay off. The Bell is a much-loved local institution: spotless, smart, uncluttered and wonderfully comfortable, with the warm glow of Cotswold stone inside and out. A well thought-out repertoire, plus daily specials, finds room for pub favourites and appetising modern dishes which make the most of whatever's in season: fortifying midwinter fare includes local pheasant and wild mushrooms braised in wine – tender, earthy and rich – and a moist, dark date and toffee pudding. There are some invigorating walks through woods and meadows, and a log fire and a big wood-burning range to welcome you back, or tables in the courtyard if the sun is shining

Food serving times:
Monday-Sunday:
12pm-2pm, 7pm-9pm
Closed 25 December
Prices:
Meals: a la carte 21.00/35.00

Typical Dishes

Baked pigeon faggot

Slow braised Old Spot belly pork

Fresh berries in Cointreau

5mi West of Cirencester by A419. Parking

Southrop

057 **The Swan**

Southrop GL7 2NU
Tel.: (01367) 850205 - Fax: (01367) 850555

VISA **MC**

 Hook Norton, Wadworth 6X, Adnams Best, Timothy Taylor Landlord

Looking little changed by the centuries, the ivy-covered inn has kept its characterful beamed ceiling, its log fire and its public bar, good for lighter lunches. The main dining room, though, is an altogether more formal affair, but no less welcoming for that. Here, the manager and chef bring their experience from Terence Conran's Bibendum to a contemporary menu with a subtle Mediterranean flavour and a touch of West End sophistication: expect anything from Spanish cured meats and foie gras terrine to monkfish with artichoke risotto or steak tartare. To round off the evening with some healthy competition, they even have a skittle alley for hire: try finding one of those in Kensington!

Food serving times:
Monday-Sunday:
    12pm-2.30pm, 7pm-10pm
Closed 25 and 26 December
Prices:
Meals: a la carte 23.00/27.00

Typical Dishes

Steak Tartare

Smoked haddock, saffron risotto

Passion fruit cream pot

3mi North of Lechlade on Eastleach Rd. Parking on road

Stow-on-the-Wold

058 **Eagle & Child**

Digbeth St, Stow-on-the-Wold GL54 1BN

Tel.: (01451) 830670 - Fax: (01451) 870048

e-mail: info@theroyalisthotel.co.uk - Website: www.theroyalisthotel.co.uk

   VISA

Hook Norton

Not many pubs can boast a leper hole in their armoury (well, in the cellar, to be precise). But that's the case here, in a building that, over a thousand years ago, was a hospice sheltering lepers. It claims to be England's oldest inn, and can certainly boast some impressive history: the discovery of a Civil War Royalist commander's letter, a tunnel leading from the bar to the church opposite, and an ancient frieze. The rooms themselves have thousand year-old timbers. To get to them, go through the reception to the Royalist Hotel and cross the threshold of a pub where you'd feel cheated if there wasn't the tangible whiff of history and rustic charm (don't worry, there is). There's also a sunny, bright conservatory and a restaurant with soft lighting and beams serving well-priced modern menus with a distinct French influence.

Food serving times:
Monday-Sunday:
  12pm-2.30pm, 6pm-9.30pm
Prices:
Meals: a la carte 19.00/41.00
12 rooms : 60.00/140.00

At the Royalist Hotel.

Typical Dishes

Baked goats cheese wrapped in filo pastry

Salmon, buttered asparagus, sauce Maltaise

Vanilla and rum panna cotta

Tetbury

059 ## The Trouble House

Cirencester Road, Tetbury GL8 8SG
Tel.: (01666) 502206 - Fax: (01666) 504508
e-mail: enquiries@troublehouse.co.uk - Website: www.troublehouse.co.uk

Wadworth IPA, 6X, Henrys IPA

You might easily speed past this nondescript roadside inn, but you'd be missing some of the best pub food in England, known far and wide. Imagination and quiet finesse bring out some great natural combinations of flavours in classic and modern British recipes. These can be deliciously simple and satisfying, like lardy cake and custard or tender liver with bacon, but more refined dishes lose none of their robust and moreish appeal: honey lacquered pork with cabbage in garlic and bacon cream, and rabbit with linguine, beans and peas are among the best. Grab a seat where you can in one of three low-beamed bars, with roaring fires and hop-trimmed beams: neat, down-to-earth and very welcoming.

Food serving times:
Tuesday-Saturday:
12pm-2pm, 7pm-9.30pm
Sunday: 12pm-2pm
Closed 25 December-4 January, Sunday dinner, Monday and Bank Holidays
Prices:
Meals: a la carte 27.00/35.00

Typical Dishes

Foie gras and apple terrine
Ribeye steak béarnaise
Dessert plate

2mi Northeast on the A433. Parking

Upper Oddington

060 **Horse and Groom**

Upper Oddington GL56 0XH

Tel.: (01451) 830584 - Fax: (01451) 831496
e-mail: info@horseandgroom.co.uk - Website: www.horseandgroom.uk.com

    room **VISA** ⓜ③

Hook Norton, Wye Valley, Brakspear, Hereford, Butty Bach, Archers, Arkeus

More "well-kept" than "well-kept secret", this busy, part 16C former coaching inn loses nothing by its rural hamlet location. Indeed, the Irish owner's conviviality is a firm guarantee that word will spread. The interior is charming, its timbers and crackling fires distributed over a spacious three rooms; they're invariably buzzing as the staff weave from kitchen to table with honest, tasty home-made dishes. Service, mostly from efficient young travellers, is never less than warm and cordial. Those wanting to steer clear of Stow's heaving guesthouses can stay here – the single rooms have plenty of character, but their sloped ceilings and beams may prove a nuisance after a healthy intake of the inn's wet stuff!

Food serving times:
Monday-Sunday:
12pm-2pm, 6.30pm (7pm Sunday)-9pm

Prices:
Meals: a la carte 18.00/27.00
7 rooms : 55.00/69.00

Typical Dishes

Scallops with pancetta

Smoked haddock rarebit

Lemon and passion fruit tart with ginger ice cream

2mi East of Stow-on-the-Wold by A436. Parking

Winchcombe

061 White Hart Inn

High St, Winchcombe GL54 5LJ

Tel.: (01242) 602359 - Fax: (01242) 602703

e-mail: enquiries@the-white-hart-inn.com - Website: www.the-white-hart-inn.com

  ⟶room **VISA** **AE**

 Old Speckled Hen, Wadworth 6X, Greene King IPA, Uley Old Spot

Over the last few years, the team at The White Hart have transformed a neglected black-and-white timbered inn and built a devoted local following. The secret of their success? It's not the traditional look of the place so much as the feeling of heartfelt hospitality; the cheerfully attentive service brims with personality, and there's a pleasant surprise on the menu too. A broad selection offers a good spread of English and International dishes, but the Swedish specialities are the real treat: gravadlax and herring platters, meatballs, smorgasbord and fruit pancakes are all flavourful, authentic and moreish. Refurbished bedrooms are decorated on a theme: choose from Scottish, Swedish, New England and Moroccan.

Food serving times:
Monday-Sunday:
10am-10pm
Closed 25 December
Prices:
Meals: a la carte 20.00/30.00
10 rooms : 55.00/125.00

Typical Dishes

Gravadlax

Rack of English lamb, rosemary jus

Baileys crème brûlée

In town centre. Parking ⟩⟩

Appley

062 The Globe Inn

Appley TA21 0HJ
Tel.: (01823) 672327
Website: www.theglobeinnappley.co.uk

    VISA **M©**

Cotleigh Tawny, Butcombe Blonde and guest ales

Cosy and traditional, even pleasantly old-fashioned in some ways, the inn's welcoming interior shows the influence of a genial man who clearly sees himself as custodian of the Globe as well as its chef and long-standing landlord. The building itself has origins in the 1400s, but there's nautical history too, in the pictures, prints and photos of the Titanic decorating one wall, and a touch of nostalgia in the display case of die-cast Dinky and Corgi cars and vans. Hard to fault for generosity, the tasty, substantial pub cooking often has a subtle international touch; service is well-organised and invariably polite. If the sun's out, lounge with lunch and beers in the garden before setting off on a walk near the Devon border; if it's not, you could always ask to book the skittle alley.

Food serving times:
Tuesday-Sunday:
12pm-2pm, 7pm-9.30pm
Closed 25-26 December.
Open Bank Holiday Mondays
Prices:
Meals: a la carte 18.00/32.00

Typical Dishes

Haddock chowder

Breast of duck, plum and
spring onion sauce

Raspberry trifle

6mi West of Wellington on A38
(Appley is signposted). Parking

Babcary

063 Red Lion inn

Babcary TA11 7ED
Tel.: (01458) 223230 - Fax: (01458) 224510

Hopback Crop Circle, Teignworthy, O'Hanlons Yellow Hammer

et to one side, the bar of the Red
Lion Inn- complete with bar skittles-
cedes pride of place to two spacious,
airy lounges. One's more particularly
given over to eating, but they share a
contemporary country style: oriental rugs,
neatly set, rustic wooden tables and
framed paintings and Red Lion posters on
the walls. It's not over-formal, and this
clearly suits a lively crowd of lunchers,
from local families to passers-by who
were lucky enough to drop in on spec.;
service might slow a fraction on the
busiest days, but a young team stays
positive and polite. Exciting menus and
regularly changing blackboard feature
contemporary combinations and locally
reared Somerset beef.

Food serving times:
Monday-Saturday:
    12pm-3pm, 6pm-10pm
Sunday: 12pm-3pm
Closed 25 December
Prices:
Meals: a la carte 18.50/25.00

Typical Dishes

Fish cake, hollandaise sauce
Roast chicken tagliatelle
Lime panna cotta

4.5mi Northeast of Ilchester by A37.
Parking

Batcombe

064 ## Three Horseshoes Inn 🛏

Batcombe BA4 6HE
Tel.: (01749) 850359 - Fax: (01749) 850615

Butcombe Bitter

This delightfully set rural pub is reached in true country fashion: down twisty country lanes until you get to the village church. The long, low bar which gives The Three Horseshoes its internal character is distinguished by its beams and painted stone walls; an inglenook boasts a wood-burning stove, there are cosy, cushioned window seats and a wonderfully characterful snug. The menus are of the modern variety, and come with some interesting combinations. You can indulge in a pretty, converted barn dining room with exposed stone, while a back terrace is an ideal place to sit on the grass in summer and inhale the sweet Somerset air.

Food serving times:
Monday-Sunday:
12pm-2pm, 7pm-9pm
Prices:
Meals: a la carte 15.00/30.00
🛏 **3 rooms :** 45.00/60.00

Typical Dishes

Prawn and Cromer crab tian

Medallions of local beef

Brioche bread and butter pudding

Signposted off the A359, midway between Castle Carey and Frome. Tucked away behind the church. Parking

Corton Denham

065 **The Queen's Arms**

Corton Denham DT9 4LR

Tel.: 01963 220317

e-mail: relax@thequeens-arms.co.uk - Website: www.thequeens-arms.co.uk

Butcombe, Timothy Taylors Landlord, Bath SPA

Tucked away in a quiet village between the lovely town of Sherborne and the roaring A303 stands this pleasant 18th century stone built pub, personally run by young owners. Appearances can deceive: the traditional façade here hides an interior where the 'usual' rustic pubby staples have been pretty much jettisoned for a relaxed, contemporary, informal feel, typified by armchairs and sofas you can sink into while sipping your real ale or bottled beer, of which there is a fine worldwide range. British dishes using fine local produce form the backbone of the menus: you can eat in the bar or book for the smart adjacent dining room. There's a delightful rear terrace, too. Bedrooms are more than a cut above the pub norm, offering individually styled luxury with superb bathrooms.

Food serving times:
Monday-Friday:
  12pm-3pm, 6pm-10pm
Prices:
Meals: a la carte 15.00/19.00
5 rooms : 70.00/120.00

Typical Dishes

Marinated fillet of beef
Lamb with minted vegetables
Chocolate pudding

Parking

Ilchester

066 Ilchester Arms 🛏

The Square, Ilchester BA22 8LN

Tel.: (01935) 840220 - Fax: (01935) 841353

Website: www.the-ilchester-arms-hotel.co.uk

🍷 ✕rest ✕ **VISA** **AE** **MC**

Butcombe Bitter

First licensed in 1686, this impressive looking Somerset pub shows its age with appropriate dignity, the profusion of ivy on its exterior just adds a little more rural charm. It stands proudly in the village centre, a relaxing oasis from the hustle and bustle of nearby Yeovil. Public areas are relaxing and intimate, typified by two small lounges and an airy, wood decorated bar - like being down at the local, which many of the customers are. A bistro continues this informal theme, its daily changing blackboard menus have a hearty and familiar ring. At any given time you might try rich, rosemary scented lamb casserole with spring vegetables, confit of duck with garlic crust and cassoulet beans or seared calves liver with onions, bacon and mash. Sizable bedrooms have a good range of facilities.

Food serving times:
Monday-Saturday:
  12pm-2.30pm, 7pm-9.30pm
Sunday: 12pm-2.30pm
closed 26 December
(bar lunch)
Prices:
Meals: a la carte 15.00/26.00
🛏 **7 rooms :** 60.00/75.00

Typical Dishes

Salad of sautéed langoustine

Cannon of lamb aubergine gateau

Iced orange and espresso pudding

Parking

Kingsdon

067 ## Kingsdon Inn

Kingsdon TA11 7LG
Tel.: (01935) 840543 - Fax: (01935) 840916

Otter, Buttcombe, Cotleigh Barn Owl

This part 17C thatched inn knows how to pack 'em in. The best advice is: "Get here early!" Punters are drawn by the unadulterated charm of the place, as well as its rather handy position just off the A303 in a picturesque village near the attractive town of Somerton. It possesses bags of character: low bowed ceiling, wood burning stove, stripped pine built-in wall seat, scatter cushions and stone floors. Four snug, adjoining rooms provide dining options; there's a pleasant garden too. Traditional, popular dishes – and lots of them – show up on a busy looking blackboard menu: everything from whitebait to lambs liver to goats' cheese salad.

Food serving times:
Monday-Saturday:
   12pm-2pm, 7pm-9.30pm
Sunday:
   12pm-2pm, 7pm-9pm
Closed 25-26 December and 1 January
Prices:
Meals: 12.60 (Sunday set lunch) and a la carte 15.00/ 23.20

Typical Dishes

Crab and prawn mornay
Duck in scrumpy sauce
Banana fudge pie

2.5 mi South East of Somerton on B3151. Parking

Lovington

068 ## The Pilgrims

Lovington BA7 7PT

Tel.: (01963) 240600
e-mail: thejools@btinternet.com - Website: www.thepilgrimsatlovington.co.uk

VISA **AE** **MC**

Cottage Champflower Ale

You'd probably not stop here at first sight: Pilgrims doesn't look anything special from the outside. But its slogan – 'the pub that thinks it's a restaurant' – gives a hint of what to expect inside. Beyond the front door, there's a transformation. It does, indeed, have a smart, pleasant restaurant style: deep burgundy and exposed stone walls, coir mat flooring and bright, cheerful watercolours mostly by a local village artist. The bar isn't forgotten; it's traditional in character, with flag floors and low beams. Cookery books are piled on a piano and matchboxes from around the world decorate the walls. Menus, in the modern style, revel in interesting variations.

Food serving times:
Tuesday-Saturday:
    12pm-2pm, 7pm-11pm
Sunday: 12pm-2pm
Closed last 3 weeks October
Closed Tuesday lunch
Prices:
Meals: a la carte 20.00/34.00

Typical Dishes

Trio of smoked fish

Monkfish, scallops, bacon and mushrooms

West Country cheeses

4mi South West of Castle Cary by B3153 signposted Somerton and A371 on B3153. Parking

Lower Vobster

069 ## The Vobster Inn

Lower Vobster BA3 5RJ

Tel.: (01373) 812920 - Fax: (01373) 812350
e-mail: vobsterinn@btinternet.com

     VISA M

Butcombe Bitter, Fuller's London Pride, Tunnel Vision

Very much the centre of its tiny Somerset village, the Vobster Inn, run by a husband and wife team, takes its duty seriously and does its best to keep everyone happy, from young families and older couples, out enjoying the sun at the terrace tables, to the unhurried neighbours enjoying a slow pint inside. Adjoining the bar, a long lounge serves as the restaurant, its walls painted with grapes and lined with posters, labels, wine racks and even old wine cases. Sensibly allowing room for market-fresh specials, fish and seafood are always on the menu and there's always a good selection of hand-crafted West Country cheeses on offer.

Food serving times:
Monday-Sunday:
12pm-2pm, 7pm-9.30pm
Closed 25 December
¨Seafood¨
Prices:
Meals: a la carte 16.00/25.00

Typical Dishes

Selection of charcuterie

Griddled scallops with black pudding

Chocolate nemesis

From Frome head northwest to Radstock on the A362. Vobster is signposted approx 5.5mi off the A362. Parking

Luxborough

070 Royal Oak Inn of Luxborough

Exmoor National Park, Luxborough TA23 0SH

Tel.: (01984) 640319 - Fax: (01984) 641561
e-mail: info@theroyaloakinnluxborough.co.uk - Website: www.theroyaloakinnluxborough.co.uk

   VISA ⓜⓒ

Cotleigh Tawny, Exmoor Gold, Palmers 200, IPA

In a fold of the rolling Brendon Hills, surrounded by picture postcard cottages, the Royal Oak is in the most idyllic position possible. Once you've located the pub among the many lanes of the area, step into a low beamed and log fired bar featuring an impishly accurate cartoon of one of the regulars (who may well be sitting there with pipe and pint). Invitingly furnished dining rooms in deep olive tones lead off from here; another rustic bar keeps them company and the atmosphere carries over from here. Suppliers knock at the front door with their produce, so there's no shortage of local inspiration: chicken with bacon lardons, cider, cream and local apple brandy is a satisfying blend of West Country flavours. There are a dozen en-suite bedrooms for those wishing to stay on.

Food serving times:
Monday-Sunday:
    12pm-2pm, 7pm-9pm
Closed 25 December
Prices:
Meals: a la carte 15.00/25.00
🛏 **12 rooms :** 55.00/85.00

Typical Dishes

Filo basket of mussels
Roast rack of Exmoor lamb
Mango cheesecake

Luxborough is signposted off the A39 East of Minehead or off the B3224 Exford to Taunton road. Parking

Mells

071 Talbot Inn 🛏

Selwood St, Mells BA11 3PN
Tel.: (01373) 812254 - Fax: (01373) 813599
e-mail: roger@talbotinn.com - Website: www.talbotinn.com

VISA ⓞ ⓜⓒ

Butcombe Best

This utterly charming 15C stone-built coaching inn boasts an immediate impact with its cobbled courtyard and walled garden with pétanque piste and vine-covered pergola. The effect continues in a pleasant, intimate main bar, where dried hops cling to the beams and green candles flicker in old wine bottles. Here, indulge in hearty, traditional bar meals with daily changing blackboard dishes or a more serious dinner menu with fish specials from Brixham. You can also drink in a large tythe barn, its ancient character recently enhanced by a mural depicting life in Mells through the ages. Bright, pretty, individually appointed bedrooms make a night's stopover worthwhile.

Food serving times:
Monday-Sunday:
12pm-2.30pm, 6.30pm-11pm
Prices:
Meals: a la carte 16.00/27.00
🛏 **8 rooms :** 75.00/145.00

Typical Dishes

Duck liver pâte
Pot roast gigot of lamb
Mango crème brûlée

4mi West of Frome. 〉〉

Montacute

072 Phelips Arms

The Borough, Montacute TA15 6XB

Tel.: (01935) 822557 - Fax: (01935) 822557
e-mail: infophelipsarms@aol.com - Website: www.phelipsarms.co.uk

 VISA

Palmers Copper Ale, IPA and Zoo

M ontacute derives most of its fame from the stirring Montacute House, owned by the National Trust and 100 yards down the road, but this attractive part-17C sand coloured inn provides another reason to turn off the A303. It's a good, traditional pub, but very small - there are only 11 tables. Bright lights and swirly carpet are offset with dark wood tables and chairs given a modern lift by bright red and blue curtains and cushions with the owner's own photos and paintings displayed on the walls. The contemporary touches carry over to the cooking, which boasts some interesting, eclectic choices which are cooked to perfection and well presented. Long back garden with benches.

Food serving times:
Monday-Saturday:
12pm-2pm, 7pm-9pm
Sunday:
12pm-2.30pm, 7pm-9pm
Closed 25 December
Prices:
Meals: a la carte 20.25/31.75

Typical Dishes

Fillet of red mullet, sauce vierge

Venison, braised chicory chocolate sauce

Triple chocolate mousse

5mi Northwest of Yeovil by A3088 (Montacute is signposted). Public parking in the square opposite

South Cadbury

073 **The Camelot** we most liked

Chapel Rd, South Cadbury BU22 7EX
Tel: 01963 440448 - Fax: 01963 441462
Website: www.thecamelot.co.uk

Butcombe, Cottage, Bath Ales, Dorset Brewing Co

So named because (allegedly) a hill in Cadbury is the original site of King Arthur's Camelot. True or not, one thing's for sure…good food here is no myth. Owned by the Montgomery family – well known in these parts for producing award-winning cheeses for nearly 100 years – this little pub was modernised in 2004 to give it a light, airy, uncluttered ambience, enhanced by stylish local artwork on the walls. Modish wood tables are dotted about and laid for eating, but there's still plenty of space for locals to enjoy a pint; in fact, they've restored the skittle alley here. Lunch features home-made pies and sandwiches, whereas at night a distinctly more modern selection, precisely cooked with local produce and offering great value, tempts the palate: there's a large first-floor area resembling a restaurant catering for the influx of weekend diners.

Food serving times:
Monday-Sunday:
 12pm-2.30pm, 7pm-9.30pm.
Prices:
Meals: a la carte 16.50/27.10

Typical Dishes

Pea soup with chargrilled scallops

Confit duck with egg noodle stir-fry

Passion fruit crème brûlée

4.5mi South of Castle Cary by B3152 off A359. Parking

Stanton Wick

074 Carpenters Arms

Stanton Wick BS39 4BX

Tel.: (01761) 490202 - Fax: (01761) 490763
e-mail: carpenters@buccaneer.co.uk - Website: www.the-carpenters-arms.co.uk

Butcombe, Wadworth 6X, Courage Best

The Carpenters Arms is actually a group of 300-year old converted miners' cottages. Now it glows with a pubby contentment, typified by dark wooden furniture, candles in wine bottles, built-in wall seats and, of course, the original exposed stone walls. A big log fire roars in winter. Its long, low exterior is offset with hanging baskets, bright flowers and the tranquility of the surrounding countryside. For diners, a snug inner "parlour" awaits with fresh flowers on the tables and beams above. Modern cooking prevails, proof of popularity confirmed by the number of tables taken. Upstairs: sizable, pine furnished bedrooms in subtle floral patterns and modern bathrooms.

Food serving times:
Monday-Saturday:
    12pm-2pm, 7pm-10pm
Sunday:
    12pm-2.30pm, 7pm-9pm
Closed dinner 25-26 December
Prices:
Meals: a la carte 21.00/25.00
 12 rooms : 64.50/89.50

Typical Dishes

Seared scallops, herb salad
Grilled Tew Valley trout
Rosemary crème brûlee

9mi South of Bristol (just off the A37) signposted off A368. Parking

Tarr Steps

Tarr Farm Inn We most liked

Tarr Steps TA22 9PY

Tel.: 01643 851507 - Fax: 01643 851111
e-mail: enquiries@tarrfarm.co.uk - Website: www.tarrfarm.co.uk

 🍴 🍷 ✂ **VISA** ⓜⓒ

The old clapper bridge at Tarr Steps has crossed the River Barle since time immemorial, and Tarr Farm has had privileged access to this unchanging tranquillity since the Elizabethan age. In the heart of Exmoor, it's one of the more gloriously remote inns of the West Country, and its neat garden is a fine spot to absorb the peaceful surroundings. Your rapture may well continue when you step inside…there's a hugely characterful and cosy beamed bar serving Exmoor ales. Typical pubby lunchtime dishes give way to a comprehensive evening menu of accomplished, interesting dishes featuring a wealth of fine local produce, served in the bar or intimate restaurant. Bedrooms here are special, too. Comfy, spacious and furnished in an eye-catching way, they offer every conceivable luxury, while, for the more adventurous, a host of Exmoor outdoor pursuits are on the doorstep, and can be arranged by the hosts.

Food serving times:
Monday to Sunday:
12pm-3pm, 6.30pm-9.30pm
Prices:
Meals: a la carte 14.50/29.75
🛏 **9 rooms :** 60.00/120.00

Signposted off the B3223 Dulverton to Exford road. Parking

Typical Dishes

Seared scallops with lentils

Fillet of beef, spinach puree

Apple bavarois with apple sorbet

Triscombe

076 **Blue Ball Inn** _We most liked_

Triscombe TA4 3HE

Tel.: (01984) 618242 - Fax: (01984) 618371
Website: www.blueballinn.co.uk

🏕️ 🍷 _VISA_ Ⓜ️©

Cotleigh Tawny, Exmoor Gold, Stag, HSD, Tribute, Otter

A walk in the gorgeous Quantocks requires sustenance along the way, so arm yourself with a map and pitch up at the Blue Ball in good time for lunch. It's a wonderfully inviting place: you can't go far wrong with a 15C thatched and stone-built former stables. There are exposed roof timbers, wooden floors and a large picture window with beautiful views over the surrounding countryside. The menus are imaginative, wide ranging and full of local ingredients. Hungry ramblers can get chunky baguettes at lunchtime; more serious diners can feast on modern and traditional British pub classics. Two modern, stylish and open-plan bedrooms with luxury bathrooms are set in what was the original pub next door.

Food serving times:
Closed 25 December, dinner 26 December and dinner 1 January
(booking essential)
Prices:
Meals: a la carte 22.00/32.00
🛏️ **2 rooms :** 30.00/80.00

4.5mi North of Bishops Lydeard by A358. Parking

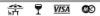

Typical Dishes

Carpaccio of beef

Rabbit with lemongrass

Chocolate and pistachio dessert

393

West Bagborough

077 ## The Rising Sun 🛏

West Bagborough TA4 3 3EF

Tel.: (01823) 432575

e-mail: enquiries@theriser.co.uk - Website: www.theriser.co.uk

 VISA **MC**

Cotleigh Tawny and Golden Eagle, Butcombe and Exmoor Gold

G rab a pint, sit for a while on one of the outside benches hard up against the front of this pretty stone pub, and take in the invigorating air of one of Somerset's most elevated and delightfully located pubs: indeed, it feels like the whole village is on the verge of dropping off the side of the Quantocks. The Rising Sun has 16th century origins, but was rebuilt a few years ago after a fire that lit up the surrounding hillside. There's oak in the beams and slate on the floors, but a modern feel prevails. It's not a big place, and you'll find locals at the bar in close proximity to diners from far afield. A smart upstairs room has exposed trusses, local artwork and a wonderful rural view from big windows. Light, traditional pub lunches give way in the evening to more interesting modern dishes with fresh Somerset ingredients. Wake up to a stylish bedroom with exposed beams.

Food serving times:
Tuesday-Sunday:
12pm-2pm, 7pm-9pm
Closed Mondays except
Bank Holidays
Prices:
Meals: a la carte 18.00/26.00
🛏 **2 rooms :** 45.00/75.00

10.5mi North West of Taunton off
A358 〉〉

Typical Dishes

Grilled Somerset goats cheese with marinated figs

Braised Exmoor lamb shank

Caramelised apple tart, pear sorbet

Winsford

078 ## Royal Oak Inn

Exmoor National Park, Winsford TA24 7JE

Tel.: (01643) 851455 - Fax: (01643) 851009
e-mail: enquiries@royaloak-somerset.co.uk - Website: www.royaloak-somerset.co.uk

VISA **AE** **D** **MC**

Butcombe, Brakspear

Facing the shaded green and its trim cottages, the old Royal Oak, its thatched roof turned and folded, stands at the heart of Winsford, a charming village best known for its little interlacing streams and its old packhorse bridge across the River Exe. Inside the pub, one cosy lounge leads into another, their original rural style proudly preserved, to the delight of visitors from out of town; cushioned benches are grouped to form intimate little booths. Out-and-out English cooking seems right at home here, and a no-nonsense menu sticks to the classics, from lunchtime pies and sandwiches in the bar to generous plates of steak and kidney pudding with tasty rhubarb crumble and cream to follow. After lunch, Exmoor beckons, with mile upon mile of heather upland and wooded valleys to be explored

Food serving times:
Monday-Sunday:
   12pm-2pm, 6.30pm-9pm
Prices:
Meals: a la carte 20.20/25.95
🛏 **14 rooms :** 75.00/136.00

Typical Dishes

Salad of Gravadlax

Roast English lamb, mint sauce

Apple crumble

5mi North of Dulverston by B3223. Opposite the village green. Parking

Axford

079 Red Lion Inn

Axford SN8 2HA

Tel.: (01672) 520271 - Fax: (01672) 521011
e-mail: indo@redlionaxford.com - Website: www.redlionaxford.com

VISA **M⊙** **JCB**

Hook Norton Best, Ramsbury Gold, Cottage Brewing Company

This brick-and-flint inn of 17C pedigree immediately impresses as a warm and welcoming place. The top area is a lovely lounge bar with roaring fire and a gaggle of contented smokers, and there are fresh flowers on the main bar. Throughout the remainder of the inn a wide range of pictures by local artists is on sale. The blackboard choice of dishes is split into starters, mains and fish and are, largely speaking, from a traditional base. They're served in either the neatly kept dining room, full of old and new silver and china jostling for attention, or conservatory, where tankards and water jugs hang beseechingly from the ceiling. There's one more blackboard, announcing wines by the glass, and when the scoffing and quaffing are done, diners are invited to fill in a card and be kept informed on future menus and events.

Food serving times:
Monday-Sunday:
      12pm-2pm, 7pm-9pm
Closed 25 dinner 26
December
Prices:
Meals: a la carte 16.75/26.00

Follow signs for Axford from Marlborough. Parking

Typical Dishes

Seared scallops with lime and ginger

Tenderloin of pork, prune stuffing

Caramelised Banana

Box

080 **The Northey**

Bath Rd, Box SN13 8AE
Tel.: 01225 742333 - Fax: 01225 742333

VISA MC

Wadworth 6X, IPA

There's not really anything remarkable about this roadside pub, at least, not from the outside. It's worth pulling over all the same, though. A thorough makeover has worked wonders on the old, slightly charmless interior and, while the bar remains, with a few sofas, much of the space is given over to simply set dining tables. It's less of a drinking "local" than it was before, but you can hardly blame the friendly team at The Northey for sticking to what they do best: well-weighed flavours are a constant theme in their appetising, well-judged dishes, which are served with tidy efficiency, and all for a very fair price. You could just have a sandwich but, with good modern cooking for the asking, you might feel you were missing out.

Food serving times:
Monday-Sunday:
12pm-2pm, 7pm-10pm
(-9pm Sunday)
Closed 25-26 December,
31 December (dinner) and
1 January (dinner)
Prices:
Meals: a la carte 20.00/30.00

Typical Dishes

Carpaccio of tuna
Beef with whiskey jus
Fig and almond tart

4,75 mi from Bath on A4. Parking

Burcombe

081 The Ship Inn

Burcombe Lane, Burcombe SP2 0EJ

Tel.: 01722 743182 - Fax: 01722 743182

e-mail: theshipburcombe@mail.com - Website: www.theshipburcombe.co.uk

 VISA **AE** **M©**

Courage Best, Flowers IPA, Wadworth 6x

L ooking traditional and well cared-for, the trim, part 17C Ship Inn lives up to expectations on the inside. Pass under the model of a man o' war in full sail, fixed in a gabled niche above the door, and into a nicely modernised open-plan bar: old exposed timbers and open fires are still in place, and so too is the rural atmosphere you'd expect. Diners and drinkers take their seats where they like and a fresh and tasty seasonal menu with a modern touch, together with traditional classics and a blackboard full of specials, offers plenty of choice: regular themed dinners and summer barbecues lend further variety. But one of the nicest things about the Ship is its lovely rear garden which runs down to a tributary of the river Nadder – find a table in the sun and make yourself comfortable.

Food serving times:
Monday-Sunday:
   12pm-2.30pm, 6.30pm-9pm
Closed 5 -20 January
Prices:
Meals: a la carte 18.20/26.45

Typical Dishes

Crab , avocado and lime timbale

Char grilled lamb chops

White chocolate and Baileys mousse

5,25 mi West of Salisbury by the A36 Off A30.Parking

Codford St Mary

082 **George**

High St, Codford St Mary BA12 0NG

Tel.: (01985) 850270

  ⚞room **VISA** Ⓜ︎Ⓒ

Ringwood Best, Timothy Taylor Landlord

The wild expanse of Salisbury Plain stretches away from this whitewashed 18C pub-hotel in a pretty village. Culture prevails in the Woolstone Theatre opposite; The George, meanwhile, makes a successful appeal to other senses. Although not the place for a cosy meal à deux - there are no beams or cosy decor - the strength of this place lies in the food. The experienced chef-patron uses seasonally changing, locally-sourced ingredients with daily specials appearing on a blackboard. Lunch menus are simpler in style and give way to a concise, regularly changing evening menu. Whet the appetite first by relaxing with a drink and a magazine in the comfortable lounge. If thoughts of the dark Plain are too much to contemplate at night, stay in one of their clean, simple bedrooms.

Food serving times:
closed Sunday dinner and Tuesday

Prices:
Meals: a la carte 18.00/35.00
🛏 **3 rooms :** 45.00/65.00

Typical Dishes

Rillette of guinea fowl, gooseberry chutney

Steamed turbot, watercress risotto

Iced white chocolate

Village signposted off the A36, southeast of Warminster, or use the A303 which is close by

Corsley

083 Cross Keys

Lyes Green, Corsley BA12 7PB

Tel.: (01373) 832406 - Fax: (01373) 832934
Website: www.crosskeysatcorsley.com

Y **VISA**

 Henry's IPA, Wadworth 6X, Summersault plus guest beers

A typically rural pub in a typically rural area: all the credentials for a satisfying experience in deepest Wiltshire. The owners of this charming 14th century pub go out of their way to create a warm, relaxed feel, with the bright, colourful walls filled with local photos and prints of outdoor pursuits, the open fires and the friendly, even lightly jokey service. Choose between dining areas either embellished by fresh flowers or tubby candles. Either way you'll eat at scrubbed tables from an extensive menu featured on three blackboards. Dishes are keenly priced, freshly prepared, and very tasty, carefully utilising local supplies and suppliers. Try something from the notable fish range.

Food serving times:
Monday-Saturday:
 12pm-2.15pm, 7pm-9.30pm
Sunday:
 12pm-2.15pm, 7.15pm-9pm
Restricted opening Christmas
Prices:
Meals: a la carte 10.50/27.75

Typical Dishes

Scallops, bacon and mushrooms

Halibut, Brixham crab risotto

Apple and cinnamon sponge

Midway between Frome and Warminster. Village is on A362 and pub is signposted. Parking

Donhead St Andrew

084 **Forester Inn** 🛏️

Lower St, Donhead St Andrew SP7 9EE

Tel.: 01747 828038 - Fax: 01747 828050

e-mail: enquiries@foresterinndonheadstandrew.co.uk - Website: www.foresterinndonheadstandrew.co.uk

 Ringwood, Hampshire, Doombar, Sharps, Wadsworth 6X

If you've a penchant for stone-built, thatched pubs with 13th century origins, then this most definitely is the place for you. The Forester is tucked away in a quaint village on the Dorset/Wiltshire border, and its beguiling exterior is enhanced by a small garden and lovely terraced area that surrounds one of its sides. All that's missing is the sea… The main bar is just like you'd expect: beamed, exposed stone walls, large inglenooks; with an attractive extension which resembles the interior of a barn: a big space with exposed roof trusses and doors and windows out onto the terrace. Menus here offer ample choice, and locally sourced ingredients make a plentiful showing; cooking is firmly in the modern bracket. Upstairs, the spacious bedrooms are done out in a pleasant contemporary style – a surprising juxtaposition to the pub's more rustic charms.

Food serving times:

Monday-Sunday:
   12pm-2pm, 6.30pm-9pm

Closed for dinner
25 December

Prices:

Meals: a la carte 20.00/30.00

🛏️ **2 rooms :** 57.50/95.00

☕ 6.00

5 mi East of Shaftesbury by A30.Parking

Typical Dishes

Chargrilled asparagus

Roasted venison with colcannon

Passion fruit soufflé

Heytesbury

085 The Angel Inn

High St, Heytesbury BA12 0ED

Tel.: (01985) 840330 - Fax: (01985) 840931

e-mail: admin@theangelheytesbury.co.uk - Website: www.theangelheytesbury.co.uk

Moorland Original, Greene King IPA and regularly changing guest ales

In a pretty village on the edge of Salisbury Plain stands this attractive roadside 17C inn. There's a delightful courtyard terrace and stylish, refurbished ground floor, boasting a cosy lounge with soft leather tub seats, roaring fire, and, further along, a snug though spacious bar. To one side, an elegant, contemporary restaurant completes the picture. Modern pub classics go down well at lunch, as you would expect but, in the evening, things move on with a particularly interesting à la carte that's well prepared and cooked with precision with steak a speciality. Staying overnight is a wise move here. Cosy, well-appointed bedrooms have been undergoing refurbishment.

Food serving times:
Monday-Sunday:
    12pm-2.30pm, 7pm-9.30pm
        (Sunday 9pm)
Closed dinner 25 December
Prices:
Meals: a la carte 12.00/35.00
🛏 **8 rooms :** 60.00/75.00

Typical Dishes

Home-cured salmon

Pork fillet, black pudding croquette

Hot chocolate brownie, white chocolate ice cream

On the A36 4 mi Southwest of Warminster by B3414, or off the A303. Parking

Hindon

086 The Lamb Inn

High St, Hindon SP3 6DP

Tel.: 01747 820573 - Fax: 01747 820605
e-mail: info@lambathindon.co.uk - Website: www.lambathindon.co.uk

Young's Special, Young's Ordinary, Brains

The Lamb has a substantial reputation for feeding travellers as it used to be a much-frequented coaching inn. The 21st century sees it adequately keeping up the tradition: its attractive creeper-clad façade is the destination for a steady stream of hungry diners, many of them passing nearby on their way to the West Country. Conveniently set just off the A303, it has a most beguiling interior of deep burgundy walls, wood and flagged floors, rafters, a gallery's worth of pictures, and higgledy-piggledy tables and chairs filling every conceivable space. A large blackboard menu forms the core of the dishes offered: expect game and traditional English fare, peppered with lighter and more traditional pub favourites. As befits an inn, there are 14 bedrooms pleasantly furnished and not without some character…especially their tartan carpets.

Food serving times:
Monday-Saturday:
12pm-2.30pm,
6.30pm-9.30pm

Prices:
Meals: a la carte 18.00/30.00
14 rooms : 65.00/90.00

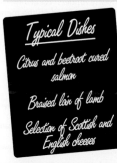

Typical Dishes

Citrus and beetroot cured salmon

Braised loin of lamb

Selection of Scottish and English cheeses

Parking

Holt

087 Tollgate Inn

Ham Green, Holt BA14 6PX

Tel.: (01225) 782326 - Fax: (01225) 782805
e-mail: alison@tollgateholt.co.uk - Website: www.tollgateholt.co.uk

  VISA M③

 A selection real ales from Exmoor, Box and Cambridge Breweries

Despite its rather noisy location at a busy road junction, the locals of Holt have made this hearty old pub of Bath stone a wonderfully friendly place to be. Conviviality stretches across all areas, aided and abetted by strategically placed sofas and a log-burning stove. No one seems in a rush as they linger over newspapers and magazines. If and when you decide to eat you have a choice of two venues. A cosy room adjacent to the bar offers a traditional feel, while upstairs, in a former chapel, is a more formal restaurant with original chapel windows and lofty timbers. Local ingredients are proudly advertised on the menus, and dishes exhibit distinctly modern overtures. Bedrooms have a more traditional outlook, but are cosy and comfortable.

Food serving times:
Tuesday-Saturday:
12pm-2pm, 7pm-9.30pm
Sunday: 12pm-2pm
Closed 25-26 December and first week January

Prices:
Meals: 11.95 (fixed price lunch) and a la carte 20.00/29.00
4 rooms : 50.00/95.00

Typical Dishes
Foie gras terrine

Pan fried sea bass, crayfish sauce

Caramelised bananas vanilla ice cream

On B3107 midway between Bradford-on-Avon and Melksham. Parking

Marden

088 The Millstream

Marden SN10 3RH

Tel.: (01380) 848308 - Fax: (01380) 848337
e-mail: mill.stream@virgin.net - Website: www.the-millstream.co.uk

 Wadworths JCB, 6X, Henrys IPA and a guest beer

Look across the delightful garden with its unusual peacock sculpture to the river Avon from this recently enlarged, Vale of Pewsey pub. The pastoral delights to be enjoyed here are timeless; inside an appealing refurbishment has taken place: champagne is served by the glass in a bar that stays open all day. This old pub's recent makeover has nevertheless left it with much original character: pale beams, thick wattle walls in a mustard palette, log burners and antiques enliven the open-plan section. There are several dining areas, with vertical beams acting as dividers. Tables are in antique wood but the menus are of more recent vintage: if you need help, the bubbly owner is only too keen to please. Much of the local produce is organic and fish is fresh from Looe.

Food serving times:
Monday: 7pm-9.30pm
Tuesday-Sunday:
        12pm-3pm, 7pm-9.30pm
Closed 25 December and Monday lunch
Prices:
Meals: a la carte 20.00/37.50

Take the A342 to Andover. Marden is 6.5mi Southeast of Devizes. Parking

Typical Dishes

Seared scallops with celeriac puree

Fillet of beef with roasted roots

Clotted cream ice cream

Oaksey

089 The Wheatsheaf

Wheatsheaf Lane, Oaksey SN16 9TB
Tel.: 01666 577348

Butcombe Gold, London Pride, Summer Lightning

Neatly flanked by the attractive trio of Malmesbury, Tetbury and Cirencester, this charming little inn reflects the minimalist appeal of the gloriously rural village from which it takes its name. There's lots of pubby character here: the original bar in situ, solid beams, wood floor, and exposed walls of stone decorated with farming implements above an inglenook fire. Rubbing shoulders with locals having a pint, you can eat at the simple tables or repair for a touch more comfort to the rear of the bar where a hint of modernisation has taken place. A tiny front terrace is popular in clement weather. Food is important here. Menus offer a concise choice of simple lunch fare to far more ambitious modern British dishes cooked with care and accomplished assurance. For the athletic, there's a skittle alley across the road!

Food serving times:
Monday-Sunday:
  12pm-2pm, 6.30pm-9.30pm
Prices:
Meals: a la carte 21.00/30.00

Typical Dishes

Smoked Coln trout salad

Poached guinea fowl, foie gras sauce

Selection of cheeses

5.5mi North of Malmesbury; signposted off the A429. Parking

Ramsbury

090 **The Bell**

The Square, Ramsbury SN8 2PE

Tel.: (01672) 520230 - Fax: (01672) 520832

e-mail: info@thebellramsbury.com - Website: www.thebellramsbury.com

 VISA **MC**

Ramsbury Brewery Ales

If this handsome period pub has a new lease of life, it's probably thanks to the new leaseholder. Though he's happiest on the first tee or the rugby touchline, behind the bar comes a close second, and he's found time to direct a renovation that feels true to the origins of the place. One half is given over to dining, the other, filled with light from the bow window, matches old pew seats with framed black and white photos - each with a bell theme; even with an encouraging crowd of regular drinkers and diners, it feels pleasantly spacious. An abbreviated lunch menu manages to offer decent variety, from pints of prawns and gazpacho to haddock risotto or sausage and mash, and is just as well-presented as the evening list, which introduces a few surprises: when was the last time you saw lamb sweetbreads on a pub menu? Don't forget the shaded garden in hot weather.

Food serving times:
Monday-Saturday:
   12pm-2.30pm, 7pm-9.30pm
Sunday: 12pm-2.30pm
Prices:
Meals: a la carte 20.00/24.00

Typical Dishes

Warm crottin of Goats cheese

Fillet steak with horseradish mash

Rhubarb and saffron creme brûlée

Ramsbury is between Marlborough and Hungerford; signposted off the B4192 Northwest of Hungerford

Rowde

091 The George & Dragon

High Street, Rowde SN10 2PN

Tel.: (01380) 723053
e-mail: thegandd@tiscali.co.uk

Butcombe and 1 guest ale

The lazy waters of the nearby Kennet and Avon Canal create the ideal mood for a visit to this divinely characterful pub in the Vale of Pewsey. Its epicentre is a gorgeous stone fireplace crackling heartily in the darker months. The low timbered ceiling just adds to the feeling of rich warmth; outside, summer sunshine can be enjoyed in a smart little garden. There are two small areas in which to dine - adjacent to the fire or in the dining room - but either way, you can't go wrong, but be sure to book as it gets very busy. Keenly-priced menus place the emphasis on plenty of daily changing specials, and the cooking is simple, robust and classic, with the emphasis on seafood specialities. As well as good value menus, you can also rely on polite, friendly service from the young owners.

Food serving times:
Tuesday-Saturday:
12pm-2pm, 7pm-9pm
Closed 1-8 January
(booking essential)
Prices:
Meals: 14.50 (fixed price lunch) and a la carte 25.00/40.00

Typical Dishes

Double baked goats cheese souffle

Sea bass with ginger and soy

3 puddings on a plate

Just North of Devizes on A342. Parking

Semington

092 ## The Lamb on the Strand

99 The Strand, Semington BA14 6LL
Tel.: (01380) 870263 - Fax: (01380) 871203

Butcombe Bitter, Ringwood Best, Thwaites Lancaster Bomber, Marstons Pedigree

This ivy clad, red brick inn is a rather diverting attraction on the busy road out of Trowbridge. It has a characterful feel, its 18C origins typified by the low beams; a woodburner and log fire adds to the pleasing ambience. A series of pleasantly furnished rooms affords lots of space to relax with a pint of real ale or a glass of wine from the landlord's carefully selected list. If the weather's good, eat outside in the attractive walled garden. Menus are traditional and extensive; consistently fresh food is served with abundant use of local produce: the mouth-watering cheese pudding is a sure-fire hit. Service at this family-run establishment is invariably efficient, friendly and helpful.

Food serving times:
Monday-Saturday:
    12pm-2pm, 6.30pm-9pm
Sunday: 12pm-2pm
Closed 25-26 December
(booking essential)
Prices:
Meals: a la carte 15.50/19.50

Typical Dishes

Roasted asparagus wrapped in air dried ham

Smoked haddock with poached egg

Crème brûlée

Between Trowbridge and Devizes on the A361 near Semington village. Parking

Upton Scudamore

093 Angel Inn

Upton Scudamore BA12 0AG

Tel.: (01985) 213225 - Fax: (01985) 218182

e-mail: theangelinn.uptonscudamore@btopenworld.com - Website: www.theangelinn-wiltshire.co.uk

   VISA

Wadworth 6X, Butcombe and 1 guest ale

To the east the vast expanses of Salisbury Plain offer a rather forbidding prospect, but in this cosy 16C inn all is relaxed and cheerful. The patrons see to that, running the Angel in their own personalised and dedicated way; the warm character of the establishment all adds to the experience. There's a lovely, sunny rear terrace with barbeque for summer days, but the interior's no less inviting, rustic charm seamlessly linked to rural setting. Scrubbed wooden floors, original artwork and candlelight will make you want to linger. Fine cooking will have much the same effect. Appealing, modern dishes are supplemented by blackboard fish specials: try, perhaps, roast scallops with chilli jam followed by roast monkfish with spinach and new potatoes. The comfortable rooms are invariably spotless.

Food serving times:
Monday-Sunday:
    12pm-2pm, 7pm-9.30pm
Closed 25-26 December and 1 January
Prices:
Meals: a la carte 16.00/30.00
10 rooms : 70.00/80.00

Typical Dishes

Seared scallops, sweet chilli dressing

Roast rump of lamb, mint creme fraiche

Chocolate marquise

Village signposted off the A350 to the north of Warminster. Parking

Whitley

094 **Pear Tree Inn** We most liked

Top Lane, Whitley SN12 8QX

Tel.: (01225) 709131 - Fax: (01225) 702276
e-mail: sales@peartreeinn.co.uk

      VISA

 Stonehenge Pigswill and Spire, Palmers Copper and Gold

Though not far from Bath, visitors to this attractive Cotswold stone inn may be tempted to stay put once they've indulged what's on offer here. A pleasant front garden leads in to what can best be described as a stylish country dining pub and restaurant. Owners are keen to stress the amount of home produced food that goes into their menus: soups, sausages, bread, sorbets and ice cream are all made on the premises and Wiltshire suppliers provide game and meat. End results are a pleasing amalgam of traditional and modern dishes with a European accent. Staying overnight is a pleasure: bedrooms drip with contemporary style. There's impressive use of beautiful local oak and re-claimed barn doors; you'll also find top quality linen, the very best toiletries, and super-smart chrome fittings.

Food serving times:
Monday-Thursday:
12.30pm-2pm,
6.30pm-9.30pm
Friday-Saturday:
12pm-2.30pm, 6.30pm-10pm
Closed 25-26 December, dinner 31 December and 1 January
Prices:
Meals: 16.50 (fixed price lunch) and a la carte 21.00/30.00
8 rooms : 75.00/110.00

Northwest of Melksham. Whitley is signposted off the A365. Parking

Typical Dishes
Goats cheese salad
Skate wing, potato gnocchi and broad beans
Roast white peach, vanilla ice cream

*I*n recent years, the restored Jewellery Quarter, Brindleyplace and Centenary Square, not to mention the shops and bars of Mailbox and the new Bullring, have brought revival and recognition to ever-evolving Birmingham. But not far from Britain's hard-wrought second city, Coalbrookdale, picturesque Ironbridge and the towns of The Potteries and The Black Country offer poignant reminders of the industries that made them and shaped their working way of life. Further afield, and further back in time, Warwick and world-famous Stratford span the centuries, while the reflections of Viking and Celtic art at Kilpeck Church look back to a more ancient past. Explore prosperous period towns like Ludlow and Lichfield, visit the cathedral cities of Hereford and Worcester or take in some of England's most captivating countryside, from the upper Wye to the lower Peaks, by way of Elgar's beloved Malverns and Housman's "blue remembered hills". The discoveries continue in the region's pubs and inns, with cider and orchard fruits from the Vale of Evesham, Herefordshire beef, Gloucester's well-known cheeses and, most famously of all, the Burton beers which transformed the great British pint over 200 years ago.

Bransford

001 Bear and Ragged Staff

Station Rd, Bransford WR6 5JH

Tel.: 01886 833399 - Fax: 01886 833106
e-mail: enquiries@bear.uk.com - Website: www.bear.uk.com

 VISA AE ⓘ Ⓜ©

Robinsons Unicorn and St. Georges

Satisfyingly familiar pub classics and more formal restaurant recipes run side by side on the Bear and Ragged Staff's huge blackboards; add to this the occasional fish specials and there's sure to be something that appeals. What's more, even with such a big choice, it's safe to assume the cooking will be tasty and prepared with sound culinary know-how. In fact, it would be easy to take this country pub for granted: unremarkable on the outside, comfortable and traditional within, it seems almost too pleasant and unassuming for its own good, but fortunately the locals know a good thing when they see it. Service is friendly with no standing on ceremony: though the pub is divided into a classically styled dining room and bar, you can order what you like and eat it where you choose.

Food serving times:
Monday-Sunday:
    12pm-2pm, 6.30pm-9pm
Closed dinner 25 December
Prices:
Meals: a la carte 18.70/31.25

4,5 mi Southwest of Worcester by A44 and A4103. From Bransford follow signs to Powick. Parking

Typical Dishes

Scallops, black pasta and Sancerre veloute

Fillet steak with Stilton, Port jus

Raspberry crème brûlée

Clent

002 **Bell & Cross**

Holy Cross, Clent DY9 9QL

Tel.: (01562) 730319 · Fax: (01562) 731733
Website: www.bellandcrossclent.co.uk

  VISA **MC**

 Banks Bitter, Mild, Marstons Pedigree, Timothy Taylor

A pretty garden and a little terrace make this pretty, early-19C inn a natural choice for summer days, but it's far from just a fair-weather pub. Five charmingly petite rooms and a traditional tap room – with a listed bar, no less – are so cosy that you'll be tempted to linger over that last drink, and attentive young staff certainly make you feel welcome. A tasty seasonal menu, with blackboard specials, is devised in part by the England football team's chef-by-appointment, who takes charge in the kitchen when not putting fire in the bellies of Sven's Men. Diners without a big match after lunch should let the training regime slide and treat themselves to the delicious cooking.

Food serving times:
Monday-Sunday:
                     12pm-2pm
Monday-Thursday:
                          6.30pm-
Friday-Saturday:
          6.30pm-9.30pm
Sunday: 7pm-9pm
Closed 25 December
Prices:
Meals: 15.00 (dinner) and a la carte 18.50/24.50

Typical Dishes

Smoked chicken and avocado salad

Belly of pork, honey glazed apple

Treacle tart, custard

Mid-way between Stourbridge and Bromsgrove. Clent is signposted off the Northbound A491. The pub is on the left hand side in Holy Cross.

Cutnall Green

003 **The Chequers**

Kidderminster Road, Cutnall Green WR9 0PJ

Tel.: (01299) 851292 - Fax: (01299) 851744
Website: www.chequerscutnallgreen.co.uk

 VISA

 Timothy Taylor Landlord, Hook Norton, Ruddles Bitter

This half-timbered roadside pub isn't too much to look at, but inside it's a different story. The bar boasts modern décor in traditional surroundings, typified by sandblasted pale beams, tiled floor and leather tub chairs. There's an adjacent, most welcoming Garden Room: lilac soft furnishings and a plush sofa, surrounded by hanging tankards. Richly coloured walls with wine-themed paintings invoke a modern country style. The pub's owner is Roger Narbett, who's chef to the England football team, but expect more than pasta or chicken: menus boast great choice from traditional favourites to up-to-the-minute and highly interesting. Service is invariably courteous, efficient and enthusiastic.

Food serving times:
Monday-Saturday:
12pm-2pm, 6.30pm-9.15pm
Sunday:
12pm-2.30pm, 7pm-9pm
Closed 25 December
Prices:
Meals: a la carte 18.50/24.50

Typical Dishes

King prawns, thai salad, chilli dressing

Calves liver, garlic and thyme

Lemon curd pavlova

3mi North of Droitwich Spa on A442. Parking

Dunhampton

004 **Epic**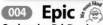

Ombersley Rd, Dunhampton DY13 9SW

Tel.: (01905) 620000 - Fax: (01905) 621123
Website: www.epicbrasseries.com

 VISA AE MC

Timothy Taylor Landlord, Hook Norton Best Bitter

If ever an establishment was named with simple, pinpoint accuracy, then surely this is it. Epic, standing hard on a West Midlands A road, is a pub conversion of suitably large proportions. The spacious interior has a slightly retro ambience; the open-plan design allows for some banquette seating in a pleasingly simple, airy format of well-spaced wooden tables. There's an al fresco alternative enabled by a small garden and decking area. Choose from a menu that offers a balanced, varied selection of tried-and-tested favourites alongside sound contemporary dishes. Seasonal, fresh ingredients are used to good effect, and well-drilled staff offer a friendly and efficient service.

Food serving times:
Monday-Saturday :
   12pm-3pm, 6.30pm-9.30pm
Sunday: 12pm-3pm
Prices:
Meals: a la carte 30.00/40.00

Typical Dishes

Tuscan bean soup

Chilli and lime squid linguini

Coconut and dark rum ice cream

2mi north of Ombersley on the southbound side of the A449.
Parking

Leintwardine

005 Jolly Frog

The Todden, Leintwardine SY7 0LX

Tel.: (01547) 540298

e-mail: jaynejollyfrog@aol.com - Website: www.jolly-frog.com

1 weekly changing guest beers

Run with personality and imagination, the Jolly Frog is the kind of place that rewards a little light curiosity, hidden around the next hedgerow bend in the gentle folds of Herefordshire. Once inside, you'll discover four cosy adjoining rooms and a conservatory with a fascinating collection of rustic bits and pieces, a library of over 850 cookery books and a small shop, but the cuisine itself more than holds the attention, spanning a commendably well-priced table d'hôte menu, an extensive choice of shellfish and interesting specials-board diversions: enthusiastic staff take the time to put you in the picture and remain quick off the mark with smooth and effective service. Though less French than the name might imply, it's informal, cosy, casual and true to its surroundings.

Food serving times:
Tuesday-Sunday:
12pm-2.30pm
Tuesday-Saturday:
6pm-10.30pm
Sunday: 12pm-2,30pm
Closed 25 December
- Seafood specialities -

Prices:
Meals: 14.00 (lunch and dinner until 7pm) and a la carte 16.00/ 26.30

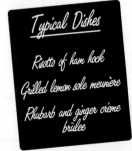

Typical Dishes

Risotto of ham hock

Grilled lemon sole meunière

Rhubarb and ginger crème brûlée

7mi West of Ludlow on A4113. Parking

Ross-on-Wye

006 **The Lough Pool Inn**

Sellack, Ross-on-Wye HR9 6LX
Tel.: (01989) 730236

   VISA MC

Wye Valley Bitter, Butty Bach, Adnams Regatta, Hereford Pale Ale, London Pride, Dorothy Goodbodys

This 16C black and white timbered inn is in a wonderfully rural spot tucked away among the country lanes of Herefordshire - an ideal location for garden and terrace dining in the summer months. It's a solid traditional establishment with exposed stone, flag flooring and lots of space to wander around with a pint of local ale. No trouble in spotting the dining areas: they're painted bright yellow with red cedar-stained pine flooring. Menus change frequently, depending on ingredients. The Lough Pool serves excellent modern style cooking where good local produce is unerringly to the fore: look out for the blackboard specials.

Food serving times:
Monday-Sunday:
12pm-2pm, 7pm-9pm
Closed 1 week January,
25 December, Sunday
dinner and Monday
October-March
Prices:
Meals: a la carte 19.00/30.50

Typical Dishes

Maple roasted scallops, chorizo and rocket

Braised beef shin, oxtail and horseradish dumpling

Treacle tart

3.25mi Northwest of Ross-on-Wye.
Turn right off the A49 (Hereford) and
follow the signs for Hoarwithy.
Parking

Ruckhall

007 ## Ancient Camp Inn

Ruckhall HR2 9QX
Tel.: (01981) 250449 - Fax: (01981) 251581
Website: www.theancientcampinn.co.uk

    VISA

Wye Valley Butty Back, Golden Valley Ciders

A Gallic touch near the Welsh border. The owners of the Ancient Camp lived in the South of France for 16 years and there are instant giveaways, like the wall-mounted Provencal posters. Meanwhile, the pub's exterior is pure rustic English: elevated whitewashed cottages – lurking snugly down a country road - staring out over the meandering River Wye. Visitors from nearby Hay might appreciate the gentle, bookish appeal of a sofa-strewn lounge, an ideal spot to sample the local Wye Valley Ale or perrys produced just a few miles down the road. Dining is an atmospheric affair, in a room that's flagged, with stone walls and traditionally styled wooden tables. French influences are strongly in evidence on the menus: the owners' son is the chef and he trained across the Channel. Expect Mediterranean dishes using local produce, like Hereford beef. Simple rooms with cotton bedding await overnighters.

Food serving times:
Wednesday-Sunday:
12pm-2pm
Wednesday-Saturday:
7pm-9pm
Closed 2 weeks February and November.
Prices:
Meals: a la carte 21.00/30.00
 5 rooms : 70.00/90.00

Typical Dishes

Rillettes of Gloucester old spot pork

Organic salmon en croute

Chocolate fondant

5 miles West of Hereford by A 49 off A 465. Parking

Stoke Prior

008 **Epic** *We most liked*

68 Hanbury rd, Stoke Prior B60 4DN

Tel.: (01527) 871929 - Fax: (01527) 575647

e-mail: epic.bromsgrove@virgin.net - Website: www.epicbrasseries.com

   **VISA** **AE**

> Hook Norton, Marston Pedigree and 1 regular guest ale

The only remnants here of its days as a roadside pub are the tiled floor and odd rafter. Otherwise this stylish establishment has benefited greatly from a major facelift and extensions. At the centre, a large modern bar with comfy sofa lounge area. All around, an airy dining space with lots of glass, brick and wood, which has been cleverly worked into the modern design. The overall feel is one of effortless style, accentuated by comfortable seating at smart wood tables with good accessories. Menus are large and dominated by popular modern classics at reasonable prices. Service is efficient from staff who are used to being busy.

Food serving times:
Monday-Saturday:
   12pm-3pm, 6.30pm-9.30pm
Sunday: 12pm-3.30pm
Prices:
Meals: 12.95 (fixed price lunch) and a la carte 25.00/32.00

Typical Dishes

Chicken liver parfait

Smoked haddock, bubble and squeak

Chocolate fondant, pistachio ice cream

2.25mi Southwest of Bromsgrove by A38 (M6 South): turn left onto B4091; pub is on the right hand side after traffic lights. Parking

Titley

009 **Stagg Inn**

Titley HR5 3RL

Tel.: (01544) 230221

e-mail: reservations@thestagg.co.uk - Website: www.thestagg.co.uk

Timothy Taylor Landlord, Hobsons Best Bitter, Brains Rev.James

In the delightful surroundings of the Welsh Marches stands this nationally renowned whitewashed landmark. A carefully cultivated network of local suppliers, a real regard for quality and exemplary belief in value for money have all contributed to its singular success. You can eat in three different areas: the cosy bar, the dining room with chunky wooden tables, or, assuming the weather is clement, the rear garden. Menus change every five or six weeks, but the cooking itself, assured and original with a hint of classic French flair, is a model of consistency, allowing fresh, natural flavours to shine through. Comfortable, softly lit surroundings and pleasant, intelligent service, contribute to a really memorable meal. If you wish to prolong the Stagg experience, there are two rooms above the pub, and more in the quieter part-Georgian vicarage down the road.

Food serving times:

Tuesday-Sunday:
12pm-2pm

Tuesday-Saturday:
6,30pm-9,30pm

Closed 1 week Spring, first 2 weeks November 25-26 December and Monday except bank holidays, when closed Tuesday

Prices:

Meals: a la carte 17.50/25.00

6 rooms : 50.00/120.00

Typical Dishes

Scallops, celeriac purée

Venison, wild mushrooms

Bread and butter pudding

3.5 mi Northeast of Kington on B4355. Parking

Trumpet

010 The Verzon

Hereford Rd, Trumpet HR8 2PZ

Tel.: 01531 670381 - Fax: 01531670830
e-mail: info@theverzon.co.uk - Website: www.theverzon.co.uk

     VISA **AE** **MC**

Wye Valley and Butty Bach

Standing just back from the main road, this attractive part-Georgian house gives no hint of its stylish modern interior. Deep leather sofas and armchairs are set invitingly around a comfortable bar with exposed brick walls; beyond is a spacious restaurant. You can eat in either, and the choice runs from a lunchtime sandwich to the full three courses of a modern menu, a concise list of classics balanced by dishes with a more original touch. Whether The Verzon is more of a pub or a bar-brasserie is a tricky question, but it's hardly likely to stop you enjoying it, particularly on a fine summer evening: its big deck terrace, under broad sunshades, gives wonderful views of the Herefordshire countryside. Large and stylish bedrooms are available.

Food serving times:
Monday-Sunday:
 12pm-2pm,7pm-9,30pm
Prices:
Meals: 18.50 (lunch) and a la carte 19.95/30.00
8 rooms : 65.00/98.00

Typical Dishes

Local game terrine

Fillet of brill, clam and bacon stew

Goat's cheese semi-freddo

3 1/4mi Northwest of Ledbury on A38.Parking

Ullingswick

011 ## Three Crowns Inn

Bleak Acre, Ullingswick HR1 3JQ

Tel.: (01432) 820279 - Fax:: 01432 820911
e-mail: info@threecrownsinn.com - Website: www.threecrownsinn.com

    VISA **MC**

 *Hobsons Best and a selection of guest ales from Wye Valley*

On one of Herefordshire's many quiet roads stands this red brick, timbered establishment blending in perfectly with its rural setting. You step straight into a wonderfully beamed bar boasting exposed brickwork and a cosy wood counter with benches and pews strewn around. Hops dangle from the rafters, sepia prints hang on the walls: all in all it's thoroughly pleasant and deserving of its loyal local following. The restaurant was refurbished to double its size in 2005, so more diners can now appreciate what's on offer. Keenly-priced food has a rustic, robust quality and tasty, local produce is proudly in evidence, not least vegetables and herbs from the kitchen garden. The good news for those who've travelled far to find this hidden-away gem: cosy bedrooms have been added, so peaceful country repose is guaranteed.

Food serving times:
Tuesday-Sunday:
    12pm-2.30pm, 7pm-9.30pm
Closed 2 weeks Christmas
Prices:
Meals: a la carte 16.75/24.75

Typical Dishes

Goat's cheese and potato terrine

Loin of pork, black pudding

Panna cotta with raspberries

1.25mi East of the village on unsigned country lane. Parking

Weobley

012 The Salutation Inn ⌐

Market Pitch, Weobley HR4 8SJ
Tel.: (01544) 318443 - Fax: (01544) 318216

VISA AE M©

Hook Norton, Fullers London Pride, Butty Bach

A old country pub through and through, this 16C cider house, in the heart of this pretty Herefordshire village, truly looks and feels the part: crooked timbers are hung with jugs, hop-bines and horse-brasses, blue and white china plates are ranged along the mantelpiece. The traditional partition of lounge and public bar is still in evidence too: one pleasant corner of the pub is set as a formal dining room, with candles and neat, white tablecloths, although the same menu is served throughout. The sound and classically based cooking seems in tune with the atmosphere of the place. Tidily kept bedrooms, some in traditional floral patterns, are kept in good order.

Food serving times:
Closed 25 December
Prices:
Meals: a la carte 15.00/35.00
⌐ **4 rooms :** 52.00/84.00

Parking ⟩⟩

Typical Dishes

Ravioli of lobster

Lightly spiced breast of Magret duck

Pineapple tart Tatin

Atcham

013 ## The Mytton and Mermaid

Atcham SY5 6QG

Tel.: (01743) 761220 - Fax: (01743) 761292
e-mail: info@myttonandmermaid.co.uk - Website: www.myttonandmermaid.co.uk

Woods Shropshire Lad, Ruddles Best, Hanby All Seasons

This redbrick, ivy-clad inn was built in 1735 and stands proudly on the banks of the Severn, opposite the National Trust's Attingham Park. The quirky bar is named after local 19C squire Mad Jack Mytton, who'd appreciate the warm, friendly atmosphere that prevails here. There's a log fire, sofa and large tables where you can linger over lunch or dinner. The easy-going restaurant – which has a separate identity but is really in the same room – sports polished tables and menus full of good, traditional dishes that change with the seasons. The relaxed style carries over into a pleasant riverside drawing room and a series of stylish, individually decorated bedrooms with antique and modern furniture.

Food serving times:
Monday-Saturday:
  12pm-2.30pm, 7pm-10pm
Sunday: 12pm-3pm
Closed 25 December
Prices:
Meals: a la carte 20.00/35.00
18 rooms : 70.00/150.00

Typical Dishes

Salmon, avocado ice cream and oyster beignets

Pork, morel and thyme cream

Assiette of lemon desserts

3mi Southeast of Shrewsbury on the B4380 Ironbridge rd. Parking

Brimfield

014 Roebuck Inn 🛏

Brimfield SY8 4NE

Tel.: (01584) 711230 - Fax: (01584) 711654

Website: www.roebuckinn.com

  VISA

Banks Best Bitter, Camerons Strong Arm, Marstons Pedigree, and monthly changing guest ales

It takes something special in the gastronomic stakes to be especially noticed in the Ludlow area, and the mustard-coloured Roebuck Inn comes up with the goods – or, rather, the inventive menus. Slap bang in the middle of an attractive village just south of the famous town, it's every inch the epitome of a classic country pub, filled with rustic objects, curios and polished older wood furniture in the bar areas - the pubby rear bar is more food oriented. A spick-and-span dining room has felt the benefits of tender loving care. Dishes are likewise freshly inspired; there's a light lunch menu, full menu and blackboard specials too. Sleep overnight in homely bedrooms.

Food serving times:
Monday-Sunday:
    12pm-3pm, 6.30pm-9pm
Prices:
Meals: a la carte 19.00/31.50
🛏 **3 rooms :** 50.00/80.00

Typical Dishes

Lemon spiced gravadlax

Fillet of venison, damson gin and bay sauce

Coconut panna cotta, pineapple

4.5mi South of Ludlow - signposted off the A49.

Brockton

015 ## The Feathers

Brockton TF13 6JR
Tel.: 01746 785202 - Fax: 01746 785202

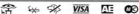

 Hobsons Best, Shropshire Pride, Secret Hop

Wenlock Edge, in the heart of the Shropshire countryside, is a popular spot for walkers, and word-of-mouth has contributed to this attractive part 16th century pub becoming one of their more favoured watering holes. The owner/chef cut his teeth in well-thought-of London establishments and dining is to the fore here, with the constantly changing blackboard menus providing interesting modern English dishes underpinned by local produce, such as Shropshire partridge or beef. Ambience is ideal: the characterful interior boasts a tiled floor, white washed stone walls, beams, and vast inglenooks with wood-burning stoves. Lots of little areas surround the central bar so a cosy feel snuggles within the rusticity. If anyone feels like splashing out, there are various examples of local artwork for sale lining the walls.

Food serving times:
Thursday-Sunday:
12pm-2pm
Tuesday-Sunday:
6.30pm-9.30pm
Closed 25-26 December
Prices:
Meals: a la carte 20.00/27.00

Typical Dishes

Scallops, black pudding

Shoulder of lamb, creamed leeks, rosemary jus

Spiced plums, honey and vanilla ice cream

5mi Southwest of Much Wenlock on B4378. Parking

Burlton

016 Burlton Inn

Burlton SY4 5TB

Tel.: (01939) 270284 - Fax: (01939) 270204
e-mail: bean@burltoninn.co.uk - Website: www.burltoninn.co.uk

   VISA **MC**

Banks, Green King Abbot, Shepherd Neame Spitfire, Ruddles county

This 18C Shropshire stalwart knows how to pack 'em in – so much so that early in 2004 some bigger, better adjustments and refurbishments gave the old place more room to breathe. Nothing of the buzzy, bustling, pubby atmosphere has been lost, though, and the Burlton is unfailingly popular with the huntin', shootin' and fishin' locals. Window boxes and hanging baskets decorate the outside in summer and in colder weather, the compact, raftered bar crackles along in sympathy with the log fire. The food – like the real ale generously stocked – goes down a treat, oiled by smooth service from a polite, friendly crew. It's rustic food, home-cooked and fresh. In the rear annexe, smart and spacious bedrooms complete the picture – make sure you don't miss out on the first rate breakfasts.

Food serving times:

Monday-Sunday:
12pm-2pm

Monday-Saturday:
6.30pm-9.45pm

Sunday:
7pm-9.30pm

Closed 25-26 December, 1 January and lunch Bank Holiday Monday

Prices:

Meals: a la carte 17.00/29.65

6 rooms : 50.00/80.00

8mi North of Shrewsbury on A528. Parking

Typical Dishes
Smoked salmon and avocado mousse
Pork steak, caramelised onion and pear chutney
Lemon meringue roulade

Marton

017 The Sun Inn

Marton SY21 8JP

Tel.: (01938) 561211

e-mail: info@suninn.biz - Website: www.suninn.biz

 VISA

Hobsons Best Bitter and Real Mild

The simply styled Sun with its neat and tidy stone facade is a credit to this quiet Marches village on the English-Welsh border. The owners previously ran a restaurant in the New Forest and their cooking experience shows to good effect, even down to tasty home-made bread. Light snacks are available all day in the rather spartan little front bar while dinner is served in the recently refurbished dining room, now resplendent in pine. The chef makes a point of using local ingredients and the well-prepared cooking, nourishing and enjoyable, has a real flavour of the season to it. Genial service from the experienced young owners helps things along nicely, as do the extensive selection of wines by the glass and real ales. An ever-increasing number of regulars and visitors who've picked up on the Sun - often by word of mouth - are proof positive of its widening appeal.

Food serving times:

Tuesday: 7pm-9.30pm

Wednesday-Saturday:
12pm-2pm, 7pm-9pm

Sunday: 12pm-2pm
(booking essential)

Prices:

Meals: a la carte 12.00/29.00

Typical Dishes

Smoked salmon and prawn terrine

Chump of lamb, pea mash

Cinnamon and honey crêpes

8.5mi Southeast of Welshpool on the B4386. Parking

Munslow

018 ## The Crown Country Inn

Munslow SY7 9ET

Tel.: 01584 841205 - Fax: 01584 841255
e-mail: info@crowncountryinn.co.uk - Website: www.crowncountryinn.co.uk

Holdens Golden Glow, Black Country, Three Tuns, Clerics

Quite how old the Crown really is, no-one really knows, but it was already long-established when it served as a "hundred house" for travelling magistrates. Warm and characterful, it certainly has all the hallmarks of a charming old rural inn, with stout beams propping up its cosy taproom, a well-stoked fire and trains of hops dangling from the woodwork. Its cuisine is not bound by tradition, though: light but still substantial modern dishes are served in the bar at lunch, while the evening menu is planned and prepared with a dash of imagination. Local vegetables, rare-breed meats, a fine English cheeseboard and even local spring water demonstrate a taste for regional produce. The large garden and terrace are popular with walkers from nearby Wenlock Edge.

Food serving times:
Tuesday-Sunday:
  12pm-2pm, 6.45pm-9pm
Closed 25 December
Prices:
Meals: a la carte 19.25/29.95
3 rooms : 40.00/70.00

Typical Dishes

Scallops, red pepper hummus, salsa verde

Duck breast, beetroot and sweet potato chutney

Crème brûlée

On the B4378 between Much Wenlock and Craven Arms. Parking

Newport

Munslow

019 ## The Fox

Pave Lane, Chetwynd Aston, Newport TF10 9LQ
Tel.: 01952 815940 - Fax: 01952 815941
e-mail: fox@brunningandprice.co.uk - Website: www.fox-newport.co.uk

Shropshire Lad, Timothy Taylor Landlord, Thwaites Original, Kelham Island Pale Rider

Bright and uncluttered, the Fox has a welcoming feel to it. The old pattern of nooks, parlours and lounges has been opened up and the well-chosen furnishings, though mostly restored or reclaimed, fit this more modern layout very well. A collection of framed fashion-plates and cigarette cards, rural scenes and period caricatures run the length of the walls and into the more intimate rooms off to the sides. It's nearly always possible to find a quieter corner somewhere, but the Fox really excels at the big get-together. Long dining tables are perfect for eating out in eights and tens: family brunches on a Sunday or an evening catching up with friends. A sizeable menu of modern classics is delivered with friendly efficiency. Big rear terrace and garden.

Food serving times:
Monday-Sunday:
12pm-10pm
Closed 25 and 26 December
Prices:
Meals: a la carte 12.85/27.15

Typical Dishes
Corned beef hash
Venison steak with celeriac and apple mash
Bread and butter pudding, apricot sauce

Parking; 1,5 mi South of Newport by A41 (Wolverhamton rd)

Norton

020 Hundred House ⊨

Bridgnorth Rd, Norton TF11 9EE

Tel.: (01952) 730353 - Fax: (01952) 730355
e-mail: reservations@hundredhouse.co.uk - Website: www.hundredhouse.co.uk

  VISA

 A selection of guest ales offered

You know you've arrived somewhere with a hugely individual character when you arrive at Hundred House. The extensive rear herb garden is a particular joy and supplies the kitchen with much delightful produce, not least the delectable soft fruit for dessert, or the dried flowers that cascade from beams. The inn has its origins in the 14C and, in the best sense, it shows: rafters, quarry tiled floors, open fires and venerable dark oak. After a hike along the Wrekin has bolstered a hearty appetite, you can eat almost anywhere. Lovely bedrooms offer a boundless variety of country comforts and character features – including half testers, four posters and swings in some of the rooms!

Food serving times:
Monday-Sunday:
  12pm-2.15pm, 6pm-9.30pm
Closed 25 December
(dinner), 26 December
Prices:
Meals: 18.95 (Sunday lunch)
and a la carte 24.00/33.00
⊨ **10 rooms :** 69.00/135.00

Typical Dishes
Wild mushroom risotto

Black pudding with apple,
sage and mint sausage

Poached pears with honey,
ginger and rosemary ice

7 mi. South of Telford on A 442.
Parking

Shrewsbury

021 **The Armoury**

Victoria Quay, Welsh Bridge, Shrewsbury SY1 1HH

Tel.: 01743 340525 - Fax: 01743 340526

e-mail: armoury@brunningandprice.co.uk - Website: www.armoury-shrewsbury.co.uk

 VISA **AE** **MC**

 Salopian Heaven Sent, Shropshire Lad, Boddingtons

This 18C former warehouse has a fascinating history: built for military use, it's done service as a bakery and a World War II convalescent home, and even been moved brick by brick to this spot in sight of the old bridge, where it cries out for a bankside terrace to enjoy the summer sunshine. Inside, gilt-framed mirrors, engravings and Edwardiana cover the brick walls, yard upon yard of old books are rivalled only by row upon rows of malts and liqueurs behind the bar, and a huge ceiling and tall arched windows make the open-plan room feel light and spacious. Lots of big tables, with a hotch-potch of second-hand chairs, make it ideal for a big get-together: its great popularity means there's usually a buzzy atmosphere, and the daily changing menu of modern favourites offers something for everyone.

Food serving times:
Monday-Saturday:
12pm-9.30pm
Sunday: 12pm-9pm
Closed 25-26 December
Prices:
Meals: a la carte 19.00/30.00

By the Welsh Bridge

Typical Dishes

Black pudding with cider and mustard mash

Rump steak, hand-cut chips

Sticky toffee pudding

Alrewas

022 **The Old Boat**

Kings Bromley Rd, Alrewas DE13 7DB

Tel.: 01283 791468
Website: www.oldboat.co.uk

VISA

Marstons Pedigree, Courage Directors and Hook Norton Old Hooky

Tucked away at the edge of the village, the easiest way to find the Old Boat is almost certainly from the canal. Though they've raised the tone since navvies and barges made this their drinking haunt, some of their customers still come by water, pottering up in their narrow boats. Anyone with an aversion to maritime knick-knacks might fear the worst at the sight of a massive anchor attached to the wall, but inside it's as much like an informal restaurant as a pub, with chunky wooden chairs and tables dotted around. Food is a big part of what they do here and regulars who come for a well-kept Burton beer may be tempted to stay for lunchtime sandwiches, set price and à la carte menus or something from an impressive variety of specials, either classic or modern in style. Friendly service.

Food serving times:
Monday-Saturday:
12pm-2pm, 6pm-9pm
Sunday: 12pm-3pm
Closed Sunday dinner

Prices:
Meals: 10.95 (fixed price lunch) and a la carte 18.00/29.00

Typical Dishes

Collar of bacon, black pudding salad

Slow roast shoulder and fillet of spring lamb

Vanilla brûlee

4,5 mi Northeast of Lichfield by A38. Parking

Stafford

023 the sun

7 Lichfield Rd, Stafford ST17 4JX

Tel.: 01785 229700 · Fax: 01785 215015

e-mail: admin@thesunstafford.co.uk · Website: www.thesunstafford.co.uk

 No real ales

Samuel L. Jackson and Brigitte Bardot, Steve McQueen, with holster and rollneck, and gangsta rapper Tupac Shakur are an unexpected quartet to find in a Staffordshire pub, but then 'the sun' is determined to set itself apart from the local competition. Their striking Pop Art portraits direct sidelong stares and moody glances around a trendily soigné modern bar area, and the dining room, very much the focus of the place, continues in the same smooth and attractively formal style. More elaborate at dinner, the cooking shows originality in its Modern British variations. Ask about their weekday set menu, served at lunchtime and in the evening. Some traditionalists may feel this is not a pub in the traditional, local mould, and they'd be right. But for a smarter evening out, it's well worth a try.

Food serving times:
Tuesday-Saturday:
        12pm-3pm, 6pm-10pm
Closed Sunday and Monday
Prices:
Meals: 13.95 and a la carte
15.50/29.40

Typical Dishes

Chicken liver parfait, chutney

Belly pork, asian greens and sweet chilli

Roast plums

Parking ❯❯

Alveston

024 **Baraset Barn**

1 Pimlico Lane, Alveston CV37 7RF

Tel.: 01789 295510 - Fax: 01789 292961

Website: www.barasetbarn.co.uk

☝ 🍷 ⇥ 🚯 **VISA** **AE** **M©**

Bass Cask

The historic structure of the old barn is still apparent in the lofty ceilings and rich, golden beams, but the main impression of this very contemporary pub is of one stylish setting after another: a smart lilac-and-white lounge conservatory, a main dining area in brick, pewter, oak and crushed velvet, an intimate rear mezzanine, and a dark, moody cigar bar for savouring an after-dinner drink and clustering round the log burner. A modern British and Mediterranean menu changes a couple of times a year: favourite signature dishes, grills, steaks, and their popular lobster and chips remain ever-present and sum up the bold, fresh culinary style. Bright, prompt service is the other key ingredient in a pleasant, unhurried lunch or evening out.

Food serving times:

Monday-Saturday:
12pm-2.30pm,
6.30pm-9.30pm

Sunday: 12pm-4pm

Closed 25 December

Prices:

Meals: a la carte 23.00/35.00

Typical Dishes

Chicken, leek and foie gras terrine

Assiette of duck, burgundy sauce

Chocolate fondant

2mi East of Stratford- upon- Avon on B4086

Ardens Grafton

025 Golden Cross

Wixford Road, Ardens Grafton B50 4LG
Tel.: (01789) 772420

Hooky Bitter, Spitfire and guest ales offered

Popular destinations in this part of the world are not confined to nearby Stratford, as witnessed by the large number of satisfied visitors enjoying the ambience of this slickly run pub. It has a very pleasant feel, both inside and out. A large rear garden and terrace is ideal for summer dining; the roomy interior has a distinctly rural character, typified by the exposed beams, open fire and scrubbed wooden tables and chairs. A separate dining room gives off a more formal air; à la carte menus bear the hallmarks of modern British tastes and are very freshly prepared with vibrant use of local ingredients; the blackboard daily specials offer a distinct seasonal base.

Food serving times:
Monday-Friday:
    12pm-2.30pm, 6pm-9.pm
Saturday:
    12pm-2pm, 6pm-9.30pm
Sunday: 12pm-2.30pm
Prices:
Meals: 12.95 and a la carte 17.95/27.00

Typical Dishes

Salmon roulade,
Rump of lamb, thyme jus
Treacle tart, vanilla
Anglaise

5mi South West of Stratford-upon-Avon by A46. Parking

Armscote

026 ## The Fox and Goose Inn 🛏️

Armscote CV37 8DD

Tel.: (01608) 682293 - Fax:: (01608) 682293
e-mail: email@foxandgoose.co.uk - Website: www.foxandgoose.co.uk

   VISA **M©**

 JW Lees, Hook Norton

The blacksmith who once worked here at his forge would be amazed at its 21C transformation. The Fox and Goose embraces modernity but doesn't forget its past. Flagstones, wooden pews and a log fire all have pride of place here. They syncopate smoothly with an upmarket ambience elsewhere in the pub. The small bar has warm red walls; they're cream in the larger, stylish eating area. Imaginative and traditional blend cleverly in the cooking stakes: you might try roast lamb shoulder with rosemary and redcurrant jus; or poached smoked haddock with spinach, poached egg and chive sauce. Service is helpful and attentive; bedrooms, eccentrically styled, are named after Cluedo characters - candlestick and lead piping not included, thank goodness...

Food serving times:
Monday-Sunday:
  12pm-2.30pm, 7pm-9.30pm
Closed 25 December and 1 January
Prices:
Meals: a la carte 20.00/30.00
🛏️ **4 rooms :** 55.00/120.00

Typical Dishes

Chicken liver parfait

Chump of lamb, cranberry and mint jus

Sticky toffee pudding

2.5 mi North of Shipston-on-Stour by A3400. Parking

Aston Cantlow

027 King's Head

Bearley Rd, Aston Cantlow B95 6HY
Tel.: (01789) 488242 - Fax: (01789) 488137

Brew 11, Greene King IPA, Abbot

This is a pub that's used to welcoming Stratford overspill, those who need a little respite from the intensity of Shakespeare's birthplace. It's a 15C whitewashed inn with black timbers set in a pretty village, with pleasant terrace and garden for summer visitors. The interior oozes charm with several cosy areas to choose from. There's a crackling log fire, low ceiling and polished flag flooring, plus rustic benches next to window tables, where you can watch the world go by. The attractive restaurant has a modern country style, reflecting the modish appeal of the menus, whose influence ranges from British and Mediterranean to the downright exotic (as in chilli and lime chicken kebabs with peanut dressing). Expect great service, too, generally with an Antipodean accent.

Food serving times:
Monday-Sunday:
12pm-2pm, 7pm-9.45pm
Closed 25-26 December
Prices:
Meals: a la carte 18.00/27.00

Typical Dishes

Crab, crayfish and avocado tian

Duck supper

Trio of chocolate mousse

3mi South of Henley-in-Arden, off B4089. Parking

Farnborough

028 Inn at Farnborough

Farnborough OX17 1DZ

Tel.: (01295) 690615
e-mail: enquiries@innatfarnborough.co.uk - Website: www.innatfarnborough.co.uk

 VISA AE D MC

 Greene King Abbot, Hook Norton, Charles Wells Bombadier, Ruddles County

The historic village of Farnborough is home to two distinctive buildings: the National Trust owned Farnborough Hall and this Grade II listed 17C inn, at the heart of the community for nearly 400 years. Expectations are fully endorsed upon crossing the threshold. A homely interior is dressed in full sympathy with the age of the building: there's a warm glow from the open fire, flag stoned floor and country knick-knacks. A homely bar offers a promising selection of real ales and diners will appreciate the frequently changing menus; much time and effort goes into sourcing local ingredients, resulting in carefully prepared, tasty dishes with a modern flourish. Upstairs, in a sharp break from the rural treats below, is an eye-catching private meeting room with a zebra-striped ceiling.

Food serving times:
Monday-Sunday:
12pm-3pm, 6pm-10pm
Closed 25 December
Prices:
Meals: 12.95 and a la carte
20.00/35.00

Typical Dishes

Ham hock and foie gras terrine

Confit of lamb, roast pepper jus

Sticky toffee pudding

6mi North of Banbury on A423. Parking

Great Wolford

029 **Fox & Hounds Inn**

Great Wolford CV36 5NQ

Tel.: (01608) 674220 - Fax: (01608) 674160
e-mail: info@thefoxandhounds.com - Website: www.thefoxandhounds.com

⟷room **VISA** **MC**

 Hook Norton and two guest ales

It takes something special to catch the eye in an area as rich in delights as the Cotswolds, but this 16C inn passes the test with flying colours. It's located in the heart of a delightful village, its honey coloured exterior luring the visitor into a series of hugely characterful rooms with bags of period appeal, typified by exposed beams with hop bines, an ancient bread oven, lovely open log fire and solid stone floor. Select from a good array of wines and local real ales and dine at candlelit tables; there's a daily changing blackboard menu of well executed, hearty, fresh fare, that puts many local ingredients to good use. In warmer months, make for the summer terrace. Stay overnight in cosy, well-kept bedrooms.

Food serving times:
Tuesday-Saturday:
12pm-2pm, 7pm-9pm
Sunday:
12pm-2pm
Closed 1 week January
Prices:
Meals: 12.95 (lunch) and a la carte 17.75/30.00
🛏 **3 rooms :** 45.00/70.00

Typical Dishes

Warm smoked duck salad

Medallions of ostrich, red wine and thyme jus

Brioche bread and butter pudding

4 mi Northeast of Moreton-in-Marsh by A44. Parking

Henley-in-Arden

030 **Crabmill**

Preston Bagot, Claverdon, Henley-in-Arden B95 5EE
Tel.: (01926) 843342 - Fax: (01926) 843989
e-mail: thecrabmill@aol.com - Website: www.thecrabmill.biz

 VISA AE M©

Tetleys, Wadworth 6X, Greene King Abbot Ale

A delightful rural hideaway, but one which doesn't quite leave its urbane smartness behind: a surprisingly spacious contemporary interior mixes smooth blond wood with ancient cross-beams and wattle walls, the warmth of a real fire and squishy tan leather sofas, so comfortable they demand a real battle of wills for a trip to the bar. A touch of brasserie style comes across in the competent cooking, with dishes like roast pigeon breast and mash, or pepper sirloin and chips, but it's the kind of food you can linger over, and you may find that hearty ramble up and down the Warwickshire hills being put back by another round. The staff look almost as nonchalant as the customers – the emblemed T-shirts are the clue – but provide prompt and conversational service with that noticeable bit extra. Justifiably popular, so consider booking.

1mi East of Henley-in-Arden on A4189. Parking

Food serving times:
Monday-Sunday:
12pm-2.30pm
Monday-Saturday:
6.30pm-9.30pm
Closed 25 December
(booking essential)
Prices:
Meals: a la carte 22.00/32.00

Typical Dishes

Lamb's Kidneys, apple and black pudding

Seabass, rösti and crab bisque

Poached pear, chocolate shortbread

Ilmington

031 The Howard Arms   We most liked

Lower Green, Ilmington CV36 4LT

Tel.: (01608) 682226 - Fax: (01608) 682226
e-mail: info@howardarms.com - Website: www.howardarms.com

 VISA

 Everards Tiger, North Cotswold Genesis, Timothy Taylor Landlord, Butcombe Gold

Wander in to this charming 16C inn for a quiet lunchtime pint and you may be surprised by the buzz of activity, but there's usually room for everyone in a spread of smartly kept rooms and snugs, decorated with prints, portraits and old photographs. Cheerful local staff are used to being busy and will talk you through the large weekly menu chalked up above the fireplace. Classic country cooking, done well, takes in dishes like steak and ale pie, pork in sage, honey and cider and pigeon with carrot and ginger purée. Three well-fitted bedrooms with an agreeable mix of antiques and country fabrics all share a view of the village green: if you do decide to stay, don't miss the famous paintings and porcelain at nearby Upton House, a stroll around the enchanting Hidcote Manor Gardens or a trip to Stratford-upon-Avon.

Food serving times:
Monday-Thursday:
12pm-2pm, 7pm-9pm
Friday-Saturday:
12pm-2pm, 7pm-9.30pm
Sunday:
12pm-2.30pm,
6.30pm-8.30pm
Closed 25 December
Prices:
Meals: 20.50 (Sunday lunch) and a la carte 25.00/30.00
3 rooms : 77.50/115.00

4 mi Northwest of Shipston-on-Stour. Located in the centre of the village. Parking

Typical Dishes

Chicken liver parfait, onion marmalade

Traditional fish pie

Pear and walnut tart, nutmeg ice cream

Tanworth-in-Arden

032 **The Bell**

The Green, Tanworth-in-Arden B94 5AL

Tel.: (01564) 742212

e-mail: info@thebellattanworthinarden.co.uk - Website: www.thebellattanworthinarden.co.uk

 VISA

Black Sheep, Timothy Taylors, Pedigree

A very handily located pub, only 20 minutes from Stratford and five minutes from main motorway access, The Bell sits proudly in its pretty village location, close to an 11C church and providing sustenance to the occasional summer invasion of Morris dancers. Its premises embrace a recently added delicatessen and post office; a good deal of time, effort and money has been invested in the pub, too, and there's now a pleasing rustic-contemporary mix with a spacious, popular bar and an intimate main dining room that boasts squashy leather sofas and polished wooden tables. The wide ranging menus cover an interesting modern range: for instance, you might order baby Thai fish and oatmeal cakes with ginger and tomato sauce, followed by Moroccan chicken, couscous and raita. The modern theme is continued with designer-led bedrooms

Food serving times:
Monday-Saturday:
    12pm-2pm, 6.30pm-9pm
Sunday: 12pm-3pm
Prices:
Meals: a la carte 16.00/22.00
 4 rooms : 55.00/75.00

Typical Dishes

Thai fish cake

Baked wild seabass, almond and mascarpone mash

Selection of cheeses

4.5mi North West from Henley-in-Arden by A3400 and Tanworth Road. 5 minutes from main motorways. Close to Church. Parking

Barston

033 ## Malt Shovel

Barston Lane, Barston B92 0JP

Tel.: (01675) 443223 - Fax: (01675) 443223
Website: www.themaltshovelatbarston.co.uk

     VISA AE M©

Old Speckled Hen, Fullers London Pride

East of the M42 and right out into the countryside, this well-managed rural pub is worth having up your sleeve for a city getaway; you shouldn't expect to have it all to yourself – it's not a ticking-clock-snoozing-dog local – but the bustling atmosphere is at least half the pleasure. Lunchtime in particular tends to be busy, so get there early to be sure of a table. The terrace at the back, overlooking a large lawned garden, makes for pleasant al fresco eating. With its banquettes, colourful paintings, big metal-topped bar and busy kitchen on view behind glass, the main part of the pub has made a subtly modern style its own, without losing too much of its country character: the same could be said for its robust cooking which features daily fish specials and uses seasonings from the pub's own herb garden.

Food serving times:
Monday-Saturday:
12pm-2.30pm,
6.30pm-9.30pm
**Closed 25 December
(lunch bookings not accepted)**
Prices:
Meals: 25.00 (fixed price dinner) and a la carte 21.00/29.95

Typical Dishes

Bang Bang Chicken

Gammon on butterbean mash

Chocolate marmalade tart

Off the A452 just South of Hampton-in-Arden: follow signs for Barston village; pub is on left hand side to the West of the village. Parking

Chadwick End

034 ## The Orange Tree

Warwick End, Chadwick End B93 0BN

Tel.: (01564) 785364 - Fax: (01564) 782988

Website: www.theorangetreepub.co.uk

⌂ 🍸 *VISA* AE MC

Tetleys, Abbots, IPA

Bay trees adorn the entrance to this smart pale-green painted pub conversion with definite restaurant sensibilities. Though pubby in style, the Orange Tree attracts ladies who lunch and sits firmly in the country dining league. Sumptuous leather sofas, cushioned chairs and banquettes beckon you into a contemporary sub-divided lounge and bar with views into the kitchen area. Unless you're making your way outside to the attractive terrace, settle down at one of the varnished wooden tables, and select a dish from the simple, up-to-the-minute menu which concentrates on oven-fired pizza, pasta and grills.

Food serving times:
Monday-Saturday:
  12pm-2.30pm, 6pm-9.30pm
Sunday: 12pm-4.30pm
Closed 25 December
(booking essential)
Prices:
Meals: a la carte 25.00/35.00

Typical Dishes

Mushrooms and dolcelatte on toast

Suckling pig, apple and black pudding

Summer fruit trifle

On A4141 midway between Solihull and Warwick. Parking

Hampton-in-Arden

035 ## The White Lion 🛏

10 High St, Hampton-in-Arden B92 0AA

Tel.: (01675) 442833 - Fax: (01675) 443168

Website: www.thewhitelionathampton.com

 ➲room *VISA* **M©**

Hook Norton, Black Sheep

Set in a leafy village opposite the church, and very handy for the NEC in Birmingham, this 17C pub has Grade II listed status; surprisingly, though, when you step through the front door, there's an appealing rusticity on show, exemplified by stripped pine floors, pale beams and fresh flowers. The cosy front bar is where the locals gather, impressed by a fine range of real ales on offer; a separate side bar boasts welcoming, modern touches. To the rear, soft, neutral colours announce the dining room where dinner is served, a stylish place to eat, with ranks of mirrors and smart Lloyd Loom chairs. Well cooked, interesting dishes offer a predominantly light touch, full of Italian elements, but reaching further afield for added inspiration in other dishes. The comfortable bedrooms – 4 in the pub and a further 4 in the outside annexe – reflect the simple, modern style of the restaurant.

Food serving times:

Tuesday-Saturday:
12pm-2.30pm

Tuesday-Friday: 7pm-9pm

Saturday: 7pm-9.30pm

Prices:

Meals: a la carte 19.50/29.95

🛏 **8 rooms :** 49.00/59.00

☕ 7.50

In the centre of the village. Parking ▶▶

Typical Dishes

Crispy duck salad

Honey and mustard glazed ham, leek mash

Chocolate cake, amaretto ice cream

Lapworth

036 Boot Inn

Old Warwick Rd, Lapworth B94 6JU

Tel.: (01564) 782464 · Fax: (01564) 784989
e-mail: bootinn@hotmail.com · Website: www.thebootatlapworth.co.uk

      VISA **AE** **MC**

Old Speckled Hen, Wadworth 6X, Tetley Bitter

Who'd believe Birmingham's just 10 miles up the road? Take a step outside the pretty village of Lapworth and discover this wonderfully rustic inn that pre-dates the adjacent Grand Union Canal by a few hundred years. It boasts a rabbit warren of beamed rooms to lunch in, the slightly gnarled tables adding to the charmingly frayed-round-the-edges feel. The Boot gets busy, so book or arrive early, and don't look for an area set for dining, as cutlery arrives after you've ordered. There's a wide mix of styles from classic rustic pub fare to dishes with a decided European and Oriental influence - whatever takes your gastronomic fancy. As well as the bars, you can eat in a timbered upstairs dining room or on the terrace.

Food serving times:
Monday-Sunday:
12pm-3pm, 6.30pm-10pm
Closed 25 December
(booking essential)
Prices:
Meals: 21.95/25.00 and a la carte 18.50/25.00

Typical Dishes

Bubble and squeak

Beef, horseradish mash

Cappuccino crème brûlée

2mi Southeast of Hockley Heath on B4439; on the left hand side just before the village. Parking

Sutton Coldfield

037 The Cock Inn

Bulls Lane, Wishaw, Sutton Coldfield B76 9QL

Tel.: 0121 313 3960 - Fax: 0121 313 3964
Website: www.cockinnwishaw.co.uk

Bass, Hook Norton, Pedigree, Tim Taylors

Traditional on the outside, splendidly modern within. There's a confident, stylish ambience here, reflected in the buzz of the place. It's light and airy with wooden flooring and carvings and modern wood tables with discreet spot lighting. Some areas boast burgundy walls featuring framed wine labels; logs line another wall. There's a relaxing lounge area by the bar, and a cigar bar (apparently rather exclusive at weekends) opens onto a beer garden. Menus are original: they change seasonally, and have a section of little dishes alongside the well established grill rotisserie. The robust, modish cooking is mainly British, but other more eclectic elements vie for attention. All this, within minutes of the roaring M6 toll!

Food serving times:
Monday-Saturday:
    12-2.30pm, 6pm-9.30pm
Sunday: 12-4.30pm
Prices:
Meals: a la carte 16.00/29.00

Typical Dishes

Asparagus, poached egg, prosciutto and hollandaise

Rump of lamb and minted pears

Summer fruit pudding

7mi East of Sutton Coldfield just off the A446 following signs over the M6 toll road to Wishaw and Grove End. Parking

 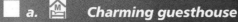

Yorkshire, for many, means the countryside: a mind's-eye landscape of fells and fields spreading out from the Pennines, neat Dales villages above the Wharfe and the Swale, and Aysgarth Falls and Hardraw Force in all their secluded beauty. But the Ridings also lay claim to the genteel charm of Harrogate and Ripon, the striking ruins of Fountains Abbey and Rievaux and the unexpected brilliance of Vanburgh's Castle Howard, to say nothing of York, its medieval walled town and its awe-inspiring Minster. Industrial change has left its mark in the pit towns and the Steel City of Sheffield, but also in Leeds' rejuvenated centre and at Saltaire, the 19C mill village painted by Bradford-born David Hockney. The counties' pubs range from the proudly classic to the ceaselessly inventive, each striking its own balance with the famous local love of tradition: roast beef and Yorkshire pudding may have been adopted by the rest of Britain, but this is still the place to go for Wensleydale cheese, York ham, moorland game and parkin, the rich spiced oatmeal cake baked specially for Bonfire Night!

Asenby

001 Crab and Lobster

Dishforth Rd, Asenby YO7 3QL
Tel.: (01845) 577286 - Fax: (01845) 577109
e-mail: reservations@crabmanor.com - Website: www.crabandlobster.com

	No real ales offered

As atmospheric in its own way as the nearby North York Moors, this bizarrely adorned thatched pub displays lobster pots, pews, a dentist's chair, rocking chair and fairground horses in its midst, but there's nothing eccentric in its widely acclaimed menus. A large conservatory, called the Pavilion, and terrace have been added, and there's also an atmospheric, pubby styled brasserie, plus a softly lit, formal restaurant. Together they concentrate primarily on one type of dish: seafood, with the same menu served in all the different areas – the result is locally acclaimed dishes. The rooms are set in a part-Georgian manor house next door, new wooden log cabins and converted outbuildings: each of them individual, some with their own hot tub.

Food serving times:
Monday-Sunday:
12pm-2.30pm, 7pm-9.30pm
- Seafood -
Prices:
Meals: a la carte 25.00/50.00
14 rooms : 200.00

Typical Dishes
King scallops, black pudding, Sherry reduction
"Posh" fish and chips
Assiette of desserts

5.25 mi Southwest of Thirsk by A168. Parking

Bilbrough

002 Three Hares

Main St, Bilbrough YO23 3PH

Tel.: (01937) 832128 - Fax: (01937) 834626
e-mail: info@thethreehares.co.uk - Website: www.thethreehares.co.uk

  VISA

 Timothy Taylor Landlord, Black Sheep, John Smiths and Hambleton Ales

This immaculately whitewashed village pub feels miles away from the eager crowds of summer visitors to York; it's a great escape, certainly, but serves Bilbrough itself well enough, too. Traditional on the outside, the ambience inside is modern and fresh. The small bar area has rafters and exposed brickwork and is great for a cosy, informal lunch of sandwiches and salads. Two other rooms provide something of a contrast for those evening visitors with heartier appetites: here is a neat and tidy, linen-clad restaurant. Bar and dining room menus vary quite considerably: if you've chosen the latter, you'll have more ambitious options to choose from. Either way, service is smooth and polite.

Food serving times:
Monday to Saturday:
  lunch 12pm-2.30pm,
  dinner 7pm-9pm
Sunday brunch: 11am-4pm
Closed Sunday dinner
Prices:
Meals: a la carte 20.00/30.00

Typical Dishes

Potted shrimps
Cottage pie, soused onions
Chocolate soufflé

5 mi Southwest of York off the A64. Parking

Burnsall

003 ## The Red Lion

Burnsall BD23 6BU

Tel.: (01756) 720204 - Fax: (01756) 720292
e-mail: redlion@daelnet.co.uk - Website: www.redlion.co.uk

VISA AE

Theakstons Best, Timothy Taylor Landlord, Folly Ales

From its haunted medieval cellars to the sedate comfort of the sitting room, history is ingrained in every nook and creaking beam of this creeper-clad inn on the River Wharfe. The 16C bar does a pleasantly busy trade in sustaining and enjoyable lunches by the fire. They'll gladly lay a table for dinner here too, but the restaurant, its windows overlooking the green and river, adds a further touch of formality and old-world service. A countryman's pub at heart, the Red Lion has its own trout and grayling waters and access to enviable grouse beats, so naturally fish and game, not to mention fine local lamb, are well represented on a extensive, classic menu with a light modern lift. Bedrooms boast sloping floors, open fires and Victorian brass bedsteads.

Food serving times:
Monday-Sunday:
   12pm-2.30pm, 6pm-9.30pm
Prices:
Meals: 21.95/31.95 and a la carte 20.00/30.00
15 rooms : 69.00/145.00

Southeast of Grassington on B6160. Parking

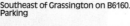

Typical Dishes

Seared king scallops

Braised brisket of beef, horseradish mash

Treacle tart

Byland Abbey

004 **Abbey Inn** 🛏

Byland Abbey YO61 4BD
Tel.: (01347) 868204 - Fax: (01347) 868678
Website: www.bylandabbeyinn.com

  ⵎⵉⵔⵉrest   **VISA** 💳

 Black Sheep, Tetley

A charming, ivy-clad, part 17C country inn with a unique monastic connection: the story goes that Ampleforth monks helped to restore the old house using the old stones of the delapidated abbey opposite. Its main rooms are full of character, as you might expect, their old beams and stonework still in place – one is open plan with an atrium roof, which works surprisingly well. Hearty, traditional cooking revolves around classic favourites supplemented with modern dishes and daily specials. Comfortable and handsomely furnished bedrooms are particularly fine, with plenty of thoughtful little extras; two rooms enjoy views of the enchanting Early Gothic abbey ruins.

Food serving times:
Monday-Saturday:
   12pm-2pm, 6.30pm-9pm
Sunday: 12pm-2pm
Closed 25 December
Closed Monday lunch
Prices:
Meals: a la carte 18.50/27.95
🛏 **3 rooms :** 70.00/155.00

Typical Dishes

Smoked salmon tartlet

Griddled rack of venison, Port sauce

Iced pistachio parfait

Opposite the ruins of Byland Abbey.
Parking

Carlton-in-Coverdale

005 **Foresters Arms**

Carlton-in-Coverdale DL8 4BB
Tel.: (01969) 640272 - Fax: (01969) 640272

   VISA **MC**

 Black sheep, Wensleydale Brewery: Poachers, Foresters, Semerwater, Rowley Mild

Between the moor and the river Cover, the quiet Dales village of Carlton is an ideal place to get away from it all. There's a pleasantly unhurried mood in the two beamed and flagged rooms of its pub (a third room, the formal dining room, also opens for dinner), and ramblers can retrace the day's walk in the maps and prints which cover the walls; there's also seating outside if you want to take your beer out into the sun. Sound cooking on a traditional base goes well with a pint and certainly gets the locals' approval. If the pictures in the bar give you an appetite for more of the great outdoors, drive north to Aysgarth and its beautiful triple flight of waterfalls, made famous by the film Robin Hood, Prince of Thieves. Three pleasant cottagey bedrooms have been comfortably refurbished by the exacting young owners.

Food serving times:
Wednesday-Sunday:
12pm-2pm
Tuesday-Saturday:
7pm-9pm
Closed 1 week February
Prices:
Meals: a la carte 16.00/25.00
3 rooms : 65.00/79.00

4.5 mi Southwest of Middleham by Coverdale rd. Parking

Typical Dishes

Wensleydale cheese and sweet onion tart

Roe deer steak, brandy sauce

Bitter chocolate tart

Constable Burton

006 **Wyvill Arms** 🛏

Constable Burton DL8 5LH
Tel.: (01677) 450581 - Fax: (01677) 450829

      rest **VISA** **AE** **MC**

Black Sheep, John Smith's, Copper Dragon, Theakstons and Hamilton

Abbeys and castles – Jervaulx, Richmond, Bolton – are all within a 10-mile radius of this early 20C pub, situated on a busy road in a small village on the eastern edge of the Dales. There are some traditional elements here – the odd beam, a stone bar area, plenty of memorabilia – but the real attraction for visitors and walkers wearied by a hike in the surrounding countryside is the good choice of ales and locally renowned dishes, steaks being a speciality. There's a blackboard menu which holds some interest, or just enjoy hearty cooking that makes the most of Yorkshire produce in the formal dining room, informal flag-floored bar dining area or the small, cosy bar. Bedrooms are neat, tidy and bright as is the small garden with its wishing well focal point.

Food serving times:
Tuesday-Sunday:
12pm-2pm, 6.30pm-9pm
Prices:
Meals: a la carte 20.00/29.00
🛏 **3 rooms :** 40.00/66.00

Typical Dishes

Asparagus wrapped in gruyere and Parma ham

Nile perch with crayfish tails, Café de Paris butter

Baked lemon cheesecake

3.5mi East of Leyburn on A684.
Parking

Crayke

007 **The Durham Ox**

Westway, Crayke YO61 4TE

Tel.: (01347) 821506 - Fax: (01347) 823326

e-mail: enquiries@thedurhamox.com - Website: www.thedurhamox.com

  rest **VISA** **AE** **MC**

John Smiths Cask and three guest beers

Seasonal Modern British cooking is the order of the day here: blackboard daily specials offer a satisfying selection which combines the robust and the sophisticated, sometimes in the same dish. A smartly set yet cosy dining room is convivial enough, but the real heart of this personally run pub is the charming main bar, with its inglenooks, open fires, gnarled beams and three centuries of character; diners are made to feel very welcome in both. A small shop at the entrance sells local deli produce and out in the converted farm buildings, attractive country-style rooms manage to marry period-style furnishings with mod cons like music systems or spa baths. A real local favourite on all counts.

Food serving times:
Monday-Friday:
  12pm-2.30pm, 6pm-9.30pm
Saturday:
  12pm-2.30pm, 6pm-10pm
Sunday:
  12pm-3pm, 6pm-9.30pm
Closed 25 December and dinner 1 January
Prices:
Meals: a la carte 15.00/32.50
8 rooms : 60.00/120.00

Typical Dishes

Scallops, Gruyère and garlic butter

Pan fried veal, lemon and parsley emulsion

Rhubarb suet sponge

2 mi East of Easingwold on Helmsley rd. Parking

Dalton

008 **The Travellers Rest**

Dalton DL11 7HU
Tel.: (01833) 621225
e-mail: annebabsa@aol.com

 VISA **MC**

Black Sheep

A traditional looking, ivy-clad pub in a tiny hamlet well off the beaten track - for anyone wanting to get away not just from the roar of the city but even from the quiet murmur of the town, this could be the place. It looks like a traditional pub inside as well as out, consisting of a bar lounge with open fire and bric-a-brac, and another room with simple wood tables, chairs and benches. But there's also a linen-laid restaurant available for dinner, where the locals tend to turn out in force, and the reason is simple: the food's good – the blackboard menu's eclectic and traditional with modern twists, and it's decent value, too. Unpretentious, with personable and friendly service.

Food serving times:
Tuesday-Saturday:
7pm-9.30pm
Closed 25, 26 December,
1 January
Prices:
Meals: a la carte 17.50/25.00

Typical Dishes

Crispy duck pancakes
Pan-fried monkfish
Citrus tart with fruits of the forest

7.5 mi Northwest of Scotch Corner by A66. Parking

465

East Witton

009 **The Blue Lion** 🛏

East Witton DL8 4SN

Tel.: (01969) 624273 - Fax: (01969) 624189
e-mail: bluelion@breathemail.net - Website: www.thebluelion.co.uk

 🍴 🍷 *VISA* ⓜ⓪

Theakstons, Black Sheep, Riggwelter

On the edge of the Yorkshire Dales, this 18C one-time coaching inn reigns supreme. It's appealing all round, from the 18C style wood floors and crimson ceiling to the old, faded pictures, open fires and beams with entwined dried flowers – and that's just the restaurant. Pop across to the bar and the character shows no sign of flagging. Or rather, the flagging spreads out right there beneath your feet. It underpins two rooms that boast a bubbly and appealing atmosphere. Wooden booths, pubby knick-knacks, simple tables and chairs and a large, self-assured, modern blackboard menu – served throughout the establishment – entice diners in large numbers: the place has a strong local reputation. No-one seems in a rush: many are staying in the comfy, individually decorated bedrooms.

Food serving times:
Monday-Sunday:
   12pm-2.15pm, 7pm-9.30pm
Closed lunch 25 December
(booking essential)
Prices:
Meals: a la carte 24.45/32.65
🛏 **12 rooms :** 59.00/99.00

3mi Southeast of Leyburn on A6108.
Parking

Typical Dishes

Black pudding salad

Slow braised leg of lamb, garlic mash

Soft baked meringue, fruit cake ice cream

Fadmoor

010 **The Plough Inn**

Main Street, Fadmoor YO62 7HY

Tel.: (01751) 431515 - Fax: (01757) 431515

  　VISA　M©

Black Sheep Best, Tetleys Cask

This neatly-kept little pub on the edge of the North York Moors has a solidly earned reputation and bustling atmosphere. Its position overlooking the village green guarantees a good smattering of walkers, and the friendly welcome ensures word-of-mouth is always positive. There's a characterful interior, a cheery balance between the rustic and the elegant: coir floors, sturdy range doubling as open fire, yellow walls, rich furnishings. Sit at simple wooden tables and chairs in the bar or head instead for a cosy, formally-laid rear dining rooms. Home cooking is to the fore, with the emphasis on fish and seafood. The same extensive menus are served throughout: a neat blend of the traditional with the more contemporary.

Food serving times:
Monday-Sunday:
　　　　12pm-1.45pm,
　　　　6.30pm-8.45pm
Closed 25-26 December and 1 January
(booking essential)
Prices:
Meals: a la carte 17.00/25.00

Typical Dishes

Duck and mango spring roll, sweet chilli dip

Slow roasted shank of lamb, rosemary sauce

Caramelised lemon tart

2.25 mi Northwest of Kirbymoorside. Parking

Ferrensby

011 ## The General Tarleton Inn

Boroughbridge Rd, Ferrensby HG5 0PZ
Tel.: (01423) 340284 - Fax: (01423) 340288
e-mail: gti@generaltarleton.co.uk - Website: www.generaltarleton.co.uk

VISA AE MC

Timothy Taylor Landlord, Black Sheep Best Bitter

The extended 18C pub, surrounded by North Yorkshire countryside, remains as characterful and well run as ever. Neatly painted beams, old stonework and open fires, not to mention a small collection of humorous prints and period pictures on some of the walls, all bring out the convivial character of the place, although the atmosphere is substantially more formal in the dining room. Blackboard specials, early evening menus and Sunday fish suppers suggest a kitchen happy to experiment and accommodate while keeping the winning combination of affordable prices and flavourful, well-judged British cooking, based on quality local produce. Polite service makes for a really enjoyable lunch or evening out.

Food serving times:
Monday-Saturday:
   12pm-2.15pm, 6pm-9.15pm
Sunday:
   12pm-1.45pm, 6pm-9.15pm
Prices:
Meals: 29.50 (dinner) and a la carte 20.00/32.00 (Sunday lunch 18,95)
14 rooms : 85.00/120.00

Typical Dishes

Smoked haddock, rarebit glaze, tomato salad

Confit of lamb, red wine thyme jus

Apple cobbler

From the A1 at Boroughbridge, take the A6055 road towards Knaresborough, the inn is on the right hand side. Parking

Galphay

012 **Galphay Arms**

Galphay HG4 3NJ
Tel.: (01765) 650133
Website: www.galphayinn.co.uk

 VISA MC

Black Sheep and 1 guest ale

Appealing and unfussy, the steady cooking at the Galphay Arms never strays far from its traditional roots, but makes good use of regional ingredients and brings out the flavours of the season with simplicity and clarity: you can't go far wrong with anything on this menu, washed down with a glass of red or a Yorkshire ale. Choose one of the neatly set, marble-topped tables to one side, or a firelit bar in true country style with wood-panelled walls, heavy wooden tables and a collection of hunting prints on the walls. All in all, a proper village pub with a relaxing, homely feel, for which the personable owners can take much of the credit.

Food serving times:
Wednesday-Monday:
12pm-2pm, 6.30pm-9.30pm
Closed Sunday dinner
Prices:
Meals: a la carte 19.00/26.00

Typical Dishes

Thai fishcakes

Duck breast, orange and cranberry sauce

Baked blueberry cheesecake

4.5mi West of Ripon by B6265.
Parking

Harome

013 **The Star Inn**

High St, Harome YO62 5JE
Tel.: (01439) 770397 - Fax: (01439) 771833
Website: www.thestaratharome.co.uk

John Smiths, Black Sheep and 1 guest ale

You'll need a hearty appetite as well as a fine palate to get the most from this deliciously characterful, 14C thatched inn at the tip of the North York Moors. The aptly named pub not only provides an utterly charming dining room, but also superb, rich dishes, prepared with balance and panache, that show pride in its Yorkshire roots. The bar loses nothing by the dining room's starring role; it boasts Mousey Thompson's famous furniture and antiques, as well as solid stone floors, walls filled with period knick-knacks, beam-and-plank ceiling, big log fire, and daily papers and magazines. As if that weren't enough, there's a cosy coffee loft in the eaves, an organic deli selling all manner of delicious goodies, al fresco options in garden or on front terrace, and contemporary bedrooms for overnighters in converted outbuildings across the road.

Food serving times:
Tuesday-Saturday:
11.30pm-2pm,
6.30pm-9.30pm
Sunday: 12pm-6pm
Closed 25 December and 2 weeks January
(booking essential)
Prices:
Meals: a la carte 25.00/40.00
11 rooms : 110.00/210.00

2.75 mi Southeast of Helmsley by A170. Parking

Typical Dishes

Black pudding with foie gras

John Dory with cauliflower purée and braised oxtail

Elderflower rice pudding

Hetton

014 **Angel Inn** We most liked

Hetton BD23 6LT

Tel.: (01756) 730263 - Fax: (01756) 730363
e-mail: info@angelhetton.co.uk - Website: www.angelhetton.co.uk

 VISA AE MC

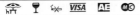

Black Sheep Bitter, Timothy Taylor Landlord

This hugely characterful pub started brewing and serving beer to cattle drovers 300 years ago. If they returned now, they'd probably recognise the same unimproved oak beams, nooks and crannies, but there's now a formal restaurant as well as a bar. The snug warren of rooms is invariably packed, so try and get there early to bag a table. Otherwise, wander around and admire the rural prints, old menus and various awards displayed around the walls. The wooden bar displays well-priced blackboard specials, made up of classic and original dishes, some taking inspiration from France and Italy. Ingredients are mostly drawn from nearby sources: meats from the Dales, Lancastrian sausages and cheese, and fish from Fleetwood. Herbs are even more indigenous: from the Angel's own back garden. The pub's smart bedrooms are set in converted farm buildings across the road.

Food serving times:
Monday-Saturday:
12pm-2.15pm, 6pm-9.30pm
Sunday: 12pm-1.45pm
Closed 25 December,
1 January and 1 week in
January
(booking essential)
Prices:
Meals: 21.00/33.00 and a la carte 23.00/30.00
5 rooms : 120.00/170.00

Typical Dishes

Seafood, lobster sauce

Roast chicken breast, leek
pomme purée

Sticky toffee pudding

5.75mi North of Skipton by B6265.
Parking

Husthwaite

015 The Roasted Pepper

Low St, Husthwaite YO61 4QA
Tel.: (01347) 868007 - Fax: (01347) 868776
e-mail: info@roastedpepper.co.uk - Website: www.roastedpepper.co.uk

hTT   **VISA**   **MC**   JCB

No real ales offered

Turn off the A19 on your way to the North York Moors for an interesting culinary diversion. In the pretty little village of Husthwaite stands this immaculately whitewashed Victorian pub, given a 21C wash and scrub-up: this amounts to an interior best described as sunny, with a bright, contemporary red and yellow palette given full reign. The 19C hasn't been totally forgotten, though – the original brick and tile flooring is still intact. There's a small bar with a couple of tables for drinkers; it all starts to get serious with the dining area, where heavy wood tables and chairs lend the air of a restaurant. Menus are keenly priced and have a distinctly Mediterranean theme, with tapas a key component. There's also a terrace which is popular in summer months.

Food serving times:
Tuesday-Saturday:
    12pm-2.30pm, 7pm-9.30pm
Sunday: 12pm-2.30pm
Prices:
Meals: a la carte 18.00/21.70

Typical Dishes

Pancetta with blue cheese, pear and walnut

Griddled marlin, fennel rice

White chocolate mousse

Between Thirsk and Easingwold off A19. Parking

Langthwaite

016 **Charles Bathurst Inn** 🛏

Langthwaite DL11 6EN
Tel.: (01748) 884567 - Fax: (01748) 884599
e-mail: info@cbinn.co.uk - Website: www.cbinn.co.uk

  VISA

Theakstons Best Bitter, Black Sheep Best and Riggwelter, John Smiths Cask

 High in the windswept hills of Arkengarthdale, the well-run 18C inn is named after the old lord of the manor, whose "CB" monogram was stamped on the local lead from which he made his fortune: any cross-country ramble – and there are plenty – is likely to skirt more than one of his long-disused mines. Wood floors, open fires and photos of Herriot country add greatly to the charm of a neatly kept bar, which is perfect for a quiet pint or two, but owes much of its strong local reputation to its half-modern, half-traditional menu, painted afresh every day on two broad mirrors: there's more choice, and more demand, in the evenings. Spacious, individually decorated bedrooms with period pine furniture are good to come back to after a long day's walk.

Food serving times:
Monday-Sunday:
   12pm-2pm, 6.30pm-9pm
Closed 25 December
Prices:
Meals: a la carte 17.50/25.00
🛏 **18 rooms :** 80.00/105.00

Typical Dishes

Avocado and crab in a filo basket

Sirloin steak, wild mushroom sauce

Southern Comfort ice cream

3.25mi Northwest of Reeth on Langthwaite rd. Parking

Leyburn

017 **Sandpiper Inn**

Market Pl, Leyburn DL8 5AT
Tel.: (01969) 622206 - Fax: (01969) 625367
e-mail: hsandpiper99@aol.com

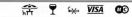

Black Sheep Best and Special, Copper Dragon

A pub ideally placed for weary ramblers making their way from the Dales, this converted 16C stone house could just as easily be missed by them, as it's tucked away at one end of the market square and needs to be sought out. The effort's not wasted. Downstairs is a traditional pub, divided into cosy alcoves nestling under dark beams, with a log fire lighting the way. In the simply stylish – though rather subdued - dining room, it's bare wood tables by day, but linen at night. Good value blackboard menus offer rich pickings in the form of traditional dishes, with local produce to the fore. For those who really are too weary, there are two comfy bedrooms upstairs and a new third room in a converted cottage across the road.

Food serving times:
Tuesday-Saturday:
  12pm-2.30pm, 6.30pm-9pm
Sunday:
    12pm-2pm, 7pm-9pm
Prices:
Meals: a la carte 21.25/29.00
3 rooms : 60.00/90.00

Typical Dishes

Belly pork, braised lentils and foie gras

Spring lamb, garlic sauce

Vanilla crème brûlée

In town centre. Limited parking available

Marton

018 ## The Appletree Country Inn

Marton YO62 6RD

Tel.: (01751) 431457

e-mail: appletreeinn@supanet.com - Website: www.appletreeinn.co.uk

     VISA MC

John Smiths and 3 regularly changing guest ales

Spacious, warm and comfortable, a typical Yorkshire inn run by a friendly couple and set in a quiet village on the banks of the Seven, where the river runs down to the Vale of Pickering. In a rustic interior of exposed brick and timbers, well-spaced tables through three adjoining rooms mark this out as a dining pub first and foremost, so it's no surprise to find a touch of rather proper formality in the service. The cooking, too, works in its presentational flourishes, but it's not without its traditional, homespun side as well, with beef to the fore.

Food serving times:
Wednesday-Saturday:
12pm-2pm, 6.30pm-9.30pm
Sunday: 12pm-2pm,
               7pm-9pm
Closed 25 December and
2 weeks January
Prices:
Meals: a la carte 17.00/33.00

Typical Dishes

Crab cheesecake

Beef, red onion marmalade

Chocolate fondant tart

7mi Southeast of Welshpool on
B4386. Parking

Middleham

019 White Swan 🛏

Market Pl, Middleham DL8 4PE

Tel.: (01969) 622093 - Fax: (01969) 624551

e-mail: whiteswan@easynet.co.uk - Website: www.whiteswanhotel.co.uk

🍷 **VISA**

Black Sheep, John Smith's Cask

In a town now best known for its racehorses, where Richard III's white boar standard once flew from the now-ruined castle, The White Swan proves there's no accounting for some choices of pub names. A pleasant but unremarkable part of the market place, the old coaching inn saves the best for inside: the stone-floored bar with stove and inglenook is inviting enough, but the two cosy little rooms at the back are even nicer on a cold evening, and the neatly decorated bedrooms could be useful for an overnight stop. A sound, locally sourced English menu sticks to what it knows best with no over-reaching modern flourishes, preferring trusty favourites. Run with quiet Yorkshire competence, it's a real asset to the town: expect it to be even better by the end of 2005 with a new bar and refurbished bedrooms promised.

Food serving times:
Monday-Sunday:
12pm-2.15pm,
6.30pm-9.15pm
Closed 25 December
Prices:
Meals: 13.95 (set lunch) and a la carte 16.50/23.50
🛏 **19 rooms :** 47.50/90.00

1mi from Leyburn on A6108. Parking ❯

Typical Dishes

Black pudding and bacon salad

Cod fillet with proscuito

Fruits of the forest panna cotta

Moulton

020 Black Bull Inn

Moulton DL10 6QJ

Tel.: (01325) 377289 - Fax: (01325) 377422
e-mail: sarah@blackbullinn.demon.co.uk

  VISA

 No real ales

There seems little to set the Black Bull apart from the other extended cottages in this North Yorkshire village, until you step inside and find a long-established, traditional place of the sort that inspires real affection in its regulars. With a comfy seat and a pre-dinner drink in your hand, it's unexpectedly easy to feel at home in the neat, unshowy lounge bar, but though they serve a full menu here, the main feature is still to come. Besides the conservatory of the main house, you can also sit down to dinner in a sumptuously comfortable 1930s Brighton Belle Pullman carriage: all of the respectful elegance of the Age of Steam, none of the points failures. Whatever you choose, a classic menu with an emphasis on seafood is served with a nice, straightforward friendliness.

Food serving times:
Monday-Saturday:
    12pm-2pm, 6.45pm-10pm
Closed 24-26 December
- Seafood specialities -(Bar snacks only Saturday lunch)

Prices:
Meals: 18.95 (fixed price lunch) and a la carte 35.00/45.00

Typical Dishes

Seafood pancake Thermidor
Grilled Dover sole
Crème brûlee, shortbread

4.25 mi Northeast of Richmond by A6108. Parking

Osmotherley

021 ## Golden Lion

6 West End, Osmotherley DL6 3AA
Tel.: (01609) 883526 - Fax: (01609) 884000

  VISA

Timothy Taylor Landlord, Jennings Bitter, Deuchars IPA, Hambleton Best Bitter, John Smiths cask

If you're walking the Cleveland Way, this old stone faced pub is like manna from heaven – it turns up right there on the path, so if you pay a visit, you're likely to meet fellow hikers. It's nothing very special to look at, and the interior isn't too much more than white walls and a few old pews, but the mix of ramblers, locals and those in search of a decent meal keeps the atmosphere lively and friendly. What draws the dining fraternity here are the simple, well-constructed, keenly priced dishes that consistently hit the spot. Tried-and-tested meals are prepared with real care; extensive menus offer hearty fuel for heading to the hills.

Food serving times:
Monday-Sunday:
   12pm-3.30pm, 6pm-10pm
Closed 25 December
Prices:
Meals: a la carte 15.00/25.00

Typical Dishes

Crab mayonnaise

Steak and kidney suet pudding

Orange cake, marmalade cream

6 mi Northeast of Northallerton by A684. Parking in village

Osmotherley

022 **The 3 Tuns** 🛏️

9 South End, Osmotherley DL6 3BN

Tel.: (01609) 883301 - Fax: (01609) 883988
e-mail: enquiries@the3tuns.net

🏕️ &✕rest 🚫 **VISA** **AE** **MC**

Timothy Taylor Landlord

Set in a pretty village, this is an unassuming pub on first sight – the modern sign outside is the first hint at the sympathetic refit that's taken place indoors. Pale oak panelling lightens rather than darkens the bar and restaurant, and combines surprisingly well with the retro design – there's more than a touch of re-interpreted Rennie Mackintosh in the pub's style. Three bedrooms in the pub and four in the cottage next door – formerly the village bakery – have been designed with similar care: they're comfortable and nicely maintained. Though you can wander in for a drink – and people do – the focus here is on food, served in a neatly set back room and also out on the front and back terraces, with modern menus which are a touch popular in places, as well as offering some more original dishes.

Food serving times:
Monday-Saturday:
12pm-2.30pm,
5.30pm-9.30pm
Sunday: 12pm-8pm
Prices:
Meals: 13.95 and a la carte 23.00/30.00
🛏️ **7 rooms :** 55.00/75.00

Typical Dishes

Thai-spiced fishcakes

Calves liver with pancetta

Bitter chocolate and orange truffle cake

6mi Northeast of Northallerton by A684. Parking in village

Ramsgill-in-Nidderdale

023 **Yorke Arms**

Ramsgill-in-Nidderdale HG3 5RL
Tel.: (01423) 755243 - Fax: (01423) 755330
e-mail: enquiries@yorke-arms.co.uk - Website: www.yorke-arms.co.uk

    VISA **AE** **D** **MC**

Black Sheep Special

Set in unspoilt countryside near Gouthwaite reservoir, this part 17C, delightfully ivy clad former shooting lodge is quite simply one of England's most charming inns. Handsomely styled with carved wooden furniture, antiques, oriental rugs and bright, gilt-framed oils, two welcoming dining rooms feel closer in atmosphere to a country house than a village pub, and the formal, structured service is that of a restaurant rather than an inn, but as a dining experience it's calm, refined and, at its best, quite delightful. Precise and consistent seasonal cooking balances classical style with a subtle regional identity. Good value lunch Monday to Saturday and you can make the most of a lovely riverside terrace and gardens, or flop onto the squashy sofas in the lounge. Superlative, stylish and contemporary bedrooms have been recently refurbished.

Food serving times:
Monday-Sunday:
12pm-2pm, 7pm-9pm
Accommodation rates include dinner
Prices:
Meals: 21.00 (lunch) and a la carte 35.00/45.00
13 rooms : 120.00/380.00

Typical Dishes
Potted beef, ham hock and foie gras terrine
Roast halibut, morel and artichoke
Four textures in chocolate

5 mi Northwest of Pateley Bridge by Low Wath rd. Parking

Sinnington

024 Fox and Hounds 🛏

Main St, Sinnington YO62 6SQ

Tel.: (01751) 431577 - Fax: (01751) 432791
e-mail: foxhoundsinn@easynet.co.uk - Website: www.thefoxandhoundsinn.co.uk

 🍷 ✂ *VISA* AE MC

Camerons, Black Sheep Special

D rive four miles out from the attractive market town of Pickering and you arrive in sleepy Sinnington on the river Seven, at the southern end of the North York Moors. The Fox And Hounds, an attractively extended 18C coaching inn, is the pivot around which community life revolves. Its characterful front bar is beamed and panelled in ancient oak, with old artefacts and a woodburner. Flop down there or retreat to the smart residents lounge with a pint of local ale. The restaurant, housed in a rear extension, has smart, linen-clad tables; the impressive menu is served in both dining areas. Bedrooms are neat and tidy with a cottagey feel and style.

Food serving times:
Monday-Saturday:
  12pm-2pm, 6.30pm-9pm
Sunday:
  12pm-2pm, 6.30pm-8.30pm
Closed 25 December
Prices:
Meals: a la carte 15.90/25.00
🛏 **3 rooms :** 69.00/120.00

Typical Dishes

Pancakes, crispy duck and chilli jam

Char grilled lamb, salad of red onion

Orange and maple reduction

Just off A170 between Pickering and Kirkymoorside. Parking

Skipton

The Bull

Broughton, Skipton BD23 3AE
Tel.: (01756) 792065 - Fax: (01756) 792065
e-mail: janeneil@thebullatbroughton.co.uk - Website: www.thebullatbroughton.co.uk

 Bull Bitter, Copper Dragon

Don't let the busy A59 send you roaring off into the Pennines without a stop at this delightful country pub, located within the grounds of Broughton Hall Country Park Estate amid 3000 Yorkshire acres. It's a lovely old building which has been carefully refurbished to bring out the open log fire, rustic décor and intimate seating areas. The greetings are effusive, even from the pub cat. A selection of hand-drawn cask ales is always available, but pride of place-mat goes to the Bull's own beer brewed specially for them. The relaxing feel stretches to the dining rooms which envelop you in a web of warm stone. Chef makes good use of ingredients close to hand with produce from the Dales never far from your knife and fork; the pub's "everything home-made" credentials are worn as a badge of honour.

Food serving times:
Monday-Thursday:
12pm-2pm, 6pm-9pm
Friday-Saturday:
12pm-2pm, 6pm-9.30pm
Sunday and Bank holiday Mondays:
12pm-6pm
Prices:
Meals: a la carte 18.10/25.94

Typical Dishes

Fishcake on mixed leaves

Sausage and mash

Home-made ice cream

3mi West of Skipton town centre on A59. In the grounds of Broughton Hall Country Park Estate. Parking

Snainton

026 Coachman Inn

Pickering Road West, Snainton YO13 9PL

Tel.: 01723 859231 - Fax: 01723 850008
Website: www.coachmaninn.co.uk

   rest **VISA** Ⓜ©

Black Sheep Bitter

The very image of a Georgian posting inn, the Coachman stands on the edge of the North York Moors and must have been a welcome sight to travellers on the York to Scarborough road. Inside, a modern dining room has a view over the lawn – if you're planning on a formal meal, this is probably better, not to mention more spacious, but the little bar takes some beating for warmth and character. Cushioned pews, old elm tables, framed prints, hunting curios and a stuffed otter called Tarquin all, in their way, add to the traditional cosiness, and the friendly atmosphere deserves pointing out. Modern British cooking incorporates Yorkshire-reared meats, locally landed fish, and a few other specialities like Dales goat's cheese. Individually styled bedrooms.

Food serving times:
Monday-Sunday:
12pm-2pm
(2.30pm Saturday and Sunday),
7pm-9pm
(9.30pm Friday and Saturday)
Closed Wednesday
Prices:
Meals: a la carte 19.00/25.00
4 rooms : 66.00/85.00

Typical Dishes

'Whitby' crab salad

'Harome' duck breast, shallot tart and orange sauce

Sticky toffee pudding, 'Black Sheep' ice cream

0,5 mi West by A170 on B1258. Parking

Sutton-on-the-Forest

027 **Rose & Crown**

Main St, Sutton-on-the-Forest YO61 1DP
Tel.: (01347) 811333 - Fax: (01347) 811444

 Black Sheep Best, Timothy Taylors Landlord, Yorkshire Terrier

Everyday pub name, exceptional pub cooking typical of a carefully sourced and precisely prepared repertoire that's won plaudits around the county and beyond and has a loyal following of locals and other regulars. There's a lovely enclosed rear terrace and lawned garden and the smart, modern feel is softened slightly in a cosily rustic interior: it's unobtrusively stylish but still feels relaxed. Service is smooth and attentive without ever seeming stifling. The little seating and dining areas add a touch of intimacy, while the firelit bar, and the fair-minded value-for-money ethic, are in the best Yorkshire tradition. Small, but frequently changing wine list.

Food serving times:
Tuesday-Saturday:
12pm-2pm, 6pm-9pm
Sunday: 12pm-2pm
Closed first week January
Prices:
Meals: 9.95 and a la carte 25.00/35.00

Typical Dishes

Terrine of smoked salmon

Rump of Yorkshire Dales lamb, pesto mash

Crème brûlée

On B1363 North of York. Parking

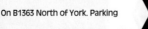

West Tanfield

028 The Bruce Arms

Main St, West Tanfield HG4 5JJ

Tel.: (01677) 470325 - Fax: (01677) 470796

Website: www.brucearms.com

   room   **VISA** MC

Black sheep

This thriving little Yorkshire pub looks no great shakes from the outside, set as it is on a roundabout, despite the rather fetching creepers. Inside, though, a mini success story unfolds. Dating from 1820, it crams in timber beams, log fire, heaps of local memorabilia, and a good local ale on tap. In 1997, it re-styled itself as a bistro and its well-prepared, interesting dishes get the thumbs-up from all comers. Enjoy pre-dinner drinks in the leather furnished seating area just inside the entrance, then settle down for a meal in the cosy dining room, or on the vine covered terrace in warmer weather. Refurbished bedrooms offer rustic charm.

Food serving times:
Tuesday-Saturday:
  12pm-2pm, 6.30pm-9.30pm
Sunday: 12pm-2pm
Closed Monday lunch
Prices:
Meals: a la carte 20.00/30.00
3 rooms : 45.00/100.00

Typical Dishes

Blue cheese and red onion tart

Chargrilled swordfish

Apple and rhubarb brown betty

Between Masham and Ripon on A6108. Parking

Westow

029   The Blacksmiths Inn 🛏

Main St, Westow YO60 7NE

Tel.: 01653 618365 - Fax: 01653 618394
e-mail: info@blacksmithsinn.co.uk - Website: www.blacksmithsinn.co.uk

  🍷   rest   *VISA*   Ⓜ©

 Tetleys, Timothy Taylor Landlord, John Smiths

Although it's fair to say that the Blacksmiths Inn is a modern dining pub, the move has taken it closer to, not further from, its country roots. There's a quiet glow from the wood-burning stove, and framed pictures, postcards, cartoons, Yorkshire landscapes and other themed artwork cover the walls. The local connection rings particularly true in the two trimly set dining rooms: vegetables from the pub's own farm, home-ground flour, and local sloe berries – in gin, jam, even chutneys and chocolates - play their part in a couple of specials and a concise, modern menu which changes by the week. Drinkers are made very welcome in the front lounge, with bowls of rustic, home-made nibbles like parsnip crisps and crackling set out on the bar. Knowledgeable and thoroughly pleasant service. Beamed, cottage-style bedrooms furnished in dark wood.

Food serving times:
Wednesday-Saturday:
           6.30pm-9.30pm
Sunday: 12pm-3.30pm
Prices:
Meals: a la carte 21.00/27.00
🛏 **6 rooms :** 34.00/68.00

6,5 mi Southwest of Moulton off the A64 past Kirkham Priory. Parking

Typical Dishes

Honey glazed pork belly, pease pudding

Duck breast, rhubarb and foie gras macaroni

Banana Tatin

Whitwell-on-the-Hill

030 ## The Stone Trough Inn

Kirkham Abbey, Whitwell-on-the-Hill YO60 7JS

Tel.: (01653) 618713 - Fax: (01653) 618819

e-mail: info@stonetroughinn.co.uk - Website: www.stonetroughinn.co.uk

 *VISA* 💳

> *Black Sheep Best, Timothy Taylor Landlord, Tetley, Theakstons Old Peculier, Suddaby's Golden Chance and 1 guest beer*

A truly idyllic spot on a summer's day – the Stone Trough Inn is close to the ruins of 12C Kirkham Abbey and the long bend of the River Derwent. The pub itself is newer than it might first seem, and the skillful and sympathetic reconstruction looks still more authentic from the inside; a charmingly rustic, heavily beamed bar built of Yorkshire stone is full of little nooks and snugs. You can dine here, choosing from a varied selection of Modern British dishes and blackboard specials, or take your drinks through to the restaurant, which actually feels more like a big farmhouse kitchen, complete with pine tables and chairs.

Food serving times:
Tuesday-Saturday:
  12pm-2pm, 6.45pm-9.30pm
Sunday: 12pm-2.15pm
Closed 25 December. Open
Bank Holiday Mondays
Prices:
Meals: a la carte 20.00/25.00

Typical Dishes

Chicken liver terrine

Chicken with wild mushroom risotto

Spiced apple and pear crumble

5mi Southwest of Malton off A64 following signs for Kirkham Priory. Parking

Sheffield

031 Lions Lair

31 Burgess St, Sheffield S1 2HF

Tel.: (0114) 263 4264 - Fax: (0114) 263 4265

e-mail: info@lionslair.co.uk - Website: www.lionslair.co.uk

Tetleys, Black Sheep

The centre of Sheffield may not be the automatic choice for those in search of cosy rusticity, but this neat little pub hidden away in the heart of the city provides a number of pleasant surprises. It boasts a lovely enclosed rear terrace with the added attraction of stylishly-nautical decking where summer barbeques and live music rustle the Yorkshire air and a snug interior dining room with leather banquettes, open fires, a pleasing mix of tables and popular, wide-ranging menus which are unfussy and freshly prepared, with dishes heavily influenced by the patron's French roots.

Food serving times:
Monday-Friday:
12pm-9pm
Saturday-Sunday:
12pm-8.30pm
Closed 25 December and 1 January
Prices:
Meals: a la carte 17.00/22.00

Typical Dishes

Seared beef fillet, tomato salsa

Rack of lamb, garlic mash

Apple crumble, vanilla ice cream

Burgess St is off Parker's Pool, to the South of City Hall. Public parking nearby

Totley

032 The Cricket

Penny Lane, Totley S17 3AZ

Tel.: (0114) 236 5256 - Fax: (0114) 235 6582
e-mail: enquiries@the-cricket.com - Website: www.the-cricket.com

    rest **VISA** **M©**

Timothy Taylor Landlord, Stones Best Bitter

Among the copses and fields, where Sheffield's outermost suburbs blend into countryside, you'll find the home ground of Totley Cricket Club and, next to it, the trimly kept Cricket Inn. A traditionally informal bar is filled with the team's memorablia; bats and bails, team photos, shots of cavalier strokemakers and hurricane 'quicks' all reflect the first love of the White Rose county. Nourishing and enjoyable food, prepared with culinary good sense, is served here: the formal restaurant, with a menu to match, opens in the evening and for Sunday lunch; service is polite and friendly throughout. Afterwards, you could always stroll to the boundary and see if you can spot the next Trueman, Boycott or Vaughan...

Food serving times:
Tuesday-Saturday:
12pm-2.30pm, 6pm-10pm
Sunday: 12pm-2.30pm
Closed 25 December and
1 January
Prices:
Meals: 18.95 (dinner) and a la carte 14.00/30.00

Typical Dishes

Sesame coated beef salad

Rack of lamb, black pudding stuffing and thyme jus

Chocolate and chilli tart

At the South end of the village: turn into Lane Head Road and go down the hill into Penny Lane. Parking

Addingham

033 **Fleece**

154 Main St., Addingham LS29 0LY

Tel.: (01943) 830491

e-mail: chris@monkmansbistro.fsbusiness.co.uk

VISA **MC**

Tetleys Cask, Timothy Taylor Landlord, Black Sheep

This good-looking, ivy-clad pub sits on the busy main street in Addingham, close to the southern 'gateway' to the Yorkshire Dales National Park. Its pleasing features extend across the threshold, where can be found open fires to entice chilled walkers on cold days, a solid stone floor, and rustic walls filled with country oriented prints, oils and general nick-nacks. It's all overseen in a very personally run style by the charming owner, and the homely ambience extends to the dining area, which boasts 1930s style tables. There's an appealing mix of dishes from the blackboard menu, the repertoire covering anything from classic and traditional pub dishes to more contemporary offerings, all served in generous portions.

Food serving times:
Monday-Saturday:
  12pm-2.15pm, 6pm-9.15pm
Sunday: 12pm-8pm
Prices:
Meals: a la carte 15.00/25.00

Typical Dishes

Mussels with garlic, thyme and white wine

Lamb with red wine jus

Apricot bread and butter pudding

On the busy through road in the centre of Addingham. Parking

Halifax

034 **Shibden Mill Inn** 🛏

Shibden Mill Fold, Halifax HX3 7UL

Tel.: (01422) 365840 - Fax: (01422) 362971
Website: www.shibdenmillinn.com

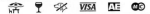

 Shibden Mill Bitter, Theakstons XB, John Smiths and 2 weekly changing guest bitters

Only a mile or two outside the centre of Halifax, and the landscape of the Shibden Valley already feels properly rural. The old millpond has long since run dry, and the formal split-level dining room gives away little of the mill's history, but there's a more authentic country feel to the main bar. With a pleasantly haphazard mix of landscape prints, plates and bottles for decoration, it's spacious but still intimate, and frankly the more inviting choice, although the frequently changing menu, served throughout, has more in common with restaurant dining. Served in hefty pub portions, the rather complex dishes bear the hallmarks of fashionable cooking over the last decade and reveal a solid background in the Modern British kitchen. Individually styled rooms, being refurbished one by one, make this a useful overnight stop

Food serving times:
Monday-Sunday:
12pm-2pm, 6pm-9.30pm
Closed dinner 25-26 December and 1 January
Prices:
Meals: 11.95 (fixed price lunch) and a la carte 19.00/29.65
🛏 **12 rooms :** 68.00/130.00

2.25 mi Northeast by A58 and Kell Lane (turning left at Stump Cross Pub), on Blake Hill Rd. Parking

Typical Dishes

Hand dived scallops, saffron risotto

Fillet of beef, Drambuie sauce

Prune and Armagnac bread

Marsden

035 ## Olive Branch ⊨

Manchester Rd, Marsden HD7 6LU
Tel.: (01484) 844487
Website: www.olivebranch.uk.com

Holme Valley

Three wonderfully cosy rooms – feeling almost like interlinking snugs – together with the rear contemporary restaurant make up the heart of this part 16C former cattle-drover's inn that matches exposed brick, pine antiques and framed sepia photographs with a light dash of modernity. Add to this the personable approach of the owners and its easy to see why the Olive Branch's reputation reaches well beyond Marsden itself. Up on the wall, large Post-it notes announce menu changes at the rate of a departures board: this might disconcert any chronically indecisive diners, but speaks well for the freshness of the diverse and tasty cooking. Flavourful seafood specialities are guaranteed, in any case, along with other contemporary country dishes.
Comfortable, smart and stylish bedrooms. Moorland and canalside walks.

Food serving times:
Tuesday-Friday:
  12pm-2pm, 6.30pm-9.30pm
Saturday: 6.30pm-9.30pm
Sunday: 1pm-8.30pm
Closed 26 December and first 2 weeks January
Closed Tuesday and Saturday lunch
Prices:
Meals: 13.95/18.50 and a la carte 24.65/34.95
⊨ **3 rooms :** 55.00/70.00
☕ 10.50

1 mi Northeast on A62. Parking

Typical Dishes

Scallops, herb risotto and white truffle oil

Duck, onion and sultana marmalade

Lemon tart

Silsden

036 The Grouse

Keighley Rd, Silsden BD20 0EH
Tel.: (01535) 657788 - Fax: (01535) 655742

   VISA

Timothy Taylor Golden Best, Landlord

A buzzy pub, busy and popular, and refurbished in late 2003, at the bottom of the town: in the latter part of the 18C, there were three cottages here but for many years it's served as an inn. As you approach, the modernisation is apparent, announced by frosted glass and aubergine coloured signs. Inside, halogen lighting, wood floors, muted tones and stark browns reflect the zeitgeist. David, the manager, and Matthew, the chef, are brothers whose teamwork gels smoothly. Not a pub popular with drinkers, diners order drinks at the small bar and eat at the uncovered tables; light lunches give way to handsomely endowed dinners, whose more formal character still manages to satisfy the local demand for steaks.

Food serving times:
Tuesday: 6pm-9.30pm
Wednesday-Saturday:
12pm-2pm, 6pm-9.30pm
Sunday: 12pm-3pm
Prices:
Meals: 14.95 (Sunday lunch and weekdays 6pm-7.30pm) and a la carte 15.00/26.00

Typical Dishes

Seared scallops with chorizo picante

Lamb with rosemary jus

White peach and green tea sorbet

Parking at rear

Sowerby Bridge

037 ## The Millbank We most liked

Mill Bank Road, Sowerby Bridge HX6 3DY
Tel.: (01422) 825588
e-mail: themillbank@yahoo.co.uk - Website: www.themillbank.com

Tetley Bitter, Timothy Taylor Landlord

H ere's a proper pub with wooden floors and exposed stone in an invigorating position in the Pennines. It caters just as readily for drinkers as for those who've come in to eat, even though its contemporary interior and modern artwork certainly put it firmly into the dining pub league. Chunky wooden tables and chairs, a ready warmth of service, allied to interesting modern cooking, guarantee customers from far and wide, and booking is essential. Dine in the conservatory for beautiful countryside views; a neat little terrace helps take the strain. Place your order with the smartly uniformed staff - whatever you choose from the menu, there's guaranteed good food at a modest price. Well-kept bedrooms add to the inn's reputation.

Food serving times:
Tuesday-Thursday:
   12pm-2.30pm, 6pm-9.30pm
Friday-Saturday:
   12pm-2.30pm, 6pm-10pm
Sunday:
   12.30pm-4.30pm, 6pm-8pm
Closed first 2 weeks January and October
(booking essential)
Prices:
Meals: a la carte 19.95/34.95

Typical Dishes

Foie gras brûlée
Roast Goosnargh Duck
Chocolate fondant cake

2.25 mi Southwest by A58. Parking on the road in front of the pub

Thunderbridge

038 Woodman Inn

Thunderbridge HD8 0PX

Tel.: (01484) 605778 - Fax: (01484) 604110
e-mail: thewoodman@connectfree.co.uk - Website: www.woodman-inn.co.uk

♀ ✗=rest **VISA** **MC**

Timothy Taylor Landlord, Best, Tetleys

T ake the road south from Huddersfield and you're soon in 'Last of the Summer Wine' country, the ideal setting for this 19C inn of Yorkshire stone which, nearly a decade ago, was extended by the owners to include the adjacent old weavers' cottages. Thus was created a host of well thought out bedrooms, the perfect final destination after an invigorating day in the nearby Southern Pennines. Bar and restaurant – set away from the bar on the first floor – are of more recent vintage, having both been refurbished in 2003. You can eat formally, at linen-clad tables, in the latter, while scrubbed tables and a more free and easy ambience set the mood for dining in the rest of the pub. Tasty, unfussy dishes appear on an appealing menu that utilises freshly prepared, local ingredients in a traditional manner.

Food serving times:
Monday-Saturday:
    12pm-3pm, 6.30pm-9pm
Sunday: 12pm-6pm
Prices:
Meals: a la carte 14.00/20.00
🛏 **12 rooms :** 45.00/65.00

Typical Dishes

Sundried tomato and goat's cheese feuillete

Marinated pork steak

Sticky toffee pudding

5.75mi South East of Huddersfield by A629, after Kirkburton follow signs to Thunderbridge. Parking

*W*indswept peaks and misty lochs from the pages of Burns and Scott or the urban grit of modern film and fiction? Visitors could be forgiven for wondering what to expect in this country of contrasts, but it's all here: the wild beauty of Wester Ross and the Neoclassical elegance of Edinburgh's New Town, the fishing villages of the East Neuk, the lush gardens of Inverewe, warmed by the Gulf Stream in the west, as well as the vibrance of straight-talking Glasgow. This is a land where tradition can mean etiquette and fellowship on the first tee or the raw energy of Shetland's Viking fire festival, centuries of pre-eminence in British science and letters, or a turbulent social history which has left its mark on every part of life. There's a difference in town and country pub culture, too. Perhaps more than anywhere else in Britain, inns in the countryside are often the centres for a widespread community: pub, hotel, restaurant and even shop in one, with a wise word behind the bar on anything from fishing lures to football scores. In Glasgow and Edinburgh, however, dining pubs are only a tiny part of a busy year-round cultural life, which hits fever pitch with the creativity and sheer variety of the summer festivals. One thing is for sure, traditional inns and modern gastropubs take equal pride in their national specialities: smoked or fresh salmon and trout, Loch Linnhe prawns, seafood soups like Cullen Skink and Partan Bree, prime beef, Highland game and haggis.

Netherley

001 Lairhillock Inn

Netherley AB39 3QS

Tel.: (01569) 730001 - Fax: (01569) 731175
e-mail: lairhillock@breathemail.net - Website: www.lairhillock.co.uk

Timothy Taylor Landlord, Courage Directors and a selection of Isle of Skye ales

Beautiful Deeside country stretches away to either side, and the Granite City is only a 15-minute drive, but tearing yourself away from a ramble in the hills is not an altogether bad idea when the wonderfully atmospheric front snug bar is the destination. A former coaching inn, the Lairhillock remains the beating heart of the village, and the snug exerts a gravitational pull. It's an invariably busy and friendly bar, but if you find the bustle a bit too much, then there are other areas to discover: there's a lounge with an altogether more relaxed feel, and a conservatory with open fires, which is the place to dig into a good choice of satisfying, rustic dishes chock full of local produce: Gourdon langoustines, salmon from the Dee and Don, Highland venison and boar, and Shetland mussels.

Food serving times:
Monday-Thursday:
      12pm-2pm, 6pm-9.30pm
Friday-Saturday:
        12pm-2pm, 6pm-10pm
Sunday:
      12pm-2pm, 5.30pm-9pm
Closed 25-26 December and 1-2 January
Prices:
Meals: a la carte 19.15/32.55

Typical Dishes

Grilled pigeon salad

Salmon, pepper and parmesan crust

Cranachan and shortbread tower

Parking

Bridgend of Lintrathen

002 The Steading
**(at Lochside Lodge and Roundhouse restaurant) Angus,
Bridgend of Lintrathen DD8 5JJ**   Tel.: 01575 560340 - Fax: 01575 560202
e-mail: enquiries@lochsidelodge.com - Website: www.lochsidelodge.com

VISA **M©**

 1 ale from Inveralmond brewery

The more informal counterpart to the Roundhouse restaurant, the Steading's name is a reminder of its humble origins as an old farm building. The original stone walls are now decorated with all sorts of agricultural tools, rural fitments, and some country sports memorabilia, some of the mystery items look like they might fall into all three categories. Cushioned pews are pulled up to solid wood tables and a brasserie style lunch menu is served along with the same menu on offer in the Roundhouse restaurant at dinner. If you're just after a drink, there's a little bar to one side, with newspapers and magazines within easy reach of the leather seats. Four pine-fitted bedrooms, in the converted hayloft, all have a dash of tartan or floral colour and plenty in the way of thoughtful, homely touches.

Food serving times:
Tuesday-Saturday:
    12pm-1.30pm,
    6.30pm-8.30pm
Sunday: 12pm-1.30pm
Closed 1-21 January, 1 week
October, 25-27 December
Prices:
Meals: a la carte 16.00/32.00
🛏 **6 rooms :** 50.00/100.00

Typical Dishes

*Dunsyre blue cheese brûlée,
plum chutney*

*Angus rib-eye, tarragon and
shallot butter*

Glazed lemon tart

Parking >

Crinan

003 Crinan (Bar) ⇌

Crinan PA31 8SR
Tel.: (01546) 830261 - Fax: (01546) 830292
e-mail: nryan@crinanhotel.com - Website: www.crinanhotel.com

⇌rest **VISA** **AE** **MC**

Piper's Gold, Belhaven, Maverick

Superbly located in a commanding position with exceptional views of Loch Crinan and Sound of Jura, this elegant, whitewashed building has picture windows that let guests take in superb views of fishing boats chugging out towards the Hebrides. Naturally enough, the bar has a nautical theme, while there are two homely lounges to sit and watch the world go by. There's a Gallery bar, too, which overlooks the loch. With all this natural beauty in abundance, make sure you get to eat where you can take in the vista. The split-level restaurant is smart with linen clad tables, and the menus have an interesting, modern feel to them. Try, maybe, roast scallops, cauliflower puree and raisin vinaigrette for starters; skate salad with haricot vert, or fillet of beef, cubed celeriac and red wine jus for a main. Stay in pleasant, bright bedrooms.

Food serving times:
Monday-Sunday:
12pm-2.30pm, 6.30pm-9pm
Closed 19 December-
1 February
Accommodation rates
include dinner
Prices:
Meals: a la carte 15.00/22.50
⇌ **18 rooms :** 95.00/310.00

Typical Dishes

Tart of warm Loch Crinan scallops

Loch Crinan prawns with garlic butter

Lemongrass panna cotta

At the end of Crinan canal on the edge of Loch Crinan. Parking ⟫

Kintyre - Kilberry

004 **Kilberry Inn**

Kintyre - Kilberry PA29 6YD
Tel.: (01880) 770223 - Fax: (01880) 770223
e-mail: relax@kilberryinn.com - Website: www.kilberryinn.com

 VISA *MC*

Vital Spark, Piper's Gold, Highlander

Between the wooded heights and the widening Sound of Jura stands a whitewashed cottage on a long country road. It's as simple as you could wish: a parlour for lunch and dinner and a little beamed lounge in stone and pine, with local landscapes on the walls, a fire in the hearth and local whiskies behind the bar. The blackboard menu changes every day, but the fortifying home cooking always has a real local flavour to it and the ingredients are all found close to home. It's the efforts of the staff that really make the place, though, with a nice, upfront informality setting the tone. The three bedrooms are cosy and usefully equipped: you'll need a good night's sleep before touring Arran or following the Islay and Jura whisky trail!

Food serving times:
Monday-Friday:
12.30pm-2.30pm,
6.30pm-9.30pm
Closed end January-February. Closed Mondays, April-October. Closed Monday-Thursday, November, December and March.
Prices:
Meals: a la carte 17.95/26.25
3 rooms: 39.50/85.00

Typical Dishes

Scallops toasted with garlic and herb butter

Cod roasted with chorizo

Tunisian orange and almond cake

Parking

Strachur

005 **The Creggans Inn** 🛏

Strachur PA27 8BX

Tel.: (01369) 860279 - Fax: (01369) 860637
e-mail: info@creggans-inn.co.uk - Website: www.creggans-inn.co.uk

🍷 rest **VISA**

 A wide selection of ales offered

The enviable delights of Loch Fyne in wild and remote Argyll and Bute provide a haunting and spectacular backdrop to this whitewashed, roadside inn. The Creggan has a well-established and hard-earned local reputation, built up by years of smoothly run service. There's a cosy bar and small wicker-chaired conservatory, and two lounges, one of which has a fine outlook. You can eat at the bar, or the spacious dining room with its wood floor and warm colour scheme. Dishes are flavoursome and full of fine Scottish ingredients. Walks in the area are guaranteed to bring on a very restful state, and the Creggan comes up trumps with delightful, cottage style bedrooms.

Food serving times:
Monday-Sunday:
  12pm-2.45pm, 6pm-8.45pm
Closed 25-26 December
(bar lunch)/dinner
Prices:
Meals: 32.00 (dinner) and a la carte 15.00/32.00
🛏 **14 rooms :** 70.00/120.00

Typical Dishes

Loch Fyne Oysters

Beef with red wine jus

Clootie dumpling with heather honey ice cream

Parking and 2 moorings for boats

Tayvallich

006 Tayvallich Inn

Tayvallich PA31 8PL

Tel.: (01546) 870282 - Fax: (01546) 870330
e-mail: tfhanderson@aol.com - Website: www.tayvallich-inn.com

  VISA **AE** **MC**

Loch Fyne Ales, Pipers Gold, Maverick

I n glorious isolation stands Tayvallich in the Sound of Jura. It's a little coastal hamlet with cosy harbour and Gulf Stream-nourished palm trees close to the shores of Loch Sween; the Tayvallich Inn, quite rightly, is the hub of the community. Believe it or not, it was the local bus garage until the early 1970s, when it was converted into its present incarnation. It has an enviable lochside setting and a smart whitewashed exterior with pleasant summer decking at the front. Inside, at the large bar in plump cushioned chairs, is a great place to mingle with the locals. Next door the pine furnished dining room has windows on three sides for the views, and interesting menus, which rely on fresh supplies of prawns, scallops and the local catch to underpin creative dishes.

Food serving times:
Monday-Sunday:
    12pm-2.30pm, 6pm-9pm
Closed Mondays
November-March
Prices:
Meals: a la carte 17.00/24.00

On the shores of Loch Sween.
Parking

Typical Dishes

Scallops with balsamic reduction

Grilled prawns with Pernod dressing

Basil and white chocolate pot

Swinton

007 **The Wheatsheaf**

Main Street, Swinton TD11 3JJ
Tel.: (01890) 860257 - Fax: (01890) 860688
e-mail: reception@wheatsheaf-swinton.co.uk - Website: www.wheatsheaf-swinton.co.uk

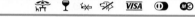

Deuchars IPA, Broughton Reiver

This cosy, attractive village inn on the Scottish borders has a welcoming stone façade, but the main delight here comes when you step through the entrance into the firelit bar with its fine array of real ales and wander through to the adjoining rooms whose nooks and crannies throw up subtle changes of character. The stylish restaurant is well renowned locally. It sources fresh seafood from Eyemouth Harbour, just 12 miles away, as well as borders beef, lamb and organic pork from local, traditional butchers. For dinner, you might try peppered breast of Gressingham duck in a thyme scented sauce with pink peppercorns, or baked fillet of local salmon with tarragon and prawns.

Food serving times:
Monday-Sunday:
      12pm-2pm, 6pm-9pm
Closed 24-27 December
Prices:
Meals: a la carte 22.00/35.00
7 rooms : 66.00/128.00

Typical Dishes

Sweet potato, coconut and paprika soup

Lamb, basil and mustard

Pear, ginger pudding

Parking

Gatehead

008 Cochrane Inn

45 Main Rd, Gatehead KA2 0AP
Tel.: (01563) 570122

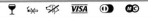

No real ales offered

A golfer's paradise: that's this traditional East Ayrshire pub, surrounded by a phalanx of courses, including the nearby Royal Troon, only five miles away on the coast. It's a fine place to relax after playing a round: the rustic stone interior or well-tended garden are ideal spots for recounting those putts that got away. The bar area boasts plenty of Scottish ales, and you can drink at little tables made from beer barrels. The separate dining room won't win any design awards, but that's how the locals like it: nice and simple, with exposed stone walls. Experienced staff serve hearty, honest, good value, well-cooked dishes with a Scottish accent and lacking any superfluous frills: try Cumberland sausage with pink peppercorn sauce and Cheddar mash, or traditional haggis with neeps and tatties.

Food serving times:
Monday-Thursday:
    12pm-2pm, 6pm-9pm
Friday and Saturday:
    12pm-2pm, 5.30pm-9pm
Sunday: 12pm-9pm
(booking essential)
Prices:
Meals: a la carte 16.00/20.00

Typical Dishes

Pickled Arctic herring, beetroot

Beefsteak and sausage pie

Sticky toffee pudding

Parking

Sorn

009 **Sorn Inn** 🛏️ We most liked 😊

35 Main St, Sorn KA5 6HU

Tel.: (01290) 551305 - Fax: (01290) 553470
e-mail: craig@sorninn.com - Website: www.sorninn.com

✄ **VISA** **MC**

No real ales offered

This traditional, family run whitewashed inn nestles enviably in the heart of the Ayrshire countryside. There's a small bar which is popular with locals and which offers the "Chop House" menu of steaks and simpler dishes. The real hub of the inn, though, is the rear dining room clothed in smart linen-clad tables and with a small lounge offshoot. It specialises in modern British cooking that's particularly good value for the accomplished cooking on offer, which specialises in using locally sourced meat, fish and game. Worth looking out for are breast of pigeon on sarladaise potato, bok choi, light Madeira and juniper berry jus, or sea trout on crushed new potatoes, pea and mint velouté. To round things off, there are four simple but modern and comfy bedrooms with showers and even DVD players.

Food serving times:
Tuesday-Saturday:
    12pm-2pm, 6.30pm-9pm
Sunday: 12.30pm-6.30pm
Open Bank Holiday Mondays
Prices:
Meals: 14.00/23.50 (set bar menu only) and a la carte 14.00/23.50
🛏️ **4 rooms :** 40.00/90.00

Parking ⟩

Typical Dishes

Rabbit with baby vegetables

Sea bass with crab dumpling

Passionfruit crème brulee

Glasgow

010 **Babbity Bowster**

16-18 Blackfriars St, Glasgow G1 1PE

Tel.: (0141) 522 5055 - Fax: (0141) 522 7774

  VISA **AE** **MC**

 Deuchars IPA, Peters Well Addlestone Cider and a regularly changing guest ale

A well-regarded Glasgow favourite in a carefully renovated townhouse, more informal than the neo-Classical façade might lead you might expect. Simple gingham-clothed tables and sketches and photos of city life set the tone in a laid-back, open-plan bar, where a short lunchtime menu of warming, substantial dishes includes Cullen Skink and stovies - meat and potato casseroles – as well as French bistro standards and croques monsieur. Upstairs, the restaurant's evening menu is a touch more formal but every bit as robust and tasty, choosing Scottish produce for its oat-crusted venison or sea bass in brandy butter. Oh, and the origin of the name? An old country dance which, like all the best folk songs, has at least two risqué interpretations to it. The friendly staff are happy to oblige with an explanation, or maybe even a rendition…

Food serving times:
Monday-Sunday:
12pm-10pm
Closed 25 December
Prices:
Meals: a la carte 12.95/25.85

Parking for hotel guests only

Typical Dishes

Scallops with red pepper

Saddle of red deer

Clootie dumpling with toffee sauce

Glasgow

011 **Rab Ha's**

83 Hutcheson St, Glasgow G1 1SH
Tel.: (0141) 572 0400 - Fax: (0141) 572 0402
e-mail: management@rabhas.com - Website: www.rabhas.com

No real ales offered

Built on the New World tobacco trade, the exchanges, halls and warehouses of Merchant City are finding a new lease of life as shops, living space and, yes, gastropubs. After the magnificence of Hutcheson's Hall and the Victorian City Chambers around the corner, Rab Ha's rather blank façade looks like a bit of a let-down. Inside, though, it's far more inviting, lively and modern and, on a cold night, discreetly cosy: there's a bit of relaxed 'take-us-as-you-find-us' about the place, but if anything the service is actually more efficient and friendly for it. As students and local businessmen squeeze onto chairs and benches, you can clink lagers and weigh up a bar menu running from Thai curry to haggis with the trimmings. A more formal restaurant selection is more likely to take in cod with leek and tomato or beef in thyme and port sauce.

Food serving times:
Monday-Sunday:
12pm-10pm
Closed 25 December
Prices:
Meals: 20.95 (fixed price dinner) and a la carte 10.00/ 20.95
4 rooms : 65.00/75.00

Typical Dishes

Pan seared scallops, citrus vinaigrette

Poached sole fillets, mustard seed mash

White and dark chocolate

Parking on the street or in nearby NCP car park in Glassford Street

Achiltibuie

 012 **Summer Isles (Bar)** 🛏

Achiltibuie IV26 2YG

Tel.: (01854) 622282 - Fax: (01854) 622251
e-mail: bar@summerislehotel.co.uk - Website: www.summerislehotel.co.uk

  VISA

Hebridean Gold, Isle of Sky Red Cuillin, Young Pretender

An idyllically named establishment for an idyllic setting – this super bar and hotel faces the eponymous isles, far away from the madding crowd at the end of a 20 mile single track road. The bar is the 'village pub', attached to the hotel but separate from it. Its simple, rustic ambience is perfect for the setting: sit in wooden booths and take in the wild, untouched landscape. You'll dine on seafood platters and rustic dishes such as casseroles and lamb shank; in the summer, don't miss the chance to eat al fresco. If you plump for the hotel, you'll be sampling precisely judged cuisine which has earned a Michelin Star for its excellence. There's every chance you'll stay the night: look forward to bedrooms ranging from simple and restrained to smart and sophisticated.

Food serving times:
Monday-Sunday:
    12pm-3pm, 5.30pm-8pm
Closed 25 December and
1 January
No food service mid
October-Easter - Seafood -
(bookings not accepted)
Prices:
Meals: a la carte 14.25/22.50
🛏 **13 rooms :** 78.00/188.00

Typical Dishes

Antipasti

Seafood platter

*Steamed chocolate pudding
and ice cream*

Parking

Applecross

013 Applecross Inn

Shore St, Applecross IV54 8LR

Tel.: (01520) 744262 - Fax: (01520) 744400
e-mail: applecrossinn@globalnet.co.uk - Website: www.applecross.uk.com

  VISA

Isle of Skye Red Cuillin, Black Cuillin, Hebridean Gold, Blaven

Not only one of the most remote pubs in the UK, but one of the trickiest to drive to as well – nevertheless, a visit to this cheerful hostelry, with stunning views to Skye's Cuillin Hills, is a truly rewarding experience. Approach via the hair-raising 'Pass of the Cattle', or the 24 mile single track road from Shieldaig: neither journey will be forgotten in a hurry. The inn is an old fisherman's cottage on the side of the loch. Its no-nonsense bar has pine panelling, exposed stone and lots of windows affording properly breathtaking views. Seafood, from extremely local sources, is the backbone of the menus: it's very fresh and certainly the thing to choose, though, local venison or sausages are also on the list. It gets busy, so be early or book! If you can't face the return journey just yet, they have bright and comfy bedrooms.

Food serving times:
Monday-Sunday: 12pm-9pm
Closed 25 December and
1 January
(booking essential)
Prices:
Meals: 30.00 (fixed price dinner) and a la carte 18.00/27.00
7 rooms : 30.00/70.00

From Kishorn via the Bealach nam Bo (Alpine pass), or round by Shieldaig and along the coast. Parking

Typical Dishes

Haggis flambeed in Drambuie

Prawns in garlic, lemon and herbs

Raspberry cranachan

Badachro

014 Badachro Inn

Badachro IV21 2AA

Tel.: (01445) 741255 - Fax: (01445) 741319
e-mail: lesley@badachroinn.com - Website: www.badachroinn.com

🛖 🍷 ✂ *VISA* **AE** **MC**

Black Isle Yellow Hammer, Isle of Skye Black Cuillin, Houston Killellan, An Teallach

Probably rather easier to get to by boat than by car, this pleasant little whitewashed pub has rather wisely invested in two moorings for visiting yachts. It's in a delightfully sheltered and remote location, right on the seashore of this small inlet, close to a little group of local houses. A cosy, lawned area with tables sits adjacent to the water. Inside, it's equally compact and traditional, with an open fire, beams, minuscule bar and local maritime charts on the walls. The nicest place to eat is the conservatory, with Loch Gairloch lapping its sides. Go for dishes from the daily changing menus featuring local seafood: all very fresh, simply prepared, and, in the majority of cases, homemade. Or take your lunch on a sunny day onto the 'terrace' and watch the world go quietly by – perfect!

Food serving times:
Monday-Sunday:
          12pm-3pm, 6pm-9pm
Closed 25 December
Prices:
Meals: a la carte 12.00/22.00

Typical Dishes

Smoked salmon with home-made bread

Gairloch prawns, salad and dip

Cranachan with shortbread

Parking and 2 moorings for boats

Cawdor

015 Cawdor Tavern

The Lane, Cawdor IV12 5XP
Tel.: (01667) 404777 - Fax: (01667) 404777
e-mail: cawdortavern@btopenworld.com - Website: www.cawdortavern.com

Highland IPA, Tradewinds

Only a few miles from Loch Ness and Moray Firth, this country inn has a tourist attraction of its own – it's only five minutes from the local castle. In fact, its links in this respect go somewhat deeper than mere proximity: it's set within the Cawdor Estate, in what used to be the joiner's workshop for the castle itself. It's now a very personally managed pub, and the owners run a tight ship. There are three separate rooms: one with pool table, one for smokers, one for non-smokers, and old oak panelling from the castle can be found here. Well-marshalled young staff serve a wide ranging menu with plenty of choice, featuring top-notch local fish, game and meats.

Food serving times:
Monday-Saturday:
    12pm-2pm, 5.30pm-9pm
Sunday:
    12.30pm-3pm, 5.30pm-9pm
Closed 25-26 December and 1-2 January
(booking essential Saturday-Sunday)
Prices:
Meals: a la carte 15.50/26.00

Typical Dishes
Scallops, bacon salad
Loin of lamb with rosemary jus
Chocolate fudge crème brulee

Parking

Glenelg

016 ## Glenelg Inn

Glenelg IV40 8JR

Tel.: (01599) 522273 - Fax: (01599) 522283

e-mail: christophermain@glenelg-inn.com - Website: www.glenelg-inn.com

VISA *AE* *MC*

  No real ales offered

Idyllically set off the beaten track in its own extensive grounds in a quiet hamlet by the lochside, this cosy inn was, in a previous incarnation, a couple of wee cottages. The Inn gloriously overlooks Glenelg Bay and the Isle of Skye. There's a very pubby bar, full of character: the locals have an amiable habit of turning it into the centre of the universe. It also boasts a beamed ceiling, dark wood panelling, and plenty of local photos on the walls. Blackboard menus offer a tried-and-tested, classic selection, utilising much local produce, of which fish and seafood are the speciality. If you're staying overnight, you can look forward to comfy, individually decorated bedrooms, followed by great Highland breakfasts in the morning.

Food serving times:

Monday-Sunday:
12.30pm-2pm, 7.30pm-9pm

Closed Christmas

Closed Sunday dinner to non residents - (booking essential) - accommodation rates include dinner

Prices:

Meals: 35.00 (fixed price dinner)

🛏 **7 rooms :** 60.00/160.00

Typical Dishes

Carrot and coriander soup

Red mullet, sweet red pepper

Chocolate torte

Parking

Kylesku

 017 **Kylesku**

Kylesku IV27 4HW
Tel.: 01971 502231 - Fax: 01971 502313
e-mail: info@kyleskuhotel.co.uk - Website: www.kyleskuhotel.co.uk

 rest **VISA** **MC**

No real ales offered

With its genuinely unforgettable view of Loch Glencoul and the mountains, the temptation would be to keep all knowledge of Kylesku to yourself. The heart of the discovery is the old hotel itself, with a very comfortable lounge in pretty patterns, and simple bedrooms, but for anyone not staying, the bar's the place to be. It's got a nice, down-to-earth feeling to it: there's a pool table, all sorts of countryside objects ranged along the wall, and a stove burning all through the long Highland winter. A blackboard menu with a strong seasonal character concentrates on the local speciality: good, just-landed shellfish in simply prepared, nicely judged dishes. Tasty and fresh, and as authentic as you could wish for.

Food serving times:
Monday-Sunday:
    12pm-2.30pm, 6pm-9pm
**Closed mid-October to
28 February**
Prices:
Meals: 27.50 (set dinner menu) and a la carte 15.00/ 25.00
8 rooms : 45.00/80.00

Typical Dishes

*Venison terrine with
Cumberland sauce*

*Grilled langoustine with
garlic mayonnaise*

Bread and butter pudding

Public car park in the village

Plockton

018 Plockton 🛏️

41 Harbour St, Plockton IV52 8TN

Tel.: (01599) 544274 - Fax: (01599) 544475
e-mail: info@plocktonhotel.co.uk - Website: www.plocktonhotel.co.uk

    VISA AE M©

Deuchars IPA, Hebridean Gold

F ine views of Loch Carron are a more than adequate reason to visit this attractive little National Trust village near the Kyle of Lochalsh. The eponymous inn – a delightful pair of wee cottages on the lochside – is the place to indulge the views while supping a pint with the locals, who flock here. The bar's the centre of activity, but if you're after a quieter environment, then you can retreat to the small rear terrace or the recently installed restaurant, where it's quite possible you'll be able to order a corn on the cob, alongside an impressive list of local seafood. Plockton isn't renowned for its road network, so for those making the wise move of staying overnight, there are plenty of recently refurbished, well-kept, comfy bedrooms to tempt you.

Food serving times:
Monday-Sunday:
   12pm-2.15pm, 6pm-9pm
Prices:
Meals: a la carte 15.50/41.40
🛏️ **15 rooms :** 55.00/100.00

Typical Dishes

Plockton Smokies

Seafood platter

Raspberry and pavlova basket

Parking 100 yards away

Plockton

019 Plockton Inn 🛏

Innes Street, Plockton IV52 8TW
Tel.: (01599) 544222 - Fax: (01599) 544487
e-mail: stay@plocktoninn.co.uk - Website: www.plocktoninn.co.uk

⊀⊁rest **VISA** **MC**

  2 regular ales offered

In the middle of a pretty harbour town on Loch Carron, this neighbourhood favourite without airs and graces is the place to come for good, unfussy seafood: platters of simply prepared shellfish and tasty dishes of locally landed fish are definitely the speciality, but they also do a good homemade hamburger! If you feel like some after-dinner entertainment, there might be a traditional music session in the bar next door. They also offer neat bedrooms in bright patterns; five of them are to be found in the annexe across the road.

Food serving times:
Monday-Sunday:
12pm-2.30pm, 6pm-8.30pm
(-9.30pm in high season)
Closed 25-26 December
Check food service times in winter
Prices:
Meals: a la carte 14.00/25.00
🛏 **14 rooms :** 35.00/70.00

Typical Dishes
Smoked seafood
Scallops with dill and lime crème fraîche
Ice cream, raspberries and whisky

Parking ❯❯

Waternish

020 **Stein Inn**

MacLeod Terr, Stein. Isle of Skye, Waternish IV55 8GA

Tel.: (01470) 592362

e-mail: angus.teresa@steininn.co.uk - Website: www.steininn.co.uk

VISA MC

Red Cuillin, Deuchars IPA, Orkney Dark Island, Skye Ale

In a breathtakingly beautiful spot on Loch Bay, the oldest inn on Skye is run with great warmth and dedication by a chatty husband and wife team. At the heart of the place is a tiny pine-clad locals bar and a lounge with rough stone walls, tall settles and an open fire; it's good for soup, sandwiches and a local ale, but it would be a shame not to try something more substantial in the little dining room – well-prepared seafood dishes, like fresh prawn tails and halibut and chips, are the pick of a tasty menu which also includes Highland venison. But for pure relaxation and peace of mind, take one of their 90 malts down to the grassy bank or the benches looking west over the bay and watch the sun set beyond the headland. Guests staying in the cosy, well-kept bedrooms – a snip at the price – can compare the view in the morning.

Food serving times:
Monday-Sunday:
 12pm-4pm, 6pm-9.30pm
 (-6.30pm-8pm in winter)
Closed 25 December,
1 January. Closed for lunch
in winter
- Seafood specialities -
Prices:
Meals: a la carte 10.65/21.65
5 rooms : 25.00/68.00

Typical Dishes

Pan fried scallops rolled in oatmeal

Highland venison pie

Raspberry cranachan

On the shore of Loch Bay. Parking

519

Howgate

021 The Howgate

Penicuik, Howgate EH26 8PY

Tel.: (01968) 670000 - Fax: (01968) 670000
e-mail: peter@howgate.com - Website: www.howgate.com

 VISA AE D MC

No real ales offered

What was at one time a stabling facility for race horses, and more recently a dairy producing Howgate cheeses, is now a characterful establishment with two distinct areas. There's a tartan carpeted bistro with bar, open log fire and stone walls with framed newspaper articles, that specialises in simple, tried-and-tested dishes; and then there's the formal restaurant, which serves slightly more adventurous cuisine, but generally covers well-rehearsed, traditional territory. Menus are generous and extensive: daily specials, which range from home-made fishcakes to dishes with locally sourced beef, lamb and venison, should appeal to those who appreciate more traditional favourites.

Food serving times:
Monday-Sunday:
    12pm-2pm, 6pm-9.30pm
Closed 25-26 December and
1 January
Prices:
Meals: a la carte 15.00/30.00

Typical Dishes

Seared pigeon breast

Sirloin steak, hand cut chips

*Banana bread and butter
pudding*

Parking >>

Ardeonaig

022 Ardeonaig

South Loch Tay, By Killin, Ardeonaig FK21 8SU

Tel.: (01567) 820400 - Fax: (01567) 820282
e-mail: info@ardeonaighotel.co.uk - Website: www.ardeonaighotel.co.uk

rest **VISA** **MC**

Innis & Gun, Heather, Black Isle

This family-run inn has its origins in the 17C, standing serenely in a wooded meadow on the south shore of Loch Tay. Its tranquil aspect is enhanced with a large garden – an ideal spot to relax in – or the library, which offers fine views. The homely, snug bar has walls filled with fishing memorabilia, and if you wander into the welcoming dining room you'll understand why: freshwater fish is a key element to the menus, alongside interesting dishes with a South African influence: the owner himself is a Springbok. There's also an enclosed courtyard, which, on a sunny day, is an ideal place to dine. Afterwards, delight in Highland walks or a slow drive alongside the Loch.

Food serving times:
Monday-Sunday:
12pm-10pm

Prices:
Meals: 27.50/35.50 and a la carte 16.00/20.00

20 rooms : 90.00/130.00

Typical Dishes

Scallops with asparagus

Roast guinea fowl with honeyed parsnips

Bourbon vanilla bean brulee

Parking

Glendevon

023 **The Tormaukin Country Inn**

Glendevon FK14 7JY

Tel.: (01259) 781252 - Fax: (01259) 781526
e-mail: enquiries@tormaukin.co.uk - Website: www.tormaukin.co.uk

Timothy Taylor Landlord, Marston's Pedigree, Harviestoun Bitter & Twisted

This extended 18C drovers' inn is tucked away in the picturesque "hidden glen" of Glendevon, with the Ochil Hills providing a splendid distant backdrop. Although a roadside establishment, it still manages to convey a character in sympathy with its surroundings. There's rustic charm in abundance: beams, flagged floors, plush softly lit bar, and log fires. A handy place for the golfing community, who create a pleasant feel, mingling with walkers and locals. You can eat in the atmospheric bar or cosy restaurant. Menus have earned a deserved standing locally: a smooth mix of popular Scottish favourites with more modern options. Ramblers – or golfers – too tired to continue can stay in comfortable bedrooms.

Food serving times:
Monday-Friday:
12pm-2.30pm,
5.30pm-9.30pm
Saturday-Sunday:
12pm-9.30pm
Closed 25 December and 2nd week January
Prices:
Meals: a la carte 20.00/45.00
 12 rooms : 60.00/90.00

Typical Dishes

Goat's cheese focaccia

Trout fillets with almond and whisky

Nougat parfait

Parking

Killearn

024 **The Black Bull**

2 The Square, Killearn G63 9NG

Tel.: (01360) 550215 - Fax: (01360) 550143
e-mail: sales@blackbullhotel.com - Website: www.blackbullhotel.com

  ⠵room **VISA** **AE**

Deuchars and regularly changing guest ales

Set in the centre of a small village half-an-hour from Glasgow and 20 minutes from Loch Lomond, this extended former coaching inn is a good base for touring the heart of Scotland. Its focus is a contemporary styled bistro/brasserie in rather striking modern browns with a large dispense bar and wood floor. Most of the locals, though, head for the adjacent pub bar which mirrors the bistro's modish style, and also allows you free reign at the extensive, popular menus, typified by steak pie, seared trout fillet, escalope of beef with fries and salad or wild mushroom and Parmesan risotto. The bedrooms are of varying shape and size but similar modern furnishings.

Food serving times:
Monday-Sunday:
12pm-10pm

Prices:
Meals: 14.95/29.50 and a la carte 15.00/29.50

14 rooms : 70.00/95.00

Typical Dishes

Lamb filled with Stornaway black pudding

Avocado mousseline with wild mushroom salad

Banana tarte tatin

Parking

Kippen

025 **The Inn at Kippen** 🛏️

Fore Rd, Kippen FK8 3DT

Tel.: (01786) 871010 - Fax: (01786) 871011

e-mail: info@theinnatkippen.co.uk - Website: www.theinnatkippen.co.uk

    VISA

Harviestoun Bitter and Twisted, Deuchars

S pacious, contemporary and open-plan, this fully refurbished village inn may not be quite what you were expecting. High-backed leather chairs and banquettes, smart glassware and casually uniformed staff set a determinedly modern tone, but it's not all out-with-the-old: framed black-and-white photos from the early 1900s show a very different way of life in this town on the edge of the Gargunnock Hills. The same wide choice is available at lunch and dinner, in the dining rooms and the rear bar, and ranges from surefire pub standards to slightly more elaborate restaurant dishes, still with a robust and straightforward style. Decorated in co-ordinated colours, the four bedrooms, named after local parishes, have a comfortable country feel to them.

Food serving times:
Monday-Saturday:
   12pm-2.30pm, 6pm-9pm
   (9.30pm Friday and Saturday).
Sunday: 12.30pm-3pm
Closed 1 January
Prices:
Meals: a la carte 15.40/28.90
🛏️ **4 rooms :** 40.00/70.00

Typical Dishes

Trio of Scottish salmon, herb pancakes

Loin of venison, sloe gin sauce

Vanilla crème brûlee

Parking ➤

Linlithgow

026 ## The Chop and Ale house

Champany, Linlithgow EH49 7LU

Tel.: (01506) 834532 - Fax: (01506) 834302

e-mail: reception@champany.com - Website: www.champany.com

 VISA **AE** **M**

Belhaven Ale

A restaurant within a restaurant, the intimate Chop and Ale House does away with most of Champany Inn's formality. Ancient exposed stone, closely set tables and a crackling log fire can't have changed much since this was the inn's public bar, while bridle bits and equestrian bric-à-brac mirror the muted prints of local squires and their prize horses. Forget dropping in for just a pint – it's cosy and relaxing, but it's just not that kind of place – but do come for well-sourced cooking, all appetising and popular with a strong Scottish flavour and a few unexpected variations. Aberdeen Angus steaks, hearty burgers and sausages, as well as piquant pickled herrings, are served with quiet professionalism by a friendly team.

Food serving times:
Monday-Friday:
12pm-2pm, 6.30pm-10pm
Saturday-Sunday:
12pm-10pm
Closed 25-26 December and
1-2 January
Prices:
Meals: a la carte 16.85/30.50
16 rooms : 95.00/125.00

Typical Dishes

Dressed salmon

Chargrilled beef sirloin

Cheesecake with apricot coulis

At the Champany Inn. Parking

"*Hiraeth*" – the longing for home – and pride in the life of the nation take their source in many parts of Welsh identity. Unity is rooted in the very language of the Cymry, or "comrades", and the strength of community famously finds its voice in the songs of an eager rugby crowd. But above all, love of Wales is inseparable from a love of the land itself. The emblematic peaks of Snowdon and Cadair Idris and the steep streets of the Rhondda live long in the memory, but the full picture is wide enough to take in Lleyn's hidden coves and holy islands, the craggy stacks of the Pembrokeshire coast, the dominating towers of King Edward's castles and the fantasia of Portmerion, a playful dreamscape of domes and colonnades. Though long overlooked, Welsh cuisine is now making up for lost time and offering a taste of home, from rare delicacies like Wye and Usk salmon to world-famous lamb, Caerphilly, cawl cenin – a leek soup – and the humble Bara Brith; increasingly diverse real ales, and even Welsh whisky, mean there's always something new to try: *Iechyd da!*

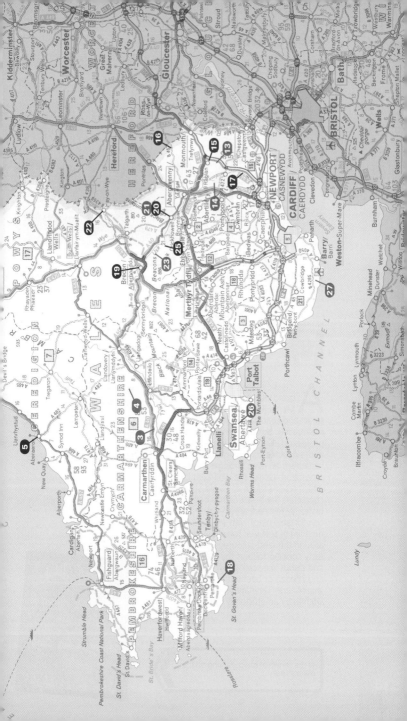

Beaumaris

001 Ye Olde Bulls Head

Castle St, Beaumaris LL58 8AP

Tel.: (01248) 810329 - Fax: (01248) 811294
e-mail: info@bullsheadinn.co.uk - Website: www.bullsheadinn.co.uk

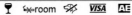

 Bass, Hancocks and 1 weekly changing guest ale

A classic market town inn and a good start for anyone crossing the Menai Strait for the first time – smart and spacious rooms are nicely maintained, but the same right-minded professionalism is in evidence throughout and a devoted following gives the restaurant an even stronger local reputation. Unlike the well-kept bar, which retains much of its old-style pub character, the brasserie has been tastefully restyled; an airy and comfortable place with seagrass matting, neat linen, soft lilac tones and lights around the sand-coloured beams. Sound, tasty cooking follows the modern lead and dishes like scallops with puy lentils and chorizo or beef with wild rice and shallot tarte Tatin are whisked from the kitchen by an efficiently drilled team.

Food serving times:
Monday-Sunday:
　　　12pm-2pm, 6pm-9pm
Closed dinner 25 December and 1 January
Prices:
Meals: a la carte 12.25/20.65

Typical Dishes

Duck rillettes wrapped in Parma ham

Fillet of sea bass, tomato salsa

White chocolate 'blondie'

In the centre of town. Parking on the main street

Red Wharf Bay

002 Ship Inn

Red Wharf Bay LL75 8RJ
Tel.: (01248) 852568

Black Sheep, Adnams, Tetleys and Brains S.A.

The neat, white-painted Ship Inn is a welcome enough sight in itself, but what makes it really special is its fabulous view: down on the shore of Red Wharf Bay, it looks out across the sands, over every play of afternoon light on the water and out to the galloping "white horses" in the open sea. In the height of summer, an empty table on the large terraces won't be free for long, but if you can tear yourself away, take a look inside. Pews and benches line the bare stone walls, which have gathered a collection of old beer adverts, pub mirrors and photographs to go with their nautical bric-a-brac, while the dining room provides a more formal setting on Saturday nights. A large menu offers anything from a lunchtime sandwich to sea bass on herb rösti or grilled pork with mustard sauce and apple compote.

Food serving times:
Monday-Sunday:
12pm-3pm, 6pm-9pm
Prices:
Meals: a la carte 15.00/30.00

Typical Dishes

Escabeche of red mullet

Char grilled rib eye, bacon and endive mash

Tarte Tatin

2.5 mi Southeast of Benilech by A5025. Parking

Nantgaredig

003 **Y Polyn**

Nantgaredig SA32 7LH

Tel.: 01267 290000
e-mail: ypolyn@hotmail.com

   VISA **MC**

 Tomos Watkins OSB and Cwrw Haf

Only a short drive from the National Botanic Gardens, this modest roadside pub doesn't look particularly eye-catching at first, but its interior gives a very different impression. Attention to detail and a love of food are clear to see in the fresh, bright interior, decorated with cookbooks, framed menus and pictures of the world's famous chefs, and in the relaxed and assured service. The food itself shows similar care and effort: classic rustic dishes – from French and Welsh traditions – are prepared to show local ingredients at their best and bring out their wholesome and natural flavours. You're welcome to stop for just a drink, though, and settle down in one of the bar's easy chairs: the pub was actually built over a stream, which was used to cool the beer in the old days.

Food serving times:
Tuesday-Friday:
          12pm-2pm, 7pm-9pm
Saturday: 7pm-9pm
Sunday: 12pm-2pm
Prices:
Meals: 27.50 (dinner) and a la carte 20.00/27.50

5mi East of Carmarthen on A40. From Nantgaredig South 1mi by B4310 on B4300. Parking

Typical Dishes

Fish soup, Gruyère, rouille and croutons

Cassoulet de Toulouse

Chocolate torte, cherry compote

Salem

004 **Angel Inn**

Salem SA19 7LY
Tel.: (01558) 823394

   VISA Ⓜ️Ⓒ

Buckleys Best and weekly changing guest beers

You'll find the welcome extended here to be as wide as the village of Salem is small; the owners took over in 2002 and their infectious enthusiasm has helped build a solid local following. Get here down a narrow road; you can't miss it, it's next to the chapel. Sink into one of the bar lounge sofas and place your order; there's a blackboard menu at lunchtimes and a more elaborate, printed a la carte in the evening. It's a spacious place, the Angel, and the sympathetic extension that is the restaurant offers large, well spaced tables, a wood floor and a subtle Victorian or Edwardian feel. By now, you'll have come to anticipate the warm, chatty service. What might surprise you are the rather complex dishes, featuring a host of local ingredients. Menus might include cannelloni of crayfish tails, Welsh spring lamb or Usk Valley venison.

Food serving times:
Tuesday-Saturday:
12pm-2pm, 7pm-9pm
Closed 1 week January
Prices:
Meals: a la carte 22.00/35.00

Typical Dishes

Confit of Welsh lamb

Seared Gower sea bass

Crème de Bananes bavarois, toffee parfait

3mi North of Llandeilo by A40 off Pen y bane road. Parking

Aberaeron

005 **Harbour Master**

Quay Parade, Aberaeron SA46 0BA

Tel.: (01545) 570755

e-mail: info@harbour-master.com - Website: www.harbour-master.com

🍷 ✗ ✗ **VISA** **MC**

Buckleys Best, Brains SA

Appealingly situated on an attractive quayside in West Wales, this listed building is painted in deep, bold blue and was, indeed, the harbourmaster's home nearly 200 years ago. It's a fine place to relax and watch the sun set over Cardigan Bay, or, if you're feeling more energetic, to take a bracing walk along the coastal path at the front door. You can eat in the bar with the locals, or in the smart, nautically themed restaurant, which specialises in local produce with a pronounced seafood bias: feast yourself on locally caught lobsters, crab, seabass and mackerel. Beef and lamb are from the land surrounding Aberaeron. For another option of watching the setting sun, climb the listed Georgian spiral staircase and stay in one of the stylish and individual bedrooms.

Food serving times:
Monday dinner--Saturday:
    12pm-2pm, 6pm-9pm
Sunday: 12pm-2pm
Closed 24 December-11 January
Prices:
Meals: a la carte 20.00/30.00
🛏 **9 rooms :** 55.00/125.00

Typical Dishes

New Quay prawns, chilli and lime butter

Chargrilled fillet of Welsh black beef

Lavender crème brûlée

In town centre overlooking the harbour. Parking

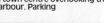

Colwyn Bay

006 Pen-y-Bryn

Pen-y-Bryn Rd, Upper Colwyn Bay, Colwyn Bay LL29 6DD

Tel.: (01492) 533360 - Fax: (01492) 535808

e-mail: penybryn@brunningandprice.co.uk - Website: www.brunningandprice.co.uk

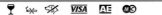 **VISA** AE MC

 5 guest ales

On the way to the local zoo, this ordinary looking 1970s pub really doesn't promise too much. But hold your horses (and your elephants and leopards). Inside there's something of a transformation, with very spacious and comfortable surroundings forcing you to change your perspective. There are oak wood floors, polished tables and tasteful décor, comprising a host of old pictures of the promenade and local scenes; one wall's packed with books and there's a real fire. To the rear is a sloped garden with benches, and a fine view of the bay is possible from some inside vantage points. A young, enthusiastic team runs the place, preparing an extensive menu, printed and replicated on a large blackboard. Welsh cooking combines with a tasty international dishes, plus good pub staples. Carefully prepared, generous portions all round.

Food serving times:
Monday-Sunday:
12pm-9.30pm
Closed 25-26 December and dinner 1 January
Prices:
Meals: a la carte 16.00/23.45

Typical Dishes

Bury black pudding, mustard mash

Shoulder of lamb with rosemary

Vanilla crème brûlée

1 mi Southwest by B5113. Parking

Glanwydden

007 ## Queens Head

Glanwydden LL31 9JP

Tel.: (01492) 546570 - Fax: (01492) 546487
e-mail: enquiries@queensheadglanwydden.co.uk - Website: www.queensheadglanwydden.co.uk

 🍷 🍴 **VISA** **MC**

Tetleys, Firkins and Burton

If popularity is the yardstick of a good pub, then here is a league champion. Holiday-makers frequent this smart, cream painted pub in droves and most of them are within the premises as there are only a few tables dotted around the tarmac outside. It's a cosy, comfortable place (if you can get a seat) with the traditional appeal of low beamed ceilings, polished wooden tables, burgundy velour sofas and walls decorated with old maps and locally inspired paintings. Menus fit neatly into the tried-and-tested category but they contain plenty of local ingredients and are invariably well cooked. Dishes you might find are goat's cheese and onion tart, baked haddock with salad and bread, and homemade sticky toffee pudding. Despite the numbers, service is notably efficient.

Food serving times:
Monday-Saturday:
12pm-2pm, 6pm-9pm
Sunday: 12pm-9pm
Closed 25 December
Prices:
Meals: a la carte 16.50/25.00

Typical Dishes

Local mussels with garlic butter

Char grilled marinated chicken

Fresh fruit pavlova

3 mi Southeast of Llandudno by A470 off Penthyn Bay rd. Parking

Tyn-y-Groes

008 Groes Inn 🛏

Tyn-y-Groes LL32 8TN
Tel.: (01492) 650545 - Fax: (01492) 650855

 Tetley, Burton Ale

On the eastern edge of the Snowdonia National Park and south of Conwy, this lays claim to being the oldest pub in Wales, and it bears its age with great charm, character and no little sense of style. There are lovely bar areas finished with great taste: historic bric-à-brac, beamed ceilings, polished oak furniture, relaxing garden and fine views. A cloth-clad dining room and conservatory are the places to dine: you'll find popular, tried-and-tested menus making good use of ingredients from North Wales. Staying overnight proves a popular option here: the bedrooms are stylish and furnished with fine fabrics; many boast superb countryside views, while two have the added distinction of a terrace.

Food serving times:
Monday-Sunday:
    12pm-2pm, 6.30pm-9pm
Prices:
Meals: 28.00 (fixed price dinner) and a la carte 15.00/25.00
🛏 **14 rooms :** 79.00/146.00

Typical Dishes

Butternut squash and sage ravioli

Poached Conwy river salmon

Home-made ice creams

From Conwy Castle take the B5106 towards Trefriw; the inn is about 2mi on the right. Parking

Llangollen

009 **The Corn Mill**

Dee Lane, Llangollen LL20 8PN

Tel.: (01978) 869555

e-mail: cornmill@brunningandprice.co.uk - Website: www.brunningandprice.co.uk

 🍷 ✗ rest 🚫 **VISA** **AE** **MC**

Boddingtons and up to 4 guest ales offered

A cleverly restructured conversion with a strong imprint of original industrial chic: joists span the spacious rooms over three levels, wooden cogs and drivewheels are braced to the rafters of the bar, period prints of riverbank landscapes hang on rough, limewashed walls and glass blocks, set into the floor, give glimpses of the old workings of the mill. Best of all, a decked terrace juts out over the fast-flowing river Dee, and on still summer days you may just hear the restored steam engines chugging up the hill to Carrog. Bold and generous cooking adds a few international influences to a British base and offers plenty of choice, including lighter bites and a big sharing platter of starters. In July, the International Eisteddfod's fringe festival of arts and world music centres on the theatre around the corner.

Food serving times:
Monday-Sunday:
12pm-9.30pm
Closed 25-26 December
Prices:
Meals: a la carte 20.00
(approx.)

Typical Dishes

Smoked haddock and salmon fishcakes

Chicken breast, apple and sage sauce

Welsh cheeses

Short walk from railway and public parking ❯❯

Mold

010 Glas Fryn

Raikes Lane, Sychdyn, Mold CH7 6LR

Tel.: (01352) 750500 - Fax: (01352) 751923
e-mail: glasfryn@brunningandprice.co.uk - Website: www.glasfryn-mold.co.uk

 Timothy Taylor Landlord, Flowers IPA, Phoenix Wobbly Bob, Deuchars IPA, Thwaites and Oakham JHB

This large red-brick pub, handily placed for visitors to the North Wales coast and Chester, may not look too promising from the outside - apart from its pleasant terrace and garden - but inside is a different story. Its modern feel is lent character by lots of old bottles, sepia photos and shelves of books, all of them lovingly kept and neatly exhibited. Institutions of local prominence are based nearby, so expect to rub shoulders at the bar with actors, lawyers, farmers, technicians and theatre-goers. There's a good choice of food with a global influence and the menu, both printed and on the blackboard, reflect traditional and modern tastes.

Food serving times:
Monday-Saturday:
        12pm-9.30pm
Sunday: 12pm-9pm
Closed 25-26 December
Prices:
Meals: a la carte 16.70/25.45

Typical Dishes

Chicken and duck pâté, onion marmalade

Braised shoulder of lamb

Waffles, honeycomb ice cream

1 mi North by A5119 on Civic Centre rd. Parking

Mold

011 ## The Stables (at Soughton Hall)

Mold CH7 6AB

Tel.: (01352) 840577 - Fax: (01352) 840382
e-mail: info@soughtonhall.co.uk - Website: www.soughtonhall.co.uk

     VISA

Plassey Bitter and 3 regularly changing guest ales

Where do you go for a decent pint in an extravagant 18C Italianate mansion? The summer house? The servants' quarters? Not quite. As relaxed and unfussy as the house is grand, the converted stable block gets slap-bang down to earth with a rustic interior of old brick and bare beams: horses' names on brass stable-plates, set into the tables, are a light-hearted touch. The approach to dining is just as informal: take your pick from sandwiches and light dishes or more substantial mains, some on the specials board - Welsh rarebit pork on a mound of apple and mustard mash sums up the generous country style here. There's also an interesting wine shop upstairs, which can only help to boost an excellent local following.

Food serving times:
Monday-Saturday: 12pm-9.30pm
Sunday: 1pm-9.30pm
(booking essential)
Prices:
Meals: a la carte 20.00/29.00
15 rooms : 170.00

Typical Dishes

Chicken liver parfait

Breast of chicken wrapped in bacon, basil and tomato butter

Sticky toffee pudding

2.5 mi North by A5119 on Alltami Rd. Parking

Aberdovey

012 **Penhelig Arms**

Aberdovey LL35 0LT

Tel.: (01654) 767215 - Fax: (01654) 767690
e-mail: info@penheligarms.com - Website: www.penheligarms.com

VISA **MC**

Old Speckled Hen, Hook Norton Old Hooky

I n the 1700s, The Little Inn was a quaint meeting place for locals in this beautiful part of West Wales. Nearly 300 years later residents and visitors are still coming, but the inn itself has grown out of all proportion, and now the Penhelig Arms, handsomely extended, stares regally out at the waters of the Dyfi Estuary. On one side is the Fisherman's Bar, where the locals gather round a log fire in the winter months. When it's warmer, you can go and sit at the sea wall. A separate dining room sports bay views, sympathetically painted light blue walls and a laid back feel. Menus change regularly and reflect the latest catch. Meat, too, comes from local sources. Try rack of local lamb, cooked pink, with aubergine chutney and rosemary gravy, or roast fillet of cod with mustard mash and prawn velouté. Cottagey bedrooms boast sea vistas.

Food serving times:
Monday-Sunday:
 12pm-2pm, 6pm-9.30pm
Closed 25-26 December
Prices:
Meals: a la carte 17.50/25.75
15 rooms : 40.00/140.00

Typical Dishes

Aberdyfi crab salad

Roasted black bream, capers and fresh herbs

Panna cotta with poached rhubarb

On A493. Parking

Llandenny

013 **Raglan Arms**

Llandenny NP15 1DL
Tel.: (01291) 690800 - Fax: (01291) 690155

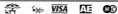

Wye Valley Bitter, Felinfoel, Brecon County Ales

The owners' years of experience go a long way to explaining the popularity of this friendly village pub that works hard to keep everyone happy, and generally succeeds. Regulars rule the roost in one half of the central bar, reserved for pool, pints and slot machines, but the other side is given over to dining. Pine tables and chairs squeeze in around leather sofas for a share of the fireside warmth, but book in good time and there's always a space, here, in the pleasant conservatory or out on the decked terrace in good weather. You risk a crick in the neck from scanning the ample blackboard menu, but it's well worth it: fairly priced dishes like duck rillettes with homemade pear chutney or a pair of sea bass fillets with garlic and coriander are typical of the refreshingly simple and ably judged cooking.

Food serving times:
Tuesday-Saturday:
    12pm-2pm, 7pm-9pm
Sunday: 12pm-2pm
Prices:
Meals: a la carte 20.50/29.75

Typical Dishes
Mussels with leeks and black pepper
Sea bass, garlic and lemon butter
White chocolate pudding

4.25mi North East of Usk by A472 off B4235. Parking

Nant-Y-Derry

014 The Foxhunter

Nant-Y-Derry NP7 9DN
Tel.: (01873) 881101 - Fax: (01873) 881378
Website: www.thefoxhunter.com

 VISA **M©**

 Old Speckled Hen, Brains SA, Marstons Pedigree

An unlikely change of use by any standards: what started life as Victorian station master's office is now a pleasant, quietly prospering pub-bistro, with appetite-awakening food-themed prints and huge arrangements of lillies taking the place of leaves on the line. The pleasant service is probably a change for the better too. Stripped back to its basics – polished floorboards, exposed timbers and original brickwork – it looks the picture of carefully styled gastropub, though the well-separated, bare wooden tables untypically allow their diners plenty of space. A wide-ranging choice with roots in rustic European cuisine spans cod goujons with aïoli, spinach and ricotta ravioli, even a choucroute garni.

Food serving times:
Tuesday-Saturday:
  12pm-2.30pm, 7pm-9.30pm
Closed 25-26 December and 2 weeks February
Prices:
Meals: 22.00 and a la carte 22.00/40.00

Typical Dishes

Tagliolini of duck

Wild sea bass, truffle sauce

Hazelnut and chocolate semi-freddo

5mi Northwest of Usk by B4598.
Parking

Raglan

015 **Clytha Arms**

Raglan NP7 9BW

Tel.: (01873) 840206

e-mail: theclythaarms@tiscali.co.uk - Website: www.clytha-arms.com

Bass, Hook Norton, Felinfoel, traditional cider and regularly changing guest ales

This relaxed and unassuming country pub is one for the traditional, 'everyday hero' category. Under the roof of the old dower house, you'll glimpse a few framed prints, a dartboard and skittles and the gleam of bar taps through a crowd of chatting locals, while the broad inglenook in the comfy lounge bar next door comes complete with a drowsy pub cat. Though the menu of familiar standards, served in the more formal dining room, is prepared with due care and attention, the food at the Clytha Arms is really at its most appealing when it forgets its restaurant manners. With greater simplicity of presentation come direct and refreshing flavours, so find a seat on the refectory benches in the bar and get stuck in to the generous servings.

Food serving times:
Monday dinner-Sunday:
12.30pm-2.15pm,
7pm-9.30pm

Closed 25 December

Prices:

Meals: 19.95 and a la carte 26.00/34.00

4 rooms : 50.00/90.00

Typical Dishes

Leek and laverbread rissole

Wild sea bass with coconut and coriander

Sauternes cream with prunes

Parking

Skenfrith

016 ## The Bell 🛏 *we most liked*

Skenfrith NP7 8UH

Tel.: (01600) 750235 - Fax: (01600) 750525
e-mail: enquiries@skenfrith.co.uk - Website: www.skenfrith.co.uk

Timothy Taylor Landlord, Hook Norton Best, Freeminer Bitter

A walk in the Monmouthshire countryside reaps rich rewards with a visit to this lovely pub: an overnight stay is highly recommended too. It's located by the river with flocks of sheep in the surrounding fields. A stylish country flavour imbues all areas: there's a stone floor, roaring log fire, bare wooden tables and chairs and lots of black-and-white photos of the locality in yesteryear. You can relax in comfy sofas or on the beautiful garden terrace. Everything, everywhere is spotlessly kept. A fresh, local and organic emphasis informs the menus, which adhere to a traditional base with modern overtones, and keen, friendly service can be relied upon. The inn's main strength, though, is its bedrooms; these are exceptional, from the inclusion of DVDs to luxurious toiletries, and practically define the term "country style".

Food serving times:
Monday-Sunday:
  12pm-2.30pm, 7pm-9.30pm
Closed late January-early
February and Mondays
November-March
Prices:
Meals: a la carte 24.00/29.00
🛏 **8 rooms :** 70.00/170.00

Typical Dishes

Tomato, basil and mozzarella salad

Duck breast, orange and coriander

Champagne jelly

11 mi West of Ross-on-Wye by A49 on B4521. Parking

Tredunnock

017 ## The Newbridge

Tredunnock NP15 1LY

Tel.: (01633) 451000 - Fax: (01633) 451001
e-mail: thenewbridge@tinyonline.co.uk - Website: www.thenewbridge.co.uk

room **VISA** **AE** **D** **MC**

Brains SA, Hancock's Bitter

The fast-flowing River Usk is the sprightly neighbour to this smartly gabled, cream painted pub which, to complete the rural picture, overlooks a winding country road and, of course, the bridge. Inside, there's a lovely open, spacious feel with stylish contemporary touches sprinkled all around. The dining element here is strong and the prevailing ambience suggests restaurant at least as much as pub. A curved iron staircase connects two levels of chunky wood tables and chairs. Lots of blackboard specials to peruse; the cooking is modern and quite adventurous but not over embellished. Afterwards, you can stay in state-of-the-art bedrooms where no expense has been spared.

Food serving times:
Monday-Saturday:
12pm-2.30pm,
6.30pm-9.30pm
Sunday: 12pm-3pm,
7pm-8.30pm
Closed 26 December and 1 January
Prices:
Meals: a la carte 25.00/32.00
6 rooms : 90.00/125.00

Typical Dishes

Oak smoked duck and poached pear salad

Loin of 'Old Spot' pork

Fine apple tart with brown bread ice cream

Five minutes drive from the centre of Caerleon, on the banks of the River Usk. Parking

Stackpole

018 The Stackpole Inn

Jasons Corner, Stackpole SA71 5DF

Tel.: (01646) 672324 - Fax: (01646) 672716
e-mail: info@stackpoleinn.co.uk

 VISA **MC**

 Brakspear, Felinfoel Double Dragon

A real fixture of the landscape, this rural pub feels as if it might almost have grown up out of the Pembrokeshire countryside: sturdy wooden slabs frame the bar-room, hops stretch their shoots towards the courses of bare brick and pint glasses shine on a Welsh slate bar. The owner, a natural hostess, superintends service with great warmth of personality and with her son in charge of the kitchen, it's a co-operative family effort. His straightforward, modern-classic cooking draws on seasonal Welsh ingredients to flavourful effect: winter in particular brings fortifying plates of warming and unfinicky country food like poached chicken with vegetable broth.

Food serving times:
Monday-Sunday:
    12pm-2.30pm, 6pm-9pm
    (winter)
    12.30pm-3pm,
    5.30pm-9pm
    (summer)
Closed Sunday dinner in Winter
Prices:
Meals: a la carte 16.00/26.00

Typical Dishes

Toasted Welsh goats cheese, walnut oil

Thai style baked sea bass

Cappuccino mousse cups

5mi South of Pembroke by B4319

Brecon

019 **Felin Fach Griffin**

Felin Fach, Brecon LD3 0UB
Tel.: (01874) 620111 - Fax: (01874) 620120
e-mail: enquiries@eatdrinksleep.ltd.uk - Website: www.eatdrinksleep.ltd.uk

Tomos Watkins OSB and CWRW Haf

The wonderfully relaxed atmosphere starts in the open bar of this converted farmhouse: antiques and reclaimed furniture, bright modern colours, sofas by the log fire and a politely inquisitive pub dog make this an easy place to feel at home in. It's the same story in the spacious bedrooms, all in light, restful tones, which prove that you can banish twee or designerish clutter and still have thoughtful extras close to hand: each has fine linens, European and Indian furniture and a selection of good books. Well-balanced cooking in a modern style makes intelligent use of local ingredients and only a very tasty breakfast, fresh from the Aga, could possibly tempt you out of such wonderfully comfortable beds!

Food serving times:

Prices:
Meals: a la carte 24.00/32.00
7 rooms : 67.50/92.50

Typical Dishes

Quail skewer, Jerusalem artichoke risotto

Rack of Welsh lamb, red pepper jus

Bitter chocolate tart

4.75 mi Northeast of Brecon by 4602 off A470. Parking.

Crickhowell

020 **The Bear** 🛏

High St, Crickhowell NP8 1BW

Tel.: (01873) 810408 - Fax: (01873) 811696

e-mail: bearhotel@aol.com - Website: www.bearhotel.co.uk

🍷 *VISA* AE M©

Bass, Reverend James, Ruddles County and Best

 n a small town in the Black Mountains, The Bear is a traditional coaching inn dating from 1435 with bags of charm and character. The snug bar at the front, with its open fire and beams, leads into an area of nooks and crannies and the lounge: lots of rafters, comfy armchairs, antique settles, and a window seat letting you to see what's happening in the market square. Don't miss out on eating here; two separate dining rooms are handsome enough on their own, with plenty of antiques and curios, but when you add the delicious food they serve – classically based with first-rate local ingredients – then you should see why the place is perennially busy. Appetising, modern bar-bistro dishes use similarly fresh produce to flavourful effect. There's also a welcoming summer garden, and bedrooms are plush and spacious.

Food serving times:
Monday-Sunday:
    12pm-2pm, 6pm-10pm
Prices:
Meals: a la carte 16.00/29.00
🛏 **35 rooms :** 58.00/144.00

In the town centre. Parking ⟩

Typical Dishes

Smoked salmon, wasabi crème fraiche

Hock of Welsh lamb

Apple and Whinberry pie

Crickhowell

021 **Nantyffin Cider Mill Inn**

Brecon Rd, Crickhowell NP8 1SG

Tel.: (01873) 810775

e-mail: info@cidermill.co.uk - Website: www.cidermill.co.uk

VISA AE M©

A selection of local real ales

This hugely characterful 16C cider mill in the heart of the Brecon Beacons is difficult to miss: apart from being a distinctive mill by a busy crossroads, it's painted in an evocative pink wash. Inside, the characterful features remain: its working parts are still in situ, and two snug bars boast open fires, comfy country style seating, rattan flooring and an interesting mix of antiques and curios. This was one of the first Welsh gastropubs, and a slightly more formal dining room is filled with old mill objects and simple wooden tables. Varied menus, apart from quite rightly highlighting cider, feature local fish and game with some prominence

Food serving times:
Tuesday-Saturday:
12pm-2.30pm,
6.30pm-9.30pm
Sunday: 12pm-2.30pm
Closed Sunday dinner and Monday except Bank Holidays
Prices:
Meals: 12.95 and a la carte 16.00/30.00

Typical Dishes

Welsh goat's cheese salad

Confit of home reared lamb, rosemary and garlic sauce

Rhubarb and ginger crumble

1.5 mi West of Crickhowell on A40.

Hay-on-Wye

022 Old Black Lion

26 Lion St, Hay-on-Wye HR3 5AD

Tel.: (01497) 820841 - Fax: (01497) 822960

e-mail: info@oldblacklion.co.uk - Website: www.oldblacklion.co.uk

 VISA M○

 Wye Valley ales

K now your JK Rowling from your DH Lawrence? After a busy round of book bazaars and seminars in the bibliophile's capital of Britain, head for dinner at this part 13C and 17C inn. The main bar is long on charm and character, lit by a real log fire: you could settle in comfortably with a pint and a good page-turner at any time, and though there's a separate formal dining room, you can choose a table and eat here, too. A dependable traditional menu holds one or two light variations, but the list of chalkboard specials is arguably the better choice – honest, tasty and prepared with good culinary understanding. Immaculate bedrooms, some in the adjacent block, are far better than the average pub, but it goes without saying that you'll have to reserve in good time for the Festival.

Food serving times:
Monday-Sunday:
12pm-2.30pm,
6.30pm-9.30pm
Closed 24-26 December and 2 weeks January
Prices:
Meals: a la carte 20.00/28.00
10 rooms : 42.50/85.00

Typical Dishes

Confit of duck, spicy noodles

Beef Wellington

Vanilla panna cotta, rhubarb compote

In the town centre. Parking

Llanfrynach

023 The White Swan

Llanfrynach LD3 7BZ

Tel.: (01874) 665276 - Fax: (01874) 665362
Website: www.the-white-swan.com

 🍴 🍷 ✂ VISA

Hancocks HB, Breconshire County Ale

Though stylishly modernised, this pub in a picturesque setting still seems as much a part of the countryside as the adjacent church and fields. The sheltered rear terrace is perfect for making the most of warm summer afternoons but, in the evening, the softly lit bar and restaurant – in Welsh slate, timber and stone – is definitely the place to be. A well thought-out menu changes with the seasons and takes the organic option wherever it can: balanced, contemporary dishes might include a simple but flavourful goat's cheese quesadilla with salsa, good sea bass served with Oriental noodles and a satisfyingly nutty iced nougat. Good value.

Food serving times:
Wednesday-Sunday:
    12pm-2pm, 7pm-9.30pm
Closed 25-26 December and 1 January
Prices:
Meals: a la carte 19.50/27.50

Typical Dishes

Mille feuille of asparagus and parmesan

Haunch of venison, fresh herb mash

Lime pie, lemon sorbet

Parking

Pontdolgoch

 024 **Talkhouse** We most liked

Pontdolgoch SY17 5JE

Tel.: (01686) 688919

e-mail: info@talkhouse.co.uk - Website: www.talkhouse.co.uk

     VISA ⓂⒸ

A cosy, unassuming exterior gives little away about the stylish goings-on inside this 17C former coaching inn tucked away on a quiet road in rural mid-Wales. It's full of charm, with lots of curios, knick-knacks and antiques adorning the rustic-styled bar, where you can slump into plush sofas in front of the log fire. French windows lead onto a lovely terrace and gardens for al fresco dining on warmer days. Eating here is a treat: considerate, personal service strikes just the right balance and a wide-ranging menu has a well-executed touch, as reassuringly local produce comes together to create well-honed seasonal dishes. There are bedrooms too: an immaculate trio with a welcoming, individual style.

Food serving times:
Tuesday-Saturday:
    12pm-2pm, 6.30pm-9pm
Sunday: 12pm-2pm
Closed first 2 weeks January
and 25 December
Prices:
Meals: a la carte 21.00/29.00
3 rooms : 70.00/95.00

Typical Dishes

Carmarthan ham, toasted goats cheese

Fillet of Welsh beef, horseradish rösti

Lemon tart

1.5 mi Northwest of Caersws on A470. Parking

Talybont-on-Usk

025 **Usk Inn**

Station Rd, Talybont-on-Usk LD3 7JE
Tel.: (01874) 676251 - Fax: (01874) 676392
e-mail: stay@uskinn.co.uk - Website: www.uskinn.co.uk

🍷 ⇆room 🚫 **VISA** **AE** **①** **⦿**

Hancocks HB, Bass, Felinfoel Double Dragon

Food serving times:
Monday-Sunday:
  12pm-2.30pm, 6.30pm-9pm
Closed 4 days at Christmas
Prices:
Meals: 14.95 and a la carte 20.00/30.00
 11 rooms : 65.00/120.00

With a blend of friendliness and professional know-how, the hospitable husband-and-wife owners can take a lot of credit for the inviting atmosphere of this rurally set inn. The generous welcome is the same if you're staying in one of the rooms – individually styled and pine-furnished – or feel like whiling away an hour in the big public bar with a drink, a light snack and a seat in one of the deep, teak-brown leather armchairs. For bigger appetites, there's the restaurant, where the native Welsh influence is unmistakeable, local produce forming the core of an extensive menu that changes through the year. If you're new to this part of Powys, you'll find no shortage of ways to explore it: a canal cruise, cycling on the Taff Trail or your first steps into the Brecon Beacons.

Typical Dishes

Baked goats cheese salad
Venison, port and liquorice jus
Treacle and almond tart

On the edge of the village, opposite the former railway station and yard. Parking

Llanrhidian

026 **The Welcome To Town**

Llanrhidian SA3 1EH

Tel.: (01792) 390015 - Fax: (01792) 390015
Website: www.thewelcometotown.co.uk

 VISA **MC**

 No real ales offered

The Welcome to Town is more of a goodbye to the city – if you're in need of the perfect mid-week escape, a ten-mile drive takes you out into the rural peace of the Gower peninsula and straight to the front door of this old pub, where the owner's enthusiasm and experience is writ large…in the framed certificates and awards decorating a traditionally styled dining room. Able, pleasant service, with the formality of a restaurant, strikes the right note, while locally influenced cooking brings out appealing, seasonal flavours, a considered, rather classical approach underpinning it all. The specials board changes by the day, and it's worth asking about their good-value lunches.

Food serving times:
Tuesday-Saturday:
    12pm-2pm, 7pm-9.30pm
Sunday: 12pm-2pm
Closed 25-26 December, last 2 weeks February and last week October

Prices:
Meals: 15.95 (fixed price lunch) and a la carte 25.00/32.00

Typical Dishes

Mille feuille of local asparagus

John Dory, braised samphire and beurre blanc

Raspberry parfait

10.5 mi West of Swansea by A4118 and B4271. Parking

East Aberthaw

027 Blue Anchor Inn

East Aberthaw CF62 3DD

Tel.: (01446) 750329
Website: www.blueanchoraberthaw.com

  VISA

Wadworth 6X, Theakstons Old Peculier, Wye Valley pale ale, Brains bitter and guest ales

Part of the original 14C thatched pub succumbed to fire in 2004, but the Blue Anchor has now been rebuilt and restored in sympathy with its old charm. Bright with overflowing hanging baskets in summer, inside, the warren of little firelit rooms and massive walls in local stone give it character to spare. It's still cosy, effortlessly pleasing and, once you get comfortable, very hard to leave, but the chatty staff wouldn't dream of hurrying you along. As you might expect, there's an extensive menu built on sound, homely foundations; restorative, traditional dishes seem to go down well with the locals.

Food serving times:
Monday-Saturday:
    12pm-2pm, 7pm-9.30pm
Sunday: 12pm-2.30pm
Prices:
Meals: a la carte 13.00/25.00

Typical Dishes

Thai style fish cakes
Glazed shank of Welsh lamb
Almond and pear tart

Turn at the cement factory and follow the road for approximately 1 mile. Car park opposite the pub

Gresford

028 Pant-yr-Ochain

Old Wrexham Rd, Gresford LL12 8TY

Tel.: (01978) 853525 - Fax: (01978) 853515
e-mail: pant.yr.ochain@brunningandprice.co.uk - Website: www.pantyrochain-gresford.co.uk

Timothy Taylor Landlord, Weetwood Old Dog, Deuchars IPA

To get an idea of this pub's vintage, look at the Tudor wattle and daub walls and timber in the alcove behind the inglenook fireplace. The Pant isn't just rather old, it's also rather vast, with several rooms running off the main bar. Overall, it's smart yet rustic, enhanced by lake views and a small model railway in the grounds. Its library bar has some dining tables, plus a good view of the lake, which makes it the pick of the rooms in which to eat. The menu is a printed sheet duplicated on the blackboard with a good choice of traditional and modern dishes ranging from light to very substantial; the cooking is robust and bold. Locally, this is a very well regarded place, but its bustling atmosphere just adds to the experience.

Food serving times:
Monday-Saturday:
12pm-9.30pm
Sunday: 12pm-9pm
Closed 25-26 December
(booking essential)
Prices:
Meals: a la carte 14.50/23.95

3.5 mi Northeast of Wrexham by A483 on B5445. Then 1 mi South from Gresford. Parking

Typical Dishes

Black pudding and caramelised apple salad

Free range chicken, pancetta sauce

Lemon tart, berry compote

*W*ith over a third of the country's population living in and around, Belfast is truly the focus of Northern Irish life. As the only city in Ireland to feel the rise and heavy fall of Britain's industrial empire, it has worked bravely to re-establish itself with a busy cultural life and a wave of new building, and perhaps it is in part the attitudes in the rest of Britain and Ireland that make us look elsewhere for easier symbols and images of the country. Though less intensely marketed than the Southern Ireland experience, the six counties contain some of the finest landscapes in the island. The incredible, innumerable columns of the Giant's Causeway, formed 60 million years ago by volcanic eruptions, attract thousands of visitors every year, while to the east lie the quiet, wooded bays of the Antrim coast and the deep inland glens. The beautiful Mourne and Sperrin Mountains stand as great Ulster landmarks, while Lough Neagh, the largest body of fresh water in the British Isles, lies in repose, a vast blue mirror in the heart of the province: here you'll find the working landscapes and the working people richly explored in Seamus Heaney's poetic memories of his youth. From the cultivated splendour of Mount Stewart Gardnes or Castle Coole to the earth-magic of Beaghmore, from the whale-backed islands of Strangford Lough to the leaping salmon and pike in Lough Erne, a feeling for the natural world of Northern Ireland goes straight to the heart.

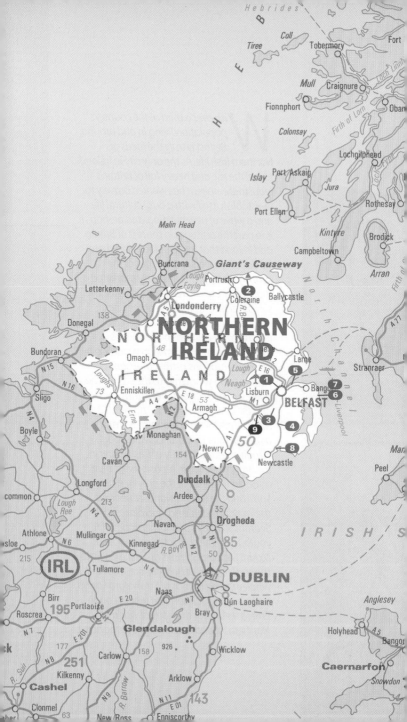

Belfast

001 ## The Errigle Inn

312-320 Ormeau Rd, Belfast BT7 2GE

Tel.: (028) 9064 1410 - Fax: (028) 9064 0772
e-mail: info@errigle.co.uk - Website: www.errigle.com

 No real ales offered

Seventy plus years in the business, this big, traditional Belfast bar remains a pub landmark in the city. Hungry newcomers can be forgiven for edging awkwardly around the maze of rooms at first: the no-nonsense Pinewood bar is really the locals' stamping ground for a beer and a smoke, but remember that the bustling Tom McGurran bar always keeps a little space for diners. For a bit more restaurant comfort, though, you're better off surrounded by handsome dark wood and green leather in the Oak Room, or in the dining room upstairs on a Friday or Saturday. Dinner dishes along traditional lines are tasty, generous and carefully prepared, whether you choose roast lamb with spinach and cabbage or pork with Thai-spiced noodles; lunches tend to be more basic: baps, grills, pastas and that dietician's nightmare, the mighty Ulster Fry.

Food serving times:
Monday-Thursday:
12pm-9.00pm
Friday-Saturday:
12pm-10pm
Closed 25 December
Prices:
Meals: a la carte 14.00/23.50

Typical Dishes

Seared duck livers, balsamic reduction

Char-grilled monkfish

White chocolate and lemon thyme mousse

Parking on the street

Bushmills

002 Distillers Arms

140 Main St, Bushmills BT57 8QE
Tel.: (028) 2073 1044 - Fax: (028) 2073 2843
e-mail: simon@distillersarms.com - Website: www.distillersarms.com

🍷 🚭 **VISA** **MC**

Theakstons Best

The smart conservation village of Bushmills has its very own smart – and stylish – pub, set conveniently on the high street. Once home to owners of the local distillery, it's seen some very plush interior renovations creating an open-plan bar and comfortable lounge with shiny wood floors, elegant coolie lampshades and chunky brown leather sofas. The rear dining area is spacious enough for groups taking in the delights of the north Antrim coast and the menus are decidedly, sometimes ambitiously modern. Typically, you could try grilled fillets of sea bass with Asian spices, wilted greens, boiled potatoes and chilled tomato, garlic and anchovy sauce or pan-seared chicken supreme, aubergine, basil couscous, tomato and red onion salsa.

Food serving times:
Monday-Sunday:
12.30pm-3pm,
5.30pm-9.30pm
Closed 25-26 December
weekends only in winter
Prices:
Meals: a la carte 15.00/25.00

Typical Dishes

Whiskey cured salmon
Steak, Guiness and oyster pie
Spiced ginger panna cotta

Close to Bushmills whiskey distillery ≫

Annahilt

003 The Pheasant

410 Upper Ballynahinch Rd, Annahilt BT26 6NR

Tel.: (028) 9263 8056
e-mail: thepheasantinn@aol.com

  VISA AE ⑆ ⑇

 No real ales offered

Even in midweek the little public bar is bustling by lunchtime: the old floorboards, mock Tudor windows and a smouldering peat fire suggest a place happy to keep 21C fads at arm's length, for the moment at least. Press through and find a table, either along the colourful banquettes or in one of the booths, and allow yourself an aperitif while you look through the menu. You'll have time for a half at least; the choice is vast – too wide, perhaps – but you're assured of generous helpings. Steak, deep-fried whitebait, pork and bacon pie, and plates of smoked salmon and smoked halibut can usually be found on a list of tasty, no-nonsense classics, served up with brisk, capable cheeriness by a young bar team.

Food serving times:
Monday-Sunday :
12pm-2.15pm, 5pm-9.30pm
Closed 25-26 December and 12-13 July
Prices:
Meals: a la carte 20.00/40.00

Typical Dishes

Steamed Japanese scallops

12oz rib eye steak

Lemon tart, passion fruit sorbet

Parking

Ballynahinch

004 ## The Primrose

30 Main St, Ballynahinch BT24 8DN
Tel.: (028) 9756 3177 - Fax: (028) 9756 5954
e-mail: info@primrosebar.co.uk - Website: www.primrosebar.co.uk

 No real ales offered

Nothing particularly draws you in to The Primrose, just one of a pretty average string of buildings along Main Street: only inside do you notice that little extra thought and effort that raises this small-town pub above the norm. Several small rooms around the double bar are all brightly decorated and feel surprisingly welcoming: you can expect an encouraging turn-out in the evening, and even at lunchtime there's a pleasant buzz of conversation from the locals, happy to have escaped the shop or the office for an hour or two. They come for burgers, steaks and baguettes, one or two daily specials or a list of well-presented dishes that includes internationally influenced choices – teriyaki beef or Indian-spiced lamb with chick peas – as well as classics like smoked salmon and prawn salad. Attentive service.

Food serving times:
Monday-Sunday:
12pm-2.30pm,
Sunday-Tuesday:
5pm-7.45pm
Wednesday-Saturday:
5pm-8.45pm
Closed 25 December
(bar meals Monday-Friday)
Prices:
Meals: a la carte 13.95/25.00

Typical Dishes

Home-made soup

Burgers with various toppings

Cassata

Parking on the street

Cultra

005 Cultra Inn
Cultra Station Rd, Cultra BT18 0EX
Tel.: (028) 9042 5840 - Fax: (028) 9042 6777

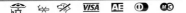

VISA AE D MC

No real ales offered

On a more intimate scale than the commanding 19C mansion on the hill, but still part of the Culloden Hotel estate, the contemporary-rustic Cultra Inn stands in its gardens. With all its clean, polished, new wood, it can feel a bit bare without the friendly sound of its regulars, but fortunately that's a pretty rare occurrence: people come in good numbers, clustering near the log fire for a moment on colder days, before sitting down to hearty lunches and dinners. A simple midday menu, beginning with potatoes and panini, extends to chicken with mushroom and bacon sauce or real classics like boiled bacon and champ or a steak sandwich on soda bread – good with a pint and live Six Nations on the big screen. A more elaborate evening choice – minus the rugby – could include pine nut and chorizo pasta or monkfish with dill cream and spinach.

Food serving times:
Monday-Saturday:
   12pm-2.30pm, 6pm-9.30pm
Sunday: 12.30pm-2.30pm
Closed 25 December
Prices:
Meals: a la carte 13.00/23.20

In the grounds of the Culloden Hotel.
Parking

Typical Dishes

Duck spring rolls

Monkfish fritters, tomato relish

White chocolate tart

Donaghadee

006 Grace Neill's

33 High St, Donaghadee BT21 0AH

Tel.: (028) 9188 4595 - Fax: (028) 9188 9631
e-mail: info@graceneills.com - Website: www.graceneills.com

No real ales offered

Reputed to be the oldest pub in Ireland, the 17C Grace Neill's has certainly seen some changes in its time. True, the traditional front bar, propped up on its massive timbers, looks as charming and timeless as ever; it's a place for slow pints and unhurried chat, with families snacking and drinking in the lounge. But at the back, the split-level brasserie is chic, formal and uncompromisingly contemporary: silk cushions, elegant storm lamps, subtle shades of chestnut and aubergine and banquettes à la parisienne. The service, even for a light lunch of omelette Arnold Bennett and lemon parfait, can get rather earnest and solicitous, but there's no mistaking the good intentions behind it.

Food serving times:
Closed 25 December and 12 July
Prices:
Meals: a la carte 22.00

Typical Dishes

Irish smoked salmon

Braised shoulder of lamb

Rhubarb and ginger crumble

Parking

Donaghadee

007 Pier 36

36 The Parade, Donaghadee BT21 0HE

Tel.: (028) 9188 4466 - Fax: (028) 9188 4636
e-mail: info@pier36.co.uk - Website: www.pier36.co.uk

VISA MC

No real ales offered

Never less than busy, this family-run harbourside pub is a real local favourite. The door opens into a thronging front bar, which manages to be comfortable and gloriously cluttered at the same time, while the semi-raised dining area, in stripped pine and bare brick, has an almost country-cottage feel to it – perhaps it's the smell of bread and home cooking from the stove. Chatty, well-marshalled bar staff keep things moving briskly, serving up enjoyable, ultra-simple seafood from plaice with lemon to lobster Thermidor, as well as tasty grills and slow-cooked roasts. It's not called Pier 36 for nothing, and a pre-dinner stroll along the waterfront can be a lovely way of sharpening the appetite.

Food serving times:
Monday-Sunday:
   12pm-2.30pm, 5pm-9.30pm
Closed 25 December
- Seafood specialities -
Prices:
Meals: a la carte 12.00/30.00

Typical Dishes

Sauteed crab claws, garlic butter

Seafood melody

Apricot brioche

Parking

Dundrum

008 Buck's Head Inn

77-79 Main St, Dundrum BT33 0LU

Tel.: (028) 4375 1868 - Fax: (028) 4481 1033
e-mail: buckshead1@aol.com - Website: www.thebucksheaddundrum.co.uk

 🍴 🍷 ⚬ 🚭 **VISA** **AE** **MC**

🍺 *No real ales offered*

L ocal watercolours on the brick walls lend a touch of intimacy and originality to this relaxing, everyday pub, where you can choose informal dining or something closer to restaurant style. Consistent and simply presented cooking with a seafood base strikes an appealing balance between traditional pub meals and more elaborate styles: dishes range from local scampi and chips and baked smokie topped with Gruyère to seared turbot on Mediterranean couscous or a light rhubarb and almond flan. There's plenty to see and do after lunch, too: visit Dundrum's ruined castle or head south into the lovely rolling landscape of the Mourne Mountains, driving the picturesque coast road or striking out on foot along part of the Ulster Way, which passes a few miles from here.

Food serving times:
Monday-Sunday:
12pm-2.30pm, 7pm-9.30pm
Closed 24-25 December and Monday October-March
- Seafood specialities -
Prices:
Meals: a la carte 15.50/24.50

Typical Dishes

Dundrum Bay oysters with Clonakilty black pudding

Pan seared Kilkeel monkfish

Caramelised banana tart Tatin

Parking on the street ⟩⟩

Hillsborough

`009` The Plough Inn

The Square, Hillsborough BT26 6AG

Tel.: (028) 9268 2985 - Fax: (028) 9268 2472
e-mail: derekpatterson@barretro.com - Website: www.barretro.com

VISA **AE** **①** **MC**

No real ales offered

In such a quiet town, The Plough Inn keeps itself surprisingly busy: there's a little coffee shop over to one side, a smarter, more modern first-floor bistro – Bar Retro – and the traditional main bar at the hub of things below. Here, the stripped floorboards and no-frills approach set a simple tone, but there are no complaints from a regular crowd of neighbourhood drinkers and diners, who can take their pick from a list of snacks and sandwiches or a broad, appealing menu with a sound Irish base: even by local standards, the portions are immense. Service may slow down a little as the lunchtime rush picks up, but the polite good humour never flags.

Food serving times:
Monday-Sunday:
12pm-9.00pm
Closed 25 December
(bar meals Monday)
Prices:
Meals: a la carte 15.00/25.00

Typical Dishes

Miso drizzled foie gras

Seared blue fin tuna, lemongrass and soy

Frozen summer berries, white chocolate fondue

Parking

Well deserving of its old epithet, 'The Emerald Isle', Ireland conjures up images of dewy fields and distant mountains. Wondrous, ever-changing cloudscapes do haul in rainfall on an almost industrial scale, accounting for the fresh atmosphere and luminous look of the landscape, but this picture of gentle, unpeopled tranquillity does no justice to the country's variety: sandy strands, flora-rich peatland and, at the westernmost edge of Europe, the natural phenomenon of the Cliffs of Moher, a five mile spectacular of shale and sandstone bounded by the Atlantic breakers and the Burren. Peaceful Cashel and Clonmacnoise evoke the spirit of Celtic Christianity and kingship, while the Republic's towns and cities throb with life, culture and chatter: Galway has grown into a bustling university and cathedral city alongside its thriving port while Killarney, near the wild south-west tip, has been attracting visitors for over 200 years. Dublin remains the heart of the nation, a fascinating focus of literary association with a vital blend of street, café, bar and restaurant life: the addictive craic of the "fair city" is played out to an accompaniment of Georgian elegance and the stunning background of the Wicklow Mountains. Away from the capital, too, friendly pubs serve up not only good stout and even better conversation, but also wholesome favourites like Irish stew, colcannon and coddle and imaginative new cuisine showcasing the finest produce the country has to offer.

Liscannor

001 **Vaughan's Anchor Inn**

Liscannor
Tel.: (065) 7081548 - Fax: (065) 7086977
e-mail: l

 VISA MC

 No real ales offered

Conveniently placed for the cliffs of Moher and the beach, this is a long-standing pub, seriously well-regarded by the locals. It boasts a charmingly unique interior: the front counter acts as a shop where you can buy corn flakes and coffee, while the walls are filled with fishing paraphernalia: nets, photos, ships' wheels and the like. Simple wooden tables make it seem like a bistro; a mix of simple and complex dishes means there's always something of interest on the menu. The more involved options might include seared scallops on a bed of crisp-fried smoked haddock and scallion mash with a white wine sauce. It gets very busy, so be prepared to wait for your dish to arrive.

Food serving times:
Monday-Sunday:
12pm-9.30pm
Closed 25 December
- seafood -
Prices:
Meals: a la carte 25.00/50.00

Typical Dishes

Pan-fried quail breasts

Grilled fillet of sea bass

Selection of Irish farmhouse cheeses

On coast road 1.5mi from Lahinch on main route to Cliffs of Moher. Parking

Newquay

002 **Linnane's Bar**

New Quay Pier, Newquay

Tel.: (065) 7078120

e-mail: linnaneslobsterbar@hotmail.com

VISA AE D MC

No real ales offered

On the crags overlooking Galway Bay, this little white-painted pub is traditional, friendly and totally relaxed. If the clouds are setting in, you can always find a table in the modest bar, decorated with black and white photos, but if there's even a hint of sun, make straight for the lovely terrace overlooking the water. A concise, all-seafood menu, concentrating on prime fresh shellfish, keeps it delightfully simple; they're open all day in summer, so you can while away the afternoon with open sandwiches, chowders, lobster, scallops, oysters, chilled Sancerre and plenty of fresh sea air! There's more seafood for sale at the pier shop. If you can tear yourself away, drive through the strange, barren Tolkien-scape of The Burren to Lahinch beach or the breathtaking Cliffs of Moher.

Food serving times:
Monday-Sunday:
12.30pm-9pm
Weekends only October-March
- Seafood -
Prices:
Meals: a la carte 18.50/38.00

Typical Dishes

Seafood chowder

Crab cakes

Apple crumble

Parking ⟩⟩

Castletownshend

003 Mary Ann's

Castletownshend

Tel.: (028) 36146 - Fax: (028) 36920
e-mail: maryanns@eircom.net - Website: www.maryannsbarrestaurant.com

No real ales offered

First find this sleepy coastal village, then follow the row of terrace houses until you come to a pleasant little 19C pub. With over fifteen years' experience, the friendly owners are old hands by now, taking real pride in their tasty, traditional home cooking and preferring not to cut corners when it comes to the important things. There's a familiar ring to much of the large menu, as well as the blackboard specials – this is food to satisfy, rather than surprise or impress – but homemade soups, good homebaked rolls, local cheeses and their real speciality, seafood, are all clearly well above the norm. If it's sunny enough, the friendly people behind the bar will offer you a seat in the garden.

Food serving times:
Monday-Sunday:
    12pm-2.30pm, 6pm-9pm
Closed 24-26 December, last 3 weeks January and Monday November to March
(bookings not accepted)
Prices:
Meals: a la carte 18.95/45.00

Typical Dishes

Mini seafood platter
Fish and chips
Assiette of desserts

Parking on main street

Clonakilty

004 An Sugán

Wolfe Tone St, Clonakilty

Tel.: (023) 33498 - Fax: (023) 33825
e-mail: ansugan4@eircom.net - Website: www.ansugan.com

   VISA MC

 No real ales offered

Personally run for ages, the unpretentious An Sugán welcomes hungry visitors as well as locals, dropping in to sink a pint and catch up on Clonakilty's news and current affairs. It's worth making time for a half in the characterful bar, all dark polished wood and frosted glass, before heading upstairs to the restaurant, decorated with memorabilia and old photos. A traditional blackboard menu doesn't try to reinvent the wheel, but offers sound, tasty home cooking with an appealing pub flavour: crisp, fresh prawn scampi are well worth trying. Relaxed and friendly service.

Food serving times:
Monday-Sunday:
　　　　　12.30pm-9.30pm
Closed 25-26 December and
Good Friday
Prices:
Meals: a la carte 20.00/35.00

Typical Dishes

Terrine of black and white pudding

Atlantic seafood basket

Brown bread ice cream

Parking available on the street

Cork

005 The Douglas Hide

63 Douglas Street, Cork

Tel.: (021) 4315695

e-mail: info@douglashide.com - Website: www.douglashide.com

No real ales offered

Somewhere, indeed, to hide away in Cork – this late Victorian pub is tucked into its cosy niche on Douglas Street, just five minutes from the city centre. The intimate little bar, with its clusters of regulars, opens out into an altogether brighter, more open area with heavy pine tables and chairs. Modern artwork, appropriately food and drink themed, adorns the walls and basks in the warm glow from candles burning on each table. County Cork is a rich provider of free range and organic produce: fish, meat, cheeses, vegetables and herbs arrive from suppliers close to hand and all the pub's desserts, breads and ice creams are made on the premises. Recent recommendations include cauliflower and soft cheese roulade with watercress salad followed by celeriac and Cashel blue cheese mousse on a turnip and thyme gratin.

Food serving times:
Monday-Friday:
    12pm-3pm, 5.30pm-9pm
Saturday: 5.30pm-9pm
Sunday: 12pm-3pm
Closed 25 December and Good Friday
Closed Saturday lunch, Sunday and Monday
Prices:
Meals: a la carte 20.00/40.00

Typical Dishes

Asparagus and Gruyère tartlet

Breast of duck, orange and ginger vinaigrette

Bread & butter pudding

> Five minutes walk from town centre over Parliament Bridge. Street parking or White Street car park 5 minutes walk

Kinsale

006 **Dalton's**

3 Market St, Kinsale

Tel.: (021) 4777957

e-mail: f.edalton@eircom.net

Kinsale Ale

Moist, tasty crab cakes with pineapple salsa, chicken satay and Cajun popcorn prawns: here's a globe-trotting chef and landlord who is determined to bring a little unexpected variety to Kinsale's dining. A loyal local following suggests he must be doing something right, and while they still offer a good pie and pint for the traditionalist, it's the more ambitious dishes which set the place apart from the countless other pubs in town. It just goes to show that you can't go by appearances, for apart from the eyecatching purple façade, the line of bar stools, the tan banquettes, the tiled floor and the glowing fire are as traditional as the easygoing ambience and the cheerful welcome.

Food serving times:
Monday-Friday:
12.30pm-3pm
Closed 25 December Good
Friday and 2 weeks August
Prices:
Meals: a la carte 15.00/25.00

2 minutes away in St Multose car park

Typical Dishes

Chowder

Baked crab cakes

Chocolate brownie cake

Dublin

007 The Cellar Bar

Upper Merrion St, Dublin D2

Tel.: (01) 603 0600 - Fax: (01) 603 0700
e-mail: info@merrionhotel.com - Website: www.merrionhotel.com

    VISA AE

 No real ales offered

One of Dublin's favourite places for lunch is hidden away behind the elegant façade of an old Georgian town house, now the Merrion Hotel. The superbly restored wine vaults are now a smart destination bar by night, a bar-brasserie by day, and a city institution all round, so beat the lunchtime rush and find an alcove table under the brick and granite arches or pull up a spare stool at the long bar. Even on the busiest days, smiling, super-efficient bar staff keep things moving, serving up everything from hot roast beef sandwiches and Caesar salad to bacon and cabbage or Irish stew; plum frangipane tart with deliciously smooth ice cream is an occasional special and deserves to be tried.

Food serving times:
Monday-Saturday:
12pm-2pm

Prices:
Meals: a la carte 22.00/30.00

Typical Dishes

Chilli marinated chicken wings

Roast Beef sandwich on sea salt bread

Chocolate fondant

At the Merrion Hotel. Parking available at a charge of 20Euro per night for guests

Ballinasloe

008 Tohers

18 Dunlo Street, Ballinasloe
Tel.: (090) 9644848 - Fax: (090) 9644844

VISA MC

No real ales offered

A bustling market town like Ballinasloe ensures that this converted pub on the high street sees its fair share of local life: Tohers' ground floor bar is a buzzing place to be. It has a rustic charm befitting its proximity to the market square, and the marina is only a short walk away. Upstairs, the atmosphere's slightly more refined: three rooms make up the restaurant with its simple linen covered tables and understated rural décor. Menus contrast sharply: bar lunches are simple but tasty – everything from freshly baked baguettes to chicken fajitas – while upstairs in the evening, ambitious dishes with global inspiration make an appearance. Menus might include spring roll of gingered crab with a marinated carrot and fennel salad; or slow cooked Moroccan spiced lamb shank with lemon and garlic couscous.

Food serving times:
Monday-Saturday:
12pm-3pm
Tuesday- Saturday:
6pm-9.30pm
Closed dinner 11 October-26 October
Closed Sunday and Monday dinner
Prices:
Meals: 25.00 and a la carte 23.50/37.50

Typical Dishes

Crispy calamari salad

Aromatic duck breast, orange and ginger sauce

Crème Brûlée, citrus fruit compôte

On street parking

Clonbur

009 John J. Burkes

Clonbur

Tel.: (094) 9546175 - Fax: (094) 9546290
e-mail: tibhurca@eircom.net - Website: www.burkes-clonbur.com

VISA M©

> No real ales offered

Between two of Ireland's finest fishing waters, it's no surprise to find cabinets and cases displaying the ones that didn't get away. The brown trout in Lough Corrib and Lough Mask are legendary, the perch and pike no less so, and where better for food and drink after a long day out than this friendly pub, still owned by the Burke family. The tiny, unassuming shopfront opens up into a big, characterful bar and simply set rear dining room, as popular with the locals as with the anglers who flock to the West Coast in the height of the season. Simple, fortifying meals will set you up for the great outdoors: try cod and chips, a pint of stout and a generous slice of home-made apple pie.

Food serving times:
Monday-Sunday:
12pm-9.30pm
Closed midweek
November-March
(live music Sunday)
Prices:
Meals: a la carte 23.40/38.50
5 rooms : 60.00/80.00

On street parking

Typical Dishes

Avocado and crabmeat salad

Sirloin steak

Rhubarb crumble

Kilcolgan

010 ## Moran's Oyster Cottage

The Weir, Kilcolgan

Tel.: (091) 796113 - Fax: (091) 796503
e-mail: moranstheweir@eircom.net - Website: www.moransoystercottage.com

 VISA **AE** **D** **MC** **JCB**

 No real ales offered

When you see the thatched roof of this pretty cottage, your mind might flash to a typical English country inn, but instead you're across the Irish Sea in a sleepy Galway village. Moran's is set in a delightful waterside location and you can watch the swans sail serenely past. Inside, this charming 18C building is full of nooks and crannies in the front bar. Settle down in one of the beamed snugs and parlours or go through to the very large dining area at the back where the walls are decorated with photos of famous customers. Local seafood dishes, unsurprisingly, make up the widely renowned menus: native oysters from their own oyster beds, lobster, mussels, crab salads, smoked salmon and seafood cocktails. Expect fairly fast and furious service from staff who are used to being busy.

Food serving times:
Monday-Sunday:
                    12pm-10pm
Closed 3 days at Christmas and Good Friday
- Seafood -
Prices:
Meals: a la carte 30.00/70.00

5 minutes from the village of Clarenbridge. Parking

Typical Dishes

Seafood chowder
Seafood special
Cheesecake

Kinvara

011 Keogh's Bar

The Square, Kinvara

Tel.: (091) 637145 - Fax: (091) 637028
e-mail: keoghsbar@eircom.net - Website: www.kinvara.com/keoghs

VISA AE MC JCB

 No real ales offered

Kinvara is a pretty harbour village on the Galway coast, renowned for the quality of its Atlantic fishing catch. Gateway to the Burren, its colourful character is echoed in this bright yellow-fronted pub whose busy bar constantly buzzes to the sound of locals chattering over a pint of dark stout. At the back is a spacious, slightly more formal dining room, which still maintains a warm, pubby ambience. The Keoghs have been here for many years, and they serve simple, well-prepared and tasty dishes, based around the plentiful supplies of local seafood. On offer, typically, are prawns, salmon, crab, mussels and seafood chowder, cooked in a hearty and traditional style.

Food serving times:
Monday-Sunday:
12pm-10pm
Closed 25 December
Prices:
Meals: a la carte 18.45/27.85

Typical Dishes

Oysters with a garlic crust
Fillet of plaice, beurre blanc
Apple crumble with strawberries

In the centre of the town. Parking ⟩⟩

Cahersiveen

012 **The Point**

Renard Point, Cahersiveen
Tel.: (066) 947 2165 - Fax: (066) 947 2165

 No real ales offered

As the beautiful Ring of Kerry runs south, hold your course to the tip of the Iveragh peninsula: down at the quay, looking out across the harbour to Valencia Island, is a neatly kept little bar that's definitely worth going a little further for. Between them, a charming couple, owners of long standing, keep the place shipshape, pull the pints and prepare a short hot and cold supper menu of local seafood; all well chosen and as fresh as it comes, as you'd expect with a fish shed next door! It's a good place for a relaxed pint and a chat – there's no food at all at lunchtime – but if you arrive in the afternoon with time to spare, just take a seat on the little pavement terrace and wait for 6pm to roll around!

Food serving times:
Monday-Sunday:
12.30pm-3.30pm, 6pm-10pm
Closed November to March
- Seafood - (bookings not accepted)(dinner only April and October)
Prices:
Meals: a la carte 30.00

Typical Dishes

Hot crab claws

Pan fried hake, garlic and olive oil

Casserole of Monkfish

Parking

Listowel

013 Allo's Bar 🛏️

41 Church St, Listowel

Tel.: (068) 22880 - Fax: (068) 22803

e-mail: allos@eircom.net

| | **VISA** | **AE** | **MC** |

No real ales offered

A discreetly set institution in the centre of Listowel, this is a wonderfully relaxed pub that proves very popular with locals and tourists alike. It's the other half of Allo's restaurant with rooms, the two gelling in a smooth and seamless symmetry. The bar is a narrow room with lots of original 19C charm. Walls feature exposed brick and the wooden bar and floor are thickly varnished; small booths and stools at the bar provide a most convivial and traditional feel. Menus change on a weekly basis and offer a good range of popular snacks and sandwiches alongside hearty daily specials. Booking really is a must, as it invariably gets packed here.

Food serving times:
Tuesday-Saturday:
　　　　　　12pm-9.00pm
Closed 25 December and Bank Holidays
(booking essential)
Prices:
Meals: a la carte 24.00/50.00
🛏️ **3 rooms :** 70.00/90.00

Typical Dishes

Boudin of Clonakilty black pudding

Crab claws on wilted spinach

White chocolate panna cotta

Parking at the rear. ⟩⟩

Carrick-on-Shannon

014 The Oarsman

Bridge St, Carrick-on-Shannon

Tel.: (071) 9621733 - Fax: (071) 9621734
e-mail: info@theoarsman.com - Website: www.theoarsman.com

🏕 🍷 🍇 ⌨-room 🚳 **VISA** **AE** **MC**

🍺 | *No real ales offered*

N o boating experience necessary, of course, but the town's club eights have been known to drop in, along with sea-anglers and tour rowers, back from a long day's pull up to Lough Key. They come for the spirited, upbeat atmosphere, light lunches and fresh, tasty dinners combining modern classics and a few popular Irish favourites; even when it's busy, alert and helpful staff will do their best find you a table in the main bar or up in the mezzanine, though propping up the bar for a half is no hardship here. Refurbished in traditional style, with some unlikely bits of bric-a-brac hanging from its exposed timbers and stone, it's an enjoyable place and worth seeking out.

Food serving times:
Monday-Wednesday :
12pm-3.30pm
Thursday-Saturday:
12pm-2.45pm,
6.45pm-9.45pm
Closed 25 December, Good Friday and Sunday
Prices:
Meals: a la carte 18.00/41.00

Typical Dishes

Confit duck leg ravioli

Rack of Paddy Sheridan's lamb

Lemon cream cheese mousse

Disc parking adjacent to pub

Terryglass

015 The Derg Inn

Terryglass
Tel.: (067) 22037 - Fax: (067) 22297
e-mail: derginn@eircom.net - Website: www.derginn.ie

   VISA **AE** **MC**

No real ales offered

Not, perhaps, typically pubby from the outside – sandwiched between the post office and Paddy's Bar – this is in fact an unmistakeable and friendly place once you're through the front door. Enthusiastically run by keen owners, it has wood and flagged floors, rafters, open fires and pot stoves; dotted round the central wood bar are chunky pine tables and an assortment of chairs, benches and pews, and there's outside seating in the summer months. As much local and organic produce appears on the menus as possible: classic Irish favourites alongside more modern dishes served in an invariably friendly manner. After which, all that remains is to take that brisk constitutional down to beautiful Lough Derg.

Food serving times:
Monday-Sunday:
11am-10pm
Closed 25 December and Good Friday
Prices:
Meals: a la carte 20.00/50.00

Parking in village

Typical Dishes

Scampi in kataifi pastry, chilli jam

Duck breast, almond marmalade

Baked Pecan pudding

Dunmore East

016 The Ship

Dock Rd, Dunmore East

Tel.: (051) 383141 - Fax: (051) 383144
e-mail: theshiprestaurant@eircom.net - Website: www.theshiprestaurant.com

VISA **AE** **①** **M©**

 No real ales offered

A small, stone-built pub happily nestling in a pleasant fishing village, The Ship's corner position makes it one of Dunmore East's most recognisable institutions and it's well received locally. There's a strong element of delightful pubby character inside: big bar, polished wood floors, beams, pillars, and lots of open fires. Nautical memorabilia, too, is spot-on for the location. Sit down at simple tables and 'barrel' shaped chairs and tuck in to menus that are not, surprisingly, dominated by seafood: you'll find meat plays an equally prominent part in the soundly cooked range of dishes. Blackboard options, though, are firmly centred on fish specials.

Food serving times:
Monday-Sunday :
   1pm-5pm, 7pm-10pm
Closed Sunday dinner and Monday October-March
- Seafood -
Prices:
Meals: 25.00 (fixed price lunch) and a la carte 25.00/50.00

Typical Dishes

Grilled Dublin Bay prawns

Baked cod with crushed chive and spring onion potatoes

Warm Belgian chocolate chip pudding

Near the harbour

Lismore

017 ## Buggys Glencairn Inn

Lismore

Tel.: (058) 56232 - Fax: (058) 56232
e-mail: info@buggys.net - Website: www.lismore.com

 ⤢room ✕ **VISA** **MC**

No real ales offered

This "pretty as a picture" cottage style inn is most homely: it even has a picket fence. A country pub writ large, it boasts everything from a little fire-lit bar to charming bedrooms with an old-world feel. The quaint bar is a good place to settle down with a pint of stout and enjoy freshly prepared dishes off a limited choice menu; or, if you prefer, the same options are on offer in a couple of small dining rooms, charmingly set up with a stylish country informality. The food is heartily rustic in nature: on the menu, you might find pot-roasted fillet of pork and apricots, or fish landed at Helvick, cooked in butter, olive oil and lemon juice. The owner is a talented artist, and it's easy to appreciate just how much of his inspiration has gone into the pub's appeal, not to mention his popular menus.

Food serving times:
Monday-Sunday:
7pm-9pm
Closed Christmas.
Weekends only in winter
Prices:
Meals: a la carte 35.00/45.00
🛏 **5 rooms :** 70.00/125.00

Typical Dishes

Duck liver pâté
Fillet of turbot
Lemon and Lime pie

Parking

Carne

018 Lobster Pot

Carne

Tel.: (053) 31110 - Fax: (053) 31401

🍷 ✂ ✂ **VISA** **AE** **◐◑**

| | *No real ales offered* |

Engagingly quirky and genuinely welcoming, this personally owned seaside pub has been over 20 years in the making: it's now covered with old metal signs on the outside, and the intimate snugs and parlours are crammed with nauticalia and pasted with old posters and advertisements from days gone by. There's also a dining room at the back and, come the evening, they add an extensive list of grills, steaks and locally landed fish to the lunchtime chowders, salads and sandwiches. The real treat, though, is the huge seafood platter, an aquarium's worth of home-smoked salmon and mackerel, freshly dressed crab, poached salmon and prawns Marie Rose, served with bushels of salad. Try it with freshly baked brown scones and a glass of stout!

Food serving times:
Tuesday-Sunday:
12pm-9pm
Closed 25 December, January and Monday except Bank Holidays when closed on a Tuesday
- Seafood - check opening times in winter
Prices:
Meals: a la carte 29.00/50.00

Typical Dishes

Baked crab mornay

Scallops and smoked haddock, leek and white wine sauce

Sticky toffee pudding

Parking

Arklow

019 Kitty's of Arklow

56 Main St, Arklow

Tel.: (0402) 31669 - Fax: (0402) 31553
Website: www.kittysofarklow.com

 No real ales offered

One of Arklow's most recognisable sights: that's the fondly regarded red building in the centre of the town. Locals flock here, and the downstairs bar is constantly bustling, the pints of stout flowing freely. It seems a shame to leave, but then again, there are two dining rooms upstairs, both rich in easy-going rustic character, decorated with everything from books and old farm equipment to pictures for sale. Arrive early for one of the most sought-after tables, which overlook the high street. Simple lunchtime menus range from panini to specials; in the evenings, more structured and elaborate options prevail; service is cheerful, efficient and as smooth as clockwork.

Food serving times:
Monday-Sunday:
     12pm-3pm, 6pm-10pm
Closed 25 December
Prices:
Meals: 25.00 (fixed price dinner) and a la carte 25.00/ 45.00

Typical Dishes

Marinated skewers of chicken

Fillet of sea bass, spring onion sauce

Raspberry crème brûlée

In the town centre. Public parking nearby.

A

B

C

D

E

Y

A

B

C

eating
out in
pubs

Michelin Travel Publications

Michelin Travel Publications
Hannay House,
39 Clarendon Rd
Watford WD17 1JA
Tel: (01923) 205247
Fax: (01923) 205241
www.ViaMichelin.com
eatingoutinpubs-
gbirl@uk.michelin.com

**Manufacture française
des pneumatiques Michelin**

Société en commandite
par actions au capital de
304 000 000 EUR.
Place des Carmes-Déchaux
63 Clermont-Ferrand (France)
R.C.S. Clermont-Fd B 855 200 507
© Michelin et Cie, Propriétaires-
Editeurs, 2006
Dépôt légal Septembre 2005
ISBN 2-06-711646-0
Printed in France 09-05

Typesetting:

Nord Compo, Villeneuve-d'Ascq
Printing and binding:
IME, Baume-les-Dames

Photography

Picture Editor: Eliane Bailly
Project manager: Alain Leprince
Agence ACSI – A Chacun Son
Image
2 r. Aristide Maillol – 75015 Paris

Location Photographs:

Jérôme Berquez, Frédéric Chales,
Ludivine Boizard, Jean-Louis
Chauveau/ACSI

Thanks to:

John Bigelow Taylor/Waddesdon,
The Rothschild Collection
(The National Trust) for the
image of The Five Arrows Hotel,
Waddesdon.

p 8: John A Rizzo/Photodisc
Vert/Getty Images

 p 12: Guy Durand/
PHOTONONSTOP

p 314: © Countryside Agency/
Marc Hill

p 560: H. Champollion/MICHELIN

GREAT BRITAIN: Based on
Ordnance Survey of Great
Britain with the permission of
the controller of Her Majesty's
Stationery Office, © Crown
Copyright 100000247

THE LAMB ON THE STRAND (PAGE 409)
99 THE STRAND
SEMINGTON
TROWBRIDGE
BA14 6LL
Tel: 01380 870263

KINGS ARMS   (PAGE 367) BEDROOMS 4
THE STREET
DIDMARTON
BADMINTON
GL9 1DT
Tel: 01454 236245

COCHRANE INN (PAGE 507)
45 MAIN ROAD
GATEHEAD
KILMARNOCK
KA2 OAP
Tel: 01563 570122

YOUR OPINION MATTERS!

To help us constantly improve this guide, please fill in this questionnaire and return to:

Eating out in Pubs
Michelin Travel Publications,
Hannay House, 39 Clarendon Road,
Watford, WD17 1JA, UK

First name: ....

Surname: ....

Address: ....

Profession: ....

< 25 years old	☐	25-34 years old	☐
35-50 years old	☐	> 50 years	☐

1. How often do you use the Internet to look for information on pubs?

Never ☐
Occasionally (once a month) ☐
Regularly (once a week) ☐
Very frequently (more than once a week) ☐

2. Have you ever bought Michelin guides?

☐ Yes   ☐ No

3. If yes, which one(s)?

The first edition of Eating out in Pubs ☐
The Michelin Guide Great Britain & Ireland ☐
The Green Guide (please specify titles) ☐
....
Other (please specify titles) ☐
....

4. If you bought the first edition of Eating out in Pubs, what made you purchase this new one?

....
....

5. If you buy the Michelin Guide Great Britain & Ireland, how often do buy it?

Every year ☐
Every 2 years ☐
Every 3 years ☐
Every 4 years or more ☐

ABOUT EATING OUT IN PUBS :

6. Did you buy this guide:

For holidays? ☐
For a weekend/short break? ☐
For business purposes? ☐
As a gift? ☐
For everyday use ☐

7. How do you rate these different elements of this guide?

NB: **1. Very Good   2. Good   3. Average   4. Poor   5. Very Poor**

	1	2	3	4	5
Selection of pubs	☐	☐	☐	☐	☐
Number of pubs in London	☐	☐	☐	☐	☐
Geographical spread of pubs	☐	☐	☐	☐	☐
Menu Prices	☐	☐	☐	☐	☐
Practical information (services, menus)	☐	☐	☐	☐	☐
Photos	☐	☐	☐	☐	☐
Description of the pubs	☐	☐	☐	☐	☐
Cover	☐	☐	☐	☐	☐
The format & size of the guide	☐	☐	☐	☐	☐
Guide Price	☐	☐	☐	☐	☐

8. Please rate the guide out of 20 ..../20

9. Which aspects could we improve?

....
....
....
....
....
....
....

10. Was there a pub you particularly liked or a choice you didn't agree with?
Perhaps you have a favourite address of your own that you would like to tell us
about? Please send us your remarks and suggestions.

....
....
....
....
....
....
....
....
....
....
....